APPROACHES TO

The Study of Politics

CONTRIBUTORS

GORDON W. BLACKWELL, University of North Carolina (Sociology)

ANGUS CAMPBELL, University of Michigan (Psychology)

CARL J. FRIEDRICH, Harvard University (Political Science)

SCOTT GREER, Metropolitan St. Louis Survey; now Northwestern University (Sociology)

HAROLD GUETZKOW, Carnegie Institute of Technology; now Northwestern University (Psychology)

CHARLES B. HAGAN, University of Illinois (Political Science)

LOUIS HARTZ, Harvard University (Political Science)

FLOYD HUNTER, University of North Carolina (Sociology)

NORMAN JACOBSON, University of California (Political Science)

MARION J. LEVY, JR., Princeton University (Sociology)

ROBERT G. MC CLOSKEY, Harvard University (Political Science)

HANS J. MORGENTHAU, The University of Chicago (Political Science)

T. M. NEWCOMB, University of Michigan (Psychology)

CHARLES E. OSGOOD, University of Illinois (Psychology)

TALCOTT PARSONS, Harvard University (Sociology)

LINDSAY ROGERS, Columbia University (Political Science)

PETER H. ROSSI, The University of Chicago (Sociology)

FOSTER H. SHERWOOD, University of California, Los Angeles (Political Science)

MULFORD Q. SIBLEY, University of Minnesota (Political Science)

RICHARD C. SNYDER, Princeton University; now Northwestern University (Political Science)

DWIGHT WALDO, University of California, Berkeley (Political Science)

FREDERICK M. WATKINS, Yale University (Political Science)

APPROACHES TO
The Study of Politics

TWENTY-TWO CONTEMPORARY ES-
SAYS EXPLORING THE NATURE OF
POLITICS AND METHODS BY WHICH
IT CAN BE STUDIED

ROLAND YOUNG, *Editor*

NORTHWESTERN UNIVERSITY PRESS

Evanston, Illinois

23769

Preface

THE ESSAYS in this volume grew out of one of those agonizing exercises in introspection which departments from time to time go through —that of re-examining their curriculum. While engaged in such an exercise, it occurred to the Department of Political Science at Northwestern University that scholars from other universities, and to some extent from other disciplines, might have some rewarding remarks to make about the study of politics. These scholars were not asked to comment on or to propose changes in the Northwestern curriculum, a task which in any event they might have approached with understandable reluctance. Instead, they were given somewhat freer scope for their talents, being asked inferentially to discuss some of the intellectual problems associated with the development of an academic discipline—and with that of political science in particular. By making the center of concern the acquisition of knowledge in the study of politics, rather than the curricular content of any single department, the discussions were raised to a level of generalization which has relevance not only for political science but for other social sciences as well.

The essays in this volume were prepared specifically for a series of four conferences held by the Department which were concerned, topically, with the formation of political concepts, the development of political theory, the use of analytic systems, and the study of the community. The categories of the various sections are not water-tight inasmuch as some essays have wider applicability than the topic of the conference suggests. No attempt has been made to edit the material in such a fashion that it will fit into a precise format, as if everything had been worked out in advance, nor yet to prepare an interpretative essay. (Minor editorial changes have been made for the sake of typographical uniformity and topical comments deleted.)

The essays represent different approaches for studying politics, some approaches being relatively new and experimental, others being more traditional and comprising well-defined schools of thought. For all of the diversity found herein, additional approaches might have been included to advantage, and the absence—to take one example—of an essay on anthropological political analysis is a regrettable omission. The variety of approaches and vocabularies in the present volume demonstrates again the vitality which exists in the study of politics as well as the lack of synthesizing themes or methods. The questions which such diversity poses for the study of politics (and for the construction of curricula) are, of course, of interest to all political scientists and social scientists as well.

In developing the conferences, the Department invited a number of scholars from other Universities to participate in discussing the essays with the paper writers. These "tall bold sluggers," to use Sandburg's phrase, did their job well, adding stimulation and occasionally provocation to the discussions. The value of the conferences as such was due in large measure to their zestful participation. Unfortunately, the stimulating aspect of the conferences, where ideas clashed and well-expressed thoughts were well defended, cannot so readily be transmitted to a broader audience through the printed word.

An extended project of this type, carried on over several years (1953–56), is the product of many hands and many minds, and in this case assisted also by monetary support from a kind benefactor. The paper writers deserve our special thanks, and so too do the discussants. The project would not have been possible without the comforting support of three University officials— Payson S. Wild, Dean of Faculties; Simeon E. Leland, Dean of the College of Liberal Arts; and Moody E. Prior, Dean of the Graduate School. All members of the Political Science Department participated in various degrees in planning and carrying out the several conferences, but a special word of appreciation is due to Professor Charles S. Hyneman, who directed the project from its inception and who presided over three of the conferences with wit, decorum, and common-sense. Other members and visiting members of the Department who were associated with the conferences include David Apter, Sidney Baldwin, Oliver Benson, George I. Blanksten, Philip Herring, Lawrence J. R. Herson, William McGovern, Roy Macridis, James Murray, Rollin B. Posey, Richard Snyder, Kenneth Thompson, and myself. Mrs. Jean Driscoll acted as Research Associate; Mrs. Ilma Roubik, secretary for the project, and Miss Catherine Bullock, secretary to the Department. James A. Robinson assisted in editing the manuscripts. Finally, a sincere word of thanks should be given to the Carnegie Corporation, not only for the welcomed financial support, which was of course gratefully received, but also for the intellectual and moral support which its staff members extended to the Department in developing and carrying out the project.

ROLAND YOUNG
Evanston, Illinois

November, 1957.

Contents

PART THREE: ANALYTIC SYSTEMS

PART FOUR: THE COMMUNITY

PART ONE

Political Concepts

The essays in this section are concerned with the formation of political concepts and the utility and relevance of some of the political concepts in current use. Several of the writers add to the value of the essays by useful personal comments on the study of politics.

RICHARD C. SNYDER

A Decision-Making Approach to the Study of Political Phenomena

I SHALL OMIT the usual disclaimers concerning the tentativeness and crudeness of the focus for political analysis suggested in this paper. At this stage in the development of political science those who take a flying leap toward more ambitious targets are bound to leave portions of their intellectual anatomy exposed or awkwardly posed. Nor should it be necessary to deny any intention to argue that the decision-making approach is *the* white hope of a more systematic political science. I believe this approach has never been fully explored and I am convinced that its rigorous development will substantially aid the search for unifying concepts.

My own feeling—indeed it is one of the assumptions upon which my interest in decision-making rests—is that the major areas of future growth in political science will be: community political analysis (not "local government" in the usual sense), the formulation and execution of public policy, the description and comparison of political systems on a high level of generalization, and the theory of complex administrative organizations. Even if we only agree that these are *some* of the directions of potential intellectual progress in our discipline, the question arises: What kinds of analytical tools and skills will be required? That the Northwestern experiment should lead ultimately to an inquiry into the nature of political science and to the quest for unifying concepts illustrates the depth and breadth of our needs provided one is courageous and skillful enough to face up to the $64 questions.

Any scheme of analysis ought to be evaluated according to two sets of criteria: first, its internal properties—assumptions, definitions, categories, logical consistency, operational qualities and so on; second, its possible contribution to the critical problems of the particular intellectual enterprise to which it is dedicated—in this case political science.

SOME MAJOR PROBLEMS OF CONTEMPORARY POLITICAL ANALYSIS

No blanket dismissal of the contributions of all of our contemporary colleagues and of the great works of the past is necessary to justify the assertion that there is currently manifest among many of us a mixed feeling of inadequacy and optimism. Whether we make real progress depends in part on how successful we are in identifying our basic difficulties. It would indeed be presumptuous of me to imply any glib grasp of these difficulties, but I

3

should like to note several briefly, even at the risk of underestimating the reader.

1) *The Boundary Problem.* Using the term boundary somewhat loosely here, there appear to be at least three sources of confusion. First, when the question: what is political science? is raised, the troublesome line between political and nonpolitical phenomena emerges and claims attention. With a very few exceptions,[1] those political scientists who write for their colleagues as well as for students have hardly clarified this problem, to say nothing of offering alternative solutions. Moreover, the different bases or criteria which might govern this division (a division only for purposes of analysis, of course) are rarely made explicit. Closely linked to the boundary between political science and, say, economics, is a second source of confusion: within any society how is the political realm to be distinguished? how is politics to be defined? Finally, within political science, there are boundary problems with respect to courses and subjects. This is not simply a matter of division of labor or different approaches in the usual sense.[2] Do all political science courses deal with the same kind of social phenomena having an agreed set of purposes in mind? Evidence suggests a negative answer.

2) *The Problem of Undergeneralization.* It would appear that a notable part of the complexity and confusion prevailing in the study of politics is due less to the phenomena than to shortcomings of observation and analysis. Some of our difficulty—particularly the "overwhelmingness" of the data— is artificial, and, hopefully, remediable. We have not paid enough attention to more inclusive categories and to the removal of untenable or trivial distinctions and dichotomies. One pathway toward economy (and this includes written words and class hours) and manageability is consciously and explicitly to analyze phenomena in terms of *common properties*. The heavy empiricism (healthy on many counts) which has historically characterized political science has tended to overemphasize the unique at the expense of the general. One of the unfortunate lacks—the more serious because of our interest in creating more convenient "handles" for political analysis—is simple, useful typologies.[3] Another way of stating this point is to say that political science has been partially imprisoned by a low level of generalization. One result has been to confuse the sheer number of data and variables with the relative complexity of possible analytical operations.

3) *The Problem of Interdisciplinary Synthesis.* It is unfortunate that there seems to be a greater amount of bad temper, ignorance, and intolerance on this matter than there is reliable knowledge and a willingness to experiment. However, my judgment here may be warped in view of my own personal experience, which has been rewarding indeed. Among others, I would cite two reasons for the apparently limited success of interdisciplinary collaboration so far. First, in the absence of a general framework of political analysis it is very difficult to select from the data and techniques of other disciplines those

most appropriate and useful for our purposes. Most political scientists are not adequately trained as analysts of social behavior and thus further risks are added. Legitimate caution or indiscriminate sampling may interfere with the building of bridges between various branches of learning. Second, we have not been able for the most part to ask meaningful questions of our colleagues in social psychology or anthropology—questions which can be answered reliably in terms of their own intellectual operations. There has been a strong tendency to ask global questions which either cannot be operationalized sufficiently or cannot be given answers transferable to political science subjects as defined.

I suggest therefore that some of our trouble in cross-disciplinary communication and problem-solving is due to our relative lack of success in minimizing the disadvantages which flow from other weaknesses already noted: under-sized concepts, limited vocabulary, and low level of generalization. The recent Dahl-Lindblom volume shows clearly the productive results which can be attained when skill and thoroughness establish a common scheme for integrating two or more social sciences.[4]

Often the possible contributions of other specialists are not fully exploited because we reject the substantive knowledge as irrelevant and do not look into the usefulness of analytical techniques. Many of our colleagues in the other social sciences have been confronted—and not entirely defeated—by some of the same kind of tough problems of observation and explanation which confront us.

One further point: those who venture into other disciplines on foraging expeditions often come back with superficially attractive loot, in some cases exemplified by a shiny new vocabulary ripped from its theoretical context and disciplinary home. In the absence of an agreed and powerful vocabulary of political analysis this is tempting, but it also opens us to those valid and accurate charges of "jargon" which give comfort to those who employ the charge essentially as insulation against any re-examination of the intellectual foundations of their own work. I have heard some political scientists reject Parsons and Shils—which they have never read—on the basis of terms used carelessly by other political scientists who never really understood the underlying system of action analysis.[5]

Admittedly I have oversimplified the problems of interdisciplinary research, but I would argue strongly that we have fumbled these problems without fully comprehending the stakes involved or the causes of our failures. If we can push political analysis to a high level of generalization and if we are careful with our unifying concepts (including their vocabularies) we may at least clarify our difficulties. One test of unifying concepts ought to be: do they permit an intellectually responsible and scientifically respectable use of the contributions of other disciplines?

4) *The Problem of an Adequate Vocabulary*. I am sure that all of us

would agree that in a broad sense the tools of our trade are words and combinations of words. For the most part, we must carry out our functions on a
symbolic level. Perhaps this has led some of us to assume too easily that we
could treat words as they are treated in daily life—as all-purpose items of
exchange and as deliberately ambiguous communicative signs. Those who
feel uneasy about this will usually go on to admit that the admonition: "define your terms" is a good starting point for discussion. Often at this point
something unfortunate develops: namely, that definitions—*à la* Alice in
Wonderland—are regarded as a kind of subjective game in which the one
who deals controls all the rules. There are available tested rules of definition
which any rigorous social analyst ought to try to employ. Sloppiness on this
score has cost us dearly, not only in the obvious ways, but because even in
our professional discourses words become "facilitators" (*i.e.,* of understanding or compromise) rather than genuine analytic tools.[6] The problem of vocabulary obviously cannot be separated from concept formation. When we
are searching for unifying concepts, we ought to face up to the necessity for
construction of the specialized vocabularies to which we—if we hope to be
good scientists—are entitled. I use the plural deliberately because I think we
need a basic vocabulary of terms which refer to our purposes, interests, and
methods and, possibly, a set of vocabularies related to a cluster of unifying
concepts. If and when we develop a general theory, we shall presumably
have a single, economical, coherent vocabulary. It seems strange that not
until after 1950 did such works as Lasswell and Kaplan's *Power and Society*
and T. H. Weldon's *The Vocabulary of Politics* appear. The first suffers
from serious logical difficulties; in the second the author does not quite follow through on his early promises. However, both stand as significant and
useful efforts. Regardless of one's posture toward political phenomena, it can
hardly be denied that at the moment such words and terms as *power, group,
organization, policy, objective, rationality, ideology, political process, informal, personality,* and *political behavior* are not all clear—either in meaning
or analytical function. Nor are we clear on why the confusion exists.[7]

I hesitate to bring up the awkward business of "technical jargon." I do so
because if we stick to the avowed purposes of this conference we shall have
to be careful of selling ourselves short or of yielding to the substantial pressures against system-building in our field.[8] There are seven factors here
which can be listed briefly:

i) Professional scholars have been guilty of using words for purposes
which have little to do with observation and interpretation of social phenomena: to engage in no-decision verbal contests with colleagues; to provide old
wine in new bottles; and to draw attention to one's existence and (hopefully)
competence.

ii) Through carelessness and faulty intellectual operations we have been caught with false dichotomies, mere labels, empirically meaningless terms, and many other defects.

iii) The few who are capable of really sophisticated analysis make just enough mistakes—usually minor if one leaves out of account value-judgments on the worthwhileness of particular scholarly purposes—to condemn their total work in the eyes of critics; instead of being shrugged off as the inevitable results of risk-taking in the scientific enterprise such imperfections are alleged to prove the case.

iv) Metaphors have an overwhelming attraction both in professional writing and in teaching; the rigorous teacher or writer sacrifices most of the major techniques for spellbinding an audience; furthermore, one can easily slip from metaphor as felicity of expression to metaphor as disguised conceptualization without having to face up to logical and other requirements.

v) Those of us who have tried (albeit by small steps) to improve the conceptualization and theoretical work in political science have added to the enemy's ammunition by not always—or often—taking care to make clear "the difference it makes" to be explicit and rigorous about concepts; this is not easy but it is both a test and a good communicative strategy.

vi) Under pressure of verbal combat, we often allow the anti-generalizers and the metaphorists to destroy confidence in our claims to more effective analysis by succumbing to this gambit: "what you're really saying is . . . Right?" Upon answering "yes" we often allow a mere illustration to pass for an explanation of a concept.

vii) One of the toughest handicaps is the pressure to reduce the level of professional analysis to the lowest student denominator; there seems little doubt that many, many teachers become so accustomed to the successful communicative strategies of the class room that these become, in subtle fashion, an intellectual way of life.

These are familiar enough to all of us. I mention them in order to suggest that in our search for unifying concepts we must keep separate the criteria for deciding what methods will enhance our knowledge, from the criteria for deciding on how our knowledge is to be transmitted or packaged. I do not minimize the translation problem or the interest-arousal problem. But our professional life—our life as scholars—ought not to be governed by whether the *technical apparatus* we employ can or should be wheeled into the class room. The notion that the scholar who has an explicit scheme of analysis is forcing jargon or propaganda or theory (in its "irrelevant" sense) is firmly entrenched, and it will not be dislodged easily. Perhaps students can be led to see that the teachers who openly disavow systematic analysis are in fact theorists of a sort—especially the ones who "let the facts speak for themselves." There are two possible by-products of this kind of conference: one is that the jargon problem may be clarified—perhaps mainly by an explicit attempt to keep ourselves intellectually honest; the other is that some encouragement may be lent to text-writers in our field who will introduce their books with a clear invitation to the reader to assume a certain posture toward the human behavior to be studied—to wear temporarily the hat of the amateur analyst, not the participant in the everyday world.

5) *The Problem of "Real" People, the "Real" World, and "Concrete Entities."* [9] While it may be carrying coals to Newcastle to continue doing so, I wish to suggest another characteristic of political science which bears on this conference and on the approach discussed in this paper. We may have imposed an unnecessary handicap on ourselves by virtually imprisoning much of our analysis within the framework of the common-sense world: *i.e.*, we have been impaled on *reality* experienced as ordinary humans, not as observers—on "real" persons and "real" entities. This opens up a bundle of problems which cannot be explored here, but the point worth emphasizing is that unifying concepts, if they are designed to help reconstruct and explain political behavior, cannot be chained to everyday concepts. The distinction between the observer and his operations on the one hand, and the social world he reconstitutes on the other, is simple yet basic. A host of confusions arise from the failure to be self-conscious about this distinction. For example, there is often evident a subtle tendency to impose the observer's rationality (either his rules of investigative procedures or his standards for conduct generally) upon persons who are being observed. At any rate, there are two portraits of the social world: one given by intuition and direct description, the other made by systematic and experimental analysis of the conditions correlated with the events initially described. The first is very close to the common-sense world, the second results from an entirely different order—the rules under which the common-sense world is to be reconstituted. These are clearly not the same. Conceptualization is, I take it, concerned with the second portrait.

Now if we were to be sound generalizers about human behavior we could not, obviously, always talk in terms of *whole, real persons;* nor should we try (even if this were possible) to recapture the complete detail, *i.e.,* the *uniqueness* of particular events and situations. So far we have neglected to explore on any noticeable scale such analytical devices as *actor, role, system, unit,* and so on—all of which are artificial creations endowed with certain properties which can, presumably, be checked against empirical evidence. The use of such devices should enable us to isolate the common elements upon which generalization can be based. No one "saw" or will "see" an actor. However, since the actor is an analytic dummy, we can build into him properties and characteristics which may be remarkably like but not identical with real persons. What this comes down to is this: analytical models of this type enable us to focus on behavioral aspects of interest to us without having to deal with whole people and reality in the usual sense.

We are therefore relieved—and *explicitly* so—from some of the insurmountable analytical barriers imposed by those who insist on realism.

There are, of course, limitations—or penalties—which accompany the attempt to use models in the description and explanation of behavior. Our statements about how real persons will behave, based upon what our model predicts, will be limited to the properties built into the model in the first place. In return, however, we have a chance to do simulated, controlled experiments of the kind social science is allegedly not capable of doing.

A related point here I shall only mention briefly because it will be covered by Marion Levy's paper. One very important—and useful—distinction in social research is that between *analytic* and *concrete structures*. A crude explanation of the difference would be this: suppose we imagine six members of the State Department sitting around a table discussing a foreign policy problem—this would be a concrete structure. But if we decided we wanted to concentrate on one aspect of the relationships among them, say, the *authority relationships,* the structure of authority relationships, either postulated or discovered, would be an analytic structure. Here again liberation from the welter of actual relationships is possible—at a price. If we speak of the political structure (or structures) of a society and the nonpolitical structures are viewed as analytic structures, we cannot say anything about causal relationships.

6) *The Problem of Comparability*. Finally, a word on comparison, which is a hallmark of any science. It would be pretentious of me to imply that I can represent the sentiments of the competent scholars who specialize in something called comparative government. Evidence suggests, however, that there is dissatisfaction and re-examination at present. A casual perusal of textbooks and articles reveals that genuine comparability (*i.e.,* comparison with the purpose of throwing light on a general class of phenomena rather than simply revealing differences) is relatively scarce. No single volume or even several volumes offer the student a conceptual basis on which the political systems of the United States, Great Britain, France, China, and the Soviet Union can be analyzed on even a moderately high level of generalization. Descriptive materials are fortunately abundant yet explanations of contrasting features is notoriously weak.

There are several other rather obvious comments which are pertinent to the purposes of this paper. First, there has been—at least it appears so —a disproportionate emphasis on *differences* with a consequent neglect of *uniformities*. Superficially it is a lot easier to detect differences and it requires no elaborate conceptual scheme to establish simple classifications of differences. Cultural bias reinforces this tendency because if the observer is not confronted by familiar symbols and institutional expressions he may *assume* fundamental differences. The structure and function, or patterns and consequences, stands out in this respect. Second, much writing in the comparative government wing of political science tends to focus on concrete structures. Thus a complete and fruitful comparative analysis of, say, Congress and Parliament is unlikely or is extremely difficult. But, to take one example, an analysis of Congress and Parliament as information systems might yield some interesting insights.

Third, the categorization of governments as "free," "totalitarian," "socialistic" and so on, while perfectly proper for some purposes (*e.g.,* for applying criteria of goodness or badness, or rightness or wrongness), may have slowed up the development of categories intended to point toward differences and uniformities of political phenomena generally. Fourth, it is somewhat puzzling that very little attention has been paid to comparative analysis within a single society. Would a comparison between a large urban council and one house of a state legislature be entirely fruitless? Or comparison between policy-making bodies at various levels of government? Comparison within the executive branch has not been carried very far. One would expect that once categories, types, concepts and other apparatus are available, the potential comparability of political phenomena within a single over-all system will be ascertainable.

Summary. I have attempted to state briefly six weaknesses or sources of difficulty which we ought to keep in mind as we discuss unifying concepts. The selective nature of my comment under each heading has undoubtedly skewed the total picture somewhat. Nevertheless, if I have directly or indirectly called attention to the fact that political science is not self-conscious enough about its major analytical problems, I shall be satisfied.

THE LOCATION OF THE DECISION-MAKING APPROACH

In order that the reader may gain some perspective on the kind of scheme outlined here, I should like to locate decision-making in terms of (*a*) its place among various types of social analysis and some of its analytic properties; (*b*) its relation to existing interests and approaches in political science; and (*c*) its relation to work going on in other disciplines.

Decision-Making and Social Analysis Generally. The decision-making approach to the study of politics clearly belongs in the category of *dynamic,* as distinct from static, analysis. I hesitate to introduce this distinction because the words are ambiguous and because the line is much fuzzier than the words suggest. Relatively speaking, dynamic analysis is *process* analysis. By process is meant here, briefly, *time* plus *change*—change in relationships and conditions. Process analysis concerns a *sequence of events,*[10] *i.e.,* behavioral events. In general, static analysis is a snapshot at one point in time. One basic difference between the two types is in the way (or ways) the time factor is handled. An important brand of static analysis [11] (namely structural-functional analysis), can yield information on the nature of change between two periods in time and on the conditions under which change took place but not on the reasons for change or how it actually unfolded.

In turn, there are two kinds of process analysis: *interaction* and *decision-making*. So far as I can see, there are only two ways of scientifically studying process in the sense employed here: the making and executing of decisions and the patterns of interaction between individuals, states, organizations, groups, jurisdictions, and so on. Interaction analysis does not and cannot yield answers to "why" questions. Thus interactions can be described and measured but the explanation of the patterns—why they evolved as they did—must rest on decision-making analysis.[12]

These distinctions are neither intended to prejudice the case for or against decision-making analysis, nor are they intended to reflect favorably or unfavorably on static and dynamic analysis. As a matter of fact, I believe these types can and should supplement each other. I do not believe they are rivals (except for the energy and attention of scholars) because there are certain things each can and cannot do.[13] Requisite analysis, for example, can aid decision-making analysis though time does not permit me to discuss the point here.

C. Wright Mills[14] has made a related and also useful distinction between what he calls macroscopic and molecular social research. This distinction, too, is one of degree and emphasis. The former embraces such things as the total social structure, global forces, great sweeps of history, and gross patterns of relationship. The latter embraces the actions and reactions of social beings in particular situations and under particular conditions. Obviously, decision-making belongs more in the latter category than in the former. It is worth noting that, as Mills says, we have as yet found no satisfactory way of relating these two types of research.

Thus decision-making is one phase or form of social action analysis. The term action has a technical meaning, not a commonsense meaning. Analytically, action depends on the empirical existence of the following components: actor (or actors), goals, means, and situation. While this formulation is borrowed from Parsons and Shils,[15] the conceptualization outlined below owes more of an intellectual debt to the writings of Alfred Schuetz.[16] Although the two schools overlap and agree in many particulars, there are fundamental differences in the observer's relationship to the actor. One such difference is that under the Parsonian scheme, a rational model of action is assumed: the observer's criteria of rationality are imposed on the actor. My own feeling is that, on balance, decision-making needs a phenomenological approach.[17] Hence no rational actor[18] is assumed in the present scheme and the observer's criteria are not imposed on the actor.

Decision-Making and Political Science. Many will probably resist the assertion that the systematic analysis of decision-making has been slighted. Yet a careful examination of the literature—particularly, of course, in public administration—reveals that this is true. Now it should be said at once that there is much discussion concerning decisions, *i.e.,* cases, administrative structure (*e.g.,* authority) and the factors which decision-makers take into account. As a matter of fact, it might be said this is what administration is about. Nonetheless, despite centuries of interest in public policy and despite the development of theory and systematic analysis in the public administration field, we have no really fruitful concept of decision-making (*i.e.,* policy-formation).[19]

Much of the conceptualization—if any—is implicit. As already noted, key words like *policy, objective, decision,* and *decision-making* remain for the most part inadequately defined or are assumed to have agreed meaning.[20] Barnard[21] and Simon[22] were among the first to insist on the primary significance of decisions in administrative organizations. Yet neither of these trail-blazers nor their contemporaries and successors have given us an answer to a very important question: if we wish to describe and explain decision-making behavior scientifically what kinds of intellectual operations are required? It is in this sense that the literature is somewhat barren. Pages and pages are available on the *substance* of decisions and *on the formal structure within which decision-making takes place,* but very few pages on *how to analyze* decisions and decision-making.[23] Problems of analysis per se are only beginning to be probed and the chief initiative has come from outside political science.[24] Although again I cannot speak as an expert in public administration, it appears to me that systematization is somewhat handicapped by implicitly different models of organization.[25]

Specifically, while in Barnard's words decision-making has been recognized "as the search for strategic factors"[26] on the part of decision-makers, no explicit categories have been established for probing why the search for these factors takes place and why it takes the forms it does. No economical set of variables has been developed for analyzing decision-making behavior. In the absence of any kind of conceptual scheme, it is difficult if not logically impossible to generalize from the abundance of case material such as is contained in Harold Stein's *Public Administration and Policy Development.* To beg all these questions is to block off interesting areas of research and to surrender too easily to "enigmas." Perhaps we ought to insist upon holding more matters problematical in political analysis. To assume is not to explain, though making assumptions is an aid to research.

At any rate, in addition to the public administration literature (I am omitting business administration for the moment), decision-making enters into the study of international politics.[27] As is true of public administration generally, there is much writing on foreign policy-making but it concerns the structural machinery (not the process) and individual cases[28] with relatively no attempt to establish categories and employ the action approach. The literature of international politics offers very fertile ground for the exploration of the decision-making approach, and some of the basic "why" questions of national behavior cannot be answered without it. American foreign policy materials lie virtually un-mined at present.[29] Closely related is the field of diplomatic history [30] where materials on particular cases, on procedures, on personalities, on precedent and so on definitely tie in with any emphasis on policy-formation.

Another paradox in political science is the lack—or so it would seem from the literature—of any systematic attention to the analysis of the decision-making behavior of judges.[31] Again there is case material and much on what judges *say* they do. Decision-making in regulatory agencies is also pertinent.[32] The third element in the triumvirate is, of course, the legislative process. Here we are somewhat better off because of the step-by-step procedures and because of some excellent case studies.[33] Nevertheless, we learn more about *what* happened (and we may learn the why of a particular bill) than about basic determinants of congressional choice. Another area of political science which relates to decision-making is personality theory—which perhaps ought to be regarded as a subhead under leadership. Increasing interest has been shown in personality traits and leadership capacity (one aspect of which is formulating alternatives) in personality types as analytic devices for explaining political responses and for demonstrating political institutional impacts on the individual, and in the social background of political decision-makers.[34] A close kin to these interests is the biographical approach, *i.e.,* case studies of individual decision-makers.

A very significant area of research and analysis is the behavior of nongovernmental groups. As David Truman has amply demonstrated,[35] it is necessary to know more than what these groups do in their attempts to influence public opinion, each other, and the various levels of government. Their organization is important and equally so is the decision-making process which in effect produces their strategies. Interactional analysis alone will not provide this. Finally, choice looms large in individual political responses. Voting behavior, group membership, and other political actions usually result from conscious decisions.

I shall omit here any reference to political theory in the sense of lore, doctrine, or values. My inclination is to believe that decision-making analysis, if it can be tested empirically, ought to throw many propositions current in our discipline into unflattering relief.

Decision-Making and Non-political Science Disciplines. Clearly there is not time to discuss all the other research (using the term broadly to include concept-formation) currently going on even if it were given to one man to know and grasp it. Only the major connections will be mentioned. An imposing and related cluster of activities can be grouped under the heading of "organizational behavior." For the most part this seems to include students of public administration,[36] sociology, business administration, economics, and social psychology. Most of the attempted synthesis and construction of analytical tools can be found reflected in the journal articles and books of non-political scientists.[37] Synthesis is seen in such collections as: Merton, *Reader in Bureaucracy;*[38] Dubin, *Human Relations in Administration;*[39] and Gouldner, *Studies in Leadership.*[40] Sociologists have been groping toward a more orderly theoretical basis for organizational analysis.[41] Lately there has been a revival of interest in the works of Max Weber who seems, incidentally, not to be a seminal writer for political scientists. The interests, and to a certain extent the researches, of students in business administration are closely related—in particular the Harvard Business School.[42] There seems little doubt that business itself has come to show greater interest in decision-making.[43] If carefully read and with explicit concepts in mind, the business administration materials can, I feel, be profitable to the political scientist.[44] Occasionally, aid comes from the strangest places. Thus what appears to be a "how-to" volume—Irwin Bross, *Design for Decision* (Macmillan, 1953)—turns out in Chapter 1 to have rather more than the normal insights into decisions and decision-making. Again, the Entrepreneurial History Project at Harvard has done some conceptual work on decisions.[45]

Psychologists and social psychologists have done substantial research in group problem-solving and in group behavior generally.[46] I believe this work is of great potential value to political science, but as I tried to say earlier, it has to be handled with care. Since we are speaking here of organizational behavior, one word of caution can be suggested. Some of the small-group experiments, though actually conducted within a business or other type organization, are nonetheless ripped out of any organization context. That is, the organizational roles and motives of the individuals observed are not under investigation; therefore, transferability of findings should remain problematical.

Turning aside from organization behavior per se, the relevant work of other groups of scholars must be noted. At the community level, tentative efforts to case social analysis in a decision-making mold are evident in Floyd Hunter's *Community Power Structure.*[47] Professional philosophers have also been concerned with decisions, but rather at the level of individual behavior.[48] As I have already mentioned, the essays of Alfred Schuetz[49] seem to me to be valuable on a number of grounds, including his incisive comments on the relationship between common sense and scientific constructs. In the field of economic analysis, there are several developments bearing on decision-making. Introduction of psychological variables has opened up the whole question of motivation in economic decisions.[50] Black[51] and others have explored the possibilities of mathematically analyzing the nature of committee decisions—particularly majority decisions. Arrow has attempted to establish a basis for discovering the "system of preferences" prevailing among a group of decision-makers.[52] The theories of Black and Arrow give special attention to the committee or small group as a decision-making body, thus suggesting, of course, a particular relevance to policy-making. Finally mention must be made of game theory.[53] There is not space here to go into the possible insights a nonmathematician can derive from the theory of games.[54] My impression is that the lines of communication are as yet too feeble to warrant political scientists rejecting game theory summarily. Karl Deutsch has made an interesting attempt to apply game theory to the study of international politics.[55] Among other things, game theory points to the central importance of information in decision-making—a point to which we will return below.

Summary. I have begged the reader's indulgence for this rather rudimentary excursion in order to make four points: (1) whether one is a specialist in public administration or whether one "buys" the decision-making approach, there is exciting work going on which the student of public policy ought to sample; (2) despite the materials cited—and these are only representative—we still lack a conceptual scheme for analyzing decision-making; (3) research and theorizing in decision-making is on the whole valuable but not integrated to any extent; (4) any decision-making scheme in political science not only has a storehouse of experience to draw on but can justify itself because of its integrative value for a wide variety of efforts. I shall argue that if a sound conceptual framework can be constructed, decision-making analysis will be appropriate for *any* area of political science where there is an interest in policy-formation or judgment of some kind.[56]

THE DECISION-MAKING APPROACH [57]

I cannot hope to say all there is to say about the decision-making concept even at this crude stage in its development. Perhaps enough will be said to enable the reader to decide whether he wishes to hear more and to stimulate discussion. I shall deliberately simplify and assume that questions lead to an expansion—or perhaps exposure—of some facets. What follows is at most a frame of reference—not a general theory.[58]

There are two fundamental purposes of the decision-making approach: to help identify and isolate the "crucial structures" in the political realm where change takes place—where action is initiated and carried out, where decisions must be made; and to help analyze systematically the decision-making behavior which leads to action and which sustains action.

Some Postulates. (1) The decision-making approach herein formulated focuses inquiry on a class of actors called decision-makers. On the assumption that *authoritative* (*i.e.,* binding on the whole society viewed as a political association or on some segment thereof also viewed as a political association, such as states, counties, and cities) action can be decided upon and initiated by *public officials,* who are formally or actually responsible for decisions and who engage in the making of decisions, our actors are official actors. These officials comprise a *reservoir* of decision-makers from which particular groups are drawn for particular decision-making purposes. We are concerned, then, primarily with the behavior of members of the total governmental organization in any society. And we are concerned therefore only with decisions made *within* that structure.[59] From past experience, I am aware that many will gag on this assumption. Without attempting to argue the case fully, let me anticipate some of the difficulty. An insistence upon a clear distinction between the governmental and nongovernmental realms for purposes of decision-making analysis *appears* to imply a narrowing of the definition of *political.*[60] This runs counter to the prevailing doctrine among behavioral political scientists and those who have been promoting "political process" research.[61] Also it seems to be a retreat from the discovery that noninstitutional social factors are basic to an understanding of political life. To focus on the behavior of official decision-makers seems to omit those powerful nongovernmental (but political by the broad definition) figures who (allegedly) *really* make the decisions.

To clarify, let it be said that this postulate does *not* imply that *all* politically important decisions are made *within* the governmental structure. I do insist that only decisions actually made by public officials are politically *authoritative.* A decision by a corporation or an organized group may be very significant politically and it may affect or be binding on certain persons, but it is not binding on the community politically organized. Furthermore, I know of no way that such nongovernmental decisions can be shown to have consequences for governmental decisions without accounting for the behavior of official decision-makers.

Earlier I made a distinction between two kinds of process analysis: *interaction* and *decision-making.* This may save some misunderstanding on the present point. Interaction process analysis does not require—and indeed would be handicapped by—a separation of decision-makers into official and nonofficial groups or a boundary line beween governmental and nongovernmental decision-making. But the limitation here is that interaction analysis per se cannot answer "why" questions of decision-making activity. To reiterate, if one wants to analyze the "why" of governmental decisions, some other conceptual scheme is required.

I have become convinced that when one shifts to decision-making analysis, it is far less troublesome methodologically to *account* only for the behavior of official decision-makers and to relate them to decision-makers outside of government by some other scheme than one which requires that *both* groups be regarded as actors *in the same social system*—which means accounting for the behavior of both according to formal rules of action analysis.

2) The behavior of official decision-makers should be described and ex-

plained in terms of action analysis. This means treating the decision-maker as an "actor in a situation." In turn, this means we make a basic choice to take as our prime analytical objective the recreation of the "social world" of the decision-makers as *they* view it. Our task is to devise a conceptual scheme which will help us to reconstruct the situation as defined by the decision-makers. The key to political action lies in the way decision-makers as actors define their situation. Definition of the situation is built around the projected action as well as the reasons for the action. Therefore, it is necessary to analyze the decision-makers in the following terms:

a) their *discrimination* and *relating* of objects, conditions, and other actors—various things are perceived or expected in a relational context;

b) the existence, establishment, or definition of *goals*—various things are wanted from the situation;

c) attachment of significance to various courses of action suggested by the situation according to some criteria of estimation;

d) application of "standards of acceptability" which (1) narrow the range of perceptions; (2) narrow the range of objects wanted; and (3) narrow the number of alternatives.

Three features of all orientations emerge: *perception, choice,* and *expectation.* Perhaps a translation of the vocabulary of action theory will be useful. We are saying that the actors' orientations to the action are reconstructed when the following kinds of questions are answered: What did the decision-makers think was relevant in a particular situation? How did they determine this? How were the relevant factors related to each other—what connections did the decision-makers see between diverse elements in the situation? How did they establish the connections? What wants and needs were deemed involved in or affected by the situation? What were the sources of these wants and needs? How were they related to the situation? What specific or general goals were considered and selected? What courses of action were deemed fitting and effective? How were fitness and effectiveness decided?

In other words, the actor-situation approach to social analysis alerts the observer to the *discrimination of relevancies*—to the *selection and valuation* of objects, events, symbols, conditions, and other actors. These relevancies are, so to speak, carved from a total number of phenomena present in the over-all setting.[62] Of the phenomena which might have been relevant, the actors (decision-makers) finally endow only some with *significance.* Relevancies may be "given" for the actors (*i.e.,* not open to their independent judgment, and among the "givens" will be certain cues to the determination of other relevancies). The situation—as defined—arises from selective perception: it is abstracted from a larger setting.

3) "Situation" is an analytical concept pointing to a pattern of relationship among events, objects, conditions, and other actors organized around a focus (objective, problem, course of action) which is the center of interest for the decision-makers.[63] As noted above, typologies are important to unifying concepts. A decision-making frame of reference will require several, among them a typology of kinds of situations. Only a crude formulation is possible here:

a) *Structured* vs. *unstructured situations*—pointing to the relative degree of ambiquity and stability; a situation for which the decision-makers find it difficult to establish meaning may be characterized by change as well as intrinsic obscurity.

b) Situations having different degrees of *requiredness, i.e.,* the amount of pressure to act and its source (from within the decisional system or from the setting).

c) The *cruciality* of situations—their relatedness to, and importance for, the basic purposes and values of the decision-makers.

d) *Kinds* of affect with which the situation is endowed by the decision-makers—threatening, hostile, avoidance-inducing, favorable, unfavorable, and so on.

e) How the problem is interpreted and how its *major functional characteristic* is assigned—political, moral, economic, military, or a combination of these.

f) The *time* dimension—the degree of permanence attributed to various situations.

g) The degree *to which objective factors impose* themselves on the decision-makers—the number of uncontrollable factors and imponderables.

Perhaps the chief advantage of such a breakdown is to remind us of the fact that certain objective properties of a situation will be partly responsible for the reactions and orientations of the decision-makers and that the assignment of properties to a situation by the decision-makers is indicative of clues to the rules which may have governed their particular responses.

The Organizational Context. All political decisions (as defined), on whatever level of government or wherever in the total structure of government, are formulated and executed in an organizational context. Having said that we will concentrate on decision-makers and how they orient to action, it is necessary to consider them as participants in a system of action. The concept of system is essentially an ordering device implying certain defined types of relationships among the decision-makers and patterns of activities which they engage in. Major characteristics of the system determine to a considerable extent the manner in which the decision-makers relate themselves to the setting. The type of social system with which we are primarily concerned is an organization. Many studies of politics ignore or merely assume the fact that decision-makers operate in a highly particular and specific context. To ignore this context omits a range of factors which significantly influence the behavior of decision-makers and omit not only the critical problem of how choices are made but also the conditions under which choices are made. I am convinced that many of the difficulties surrounding the attempt to apply personality theory, culture theory, and small-group theory have been due to a failure to consider the peculiar social system in which decision-makers function. Emphasis on personality and so-called informal factors [64] has tended to minimize the importance of formal factors. Combined with some of the consequences of the "political process" approach, the individual policy-maker has been regarded as operating in a vacuum.

Since we are interested in process analysis we shall take for granted many of the commonly recognized structural features of organization. In other words, such factors as personnel, internal specialization, authority and control, routinized relationships, professionalized positions and careers, and so on will be considered as given prerequisites.

Organizational Decision-Making.[65] Here is a tentative definition plus a commentary: *Decision-making results in the selection from a socially defined, limited number of problematical, alternative projects (i.e., courses of action) of one project to bring about the particular future state of affairs envisaged by the decision-makers.*

Explanation and Assumptions. (1) Decision-making leads to a *course of action* based on the project. *Project* is employed here to include both objectives and techniques. The course of action moves along a *path* toward the outcome envisaged. Adoption of the project signifies that the decision-makers were motivated by an intention to accomplish something. The means included in the project are also socially defined.

2) Organizational decision-making is a *sequence of activities*. The particular sequence is an *event* which for purposes of analysis may be isolated. The event chosen determines in good part what is or is not relevant. To illustrate: if the event in which the observer is interested is the making of the Japanese Peace Treaty, then the focus of attention is the system that produced the treaty and the various factors influencing the decision-making in that system. NATO, EDC, ERP, the Technical Assistance Program, etc., are not relevant. If, on the other hand, the over-all cluster of policy decisions with respect to the policy of containment is the focus, the Japanese Peace Treaty and NATO, EDC, ERP, the Technical Assistance Program and a number of other factors all become a part of the strategies of implementation.

3) The event can be considered a unified whole or it can be separated into its constituent elements. A suggested breakdown might be in terms of

the sequence of activities: (*a*) pre-decisional activities, (*b*) choice, and (*c*) implementation.

4) Some choices are made at every stage of the decision-making process. The *point of decision* is that stage in the sequence at which decision-makers having the authority choose a specific course of action to be implemented and assume responsibility for it. The weeding out of information, condensation of memoranda, etc., all involve decisions which must be recognized as such by the observer.

5) Choice involves *evaluation* in terms of a *frame of reference. Weights* and *priorities* are then assigned to alternative projects.

6) The *occasion for decision* arises from uncertainty. Some aspect of the situation is no longer taken for granted and becomes problematical in terms of the decision-maker's frame of reference.

7) The problem requiring decision may originate within the decisional system or it may originate in a change in the internal or external setting.

8) The *range of alternative projects* which the decision-makers consider is limited. Limitations exist both as to means and ends. Limitations on the range of alternative projects are due in large part to the following factors: The individual decision-maker's past experience and values, the amount of available and utilized information, situational elements, the characteristics of the organizational system, and the known available resources.

Definition of the Decisional Unit and of the Decision-Makers. It is necessary to establish boundaries which encompass the actors and activities to be observed and explained. Here we specify that the organizational system within which a decision-making event takes place is the decisional *unit* which becomes the focal point of observation. The unit embraces, analytically, the actors and the system of activities which results in decision.

By what criteria is the decisional unit to be isolated and differentiated? The single criterion which seems at the moment to be most useful is the objective or mission. Objective or mission is taken to mean a particular desired future state of affairs having a specific referent. Specificity is most crucial because it is only possible to speak of the unit (or organization or system) with respect to a specified objective. In other words, regardless of the level of government or the size of the unit, it is constituted by the observer in terms of the decision-makers responsible for, and activities geared to, a particular policy, problem, or other specific assignment. With respect to any objective or mission, there is an organizational unit so constituted as to be able to select a course of action for that objective.

In passing, it might be noted that as the concept of decision-making is refined, two other typologies will be useful: a typology of kinds of political objectives and a typology of decisional units.[66]

Immediately, a two-headed question will be asked: how can the observer be sure he has all the actors in the unit who were involved in a decision and how is "involved" to be interpreted? This is mostly a matter for empirical investigation in the particular case. Very often there are established, well defined units. In some cases it may be necessary to do some detective work to reconstruct the unit. Undoubtedly, the observer will have awkward choices to make occasionally as to whether an actor or a function is to be included or excluded. When this is true, the observer will have to choose on the basis of his analytical purposes. The one great advantage of establishing the unit on the basis of the purposes of its activities is that we can avoid having to be content only with high level abstractions such as the State Department or the city government or the company, and when several agencies or other concrete structures are engaged in policy-making, only the relevant actors and functions need be considered.

The Unit as Organization. The constituent elements of *any* decisional unit will be suggested below. Here we shall only indicate that all units will be organizational in the sense that activities and relationships will be the outcome of the operation of formal rules governing the allocation of power and responsibility, motivation, communication, performance of function, problem-solving, and so on. Each unit will have its own organization in this sense. Obviously, the particular organizational form which a unit takes will depend on how and why the unit was established, who the members are, and what its specific task is. A unit may be a one-shot affair—as in the case of the Japanese Peace Treaty or an ad hoc investigating committee in Congress. Or, a unit may represent a typical decisional system for dealing with typical objectives as in the case of an interdepartmental committee at the federal level or the city council.

The Origins of Units. I have argued that the unit is an analytical tool —a device to aid the observer in reconstituting the decision-making universe and in establishing boundaries. However, as hinted above, the empirical question underlying the concept of the unit is: who becomes involved in a decision, how, and why? How does the group of officials (actors, decision-makers) whose deliberations result in decision become assembled? Often, of course, the answer to this question is essential to an explanation of why the decision-makers decided the way they did. Two methods of unit construction may be suggested: *automatic assignment* and *negotiation*. Sometimes the selection of decision-makers from the total number who might in any substructure of government become involved is based on a simple classification of problems or decisions. The formal roles of the actors provide the clue as to whether they will be part of the unit. Also, as already noted, there are standing units (*i.e.*, committees or groups) who are expected to act on given matters. A quite different method of selection is negotiation in cases where no routine procedures exist or where new conditions require special procedure. Negotiation may be simply a matter of springing the right officials loose for a particular task or it may represent basic disagreement over the location of authority and power. Thus everywhere in government the decisions on who will decide are extremely important.

In the case of complex governmental institutions in which a great many activities and a great many officials are involved, often the unit may be created by default. That is, the unit is constituted empirically by the actors, who, in effect, select themselves into it.

The Unit and the Setting. Every group of decision-makers functions in a larger setting. Setting is felt, analytically, to be more satisfactory than environment, which has certain explicit connotations in psychology and has ambiguous connotations otherwise. Setting refers to a set of categories of *potentially relevant factors and conditions* which may affect the action of decision-makers. Relevance of particular kinds of factors and conditions *in general* and *in particular situations* will depend on the attitudes, perceptions, judgments, and purposes of particular groups of decision-makers, *i.e.,* how they react to various stimuli. Setting thus is an analytical device to suggest certain enduring kinds of relevance and to limit the number of nongovernmental factors with which the student of politics must be concerned. The setting, empirically, is constantly changing and will be composed of *what the decision-makers decide is important* or *what is "given" as important.*

Two aspects of the setting of any decisional unit deserve mention: the social setting and the political institutional setting. Normally and familiarly, social setting designates public opinion, including the possible reactions of veto-groups. For bureaucracy, this means the general public *and* the specific clientele—either for regular government services or "attentive publics" [67] or an ad hoc interest grouping based on particular issues. However, an adequate concept of decision-making will include in the social setting much more fundamental categories: major common-value orientations, major characteristics of social organization, group structures and function, major institutional patterns, basic social processes (adult socialization and opinion formation), and social differentiation and specialization. From these can be derived conditions and forces of immediate impact on decision-makers.

Several of these can be noted briefly. First, every action taken by the decision-makers has consequences in the society at large. One kind of feedback is that the society experiences its own decisions. Possible effects can range from redistribution of social power to specific complaints, from puzzlement to understanding, from acceptance to rejection. Second, policies are usually accompanied by official interpretations which may or may not agree with nongovernmental interpretations. The strategies of *legitimation* chosen by decision-makers have a very crucial effect on the way policy results are viewed. Third, the society provides decision-makers with a wide range of means—technical services in which government must rely on private sources.

Fourth, the social system has an important bearing on *who* gets recruited into decision-making posts and *how*. This raises the whole question of support for the governmental structure and this question leads to the internal adjustments in response to the social setting. In particular, this point subsumes the number of private agencies and individuals which can hold the decision-makers responsible.

The political institutional setting is perhaps a much more immediate factor. This consists of what might be called the total organizational reservoir from which the constituent elements are drawn, including constitutional prerogatives, rules of the game, responsibility equations, general purposes, concrete membership groups, roles, functions, pools of information, communication links, and so on. These are the items of traditional concern in government —government in general. Basically, the institutional setting viewed in this light is a vast pool of rules, personnel, and information for the decisional units. Within this pool, certain specialized activities—*not* concerned directly with decision-making and execution—are carried on day by day. The decision-making approach does not ignore or render unnecessary structural institutional analysis. On the contrary, it requires more and more thorough analyses of this sort, and, hopefully, it can add to their usefulness.

Unless the particular substructure is very small (*e.g.,* a village or town) any decisional unit is likely to exist simultaneously with other units. These units will be analytically connected because of the following kinds of factors: (*a*) overlapping membership; (*b*) a common set of givens—rules and precedents; (*c*) common objectives throughout the total system; (*d*) overlapping jurisdictions; (*e*) reciprocal impact of courses of action adopted.

To return to the notion of definition of the situation: the line between what is included in the definition and what is not is not just a boundary between relevance and nonrelevance. Two types of relationship appear within the defined situation. On the one hand, there will be relationships among factors within the social setting and the institutional setting and between these two aspects of the setting. On the other hand, there will be relationships between the setting *and* the plans, purposes, and programs of the decision-makers.

Limitations on Decision-Making. The concept of limitations constitutes a set of assumptions about *any* decisional system. The assumptions concern the factors or conditions which limit (*a*) alternative objectives; (*b*) alternative techniques; (*c*) the combination of *a* plus *b* into strategies or projects; (*d*) decision-making resources—time, energy, skills, information; and (*e*) degree of control of external setting. In accordance with our general phenomenological approach, we feel that the range and impact of limitations should be considered from the decision-maker's point of view, although many such assessments will be objectively verifiable. The main categories of limitations in terms of their sources are: those arising from *outside* the decisional system, those arising from the nature and functioning of the decisional system, and those arising from a combination of both of these.

Limitations Internal to the Decision-Making System. For purposes of illustration, let us list briefly some major limitations of this kind. It must be emphasized that the limitations traceable to bureaucratic pathology are perhaps the most dramatic but certainly not the only ones.

1) Information.—The decision-makers may lack information or may act on inaccurate information; in either case, the range of alternatives considered may be affected. It would appear to be a permanent liability of the decision-making process that relevant information is almost never completely adequate and testable. The necessity to adopt and employ interpretive schemes and compensatory devices such as simplification of phenomena provide a related source of limitation.

2) Communication Failures.—Reasonably full information may be present in the decisional unit but not circulate to all the decision-makers who need it to perform their roles satisfactorily. A decisional unit may be resistant to *new* information or the significance of new information may be lost because of the way messages are labeled and stored.

3) Precedent.—Previous actions and policy rules (the givens for any unit) may automatically narrow the deliberations of the decision-makers. Previous action may prohibit serious consideration of a whole range of projects. Reversal of policies is difficult in a vast organization.

4) Perception.—The selective discrimination of the setting may effectively limit action. What the decision-makers "see" is what they act upon. Through perception—and judgment—external limitations gain their significance.

5) Scarce Resources.—The fact that any unit is limited in the time, energy, and skills (and sometimes money) at its disposal also tends to limit the thoroughness of deliberation and the effectiveness with which certain related functions are performed. Time pressures may seriously restrict the number of possible courses of action which can be explored.

THE DETERMINANTS OF DECISION-MAKING BEHAVIOR

Having said that the actions of decision-makers can be conveniently analyzed in terms of a particular kind of social system which functions in an organizational unit, we come now to the factors which determine the choices of these decision-makers. I propose that any such system or unit—be it a congressional committee, a school board, the National Security Council, the Republican National Committee, a city council, or the Supreme Court—can be analyzed fruitfully in terms of three significant variables: *spheres of competence; communication and information;* and *motivation.* Discussion of these variables should be followed with the review of the literature of decision-making in mind.

Two things must be said at once. First, these variables must stand only as assumptions until empirical evidence sustains or refutes them—meanwhile I argue their logical capacity to account for *all* factors which influence decision-making. Second, one reason why this whole scheme is not a theory is that the three variables deal with decision-making from two fundamentally different perspectives: the properties of the *system* (structure and process) and the *actor* (individual decision-maker). The nature of these three variables can only be suggested briefly here.

Spheres of Competence.[68] Competence includes not only the structure of relationships and activities which results from the operation of formal rules but also the conventional methods of action necessary to achieve the organizational mission. In brief, this means the explicitly prescribed job specifications *plus* supplementary patterns of action established and sanctioned by precedent and habit. Together, the prescribed rules and the conventional rules make up what we may call the formal characteristics of the organization. Prescribed rules and conventional rules together may be viewed as a set of guides to the conduct of the decision-maker. The rules thus comprise a normative order—a legitimate normative order—to which the actor is bound and which he must interpret.

For any decisional unit, there will be a considerable amount of information generally available to the observer concerning the division of work, structure of authority, flow of information, and so on which provide the framework within which the decision-maker operates. Evidence of this kind would be sought in statutes, directives, charters, and organizational manuals. In addition, other rules—equally necessary to the system—must be sought in routine responses, precedents, and presuppositions which comprise a set of implicit understandings.

The structure of competences within the decisional unit will determine the behavior of the actor in terms of: the specific functions assigned to him and what these mean; the command or subordinate relationships between himself and other decision-makers; the horizontal relationships with other decision-makers on the same level of authority; and the expectation he has of how his action will be received by others in the system and how others act. Viewed from the standpoint of the actor, then, his competence involves his qualifications to act, his authority to act, and the expectation that he will act and that his action will be received in a certain way. The structure consists of the interrelation of numerous individual competences.

Both prescribed rules and conventional rules governing the actor's orientation toward his competence inevitably allow room for the actor's own interpretation. His job description, his powers, and the expectations concerning him cannot be perfectly appropriate for all conditions and circumstances and therefore he still has choices to make. Regardless of how simplified a model of the actor we employ, it must include at least some elements of

his value system, his prior experience, and his learned behavior in order
to explain his discretionary behavior within the formal structure. Latitude
in interpretation will also be related to the actor's position in the hierarchy
and to his expertness. Any concept of decision-making must allow for the
interaction between the actor and his competence. Thus the sphere of competence must be regarded as flexible. We are handicapped here because organization theory has rarely dealt with the problem. One thing we can say
is that an interpretative scale-of-competence is needed, ranging from the
extreme in latitude to what might be called completely strict construction.
The theoretical limits would seem to be fairly clear: at the extreme of
greatest latitude, the organizational system would cease to exist or change
into another unit; at the other extreme, obedience of the "letter of the law"
would also cause destruction of the system.

This brief discussion of sphere of competence directs our attention to
several crucial factors:

1) Decisional units may be distinguished on the basis of the tightness or
looseness of the structure of competence—the latter being characterized by
relatively wide opportunity for discretionary behavior.

2) Not all relationships will be necessarily "authority" relationships and
therefore it will be necessary to ask whether the decision-makers equally
share decision-making responsibility.

3) It will also be important to inquire under what conditions there is a
discrepancy between the authority component of competence and the ex-
pectational and functional components and what the behavioral consequences are.

4) Given the interpretation of his competency by the individual actor
and the fact that different missions may be assigned to the same unit, it
follows that the decisional unit does not have *one* and *only* one structure
of competences. Rather each unit has a number of possible structures,
though each decision can have only one associated with it. The structure
which emerges may result from internal negotiation or from expectations.

5) The negotiation leading to the formation of the unit may importantly
determine the structure of competences by determining which actors (and
hence what functions, authority, and expectations) are included in the
membership.

6) Any decisional unit will have responsibility relationships to other units
and/or to the total governmental structure or a substructure which will be
related to its structure of competences—particularly to assigned duties, degree of authority, and normative rules binding the actors.

7) Tension points and conflicts may be linked to different functional
bases of competence (line *vs.* staff; areas *vs.* subject matter expert) and
to different satisfactions with the legitimate order.

8) Bureaucratization would appear to result from a process whereby more of the rules, precedents, and methods of operation are no longer easily subject to challenge, questioning, or amendment—in other words, a narrowing of choice through conventionalization.

9) Bureaucratization may simply mean a relatively great degree of efficient routinization of decision-making activities or it can mean that the institutionalization has been undermined by the persistent behavior of the actors.

Advisory vs. *Representational Roles.*[69] Competences in the decisional system are differentiated not only by the nature of authority attached to them and by specialized functions but also by the basis of participation in decision-making. Here I can only suggest briefly what is involved. Some decision-makers are automatically members of an organizational unit because of the competence they occupy. This is fairly simple and straightforward. But it is also true that in many complex systems of action, decisional units are so constituted that *claims,* or the *basis* of claims, to participation may exist and be honored. Thus some official individuals, groups, or other institutions can or may claim participation as a matter of *right,* whether this is given explicit expression or exists as a matter of general consensus. Federal interdepartmental committees are examples of participation (by some decision-makers at least) on the basis of something more than job description or expertness; namely, as representatives of agencies which have an interest in the particular organizational mission.

The advisory basis for participation involves neither claims nor authority-responsibility relationships. Such actors are brought into the system because of the need for special skills and information. Much more is implied here than expert recommendations since experts in subtle fashion may help to establish the bases of decision. Naturally, the line between advisory and representational is often blurred and one very significant organizational phenomenon is this: through time the advisory type becomes, through subtle transformation, representational.

Communication and Information. Thus far, we have analyzed certain of the structural features of the unit in terms of a set of relationships derived from spheres of competence, by which we mean: function, authority, and expectation as normatively ordered by prescribed and conventional rules. By implication at least, it was assumed that the members of the unit could communicate with one another and with others outside the unit. Ordinarily, political analysis has assumed or neglected this vital aspect of decision-making, but I am convinced that one of the most promising tools of analysis lies in the explicit recognition of this twin-factor as a key variable.[70]

Coterminous with any decisional system will be a communication system which will also be a structural feature of the unit. The communication system will consist of *channels* which are links between points in the system—really between actors and competences. The sum total of channels will constitute the communications *net*. Among the prescribed and conventional rules discussed under spheres of competence will be those governing *who communicate with whom* among the decision-makers and *how* as well as communicative links between the unit and the setting (social and institutional). As is well-known, communications take a number of forms—telephone calls, memoranda, recommendations, personal conversation, conference procedures, and so on. It is unfortunate that we know so little about the socio-psychological impact of different communicative techniques. I would venture a prediction that ultimately social analysis will be more and more cast in terms of communicative acts and strategies.[71]

Several rather basic functions are served by the communications net: to support and confirm the structure of authority; to make possible the circulation of orders and directives; to activate particular patterns of predecisional and decisional activity; and to make possible uniform definitions of the situation among decision-makers.

If we think for a moment of a decisional system as a communication net, perhaps the familiar notion of "access"—employed to analyze some relationships between private groups and the policy-making process—can be given a somewhat different twist. Three factors may be suggested. First, any net will have different *kinds* of entrances and exits so to speak. Thus, there is a *prescribed* type of communication access such as hearings and formal petitions. In addition, there are conventional points of access such as private conversations and the personal knowledge of the decision-maker. We might also find useful a distinction between face to face and *mediated* communicative acts. Second, outside the net there will be at least several *pools of information* "available" to the decision-makers. Some or all of these may be tapped. They will exist in the social setting and the institutional setting. They may be blocked off for some reason or other. The choices as to which will be tapped will depend in part on the structure of competence, on the situation, on the mission, and on personality factors. These choices are among the crucial pre-decisional decisions. Third, one fruitful way of looking at access—including its existence and success from the outside group's point of view—is to analyze the competing kinds of information (*i.e.,* not only in terms of sources but content as well) which in effect compete to get into the net and once in compete for status. How are conflicting messages resolved? How are they checked? Are messages from the social setting "stronger" when confirmed by messages from the institutional setting? This, of course, opens up a whole range of questions.

We should note certain major kinds of consequences which may flow from the structure of a particular communications net. One of the important characteristics of a decisional unit or a governmental structure in general is the *monitoring* function—both from the standpoint of internal operations and from the standpoint of feedback from the unfolding of action decided upon. How effective is each or is there even provision for each? Again, does the net provide "easy" access to *new* information inside or outside the net? Or is there "hardening of the arteries"? Assuming full information inside the net, what are the limits on reinterpretation of old information? Finally, does the net undermine the structure of competence? Are some actors virtually rendered ineffective because channels of communication are closed to them?

Informational Analysis. A few words must be said about information itself. There are *two kinds* of information (regardless of source) which are of particular concern: information about the setting of the unit; and information about the consequences of projects already under way. Together, these may be viewed as a feedback for the decisional system. Another distinction seems useful: *primary* and *secondary* messages. It is, of course, commonplace knowledge that information in any system is *classified* and *coded*. A primary message contains raw information, *i.e.,* its contents have not been summarized or interpreted—as for example in the case of a telegram from a diplomatic officer in the field. A secondary message occurs when the telegram is stamped "urgent" or "file" or "circulate" or some other symbol is attached. Classification and coding result in *selection* and *rejection* of information and also routing.

Two considerations follow. In any system information is stored—either in files or in the heads of the actors. Thus the organization has a *memory*. Information on past activities may be "lost" in the files or it may become precedent through the remembrances of the actors. Usually one actor in any decisional unit is the walking repository of the unit's past conduct. Secondly, since information circulates through the structure of communication on the basis of choices (*i.e.,* classification, coding, routing) the question of the access of the decision-makers to all information in the net at one time arises. The distribution of this information may have a significant effect on images the decision-makers have of a situation or problem. The participation of an actor is conditioned in part by how much he knows, and withholding of information is one of the strategies employed by the actors to influence each other.

Clearly the pervasive problem or phenomenon of secrecy is pertinent here. Kinds of information can be classified according to how many people do know it, should know it, and are prohibited from knowing it. In the area of atomic weapons or other sensitive policy issues, the size of the unit may bear a direct relationship to the kind of information in this sense. The larger the unit, the larger the number of potential leaks. This would hold for any level of government. Finally, we should mention the *shutoff point*—the point at which the decision-makers refuse to consider any new information in reaching an agreement on a course of action.

The Leavening Capacity of the Decisional Unit. Organizational pathology is usually viewed in terms of structural weaknesses or the subversion of the "formal" structure by the "informal" or the unanticipated consequences of rational procedures—all of which involve communication to a certain extent. The communication and information analysis suggested might broaden this considerably. I have a hunch that the analogy of the homing weapon—as Karl Deutsch has argued—is not too far-fetched. Organizational weakness might be analyzed from the standpoint of the readjustment of responses in order to enhance goal-seeking effectiveness, inflexibility of intake of new information—particularly concerning policy consequences, and unwillingness or inability to reinterpret old information.

Motivation. We come now to the third variable. In all candor, the question of motivation has been—for reasons good and bad—a ball of snakes for most social analysts. There are many who deny any possibility of systematic investigation of the motives of political actors. Yet motivational propositions are scattered all through the literature of our discipline. One of the crudest and most misleading examples of implicit and erroneous motivational assumptions in political science is found in the field of international politics, which is my so-called specialty. Leaving this aside, I feel strongly that before anyone decides that motivational questions are ruled out as interesting but unmanageable, a few basic considerations should be laid on the table.

To begin with, I venture to reiterate again that to *assume* motivation begs many of the significant questions which arise in political analysis. To the extent that we can do *anything* with this variable, we may be able to spotlight certain aspects of decision-making which might otherwise be neglected—and have in fact been neglected because motivation has remained implicit in various conceptual schemes. If properly conceived, motivational analysis ought to provide a much more satisfactory foundation for linking the *setting* and the *unit*—one of the more troublesome areas of research. Such concepts as personality, values, learning, and attitudes have increasingly become part of the terminology which refers to the behavior of decision-makers. And motivation may possibly offer a way of synthesizing all of them.

Some Analytic Aids. One unfortunate pitfall in motivational analysis can be avoided if we understand clearly that motivation is only *one* component of action. Furthermore, if we keep in mind our actor-analytical dummy, we can assume that we are only interested in the motivational factors which may help us to account for their behavior in a particular system of activities. We are not, fortunately, interested in whole, real, discrete persons. Since the motives we are concerned with—*i.e.*, those relevant to human behavior in complex organizations—we can avoid worrying about "innate drives." The motives we are basically concerned with are *acquired*, not structurally determined (inherent in the physiology of the organism).

Our task can be rendered easier—and less dangerous—in other ways.

One is to draw a very important distinction between *because of* and *in order to* motives. If we had to trace every act back to an ultimate cause all would be lost indeed. Were we required to account for "because of" motivation, we should have to explain a particular act in terms of a sequence of past behaviors, something which would necessitate almost a psychoanalytic approach, whereas in the case of "in order to" motivation, we are concerned with the future consequence of an act—its relationship to an ultimate end from which motive can be inferred. In the first case, there is always the problem of whether one has fully reconstructed the antecedents of an act. Explanation would entail dealing with the organism and its psychic structure. One would need a full medical and psychiatric case history of the Secretary of State to account for why he lost his temper at a conference or why he yielded a point to an adversary.

I believe that we can further simplify our analysis by employing a concept of a *vocabulary of motives*. With Gerth and Mills [72] we can consider motives as terms which persons use in their interpersonal relations. Fortunately—some will say unfortunately—people talk about their motives and attribute motives to others. In a sociological sense, motive statements (concerning the actor's or others) serve a function and have consequences in any social system. Politics is a social realm where, par excellence, the participants pay a great deal of attention to the reasons they give for their actions and to arguing with others about the reasons for their action. Much of the action which results from decision-making is verbal. Political acts are verbal acts (oral or written). Much political discussion is noted by Lasswell [73] and others. Gerth and Mills argue that it is in precisely those social situations in which purposes are vocalized and carried out with close reference to the speech and actions of others where motive avowals and imputations seem to arise most prominently.

Motives, from this standpoint, are words which are adequate (in the eyes of an observer and/or other actors) explanations of conduct. An adequate motive is one which satisfies those who question an act (including the decision-maker himself and his colleagues). Motive statements thus function to coordinate social action by persuading participants to *accept* an act or acts. Motives are *acceptable justifications* for programs of action—past, present and future. However, it should be emphasized that is not *mere justification* because motive statements serve important social functions. A noteworthy point emerges: *the decision to perform or not to perform a given act may be taken on the basis of the socially adequate answers to the question: what will be said concerning the motives of the decision-makers?* In short, what acceptable motive can be attached to a contemplated act? We have paid so much attention to the common-sense interpretations of political motivation, to the substance of motives and to proving or disproving *real* motives, that we have neglected the social consequences and functions of motives—particularly in those systems of action where they are articulated and made explicit. It follows from the foregoing that in political decisions, motives are often *chosen* in the sense that the decision-makers will be more concerned about how a particular act (in a set of alternatives) can be motivated for others than about its other consequences.

By this time, the word "rationalization" has doubtless crossed the reader's mind. Can vocabularies be taken for *real* motives? Do politicians really mean what they say? If as serious researchers into the "why" of behavior we assume in advance that politics is a vast shell game, we are, to repeat, lost. First, much political behavior is verbal. The discrepancies frequently noted between alleged real motives and motive statements may be discrepancies between two kinds of action, verbal and non-verbal. Second, it is a well-known principle of behavior that an actor may influence himself by his own declarations. Motive statements originally not reflective of true motives may become guides to action. Third, motive statements do not just describe or offer reasons—they affect other actors. It is also a principle of behavior that an actor's motive statements may and usually will alter the situation through impact on other actors. Even if a decision-maker lied about his motives, we would also have to take note that many would believe his lie and act on it. The notion that a decision-maker can consistently falsify his motives without consequences for ensuing decisions is misleading indeed. Fourth, we are interested in the imputations and confession of motives among the decision-makers themselves. It seems highly unlikely that a decisional unit could survive constant falsifications of motives.

A Brief Definition of Motivation. Without entering into a detailed analysis here, we can suggest that motives refer to why questions—why does the actor (or why do the actors) *act, i.e.,* why does a decision get made at all, or not made? Why does action take the *particular form* that it does *in a particular* situation? Why do *patterns* of action evolve from decision-making? Motivation refers to a psychological state of the actor in which energy is mobilized and selectively directed toward aspects of the setting. This state is characterized by a *disposition* toward certain actions and reactions. Since there will be more than one disposition we shall speak of a set of *tendencies* (limited to the particular social system): to *respond* in uniform ways to certain stimuli in the setting; to *select* certain conditions and factors as relevant; to *value* certain objectives; to make *evaluations* of alternative courses of action; to *allocate energy* to various projects and so on.

Motivation, Attitudes, and *Frames of Reference.* Clearly such tendencies are related to familiar questions: what is the *attitude* of the decision-makers toward this kind of situation or condition? What do the decision-makers *think* about this range of problems? *How* do they think about these problems? Behind questions of this type lie complicated behavioral phenomena. To probe these further, derived components of motivational analysis must be suggested.

Attitudes, as the term is used here, are the *readiness of individual decision-makers to be motivated*—in effect, the readiness to have the tendencies noted to be *activated.* Thus the structure of official attitudes constitutes a generalized potential of responses which are triggered by some stimuli. Since we cannot assume a uniform set of attitudes shared equally by all decision-makers, we would want to investigate the *content* of the various clusters likely to be present. We would also want to inquire into the *sources* of these attitudes *and* their behavioral consequences.

These generalized potential responses leave us still one step short. For example, why does a hostile attitude take the form it does? Surely there is more than one possible specific response, and readiness must be mobilized with respect to some particular situation or problem. This brings us to a second component, *frames of reference,* which will determine the specific responses of decision-makers. In turn, frame of reference has several analytical components: *perception, valuation,* and *evaluation.* Psychologists seem generally agreed that perception involves three processes: *omitting, supplementing,* and *structuring.* Perception, then, refers to the selective aspect of motivation—the actor is in a sense prepared by the tendencies referred to, tendencies learned from experience and training which govern recognition and appraisal of events, objects, conditions, and so on. Knowledge and information will enter into recognition and relating of selected elements in the setting. Valuation refers to the nature and range of objectives which will be injected into the situation by the actors. The values brought to a problem as part of the motivational equipment of the decision-maker will include preferred paths or strategies which direct specific acts toward the objectives chosen. I have confined valuation to the general direction of the motive pattern as action unfolds. Evaluation refers to the appraisal of the relationship between specific acts and the objective envisaged. The combination of perception, valuation, and evaluation can be looked upon as embracing thinking or problem-solving. Actually, the separation of motive, attitude, and frame of reference is for analytical purposes only.

Motivational Data. I shall conclude the discussion of motivation as a basic determinant of decision-making behavior by indicating some of the major kinds of data which may be motivationally relevant:

1) *Functions and Objectives of the Total Decision-making Organization or Suborganizations.* The members of any decisional unit will be motivated in part by the responsibilities and missions of the particular governmental structure or substructure of which the unit is a part. Functions will range from the most general (national security) to the more and more specific (intelligence reports). Objectives refer to the existence of a set of strategies (containment of Soviet power) or a collection of prevailing plans and projects (action contemplated or under way).

2) *The Missions of Particular Units.* Decision-makers will be motivated

not only by general objectives but by the purposes for which a unit was established. For example, a committee in whatever political institution will be at least partially influenced by the directive which established it.

3) *Socially defined* [74] *Norms and Values Internal to the Decisional Units.* Decision-makers have a membership in a total governmental organization or suborganization. In addition, membership in the unit itself usually carries a formal assignment. Decision-makers *may* be motivated by factors which have nothing to do with the purposes of the total organization or the unit. Thus competence expectations, unwillingness to appear unorthodox, a desire not to impair communications outside the unit, these and others may operate. Especially to be noted are the traditions and loyalties with respect to particular suborganization—an example would be the Foreign Service.

4) *Socially Defined Norms and Values External to the Total Decision-Making Structure and Internalized in the Decision-Maker.* From what has been said under previous categories, it is clear that when a person becomes a decision-maker, he enters a system of purposes, preferences, and rules and becomes a group member. Yet the decision-maker comes from a larger social setting. He comes as a "culture bearer." Any conceptual scheme for analyzing political decision-making must attempt to account for the impact of cultural patterns. Of particular interest are the major common value orientations shared by most members of a given culture. These are of interest on two counts: first, the effects on the ways in which decision-makers perceive the social world with which they deal and the unproblematic (*i.e.,* not open to doubt or choice) ends which they bring to their deliberations; second, the verbal formulations which decision-makers employ to render official policies acceptable to the society (only those relating to shared values). It must also be noted that some decision-makers will be affected by subsystems of cultural values (of a region or a social role).

5) *Material Needs and Values of the Society or Community or Any Segment Thereof Not Internalized in the Decision-Maker.* The norms and values referred to under item 4 are second nature to the decision-maker and their pursuit is in his self-interest so to speak. These are brought in by the actor as part of his "preparation." The factors referred to here are "accepted" or "learned" by the actor *after* his entrance into a decision-making capacity. These needs or values enter into the motivation of decision-makers in *two* ways:

(*a*) Through *estimates* made by the decision-makers—either independent calculations of the importance, significance, or compellingness of material needs and values or calculations accepted by the decision-makers as accurate (in which case they become the calculations of the decision-makers.) Calculations will include general and particular needs and values.

(*b*) Through *expectations* of rewards and sanctions which the decision-makers feel might be the consequence of deciding to maintain or not maintain certain general conditions in the society or to accept or reject certain demands by particular groups.

6) *Personality of the Decision-Maker.* Two kinds of data are pertinent here:

(*a*) *The intellectual skills* of the decision-maker and their *application*. This can be researched in terms of the following information: (1) training and professional or technical experience inside or outside the decision-making organization; (2) continued professional affiliations; (3) working theories of knowledge—the ideas, concepts, formulas, and proverbs concerning human nature and behavior which circulate in any given culture and not necessarily inculcated through specialized training.

(*b*) *Interpretation of competence*—an assumption can be made that in the case of any competence it is possible to isolate dimensions which would persist regardless of the particular occupant. Beyond this, it is largely (apparently) a matter of individual interpretation or adjustment. The activities "added" or "substracted" to or from a competence by interpretation of a given competence may be due to ego-oriented factors (*i.e.*, purely personal need-dispositions of the actors). However, there are two basic sources of pressure for changes in competence interpretation: (1) an organizational decision; (2) a crisis situation. Neither of these has anything to do with idiosyncratic factors.

Personality and Decision-Making. It is necessary to say a further word concerning personality—another Pandora's Box. Normally, personality factors constitute a huge residual category—anything which cannot be explained by chosen variables is due to *kismet* or purely personal factors. I have implicitly argued here for facing up to the personality problem which is necessary on both common sense and theoretical grounds. Many students of politics—amateur and professional—have been attracted by the "great man approach" to historical explanation. Analyze the motives of Churchill and you have the motives of Great Britain. Recent developments in personality theory and psychoanalytic theory make it tempting to analyze decision-makers in terms of tension-reduction mechanisms and Oedipus complexes. In both cases, organizational factors are left out of account. On the other hand, we need a method of bridging the analytical gap between those portions of the scheme based on a system or structure. A personality construct, devised especially for this purpose, is needed. To repeat, if the task is defined as trying to ascertain which facets of a decision-maker's total personality structure made him behave in a certain way on a given day, we are up against a hopeless search.

We should note that analytically there is a threefold division of character structure; the physiological organism, the psychic structure, and the person, *i.e.,* the social being. What is required for our purposes is a sociological conception of personality, not a psychological. This scheme places the individual decision-maker (actor) in a special kind of social organization. Therefore, I believe we must think of a social person whose "personality" is shaped also by his interactions with other actors and by his place in the system. This does not mean that the influence of ego-related needs and tensions is rejected, but only that the behavior of the actor be explained *first* in terms of personality factors relevant to his membership and participation in the decision-making system. Thus the influence of idiosyncratic factor is isolated, and hopefully, narrowed.

THE ESSENCE OF DECISION-MAKING

I have argued that three key variables can be employed fruitfully in describing and explaining decision-making behavior: *spheres of competence* (specialized functions, authority relations, basis of participation, and reciprocal expectations); *communication and information;* and *motivation* (including personality). The six kinds of data specified as relevant imply a general concept of multiple membership for the individual actor: (1) membership in a culture and society; (2) membership in a total institutional (political) structure; (3) membership in a decisional unit; and (4) membership in noninstitutional social groupings such as professional, class, or friendship.

The analysis so far has concerned the interaction of the decision-maker with the various elements of his situation and to point to some of the consequences of this interaction. Earlier, I referred to work in economics, philosophy, and psychology dealing with the Theory of Choice.[75] The models all have two things in common (regardless of differences in mathematical or other formulation); first, the actor or decision-maker is represented by *a scale of preferences*—from the most to the least highly regarded; second, *a set of rules* governs the actions of the decision-makers—specifying the manner in which alternative choices shall be presented, the procedure of voting, etc.

Decision-makers have preferences, though the scale may not be as highly ordered in the theories noted. What is the nature of these preferences? What are the factors influencing them? In general, these preferences are *not* entirely individual but derive in part from rules of the organizational system. Precedent may structure the scale. Shared organizational experiences and similarities and differences of biography (*i.e.,* training, experience, group membership) of the actors also can be presumed to operate. Information enters in—assessed selectively in terms of the decision-maker's frame of reference.

Two meanings of "rules" should be clarified. We have used rules in connection with structural and other properties of the decisional unit. Now with respect to choice, rules refer to the methods for determining which preferences shall prevail, such as majority vote, the will of the leader of a unit, "sense of the meeting," and so on.

In sum, information is selectively perceived and evaluated in terms of the decision-maker's frame of reference. Choices are made on the basis of preferences which are in part situationally and in part biographically determined.

UNFINISHED BUSINESS: SUPPLEMENTARY ANALYTICAL TOOLS

I had intended originally to attempt to offer briefly a definition of such terms as *objective* and *policy* and to deal with such analytical problems as *chance* in the political arena—particularly as it affects the setting of decision-making, and the *simultaneity* of operations of many decision-making units in most substructures of the total governmental structure. In particular, I wanted to develop the concept of a *path of action* which carries the scheme beyond the actual decision point. I have spoken of the need for typologies in political science generally and in the decision-making approach. In the case of *situations* I did suggest, for purposes of illustration, a crude set of typical situations. But space does not permit similar illustrations for *units, decisions,* and *decision-making personalities.* Finally, I have omitted mention of the *stages* in the decision-making process which opens up possibilities of dissecting analytically otherwise inseparable factors and phenomena. Decision-making, of course, takes place *within* units and also, often, from *unit to unit.*

I should emphasize something which is implicit in my argument, namely, that the observer has many, many choices. I fear that in trying to say a lot in a short space I have given a false impression of rigidity. Nearly all phases of this scheme represent analytical devices—something like the multi-purpose household tool. At the same time, I hope the more durable properties are evident.

Two derived concepts emerge from the decision-making approach which must await later development. First, the concept of *intellectual process*—an abstraction from the unit or system of certain elements which constitute the kinds of operations which the decision-makers as a collective group went through to reach their agreed course of action. This might provide a means of exploring more systematically such intuitive notions as "military mind," the "bureaucratic mind," and so on. Second, the concept of *policy attention* which highlights the distribution of energy and resources within the unit and within a total governmental substructure with respect to problems or issues. This might provide some cues as to the conditions under which problems get lost or neglected.

CONCLUSION

I hope my capacities as an analyst can be kept separate from the possible objective (*i.e.,* intersubjective) merit my proposal might have. Inevitably, the two have fused in this paper. I should also like to make it clear that

until this scheme is tested—not only in the specific sense of empirical verification but as an exploratory, organizing, and teaching device—it must be
regarded with skepticism. In the course of presenting the concept of decision-
making in abbreviated form, I trust that I have not by implication or otherwise indicated that I regard this concept as anything more than one of
several major complementary approaches to the study of politics.

If previous experience is any guide, readers will think of many exceptions,
examples, and research problems which appear to offer difficulties. I would
only plead that I have tried to indicate both the research possibilities and
the more general organizing (*i.e.,* interpretive and teaching) functions.
Sooner or later, when pushed to more specific applications, the two part
company.

In general, I would argue that the criteria mentioned earlier should be
applied rigorously to the decision-making approach. After several years of
work, I am convinced it offers sufficient aid to some of the major analytical
problems of political science to justify a substantial investment of intellectual
energy on the part of some scholars.

Finally, I should like to conclude with two kinds of questions. First, does
this approach offer any possible help on problems of *training* at the graduate
level, both for policy-oriented positions and teaching? on problems of the
setting of decision-making (opened up by Charles Hyneman's provocative
book)? on the unexplored role of *experts* and *consultants* in complex organizations? Second, is it fruitful to ask for re-examination of certain difficult
questions of political analysis which have, in effect, been in mothballs for
a long time and despite hardheaded insistence that such questions are un-
answerable?

CHARLES B. HAGAN[1]

The Group in a Political Science

I

ONE OF THE first conditions for progress in a particular
discipline of scientific inquiry is the ability of its practitioners to communicate
with each other. Their ability to do that, in turn, depends upon at least
these two things: an agreement among them upon what problem they are
studying; and an agreement among them upon certain basic concepts, certain
categories of description, in accordance with which they can sector and
investigate their problem.

For example, despite the many disagreements among economists on such
questions as whether the progressive income tax is a good thing or whether

we are presently in a "recession," they are all agreed that the problem of economics is "the allocation of scarce goods"; and they are all agreed that the basic system by which those goods are allocated is the interplay of two forces, "supply" and "demand."

In his recent inquiry into the state of political science, entitled *The Political System,* David Easton raised this question: Do the extremely variegated and multiform writings that make up the literature of political science have anything in common that justifies their being placed under the same taxonomic tent? He concluded that they do, and that what they share is a concern with the same basic problem. That problem he defined as "the authoritative allocation of values for a society." He did not give a complete definition of the term "authoritative," and, indeed, it is probably impossible— and unnecessary—to do so.

In my opinion, Easton has come as close as anyone to making articulate the common preoccupation of the polyglot army that marches under the banner of "political science." Some of us may, in our research and writing, be working at the margins of the problem rather than at its center; but Easton has shown us that we are all working at the same problem. It is surprising that the core of concern in our study should not have been made clear to us sooner, but I think most of us will feel that Easton has come close enough to the mark to enable us to proceed from where he has left us.

The most cursory survey of the literature that appears in the political science periodicals, however, reveals an immense *lack* of agreement on the matter of *how* we should go about studying our problem. It is probably not too much to say that any essay which some political scientists regard as really significant and first-rate work hardly communicates at all to most political scientists; and an essay which most political scientists understand and approve is regarded by some of us as unimportant. In my opinion, the inability of any of us to communicate with all of us stems from our lack of an agreed-upon set of categories of description. Easton has shown us that we do have a common core of concern, just as the economists do. But we do not have any agreement upon a system of description, such as the economists' supply-and-demand system, to explain *how* values are authoritatively allocated for a society.

Some of the articles and essays can communicate only to fellow practitioners in some narrow segment of the total discipline, while other pieces are of such general character that they mainly pass on lore, if I may borrow a term from Charles Hyneman's recent memorandum on the subject matter of our discipline. The political science of a half-century ago was concerned to spell out in considerable detail the legal structure of society with especial emphasis on those aspects that related to the election of officials and the operation of the various organs within themselves and in their relations with each other. The development of the political party literature pushed the margins of inquiry out into new areas of investigation. Morality and ethics were proper questions of inquiry and logical analysis. As the probing and the inquiries explored in greater detail the operations of a political society the categories of explanation were widened to incorporate the data experienced in the research. On the whole the categories were able to swallow the data. At times on a second look from a different vantage point, it seems as if the researcher sometimes missed the point of his findings. That is merely one way of saying that a different frame of reference would have yielded different results.

The purpose of this paper is to suggest a descriptive system which, properly understood and employed, can be as useful—*and* as uniting—for political scientists as the supply-and-demand categories are for the economists. The descriptive system I propose is generally known as the "group concept," and is most simply stated thus: values are authoritatively allocated in society through the process of the conflict of groups.

II

Contemporaneously with the elaboration of the traditional categories there appeared alternative suggestions for ordering the materials relevant to political life. The new materials came from a variety of sources. One of the books which seriously challenged the usual description of the ways of political life was Lincoln Steffens' *Shame of the Cities,* a famous muckraking study. For my purpose there are two comments to be made about such a study: (1) the account which it gives of the operations of the political system differed greatly from the accounts that were to be found in the social sciences, and (2) the label attached to the situations described shows the moral indignation which points clearly to the discrepancy between the expected patterns of behavior and the ones that were found. Perhaps it ought also to be added that such observers and describers of contemporary affairs found enough materials to show that their accounts probably reflected more accurately the routine activities of political life than did the customary descriptions of the orators and genteel writers. At any rate political science has never recovered its simplicity.

The findings of the muckrakers were supplemented by studies of psychologists and sociologists. These people opened up new frames of reference for social and individual analysis. Their studies have influenced the categories of political science in the same way that "creeping socialism" is alleged to have influenced private enterprise. Often their techniques and results have been grafted on to the traditional categories. Some readers have found the results offensive to their sense of order and discipline, and there has been a search for new systems which provide more order and more system. It may be doubted that either of those results has been achieved. As evidence of that conclusion I suggest that you look at the categories borrowed from

Pendleton Herring which Stephen Bailey sought to use in his famous study, *Congress Makes a Law.*

The categories to which I refer are found in that sentence in Herring's *Politics of Democracy* (p. 421): "It is enough if we achieve a working union of interests, ideas, institutions, and individuals." There is little indication of how a working union of these four I's is to be achieved. Mr. Herring's prescription is tolerance, and that seems to accord more with an ethical prescription than with a scientific frame of reference. In neither study is there an effort to show how you commingle those items; nor, I may add, is there any effort to show how one of the I's differs from another. Most studies in political science make little or no effort to fix with any precision the range of meaning of the basic descriptive system.

I maintain that the traditional categories, as they play their role in contemporary descriptions of politics, leave a lot to the imagination of the reader, and as a result the communication process is not always precise. The four I's of Herring and Bailey are close enough to the traditional categories to illustrate my thesis. How does an interest differ from an idea and how do you tell when one is operating rather than the other? The same questions can be made about the other two categories: the institution and the individual. The answers will be just as ambiguous. These categories are usually mixed in with the notions of a legal system as formulated by John Austin or Westel W. Willoughby. At least that was the source of my descriptive apparatus until recent years. As we all know, it is difficult to fit the materials which pass for *facts* among us into those categories without doing violence to the legal system or to the facts.

Now, leaving the communication process to the imagination of the reader has several "virtues." In the first place it allows the writer to avoid the spelling out of his meaning in more precise terms; in the second place it allows the reader to supply his own meaning; in the third place it allows both to agree on one another's brilliance; and finally it avoids controversy. These are "valuable" traits, and I would be the last to decry them, but I doubt that they have any place in a scientific descriptive system. The four I's comprise the same data viewed from slightly different angles of emphasis. *Idea* emphasizes the talk and writing facet, *Institution* emphasizes the customary modes of acting, *Individual* emphasizes the part which the physiological entities play, and *Interest* usually emphasizes or explains the behavior not accounted for on the other principles. In every instance the phenomenon to be explained is a political decision of masses of people, and somehow the decision gets made. I do not see how the *Idea* could "cause" anything to occur apart from the activity of the participants in the decision. An *Institution* is more easily understood, perhaps, as expected activity of participants. And *Individuals* have meaning only as participants in the decision and only that part of them that operates in the decision-making is relevant to the analysis. *Interest* is likewise the activity of the decision-makers either pro or con the issue. Its meaning is found only in the activity. In fact the other I's get their significance from the interest or activity that is to be explained.

I recognize that the only thing more dangerous than reasoning by analogy is reasoning by bad analogy, but I want to risk that danger for a few moments. Earlier I have pointed out that Easton has shown the problem of political science to be the authoritative allocation of values. The analogy that I want to use is the development in economic speculation. There the equivalent problem is the allocation of scarce resources. The test of whether a study is an economic study or not is: does it concern itself with the allocation of scarce resources? The device used by economists to explain how such resources are allocated is the supply-and-demand situation. All economics, Professor Robbins has said in his essay, "The Nature and Significance of Economic Science," can be subsumed under those rubrics. The most recondite discussions in economics deal with these problems in more or less clear terms. The higher reaches of contemporary mathematical exercises in economics as well as the most traditional discussions are all concerned with the same issues. It may be difficult to recognize the relations but they are always there for economists.

The analogy that I want to pursue has to do with the equivalence of the supply and demand curves, since it seems to me that the authoritative allocation of values is equivalent to the allocations of scarce resources. The equivalent that I want to suggest for the supply and demand curves is the group struggle. There is no claim that I have orignated this notion, or even that I can add much to what a careful reader can find in the literature. I find that there is a great deal of confusion as to what the group struggle means, and I may hope to aid in some clarification of what is meant when one says that political science has as its chief problem the authoritative allocation of values and that the means by which those values are allocated is the group struggle.

III

There are two distinct strands in the discussions which use the group as the explanatory principle in political science. The first strand still is found primarily in the writing of A. F. Bentley. He introduced the phraseology of group interest or group or interest (these are synonyms) in his volume, *The Process of Government,* which was published in 1908. He carried the analysis a little further in his volume *Relativity in Man and Society* in 1928. In all of his writing Bentley has been concerned with a semantic or epistemological set of problems. I do not think that he would accept that characterization of his studies, but for my purposes here he has tried to elucidate some of the ambiguities that are found in the discussions of social activity.

There have been few, if any, consistent followers of Bentley in political science. Two recent authors have admitted their great debt to him. David Truman in his volume entitled *The Governmental Process* and Bertram Gross in his *The Legislative Struggle* are clearly working in the direction suggested by the earlier Bentley volume. Truman has sometimes deviated from the requirements of Bentley's "tool," but this is done deliberately and with critical acumen. Gross adheres more closely to the framework suggested in *The Process of Government*.

A second strand of writing in political science has also utilized the group as an explanatory principle. This strand has many variations and many practitioners. In these studies the group is used to supplement the individual as an explanatory phenomenon, and both of these in turn are used to supplement ideas and institutions as explanatory principles. These categories take on a real existence or in other language they are reified. In more abstract expositions they may even have essences. These "objects" would seem to have careers of their own and are capable of producing results. And as has been stated earlier these "objects" or essences intermingle one with another to cause the results in politics. The intermingling can apparently be accomplished in varying degrees, so that a given political result may be ten per cent ideas, twenty-five per cent individual, thirty per cent institution, and thirty-five per cent interest or any other mathematical arrangement which adds to a unity of one hundred per cent. I have never seen any study that undertook to establish the percentages, but it is clear implication of such approaches that it can be done. Another variation of this approach is to allocate the explanatory principles to environment, technology, education, and other such variables. The latter do not necessarily involve a group base, but these variables are frequently interjected into studies allegedly proceeding on a group base.

As an aside to this general discussion attention may be called to the explorations of the sociologists and psychologists. These studies, to which Homan's *The Human Group* is a recent addition, are undertaking basic investigations into small face-to-face groups. These clearly have potential implications for a political system, but as yet the practitioners are extremely modest in their claims. It seems to me that political scientists will have to do just such detailed investigation before there can be much advance in theoretical sophistication. However, it should also be pointed out that some of these inquiries are operating on an epistemological basis similar to that of the second strand of political studies that are indicated above. In short there are implicit or explicit notions of the group as a real entity rather than as an hypothesis for organizing data.

To make clear the basis for these remarks it may be necessary to state some of my premises. I regard all verbal formulae as principles in a system of description. The system may be implicit or explicit to the author. The task of the formulae is to organize and manage the data which the author finds it necessary to manage or organize. The system of description or theory may more or less "explain" the findings of an empirical character. If the explanation "works" it is useful, and if it doesn't it is inadequate. On the other hand, those authors who reify the phenomena that they are studying expect their verbal formulae to have some kinds of correspondence to a world external to themselves and independent of their mental constructs. In this framework "facts" exist and the function of a theory is to tie them together. If the theory does not possess this quality of "correspondence" it is wrong rather than, as I would describe it, inadequate.

So far I have tried to provide an intellectual setting to enable further analysis. One more warning and it will be possible to outline the political system of the first strand of writers about the group. It has been stated here that the second strand of writers reify the group. By this I mean that the group is somehow imagined as having an existence independent of its surroundings. The group is external to other groups or to situations or to its environment. It, the group, is an aggregation of individuals who operate as a unit. There is implicit in this analysis or approach an acceptance of traditional notions of objects. A group, so to speak, is an enlarged individual. Sometimes the discussions proceed as if the group had a brain and physique like that of the individual, the physiological entity. The assumptions that are implicit are seldom elaborated or explored, but when they are, there are qualifications made to take care of the physical aspects of the analogy. Our language, I may add, is so deeply committed to this reification process that it is almost impossible to escape from its consequences. If I do escape in the course of this discussion, it will be a major accomplishment. In order to move into an understanding of the alternative hypothesis about groups one needs a sort of brainwashing.

The group theory of the writers who follow Bentley starts from quite a different epistemological base. It is closer to Dewey's epistemological notions, and, of course, its record can be traced in philosophical literature. Its pedigree is long, but it is not as prestigious in contemporary society as the other. Perhaps the best way of conveying the basic supposition is to start with the mass of human activity out of which is to be abstracted that which is relevant to the authoritative allocation of values. In order to head off the obvious question as to how one knows what is relevant, I shall say at this point that it is a matter for investigation and research. The method of study would be the same as now, but the emphasis of explanatory principles would be different. This is a topic to which I shall return.

The mass of activity includes all of the talk and writing and all of the public meetings as well as the physical violence that takes place. The relevance of particular phases of the activity and its meaning or significance in any political problem is a matter to be determined. It is determined by the use of principles or hypotheses to explain relations between the activities that are under study. The problem for political science is to arrange the activity on one side or the other of the question that is being investigated. For example, the proposal to alter the term of the members of the House of Representatives to four years can be explained in terms of the groups pro and con the proposal. There will be a wide variety of activity pro the proposal and a wide variety con the proposal. The activity is activity of human beings, and it may take the form of writing abstract treatises on the desirability of long or short terms for such offices. It may take the form of labor unions adopting resolutions, of political parties adopting platforms, or of conversations between friends enjoying a social evening. It may take the form of providing transportation to the polls on election day and in some instances stuffing the ballot box. It may be activity engaged in keeping the bars open or closed and in fist fights or riots. In short, all activity that can be tied to the proposal by one principle or another is political activity and it is activity by groups. The political meaning of the activity is to be found in its relation to the proposal to change the term of the Representative in our example. Other aspects of the activity may also be tied to other political goings on, but that would involve organizing the activity around another issue. The distribution of the population on one issue may be quite different from that on another. It is extremely unlikely that any two issues would divide the population exactly alike. Also, it is unlikely that at present there exist any methods of counting that can give more than a very approximate notion of the distribution.

The groups in the above illustration are those activities of individuals which support or oppose the matter at issue. It is important to grasp the notion that an individual in his role on the issue may play more than one part. The individual, the physiological one, may participate in a number of organizations or associations without formal organization. David Truman has called this phenomenon "overlapping memberships." Each organization or association may play a role in the process of making a governmental decision, and their roles may be contradictory. It is a matter of common observation that not all members of an organization support the program of the organization with equal zeal. This phenomenon must be accounted for in any adequate theory of the political process. The variation in the amount of activity of any organization on different issues is a manifestation of the difference. In short, to use the terminology of Bentley, the organization is representative of the activity and is itself an activity. The activity *is* the interest. The interest is a shorthand way of saying that there is a mass of activity operating in a given direction. I am trying to say here that the terms *individual* and *interest,* which have been used above as illustrations in the reified type of analysis, can be given a function in group analysis. The individual *is* his activity, and his acts are representative of an interest. This definition of individual includes all that is useful in the explanation of the political process and leaves out the physiological aspects which are of no importance in explaining the political process. If one wants to say that without the physiology there is no individual, I would not object, but physiology does not aid in explaining politics.

Interest is often utilized to designate a kind of activity which follows as an inference from a premise. Thus one finds statements in the literature that it is to the interest of labor unions to oppose legislation prohibiting union contributions to political parties. If, on examination, it is discovered in the Congressional hearings that the unions were unopposed to such legislation, one could say that the unions acted contrary to their interest. That kind of explanation is often found in the literature. One wonders what kind of a science it is that finds activity contrary to its explanatory principles. The present assignment of meaning to interest is to find the activity and to call that the interest which the activity connotes. Interest is *a posteriori* not *a priori,* and it is consistent with the observed behavior and not contrary to it. In another way of speaking, the interest and the group are the same phenomenon observed from slightly different positions, and an interest group is a tautological expression. The interest is not a thing that exists apart from the activity or that controls activity. To make interest a phenomenon external to the behavior of the group is to reify interest and to direct attention away from the requirements of competent investigation.

The other two explanatory principles, institutions and ideas, gain meaning in this type of analysis. An institution is a way of action, and the action is clearly that of individuals. An institution is not a control outside of the persons who are acting, but it is their acting. A constitution is often defined as an institution controlling the behavior of those who live under it. Such phraseology reifies the document and makes it possess an authority of some kind. However, if the constitution possesses any authority independent of the behavior under it, then its meaning and guidance should be the same at all times. No one believes that about a constitution, and so there is need for another explanation. In the approach here suggested a constitution is the behavior that the dominant groups manifest in the operation of the community. If the groups change then the constitution changes with them. The stability of the constitution is the stability of the underlying group support. There is nothing in the group hypothesis that requires groups to be evanescent or transitory in character. Neither on the other hand is there any requirement that the group be stable or longlived. The changes in the group combinations allow a means of explaining the shifts in political behavior. To take an example from contemporary affairs: the Supreme Court has recently ruled that segregation of the young for educational purposes is a *per se* violation of the equal protection clause of the Fourteenth amendment. The decision marks a shift in the groups that are receiving representation in that Court. Previously that body had given its sanction to the view that separate but equal facilities would meet the requirements of that clause. Actually, in the years since that verbal formula was developed to meet the ideological quarrel, the facilities have been separate but hardly equal. Yet the factually unequal character of the educational facilities was not enough to bring the clause into operation in the period between 1868 and the present. The opinions that have been expressed since the recent decision suggest, at the least, that the vision of the Court as to the meaning of the Constitution is not enough to silence the partisans of the segregated school. In short, the wording of the Constitution is not a precise guide to its meaning; a better guide to its meaning is to be found in the conflicting groups that seek to clothe themselves in one or another interpretation of the words and phrases. For example, if you look at the Constitution in 1868, in 1896, and in 1954, the words in the Fourteenth Amendment remain constant, yet the actual meaning has indeed changed. Some people have called this a revolution. How to explain this? Neither the words nor the institutions have changed. What has changed is the interest groups. The interest that secured representation in 1868 and in 1896 has been supplanted by another interest—that which gained representation in the recent decisions. There is no evidence that ideas played any significant or distinctive role in "causing" this change in the judicial interpretation of the Fourteenth Amendment, for the ideas, like the words, have been constant through this period.

This brings us to the treatment of ideas. Discourses as to the meaning of the Constitution are ideas, but the word *idea* also embraces a wide range of literary productions. There are abstract and philosophical treatises, there are popular books and magazines, there are learned journals as well as the comics, there are speeches and art objects and all the other devices for conveying significance to others. Our question: What is the meaning of these in the group theory of politics? The short answer is that all of these forms of communication get their political meaning from group conflicts. All or some of the media can be used in the group struggle, and they may be used in a wide variety of ways. Propaganda has become a commonplace explanation of the political process, and I am asserting that all forms of communication may be treated as propaganda in the process. Obviously it would be foolish to say that all forms are equally important or that they convey the same meaning to all participants. I suspect that once one of these products started on its career it would be impossible to forecast the role that it would play. I mean that at one stage it may be used by one group to flay another, and again the latter group or its remnants may use it to flay the former. That is, the idea or the communication has no fixed meaning, since its meaning derives from the context in which it is used. The arrangement of groups may be such that in one layer on one side the idea may play an opposite role to that which it plays in another layer on the same side. These are hypotheses about the idea and its operation and are not to be taken as having been demonstrated. I have used them to try to convey the sense in which ideas may be construed in the group theory. The importance of the idea is in its representative quality in the underlying group struggle. The idea must ultimately be traced into the activity, and its importance for this approach lies in the activity.

Of course the same observations apply to philosophy and to ideology. In some contemporary discussions of the role of ideas, distinctions are made between ideology and philosophy. Ideology is frequently given a role closer to action than to philosophy. Both are data in the political process and both have to be given their measurable importance and significance in that process. The influence of both in the political process is denoted in activity of those pro or con the group struggle.

I have tried in this section to demonstrate that those who are seeking to develop a political science which utilizes the group as the basic unit of analysis can explain all that the other writers explain with their reified categories. The group theory has the added capacity to cope with changes and shifts in the activity of the governmental process. The *individual* has many facets and these are reflections of the groups in which he is a participant. He is not a fixed point of reference but is an act in the totality of activity that makes up social action. *Interests* are the activity, and the association of acts of physiological beings in a common effort for or against another collocation of common activity is the manifestation of the group or group interest. An *institution* is a stable group of individual activities, and a crowd or mob is a temporary group. *Ideas* are expressions in verbal or other forms of activity, and in the governmental process they also take their meaning from the group association. To illustrate, a statue of Lincoln has a meaning quite as well as the Gettysburg address, but the meaning is to be found in the group activity associated with each. In the extreme case any connection between the group significance and the original existential record is coincidental. For example, Armistice Day is currently being made over into Veterans Day.

Nothing is lost that is significant in the political process by giving meaning through this method. The gain is in the freeing of the observer from the alleged meanings so that he may observe untrammeled by the clutterings of former meanings. The framework of analysis is flexible, and it is able to incorporate all social data that is relevant to a social theory. However, to state that this is a desirable method of approach is not to deny the usefulness of other frameworks. I consider this approach more desirable than the alternative frameworks because it is so much more capable of managing the data of political science.

IV

The three preceding parts of this essay have attempted, first, to give a setting to the role which the group plays in political analysis and, second, to delineate the characteristics of the group upon which a science of politics may be based. Sizable problems remain even though acceptance is given to the preceding comments.

In the first place it should be emphasized that the method of study indicated here is dialectical, that is, one side of the proposed topic of investigation always has its other side. One side is always to be treated as related to the other. Movement may be in either direction or both. This rejects the notion of interaction of separate, independent and discrete factors, that is found in most political studies. Interaction in such studies postulates factors as the basic units of inquiry. Furthermore, each factor exists independently of the other. A combination of factors may cause a third phenomenon. All of these are real entities rather than intellectual inventions.

On the other hand, I work with the concept of the transaction which is beginning to find its way into contemporary discussions of social phenomena. The transaction regards both sides of the group struggle as a single process. Each side gets its meaning from that struggle. One does not exist without the other. The relation is not one of cause in the sense that one side exists before the other. The meaning of one side *is* its relation to the other side.

An illustration may help to clarify the position. A loan is a transaction. It involves a borrower and a lender. Neither has meaning apart from the relation to the other. In order to get the full significance of the loan it would be necessary to describe all the activities of those who provide the monetary system and its accompanying credit system plus all of the potential activity involved in collecting of the loan. The loan is embedded in a pattern of habits of activity which are widely understood and acted out easily and with dispatch.

I am concerned only with the notion of the transaction which makes the loan a dialectical process, and it is a glimpse of that feature of the political process that I want to convey. The group struggle is that sort of phenomenon.

A group is a segment of human activity focused upon by the analyst or investigator for the purposes of his particular inquiry. The membership of the group is to be determined by the purposes of the inquiry rather than by "inherent" or "essential" criteria. For example if one were to study the groups supporting and opposing classical neutrality, both groups would certainly include persons labeled for other purposes as Englishmen, Frenchmen, Brazilians, Americans, and so on. For other purposes these categories of Englishmen, Frenchmen, Brazilians, and Americans may be useful, but they would not assist in the study of the neutrality contest. National groups, in other words, are not the only or even the most important groups to describe some political struggles.

One aspect of research in the group would involve the study of the size of the group; that is, the number of persons who participate in it. This would not always be an easy task. The difficulties would vary with different kinds of issues.

On some matters there would be vast quantities of data, and on other matters there would be little or none. Crude measuring devices are used in almost all political studies, frequently without the recognition that they are measures. For example words like important, great, significant, etc. are such measures. There is need for a great deal of work on techniques for counting and on developing new methods of solving problems as they are detected and delineated. The materials compiled by polling organizations illustrate my point. These organizations started out with simple questions to determine public opinion and soon found that the answers were poor guides to political behavior. As a result they are constantly sharpening their tools. It is desirable that similar development should take place in the comparable study of the means of determining the numbers on one side or the other of the group struggle.

Political speculation has always placed a great emphasis on numbers. But the group theorist's concept of numbers or size as a facet of activity is a different concept from the traditional. In traditional investigation attention is focused on physiological entities. Each individual is counted. But when one bases his research on the group theory, attention is focused on the activity, not on the individual.

Numbers, or a better way to state it, the size of the group, is obviously not the only factor to be considered. It is a matter of common observation that the largest group's activity does not always dominate in the group struggle. Another aspect of the activity which needs investigation is what Bentley called "intensity." This does not refer to any "mental force" but to the observable variations in the nature of the activity under investigation. David Truman has called our attention to the importance of "overlapping membership." I would phrase it that the activity of an individual (and a number of individuals) is multi-directional. The activity of a relatively small group may dominate that of the larger group because the activity of the smaller number is in one direction and constant. "Hard core Communists" or "hard core Republicans" are examples of behavioral patterns of intense activity.

A third aspect of group activity has to do with technique. Technique would include such things as organization, cohesion, leadership. These are different ways of talking about the activity. It is true that group techniques have been studied in the traditional literature. But most of these studies are set within the framework of formal and informal categories. It is consistent with group theory to consider the formally organized groups as a manifestation of the group struggle representing "underlying" groups so long as it is clearly understood that the "underlying" groups are merely that part of the group which is not within the formal organization. The detection and delineation of the "underlying" groups is a matter for investigation. But what is needed is a broader view of the techniques. Traditional studies center attention on the logic of the arguments and on writing and talking activity as means of influencing others. Although they have recognized that there are other techniques of influence, they have been frowned upon and left for study by sociologists and revolutionaries. But these other kinds of activity and the relations between them and the writing and talking activity cannot be left out of account if we are to achieve our goal of adequate description.

V

A political science must reduce its problems to their simplest terms and the smallest number of explanatory principles. Under that rule only one of the above conceptions of the group can hope to become the basis for a science of politics. The conception of the group that meets the requirements of the above rule is the one of the group as activity of human beings. I have shown that all the important qualities of ideas and institutions and individuals and interests meet on common ground in that conception. I have further shown that whatever qualities those words have that are not incorporated into the group activity are irrelevant for a political science. The same can be done for all the other explanatory principles.

The reasoning that leads to the rejection of the alternative conception of the group as an explanatory device in the study of government may be briefly stated. This alternative conception expands the number of factors that are needed to explain behavior, and, moreover, it offers no means by which one factor can be related to the others. The highest level to which generalizations can rise on this basis is common sense, and by that is meant the kind of explanations that any person can give. Science seeks order and not disorder, and it is my belief that this approach attains the latter rather than the former. Disorder is inherent in the constant addition of new and different factors.

I do not mean to assert that the scientific theory will always be the one preferred. However, it should be the basis until a better one is found. In order to be better the new theory will have to manage the data relevant to an understanding of the governmental process on simpler and more comprehensive principles.

MARION J. LEVY, JR.

Some Aspects of "Structural-Functional" Analysis and Political Science

THERE HAS been a great deal of talk in the various social sciences in recent years about "structural-functional" analysis. Without speculating on the varying ratios of heat to light found therein on the part of both the presumed proponents and opponents of this "newly discovered" approach, one may say that most of these discussions have been featured by great confusion of the concepts involved. The terms "function" and "structure" have usually had implicit definitions quite important for analysis. A major source of confusion has been the fact that few analysts trouble to distinguish their several different usages of each of these terms. Sometimes they have switched from one referent to another within a single paragraph. This is no cause for despair, though it is cause for caution. The concentration of attention on the attempt to do systematic scientific work in the social field is a recent one. The field of biology makes use of essentially the same set of concepts on its more general theoretical levels and has been featured by almost precisely analogous confusion. The hopeful aspect of the situation is that the distinctions in usage have been ones that are important for analysis. The task of making these various concepts explicit is a comparatively elementary one once the fruitfulness of the different usages has been suggested, however implicitly. In the Appendix to this book there is attached a set of definitions of these concepts and some of their subcategories. Many other distinctions of this sort can be made, but I believe that these cover the major usages generally intended.[1]

Using these terms as defined in the Appendix, nothing is new and nothing is startling about "structural-functional" analysis except the discovery that it is being employed. The situation is rather like that in *Le bourgeois gentilhomme* in which M. Jourdain, well advanced in his mature years, discovers (*Act II, Sc. 6*) to his delight that he has been speaking prose for more than forty years. Even the special forms of "structural-functional" analysis such as "structural-functional requisite" analysis, "eufunctional-dysfunctional" analysis, "latent-manifest-UIR-IUR" analysis, and various combinations of those and other special forms [2] are nothing new or revolutionary. The most that can be claimed for the more recent attempts is the effort to be more ex-

52

plicit and careful in the use of these forms of analysis and to utilize them with a view to their relevance for the formulation of systems of theory.

In the work that I shall discuss here, "structural-functional requisite" analysis is the focus of interest. Many of the other concepts of structure and function are vital to this sort of analysis, but for the present at least I am concerned with them primarily in so far as they contribute to requisite analysis. The special utility of the requisite form is that it enables one to develop systematically schemes of analysis in terms of which work on widely different types of units can be carried out and compared.[3] It is from the systematic comparison of such empirical studies that major elements in a system of theory are likely to emerge and be confirmed or disproved.[4]

With some oversimplification in order to conserve space, the basic steps in "structural-functional requisite" analysis may be put as follows:

1) One must define the unit to be discussed. For these purposes the unit must be a unit in terms of which operations (or processes) can or do take place. The choice of unit will depend on the problem to which the analysis is addressed. In this case the unit chosen is *any* "society" for reasons discussed below briefly.

2) One must *discover* (at least by hypothesis) the factors setting the most general limits of possible variation for the type of unit chosen. For any human "society" the most general limiting factors are human heredity and the nonhuman environment.

3) One must try to determine what general types of conditions must be met if the unit is to persist as defined within these limits.[5] These conditions are the functional requisites. (See Appendix.)

4) One must then determine what patterns of action must be present if operation in terms of them is to result in the production of the functional requisites. These patterns are the structural requisites. (See Appendix.)

In "ordinary language" one seeks to know: "What must be done if a unit of the sort chosen is to persist?" and "How must what must be done be done?"

There are many dangers in such analysis. If it can be carried out successfully, and it is still in a highly tentative untested stage of development, it will result in a set of categories such that one can say that as a *minimum* on the level of generalization under discussion such and such patterns will be found to exist in any stable example of the unit chosen.[6]

The specific type of unit that I have used in attempts to develop a system of analysis of this sort is a "society." That term has been defined for these purposes in the following fashion:

A society is a system of action in operation which: (a) involves a plurality of interacting individuals of a given species (or group of species) whose actions are primarily oriented to the system of action concerned and who are recruited at least in part by the sexual reproduction of members of the plurality involved; (b) is at least in theory self-sufficient for the action of this plurality; and (c) is capable of existing longer than the life span of an individual of the type (or types) concerned.[7]

Whenever one uses concepts such as this, there is always a problem involved: "Is the empirical case that is supposed to be an example of such a unit in fact an example of it?" In this case the difficulty is magnified by the fact that, for reasons too complicated to state here, complete identification of it as such a unit would in all probability rest on knowing all that one seeks to learn from the use of the system of analysis. There were many reasons for the choice of the definition, but the one that is germane here is that a rather interesting hypothesis can be entertained about this type of unit. This hypothesis is as follows: "Any social system other than a society is either a subcategory of a single society or the result of interrelationships between two or more societies." Thus, for example, the United States Congress, or a given family in the United States, is a social system that is a subcategory of the United States society. The United Nations Organization is the result of the interrelations between two or more societies.

I do not think that this hypothesis is tautological. This may be a mistaken notion. If it is not tautological, it may be untenable. It has certainly not been proved in any precise form. For the moment, however, without justification of this hypothesis, I should like to explore some of its implications *if* it is correct. The first of these implications is that one need not delay analysis pending complete identification of an empirical unit deemed to be a society. If, even in a tentative fashion requiring much modification by empirical research, one has determined the structural requisites of any society, one can proceed to analyze the case in question in these terms. If the unit is in fact a society, all of the categories and subcategories of the various requisites and their cross-cuttings will be filled by data of some sort (unless we have misobserved or unless a theoretical error has been committed in the derivation of the structural requisites of any society.) [8] Furthermore, if it is not a society, the results of the analysis will at least show in what respects the unit is like and in what respects it differs from a society with regard to the structural requisites of a society.

The second implication germane here has to do with systems other than societies. If the unit analyzed in these terms is not a society, and if the hypothesis presented here is tenable, the analysis will show, in addition to what has already been mentioned, what functions must be performed by and what structures must exist in other social systems with which it is in contact, *if* it is to persist. These things can be discovered by using the structural requisites of any society to analyze any type of social system other than a society. To the extent that structural requisites for specific types of societies are determined, the implications for the subsystems within them will become more specific and detailed. For the present, interest has been confined to the most general level of consideration in this sort of analysis.

If one does not wish to use the structural requisites of any society for the analysis of other social systems—and there are many types of problems for which this procedure is not necessarily well suited—one may still proceed in terms of developing the structural requisites for any unit of the type that is the immediate focus of interest. These requisites will have corresponding implications for the subsystems of these systems.

With so much by way of general introduction to "structural-functional" analysis in general and its "requisite" form in particular, I should now like to turn to a structural distinction that bears directly on the concerns of "political science." This is the distinction between *concrete* and *analytic* structures. There is no need to repeat the definitions of those terms given in the Appendix. The fallacies of reification, the monisms, an indeterminate number of "chick-egg" problems, as well as auxiliary confusions in profusion in the social sciences attend our failures to keep straight the distinction between concrete and analytic structures. This distinction again is nothing really new, though the attempt to be explicit about it may make it seem so. The distinction is not confined to the social sciences. In fact it is somewhat easier to understand the distinction in its social science applications if it is first illustrated and discussed in physical terms. One may take for example a table. The table itself is a concrete structure in the sense intended here. Its various parts such as legs, top, sides, etc., are concrete substructures. It is at least conceivable that one place the legs of the table in one room, its top in another, and so forth. This may destroy the table, but the division and separation are at least conceivable. It is extremely useful for many purposes of analysis to be able to refer to these different "parts" or "concrete substructures."

One may also look at the table in other terms. One may distinguish its mass, its volume, its shape, its color, etc. The physical separation of its mass from its volume, its shape from its mass, or its volume from its color—these separations are not conceivable. These are not parts of the table. It is true that one can keep the volume of a table constant and increase its mass; one may change the table's color and shape without altering its volume, and so forth. Nevertheless the mass of the table cannot be put in one room and its volume in another—not even conceivably within the conceptual scheme of scientific method. Concepts like mass, volume, etc., refer to *aspects* of concrete objects rather than to their *parts*. These are the analytic aspects of objects. When they are patterned, they are the analytic structures.

The analytic structures do not refer to different things but rather to different ways of looking at the same things. As such, analytic structures cannot be spoken of as "causing" one another to do anything or even as "doing" anything. They are ways of looking at things that are "done," that "cause" or are "caused." This does not mean that these analytic structures cannot be used for purposes of setting up predictions. If one knows the volume and type of material in a table one can predict its mass. Any action that changes its volume but leaves its type of material the same will change its mass, etc. On the other hand, changes in concrete distinctions may "cause" changes in other concrete objects or operations.

In the social sciences many analytic distinctions have characteristically been used as though they were concrete ones. Among the more spectacular of these have been the distinctions between the "economic" and the "political." Either implicitly or explicitly the term "economic" has generally had to do with the allocation of goods and services, and the term "political" has had to do with the allocation of power and responsibility.[9] But there are no concrete acts that do not involve some allocation of goods and services and simultaneously some allocation of power and responsibility. Discussions of "political" as distinguished from "economic" acts or organizations are therefore inevitably misleading. If these acts are to be regarded as concretely distinct, the criteria stating where the "political" and the "economic" begin and end must be stated. If the definitions given above are used either explicitly or implicitly, no such line of demarcation can be drawn. Correspondingly, it is difficult or confusing to talk about "economic" acts "causing" "political" results or vice versa. What one can say is that a given set of concrete acts in which the "economic" aspect is crucial for given purposes had a particular set of implications for subsequent states of affairs in which the "political" aspects are crucial for given purposes.

Something similar can be done with organizations. It is possible in some situations to distinguish between "predominantly economically oriented" concrete structures (or organizations) and "predominantly politically oriented" ones. For example, it is not unreasonable from many points of view to speak of M—y's Department Store as "predominantly economically oriented" and the Executive Departments of the United States Government as "predominantly politically oriented." It is not true that the former involves no allocation of power and responsibility (or even that it involves no important allocations of power and responsibility) or that the latter has nothing to do with the allocation of goods and services.

It may seem picayune to go at such length into these matters. Actually most of the modern social scientists have come from societies that carry such specialization of organizations, in terms of a single aspect, to great lengths. But such specializations are relatively rare in social history. One result of this is that systems of analysis carried out in these terms tend to fall apart in our hands when we try to apply them to societies in which individual concrete structures have not been specialized in terms of a single "predominant orientation." Even in the societies with the more specialized structures, however, the functioning of nonspecialized structures and the interrelations among the specialized ones have been obscured by our persistent reification of these distinctions. It is not a matter of chance that much of our reasoning about the implications of the activities in terms of "predominantly economically oriented" structures for the allocation of power and responsibility have proceeded in terms of the "it's a plot" theory of social problems, and that many of our theories of the "economic" implications of the various activities of "predominantly politically oriented" structures (such as legislatures) have been in terms of graft and corruption or "drifts toward socialism" and the like. In both cases the most difficult and least analyzed problems fall well outside these extreme interpretations.

Looked at from the point of view suggested here, "political science" does not deal with different phenomena from other social sciences. If distinctions among these fields are to be drawn, "political science" deals with the same phenomena looked at from a special point of view. The Congress of the United States is certainly to be reckoned with in trying to understand decision-making in the foreign policy field. It is no less to be reckoned with in trying to understand the prospects for a period of prosperity or depression in a given European country. The same sort of thing may be said of "economics" or "sociology." The "social" is not "non-political" nor is the "political" "non-social" in this sense. Distinctions among these fields are useful in many ways, but when they are erected into barriers to analysis, they are pernicious. To say, in effect, "Those factors are relevant to my study, but they are 'political' and this is a 'sociological' study; therefore I can't use them," is a counsel of despair. It is not going too far to say that no problem has ever been solved or had its solution aided by first deciding whether it lay in the field of economics, politics, sociology, anthropology, or the like.

One of the reasons for going at some length into this distinction along with discussion of the relevance of using the society as a unit for requisite analysis is that it is difficult if not impossible at the present stage of development of the field to derive the concrete structural requisites of any society. It is not correspondingly difficult to discover at least a tentative list of the analytic structural requisites of *any* society. One of these latter is the structure of political allocation or the structure of allocation of power and responsibility.

It is in connection with the structure of political allocation that the analysis here comes directly and obviously to bear upon much of what has generally been the concern of "political scientists." [10] *Political allocation* may be defined as the distribution of power over and responsibility for the actions of the various members of the concrete structure concerned. *Power* may be defined as the ability to exercise authority and control over the actions of others. It should be noted that the use of physical force or the threat of physical force is only the extreme in one direction of the concept of power. The possibilities inherent in such forms of power have long been examined;

their limitations have not received quite so much attention. *Responsibility* may be defined as the accountability of an individual (or individuals) to other individuals or groups for his own acts and/or the acts of others. The concepts of power and responsibility fall into a peculiar class of concepts in the social sciences and in other sciences as well. What is power from one point of view is responsibility from another. This should be borne in mind, just as in the case of the concepts of production and consumption. It does not mean, however, that the distinction is either useless or imprecise or that the terms are synonymous.

Most of the work of political scientists has in some sense been rather directly concerned with the problems of allocation here referred to as political allocation. For these purposes the concepts have quite deliberately been defined on an extremely general level—they are designed after all to be used in relation to *any* society. Nevertheless they can be modified by the addition of more specific criteria and used on any more specific level desired. There is a tendency in some quarters to feel that beyond rather restricted levels of generality propositions cease to have any empirical content at all. This is, of course, not the case. The proposition that the structure of political allocation is a structural requisite of any society is an empirical proposition even though an extremely general one. It may be untenable, and it may even be uninteresting from the theoretical point of view, but it is still an empirical proposition. In what is to follow I shall present another empirical proposition that has come out of work on the structure of political allocation in any society. After presenting it in its most general form, I shall try to illustrate it by its application to two problems on different and much more specific levels. The first of these problems has to do with certain inadequacies in a frequently but, I believe, improperly described and analyzed structure of political allocation. The second has to do with the delineation of the actual system of power and responsibility in a particular segment of a particular society and certain minimal interrelationships between the political and the religious aspects of that society.

The empirical proposition may be stated as follows: any concrete structure with regard to which power and responsibility are not balanced is inherently instable.[11] For the time being I should like to leave this hypothesis in its strongest form—without qualification. This will make exceptions to it easier to detect, and hence will make it easier to modify on the basis of actual empirical data.[12] Before going on with this discussion, the term stability should be defined. A system will be called stable if its operation within its setting does not result in changes in the system on the level under consideration; *i.e.,* its operation does not result in a change in its structural requisites or their elimination. Instability may be defined as the residual category of stability. A system will be called instable if its operation within its setting does result in changes in the system on the level of generalization under consideration;

i.e., its operation does result in changes in its structural requisites or in their elimination.

I suggest this proposition as an hypothesis and not as proven in any sense. It is not really a new proposition. It is embedded in much common-sense discussion of such fields as administration and international relations. In one form or another political thinkers from time immemorial have expressed this doctrine. My interest is not in its authentic pedigree but in its explicit statement and its systematic use in the analysis of political aspects of phenomena. One further caution is in order. The proposition asserts that an imbalance of power and responsibility leads to instability. *It does not assert that stability is present whenever there is a balance of power and responsibility.* Stability and instability are not defined in terms of power and responsibility, and power and responsibility are not defined in terms of one another.[13] Whatever else the proposition may be, it is not tautological.

There is, however, another consideration that should be faced up to by those who wish to play with this sort of analysis. This is the problem of how one determines whether there is a balance or imbalance of power and responsibility. Ideally speaking such research must sooner or later get down to suggested scales for making measurements of this sort. I regret to say that I have not as yet been able to find any very satisfactory solution to this problem. I have been told of some work being carried out at the Survey Research Center of the University of Michigan which, albeit limited in scope to questions of union leadership, may turn up promising leads in this connection.

Even in the absence of such well worked out measurement techniques, however, all is not hopeless in my opinion. In the first place some of these questions seem to take an "all or none" form. Thus it may be possible to tell that there is imbalance in some cases simply because the most diligent effort turns up, let us say, some clear instance of power but no clear evidence of responsibility on the part of the power wielder at all. For example, we may be able to assert with some high probability of correctness that a dictator can order an execution, but no source in the system can hold him responsible for such an order. This does not, of course, help us in the case where some degree of both power and responsibility seem to be identifiable but the question is how to determine whether they are or are not equal. As a strategy of research for the present, pending the development of more satisfactory measurement techniques, I can only suggest the deliberate attempt to find as many "all or none" aspects as possible, keeping in mind that one runs some risk of distortion in doing so. If the results of this crude sort of measurement seem promising, the stimulus to the discovery of more precise and satisfactory measures may be greatly increased. When found these measures may enable us to destroy our original hypothesis, but if the concepts continue fruitful in other contexts this by-product of the original effort will have proved more valuable than the hypothesis that gave it rise. If one is not

willing, temporarily at least, to "sin bravely" (but explicitly and self-con-
sciously) against the best canons of scientific technique, one should face up
to the fact that progress along these lines is for the time being out of the question. There is much to be said against such purism, as tending to stifle exploration. Nevertheless this does not invalidate any of the specific criticisms
from such a purist point of view, nor does it justify pretending that the purist
objections do not exist. On the other hand, the purist position in these questions has in some unsophisticated cases resulted in what seems to me to be a
perversion of the role of technique in scientific work. Some social scientists
seem to choose their problems by first determining what can or cannot be
measured adequately at a given state of the arts rather than to seek to meas-
what is important for study in terms of an explicit system of analysis or system of theory. If this extreme is avoided, however, the only proper answer
to the purist lies in continual efforts to improve and careful efforts to be
aware of those respects in which improvement has not yet been feasible.

Let us now take our first problem and ask what the implications of this
hypothesis would be for that problem if the hypothesis were true. The problem is that of the so-called gerontocratic society. Much has been written by
anthropologists, historians, sociologists, and others about societies in which
it is stated that the aged control the society. Furthermore many of these societies appear, on superficial examination at least, to have been highly stable.
Such a situation is frequently alleged about primitive societies (or portions
of their societies), and has certainly been alleged about many parts of "traditional" Chinese society [14]—most notably about the family system on which
much of the general system of control in that society depended.

It is possible to give the aged, or even for the aged to hold, both ideal and
actual power [15] in a system. It is possible to give the aged ideal responsibility
both from their point of view and from that of others in the system. It is not
possible for them to have or be given actual responsibility. There are two
main reasons for this. In the first place there is the imminence of death for
the aged. The probability is generally much higher that the aged will not be
present to take responsibility than is the case with regard to their mature
juniors. In the second place, there is the imminence of senility. In a sense
this is more serious. Senility may well take the individual beyond the reach
of actual responsibility, but it does not necessarily take him beyond the possibility of exercising actual power. If that possibility remains, the probability
that the exercise of power may be capricious, and hence disruptive, is certainly increased. It is true that history has seen some rather remarkable
virtuosi of old age—men who have staved off senility as well as death for
unusual periods. These cases only help us to account for stability in idiosyncratic cases, however, for no systematic method of producing or discovering
such virtuosi of old age has ever been invented in social history. For a gerontocratic system to eliminate the implications of the imminence of senility

methods for developing and/or locating such virtuosi would have to be present.

Some of these societies or social systems do seem to be (or have been) stable if one places any reliance on the available decriptions. The presence of such stable systems would certainly disprove the hypothesis with which I started. I do not wish to maintain this hypothesis forever in the face of contradictory data. Nevertheless, what are the implications if I continue to assume its tenability for a bit longer? There are two major alternatives. On the one hand, the allegation about stability may be mistaken. On the other, the system may be stable but its structure may differ from the description—or perhaps, to put the matter more accurately, the apparently precise descriptions of its structure may be vague. The first alternative may be discarded for the moment. It leads nowhere save to a further contradiction—by assumption in this case—of descriptions given us. The second alternative is a more interesting one to follow. If the hypothesis is correct and if the systems are in fact stable, what could have been left out of the descriptions or what could have been presented in such a way that its inferences are misleading? For one thing there could have been a confusion between those patterns that are the actual patterns of the system and those patterns that are the ideal patterns of the members of the system. This is a very frequent source of confusion in handling social materials.[16]

Suppose that the aged in these societies have ideal power and ideal responsibility. Such a state of affairs might easily account for their description as gerontocracies. Suppose also that the aged do not have actual power and responsibility. That would permit a balance of power and responsibility by other patterns of allocation. A contradiction of the general hypothesis would not then be involved, and the apparent stability of those systems would not be contradictory either. But if this is the case, what are the other patterns of allocation of power and responsibility? How are the ideal holders of power and responsibility reconciled to this? How are others adjusted to it? It is true that not all contradictions in societies make the members thereof uneasy, but some of them do. Such a contradiction as this could easily become a source of great strain. One is led to hunt for structures that could eliminate such problems.

Precedence with regard to power and responsibility is extremely likely to be associated with other sorts of precedence. Respect and prestige frequently cluster about such allocations.[17] Suppose, in societies in which the aged have ideal power and responsibility, the aged are considered to be too honorific to be bothered with the mundane, banal, but necessary day-to-day decisions. Suppose these are made for them by representatives of some sort. Under these circumstances the actual power and responsibility in these areas will have been shifted though not necessarily the ideal ones. Furthermore, this may be done under the guise of a service to the aged and not a limitation of their roles. Such transfers will have their effects on less mundane issues as well. The less mundane issues are usually determined in important respects by the general settlements of mundane issues. Under these circumstances even if the "larger issues" are submitted to the aged, it does not follow that they exercise actual power and responsibility in connection with them. Such structures may take many forms combining all sorts of recognition of power delegated *actually* to persons who are, ideally speaking, subordinates. In some cases even outright retirement systems for the aged are present.

Now we have a derived hypothesis that may be subjected to empirical tests. It takes the general form: "There is no stable society that is a true gerontocracy" (*i.e.,* there is no stable society in which the aged possess both actual and ideal power and responsibility). From this, unless one is simply to discount completely all reports on the role of the aged in these systems, one may develop the following more specific hypotheses as a minimum: (1) There are stable societies in which the aged have ideal power and responsibility. (2) None of these stable societies are incapable of handling the problems of senescense and the death of the aged. (3) All of them are characterized by delegations of actual power and responsibility to subordinates who act as representatives of the aged, or by retirement systems, or by some combination of the two.

In the empirical examples that I have looked into such departures from "true" gerontocratic patterns have always been present. This work has not yet been carried out on a systematic basis, but I hope that with the continued development of the Human Relation Areas Files and other materials such a systematic examination need not be long delayed. I have examined this matter in some detail in one case, that of the Chinese family system. Even among the gentry this does not turn out to be a "true" gerontocracy. Furthermore the variations in these respects among different Chinese families strongly supports the line of hypothesis taken here. In those families best insulated against the effects of capricious acts on the part of the family head, the combination of ideal and actual power and responsibility is prolonged age-wise to the greatest extent. Even in these families, however, the aged eventually come to be considered too honorific to have much to do with anything apart from the ancestor rites, the maintenance of geneologies, ceremonial performance in general, etc. The more vulnerable the family to capricious acts by the family head the earlier is the son taken into "full partnership," as it were, with his father. There are cases in which there are departures from these patterns. Some peasant fathers continue to dominate their sons completely after maturity. Under these circumstances, if the father's acts are capricious relative to the family, the family is destroyed or seriously injured.

Our second, more specific, case of balance of power and responsibility may be raised now. It has been noted above that, although there is a sense in which what is power from one point of view is responsibility from another, it does not follow that if A has power over B (and correspondingly B is responsible in some sense to A) then A is responsible to anyone or anything for his power over B. It also does not follow that, if A has power over B, B has any reciprocal power over A. There are, of course, some systems in which the power-responsibility allocations are reciprocals. The total structure of political allocation of a society never takes this reciprocal form, however. In the "traditional" Chinese family system there is a typical case of the non-reciprocal allocation. At least in his junior years the son owes complete responsibility to his father and the father has complete power over his son. At many points in Chinese history this power has in fact been carried to the point of executions. It is unfilial of the son to call his father to account or to resist his exercise of power. Furthermore, if the father is also head of the family,[18] there is no other group outside the kinship organization which may legitimately hold the father responsible. Even the clan organization, when it exists, is unlikely to interfere in such relationships. On the surface this would appear to be a classic case of the imbalance of power and responsibility, and yet the "traditional" Chinese family system has certainly had these structures and been stable over long periods of time for very substantial numbers of people.

It is not possible to maintain in this connection that fathers never abuse their power over their sons or that such abuse does not destroy family units. There are plenty of examples of both. It must be borne in mind that violence is by no means the only relation between father and son that can threaten the family. If the father fails to provide a wife for the son, fails to conserve land to pass on to his son, or drives his son to the unfilial act of running away, the family may be ruined. My general hypothesis leads me to predict instability when there is an imbalance of power and responsibility. There is ample evidence in the Chinese case to show that such instability comes to pass in some individual cases. But it does not come to pass in general.

Suppose once again we assume for a moment that the general hypothesis is correct. For present purposes I have oversimplified the situation by stating that the father is not responsible for his conduct toward the son—to any group or organization other than the family in the society. As head of the family, he is not subject to accountability to other family members or parts.[19] Where then might one look for a source of balance? Or failing that, must the general hypothesis be rejected? Here, I think, the hypothesis leads us to reject certain of our own social biases and widen the field of investigation. In modern industrial societies (whence most of our social scientists come), and particularly in the United States, we are accustomed to seek these balances as between individuals or groups regarded as empirical by the actors in the systems. The "system of checks and balances" of the United States is a classic case of this sort. With regard to the governmental system of the

United States there is a sense in which *ideally speaking* it is always *supposed* to be possible to state who has power over whom (or who doesn't have power over whom) and who is responsible to whom or what. The whole matter is *supposed to be summed up* in the most general sense in a single major document. It is true that the document is often regarded as closely linked to the Deity and fully approved by Him, but the members of the system seem to regard it as too much to ask the Deity to intervene unless men have done their very best to set up their own methods of handling these problems. Miss Margaret Mead has summed up this general position in the United States (it goes far beyond the matter of the government) by reference to Cromwell's remark, "Put your trust in God; but mind to keep your powder dry!" Another way to put it is, "God helps those who help themselves." Not all societies have gone so far in taking matters into the hands of men.[20]

In the case of the "traditional" Chinese family, balance of power and responsibility is not to be sought in a system of empirical checks and balances as seen from the point of view of the members of the system. It is to be found rather in a type of orientation by the members to non-empirical considerations—toward deities from their point of view if one wishes to put it in that fashion. Whatever other religious systems the "traditional" Chinese participates in, he also participates, in the overwhelming majority of cases, in Ancestor Worship. The father ordinarily believes in the Ancestors and believes himself responsible to them for the future of the family.[21]

The "traditional" Chinese father does not regard himself as responsible *to* his son in any way. He regards himself as responsible *for* his son and *for* the future of the family. This responsibility is owed to the Ancestors. The entities to whom he regards himself responsible are non-empirical ones. The fact that he believes in them and in his obligation to them and the fact that this belief affects his actions and the structure of the family system are quite empirical and quite open to study.[22] For reasons too complicated to go into here, the general political allocation in "traditional" China rests on family stability. For these reasons the general political structure of the society is not comprehensible without attention to the religious aspects of the system. This is to be seen in part via the examination of the family structure.

Going back to the original general hypothesis it appears that our second case has not proved it. It has not disproved it either, however, and this time use of the hypothesis has led to a consideration of the interrelationship between the religious and the political aspects of "traditional" Chinese society. It has furthermore led to a distinction on a far higher level of generalization. Balances of power and responsibility may be achieved, if they are achieved, through empirical or non-empirical orientations of the members of the system or through some combination of the two. It would take a great deal of space to explore this fully, but one may at least state that the two types of orientations or varying combinations of them have widely different implications for structures of political allocation and for the general structure of societies or social systems. These are not lofty theoretical concerns either. In concern over the "development" of "underdeveloped" areas and in the maintenance of stability in the "developed" ones some of the major little-examined aspects lie precisely in this field. Many other problems, some of them practical ones, some of them age-old, some of them both, may be tackled in terms of this hypothesis. Perhaps, for example, the major problem in connection with the attempt to make use of mobs as an instrument of rule lies in the fact that mobs can be given or can take power, but they cannot be held effectively responsible. From this point of view alone the Middle East is today a particularly strategic area for study by social scientists in general and political scientists in particular.

With vast oversimplification this paper has ranged over three types of problems. The first had to do with some observations on "structural-functional" analysis in general. In particular it presented a special form of "structural-functional" analysis, "structural-functional requisite" analysis. This kind of analysis can be used to get at systems of analysis for various types of social systems. It was suggested that its use in connection with societies, defined in a particular way, has some special value because other social systems seem to be either subcategories of a particular society or the result of interrelations between two or more societies. Many of the major problems in political science as in the other social sciences hinge on our being able to do systematic analyses of different examples of a given type of unit (or of different types of units) and on our being able to compare the results of those analyses in a search for generalized propositions.

The second part of the paper has taken up one distinction between different types of structure—between analytic and concrete structures. Basically this is a distinction between aspects of social systems on the one hand and membership units on the other. This distinction was singled out because I feel that failure to appreciate its significance has underlain many of the major confusions in social science today. These confusions are particularly marked in the attempts to bring about an association between the efforts of political scientists and economists—or rather, perhaps, in the failure to bring about these associations successfully. The relevance of this distinction to the fallacy of misplaced concreteness and to the creation of monisms was suggested, and finally its use in the attempt to get a system of analysis for any example of a given type of unit (in this case, of societies) was pointed out.

The third part of this paper has gone more directly into what has in orthodox terms been considered the "proper" realm of political science. Here with regard to the structure of political allocation in any society a specific hypothesis was presented. Although "unproved," this hypothesis was explored in two different types of cases. One of these cases calls into question the tenability of an observation frequently made in common-sense terms about many societies and social systems. The results at first seem to contradict common sense. In the long run they indicate that the common-sense version of these matters is at best vague and inadequate. It also seems to develop the lines along which qualifications may be introduced in this problem and directs attention to lines of exploration for data. The second application of the hypothesis seems to be fruitful not only in opening up suggestions for sources of relevant data on a question of political allocation, but also seems to suggest certain general conditions under which the political aspects of a system are interrelated with other aspects—the religious aspects in the example cited.

The explicit use of the various forms of structural-functional analysis with some care as to their advantages and limitations has only just begun. Neither these nor any other types of analysis will ever serve as substitutes for the gathering of data and/or the imagination and creativeness required to suggest fruitful hypotheses for exploration. They do, in my opinion, promise considerable aid in developing the implications of one's data or of one's creative insights. They also promise to direct attention away from sterile prides and squabbles over disciplinary jurisdictions and toward the solution of empirical problems in such a way as to increase the possibility of the development of more and more sophisticated and fruitful systems of theory in the social sciences.

HANS J. MORGENTHAU[1]

Power as a Political Concept

ANY ATTEMPT at reorganizing political science around a central concept must come to terms with three factors which in the past have impeded such organization: its subject matter, its method, its moral orientation.

I

Political science as an academic discipline owes its existence to two factors: the breakdown in the late nineteenth century of the great philosophic systems which had dominated Western thought, concomitant with emphasis upon the empirical investigation of the social world, and the lack of interest of the established academic disciplines in the investigation of certain aspects of politics.

All the social sciences are the result of the emancipation of the Western mind from metaphysical systems which had made the social world primarily a subject for metaphysical speculation and ethical postulates. In certain fields, such as economics, that emancipation occurred early; in others, such as political science, it occurred relatively late (for reasons which, as we shall see, are inherent in the nature of political science). Yet when the first departments of political science were established in this country toward the end of the nineteenth century, they did not grow organically from a general conception as to what was covered by the field of political science, nor did they respond to a strongly felt intellectual need. Rather they reflected the negative attitude of other academic disciplines, especially law, towards certain aspects of the political world. Furthermore, they tried to satisfy certain practical needs. For instance, in that period the law schools would not deal with public law. Yet it was felt that somebody ought to deal with it, and thus it was made part of political science. There was a demand for instruction in journalism, but there was no place for it to be taught; and thus it was made part of political science. There was a local demand for guidance in certain aspects of municipal administration, such as sewage disposal; and thus a course in that subject was made part of the curriculum of political science.

In other words, political science grew not by virtue of an intellectual principle germane to the field, but in response to pressures from the outside. What could not be defined in terms of the traditional academic disciplines was defined as political science. This inorganic growth and haphazard character of political science is strikingly reflected in the curricula of the earliest departments of political science, such as those of Columbia and Michigan.

In the meantime, a process of contraction has eliminated from the curriculum the more disparate elements. But still today the curriculum of political science bears the unmistakable marks of its haphazard origin and development. To pick out at random some courses from two departments of political science with which I am familiar, what have "Plato's Political Philosophy and its Metaphysical Foundation" and "The Politics of Conservation" in common, or "General Principles of Organization and Administration" and "International Law," or "Conduct of American Foreign Relations" and "Introduction to Jurisprudence," or "Nationalism" and "Political Behavior and Public Policy," or "Russian Political and Economic Institutions" and "Public Personnel Administration"? The only common denominator which ties these courses loosely together is a general and vague orientation toward the nature and activities of the state and toward activities which have in turn a direct bearing upon the state. Beyond that orientation toward a common subject matter, defined in the most general terms, contemporary political science has no unity of outlook, method, and purpose.

II

As concerns method, political science is split in five ways, and four of these methodological positions have hardly anything in common. Their disparity is such that there is hardly even a possibility of fruitful discourse among the representatives of the different approaches beyond polemics which deny the very legitimacy of the other approaches. These approaches can be classified as philosophic theory, empirical theory, empirical science, description, and practical amelioration.

These five methodological approaches are not peculiar to political science. They have appeared in other social sciences, such as psychology, economics, and sociology, as well, but with two significant differences. First of all, the other social sciences have traditionally shown a much greater awareness of the existence, nature, and separate functions of these approaches than has political science. Second, they have been able to rid themselves in good measure of the ameliorative and vocational approach which has by itself only a minimum of intellectual relevance. Political science, on the other hand, has never squarely faced the methodological problem in terms of the intrinsic character of these different approaches and the functions which they are able to perform for the understanding of political science. These five approaches have rather coexisted indistinctively within the departments of political science, one to be emphasized over the others at different times and places according to the pressures of supply and demand. Here, too, the development has been haphazard and subject to accident rather than guided by certain fundamental theoretical requirements.

Thus political science has not generally been able to make that distinction which is a precondition for the development of any true science: the distinction between what is worth knowing intellectually and what is useful for practice. It is this distinction which economics and sociology accomplished some decades ago, when schools of business, home economics, retailing, social work and the like took over the practical concerns which at best develop practical uses for theoretical knowledge or else have but the most tenuous connection with it. Political science has taken a similar step in some instances by organizing the practical uses of political science for the amelioration of government activities in schools of administration and the like. But not only has this separation been exceptional rather than typical, it has also been made as a matter of convenience rather than in application of a generally accepted theoretical principle. In consequence, improvement of the processes of government is still generally considered not only a worthwhile activity to be engaged in by political scientists, but also a legitimate, and sometimes even the only legitimate, element of political science as an academic discipline, to be taught under any of the course headings composing the curriculum of political science.

It should be pointed out in passing that we are dealing here not with a specific subject matter, but with a particular method, a particular intellectual approach. This approach will naturally manifest itself most frequently and typically in those fields of political science which have a direct relevance to the operations of government, such as public administration, but it is by no means limited to them. The other fields of political science, such as international relations, American government, constitutional law, and parties, have at time been dominated by the practical approach seeking practical remedies for conditions regarded as being in need of amelioration.

Today, however, description is still the method most widely used in political science. Factual information arranged according to certain traditional classifications still dominates most of the textbooks in the field. While it is unnecessary to argue the case for the need for factual information, it ought to be no more necessary to argue that factual description is not science but a mere, however indispensable, preparation for the scientific understanding of the facts. It may, however, point toward a theoretical awakening that descriptive political science tends to dress up descriptive accounts of facts in theoretical garb and to use fancy classifications and terminologies in order to conceal the mere descriptive character of its substance. While the theoretical pretense of factual accounts shows an awareness of the need for theoretical understanding, that understanding itself requires more than the demonstrative use of an elaborate apparatus of classification and terminology.

With this last type of descriptive political science which overlays its descriptive substance with theoretical pretense, we are in the borderland where description and empirical science merge. Empirical science is today the most vigorous branch of political science which tends to attract many of the abler and more inventive students. Taking its cue from the natural sciences, or what it thinks the natural sciences are, it tries to develop rigorous methods of quantitative verification which are expected in good time to attain the same precision in the discovery of uniformities and in prediction to which the natural sciences owe their theoretical and practical success.

I have argued elsewhere against this analogy between the social and the natural sciences, and this is not the place to resume the controversy. It must suffice here to state dogmatically that the object of the social sciences is man, not as a product of nature but as both the creature and the creator of history in and through which his individuality and freedom of choice manifest themselves. To make susceptibility to quantitative measurement the yardstick of the scientific character of the social sciences in general and of political science in particular is to deprive these sciences of that very orientation which is adequate to the understanding of their subject matter.

The inadequacy of the quantitative method to the subject matter of political science is demonstrated by the limitation of its success to those types of political behavior which by their very nature lend themselves to a certain measure of quantification, such as voting, and the barrenness of the attempts to apply the quantitative method to phenomena which are determined by historic individuality and moral choice. It will not do to argue that this failure is due to the "backwardness" of political science which could be overcome if only more and better people would spend more time and money for quantification. For that argument to be plausible the failure is too persistent, and it becomes ever more spectacular as more and better people spend more time and money to make it a success.

Once quantification has left that narrow sphere where it can contribute to relevant knowledge, two roads are open to it. Either it can try to quantify phenomena which in their aspects relevant to political science are not susceptible to quantification, and by doing so obscure and distort what political science ought to know; thus much of quantitative political science has become a pretentious collection of trivialities. Or, dimly aware of this inadequacy, quantification may shun contact with the empirical phenomena of political life altogether and try to find out instead what the correct way of quantifying is. Basic to this methodological concern is the assumption that the failure of quantification to yield results in any way proportionate to the effort spent results from the lack of a correct quantitative method. Once that method is discovered and applied, quantification will yield the results in precise knowledge its adherents claim for it.

However, it is obvious that these methodological investigations, patently intended for the guidance of empirical research, have hardly exerted any influence upon the latter. This divorce of methodology from empirical investigation is not fortuitous. For it points not only to the inadequacy of the quantitative method for the understanding of much of the subject matter of political science, an inadequacy which must become particularly striking when quantification is confronted in its pure theoretical form with the actuality of political life. That divorce also illuminates a tendency, common to all methodological endeavors in the social sciences, to retreat ever more from contact with the empirical world into a realm of self-sufficient abstractions. This "new scholasticism," as it has been aptly called, has been most fully developed in sociology; yet it has left its impact also upon political science. The new scholastic tends to think about how to think and how to conceptualize about concepts, regressing ever further from empirical reality until he finds the logical consummation of his endeavors in mathematical symbols and other formal relations.

With this emphasis upon theoretical abstractions which have no relation to political reality, the methodology of political science joins a school which from the beginning to this day has occupied an honored but lonely place in the curriculum of political science: political theory. Political theory as an academic discipline has been traditionally the history of political philosophies in chronological succession, starting with Plato and ending, if time permits, with Laski. As an academic discipline, political theory has been hardly more than an account of what writers of the past, traditionally regarded as "great," have thought about the traditional problems of politics, without ever a systematic attempt being made to correlate that historic knowledge to the other fields of political science and to the contemporary political world. Thus political theory as an academic discipline has been intellectually sterile, and it is not by accident that some of the most important contributions to contemporary political theory have been made not by professional political scientists, but by theologians, philosophers and sociologists.

Political theory has remained an indispensable part of the curriculum not because of the vital influence it has been able to exert upon our thinking, but rather because of a vague conviction that there was something venerable and respectable in this otherwise useless exercise. Thus the academic concern with political theory has tended to become an intellectually and practically meaningless ritual which one had to engage in for reasons of tradition and prestige before one could occupy oneself with the things that really mattered.

The awareness of this contrast between the prestige of political theory and its actual lack of relevance for the understanding of contemporary political problems has led theory closer to the contemporary political world. On the other hand, the awareness of the meagerness of the insights to be gained from strictly empirical investigations have made empirical political science search for a theoretical framework. Avoiding the limitations of the traditional approaches and fusing certain of their elements, contemporary political science has revived a tradition to which most of the classics of political science owe their existence and influence. The intent of that tradition is theoretical: it wants to understand political reality in a theoretical manner. The subject matter of this theoretical concern is the contemporary political world. This branch of political science, which we call empirical theory, reflects in theoretical terms about the contemporary political world. The political world, however, poses a formidable obstacle to such understanding. This obstacle is of a moral rather than an intellectual nature. Before we turn to the requirements of such an empirical theory and its central concept, we have to dispose of the moral problem with which political science must come to terms.

III

The moral position of the political scientist in society is ambivalent; it can even be called paradoxical. For the political scientist is a product of the society which it is his mission to understand. He is also an active part, and frequently he seeks to be a leading part, of that society. To be faithful to his mission he would, then, have to overcome two limitations: the limitation of origin, which determines the perspective from which he looks at society, and the limitation of purpose, which makes him wish to remain a member in good standing of that society or even to play a leading role in it.

The stronger the trend toward conformity within the society and the stronger the social ambitions within the individual scholar, the greater will be the temptation to sacrifice the moral commitment to the truth for social advantage. It follows that a respectable political science—respectable, that is, in terms of the society to be investigated—is in a sense a contradiction in terms. For a political science which is faithful to its moral commitment of telling the truth about the political world cannot help telling society things it does not want to hear. This cannot be otherwise in view of the fact that one of the main purposes of society is to conceal the truth about man and society from its members. That concealment, that elaborate and subtle and purposeful misunderstanding of the nature of man and of society, is one of the cornerstones upon which all societies are founded.

A political science, true to its moral commitment, ought at the very least to be an unpopular undertaking. At its very best, it cannot help being a subversive and revolutionary force with regard to certain vested interests—intellectual, political, economic, and social in general. It stands to reason that political science as a social institution could never hope even to approach this ideal; for it would destroy itself in the attempt. Only individuals have achieved the distinction of unpopularity, social ostracism, and criminal penalties, which are the reward of constant dedication to the truth in matters political.

While political science as a social organization cannot hope even to approach the ideal, it could at least be aware of its existence, and the awareness of its moral commitment could at least mitigate those compromises between the moral commitment and social convenience and ambition which no political scientist can fully escape. It is the measure of the degree to which political science in America meets the needs of society rather than its moral commitment to the truth that it is not only eminently respectable and popular but—what is worse—that it is also widely regarded with indifference.

A political science which is mistreated and persecuted is likely to have earned that enmity because it has put its moral commitment to the truth above social convenience and ambition. It has penetrated beneath the ideological veil with which society conceals the true nature of political relations, disturbing the complacency of the powers-that-be and stirring up the conscience of society. It helps to cover political relations with the veil of ideologies which mollify the conscience of society; by justifying the existing power relations, it reassures the powers-that-be in their possession of power; it illuminates certain aspects of the existing power relations; and it contributes to the improvement of the technical operations of government. The relevance of this political science does not lie primarily in the discovery of the truth about politics but in its contribution to the stability of society.

A political science which is neither hated nor respected, but treated with indifference as an innocuous pastime, is likely to have retreated into a sphere that lies beyond the positive or negative interest of society. Concerning itself with issues in which nobody has a stake, this political science avoids the risk of social disapproval by even foregoing the chance of social approbation. The retreat into the trivial, the formal, the methodological, the purely theoretical—in short the politically irrelevant—is the unmistakable sign of a "non-controversial" political science which has neither friends nor enemies because it has no relevance for the great political issues in which society has a stake. By being committed to a truth which is in this sense irrelevant, it distorts the perspective under which the political world is seen. It passes in silence over such burning problems as alternative foreign policies, the political power of economic organizations and of religious and ethnic minority groups, the relation between government and public opinion, as well as most of the other fundamental problems of contemporary democracy. By doing so, it makes it appear as though these problems either did not exist or were not important or were not susceptible to theoretical understanding. By its predominant concern with the irrelevant, it devaluates by implication the really important problems of politics.

IV

The content of a theory of politics is not to be determined a priori and in the abstract. A theory is a tool for understanding. Its purpose is to bring order and meaning to a mass of phenomena which without it would remain disconnected and unintelligible. Its content, then, must be determined by the intellectual interest of the observer. What is it we want to know about politics? What concerns us most about it? What questions do we want a theory of politics to answer? The replies to these three questions determine the content of theory, and the replies may well differ not only from one period of history to another, but from one contemporaneous group of observers to the other.

Hypothetically one can imagine as many theories of politics as there are legitimate intellectual perspectives from which to approach the political scene. But in a particular culture and a particular period of history, there is likely to be one perspective which for theoretical and practical reasons takes precedence over the others. At one time theoretical interest was focused upon the constitutional arrangements within which political relations take place, and in view of the theoretical and practical problems to be solved, this was then a legitimate interest. At another time in the history of political science, theoretical interest was centered upon political institutions and their operations, and in view of what was worth knowing and doing at that time—this theoretical interest was again legitimate. Thus political science is like a spotlight which, while trying to illuminate the whole world, focuses in one period of history upon one aspect of politics and changes its focus in accordance with new theoretical and practical concerns.

In our period of history, the justice and stability of our political life is threatened, and our understanding of the political world is challenged, by the rise of totalitarianism on the domestic and international scene. The novel political phenomenon of totalitarianism puts in doubt certain assumptions about the nature of man and of society which we took for granted. It raises issues about institutions which we thought had been settled once and for all. It disrupts and overwhelms legal processes on which we had come to look as self-sufficient instruments of control. In one word, what has emerged from under the surface of legal and institutional arrangements as the distinctive, unifying element of politics is the struggle for power, elemental, undisguised, and all-pervading. As recently as a decade ago, it was still held by conservatives, liberals, and Marxists alike either that the struggle for power was at worst a raucous pastime, safely regulated by law and channeled by institutions, or that it had been replaced in its dominant influence by economic competition, or that the ultimate triumph of liberal democracy or the classless society, which were expected to be close at hand, would make an end of it altogether. These assumptions and expectations have been refuted by the experience of our age. It is to the challenge of this refutation that political science must respond, as political practice must meet the challenge of that experience.

It may be pointed out in passing that all great contributions to political science, from Plato and Aristotle to *The Federalist* and Calhoun, have been responses to such challenges arising from political reality. They have not been self-sufficient theoretical developments pursuing theoretical concerns for their own sake. Rather, they were confronted with a set of political experiences and problems which defied understanding with the theoretical tools at hand. Thus they had to face a new political experience, unencumbered by an intellectual tradition which might have been adequate to preceding experiences but which failed to illuminate the experience of the contemporary world. Thus they have been compelled to separate in the intellectual tradition at their disposal that which is historically conditioned from that which is true regardless of time and place, and to pose again the perennial problems of politics and to reformulate the perennial truths of politics in the light of the contemporary experience. This has been the task of political science throughout its history and this is the task of political science today.

By making power its central concept, a theory of politics does not presume that none but power relations control political action. What it must presume is the need for a central concept which allows the observer to distinguish the field of politics from other social spheres, to orient himself in the maze of empirical phenomena which make up the field of politics, and to establish a measure of rational order within it. A central concept, such as power, then provides a kind of rational outline of politics, a map of the political scene. Such a map does not provide a complete description of the political landscape as it is in a particular period of history. It rather provides the timeless features of its geography distinct from their everchanging historic setting. Such a map, then, will tell us what are the rational possibilities for travel from one spot on the map to another, and which road is most likely to be taken by certain travelers under certain conditions. Thus it imparts a measure of rational order to the observing mind and, by doing so, establishes one of the conditions for successful action.

A theory of politics, by the very fact of painting a rational picture of the political scene, points to the contrast between what the political scene actually is and what it tends to be, but can never completely become. The difference between the empirical reality of politics and a theory of politics is like the difference between a photograph and a painted portrait. The photograph shows everything that can be seen by the naked eye. The painted portrait does not show everything that can be seen by the naked eye, but it shows one thing that the naked eye cannot see: the human essence of the person portrayed. Thus a theory of politics must seek to depict the rational essence of its subject matter.

By doing so, a theory of politics cannot help implying that the rational elements of politics are superior in value to the contingent ones and that they are so in two respects. They are so in view of the theoretical understanding which the theory seeks; for its very possibility and the extent to which it is possible depends upon the rationality of its subject matter. A theory of politics must value that rational nature of its subject matter also for practical reasons. It must assume that a rational policy is of necessity a good policy; for only such a policy minimizes risks and maximizes benefits and, hence, complies both with the moral precept of prudence and the political requirement of success. A theory of politics must want the photographic picture of the political scene to resemble as much as possible its painted portrait.

Hence, a theory of politics presents not only a guide to understanding, but also an ideal for action. It presents a map of the political scene not only in order to understand what that scene is like, but also in order to show the shortest and safest road to a given objective. The use of theory, then, is not limited to rational explanation and anticipation. A theory of politics also contains a normative element.

V

A curriculum of political science which would try to put such a theoretical understanding of politics into practice for the purposes of teaching would have to eliminate all those subjects which do not serve this theoretical understanding. It would also have to add subjects which at present are not included, but which are essential to such understanding.

The process of elimination must move on two fronts. First, it must concern those subjects which have been traditionally included in the field but which have no organic connection with its subject matter or with the perspective from which contemporary political science ought to view it. In this category belong, for instance, all the legal subjects with which political science concerns itself because the law schools at one time did not. However, this practical consideration is unfounded today when law schools offer courses in jurisprudence, administrative, constitutional, and international law.

On the other hand, there has been a strong tendency in political science to add to the curriculum subjects which happen to be of practical importance at a particular moment, regardless of their theoretical relevance. However, what is worth knowing for practical reasons is not necessarily worth knowing on theoretical grounds. A certain innovation in municipal administration or international organization may attract at one time wide attention by virtue of the practical results it promises, or the political developments in certain areas of the world may become a matter of topical interest for public opinion. It still remains to be shown on theoretical grounds that such topics ought to be included as independent subjects in the curriculum of political science. On a limited scale this problem raises again the issue of liberal *vs.* vocational education.

The additions to the curriculum of political science, too, must be of two different kinds. On the one hand, the curriculum must take into account the fact that its central concept is a general social phenomenon which manifests itself most typically in the political sphere, but is not limited to it. The phenomenon of power and the social configurations to which it gives rise in the political sphere play an important, yet largely neglected, part in all social life. A configuration, such as the balance of power, for instance, is a general social phenomenon to be found on all levels of social interaction. The theoretical understanding of specifically political phenomena and configurations requires the understanding of the extent to which these political phenomena and configurations are merely the specific instances of general social phenomena and configurations and to which they grow out of their specific political environment. One of the cornerstones of the curriculum of political science, then, ought to be political sociology, which deals with the phenomenon of power and social configurations to which it gives rise in general, with special reference, of course, to those in the political sphere.

On the other hand, the contemporary political scene is characterized by the interaction between the political and economic spheres. This interaction runs counter to the liberal assumption and requirement of actual separation, which is reflected in the academic separation of the two fields. This interaction reverts to a situation which existed before political science was established as an academic discipline and which was reflected by the academic fusion of the two fields in the form of political economy. The curriculum of political science must take theoretical notice of the actual development of private governments in the form of giant corporations and labor unions. These organizations exercise power within their own organizational limits, in their relations to each other, and in their relations to the state. The state in turn exercises power with regard to them. These power relations constitute a new field for theoretical understanding.

A new curriculum of political science would have to rest on three cornerstones: political sociology, political theory, and political institutions. Political sociology deals with the empirical phenomena and problems to which the general social phenomenon of power gives rise. Political theory concerns itself with the theoretical attempts which have been made throughout history to understand the phenomena and solve the problems of politics. (It might be noted in passing that political theory ought not to limit itself to the understanding of the political theories of the Western world but ought to take the political theories of India and China into account.) Political institutions would be the empirical counterpart of political theory; this course would not deal exclusively with contemporary political institutions but would consider the main types of political institutions developed in the Western world as well as those of the main non-Western political societies.

On that common foundation the curriculum of political science would be divided into four wings, housing in turn American politics, international politics, foreign politics, and the politics of private government. Each of these four wings ought to be subdivided into institutions and processes. What further subdivisions as to substance and functions may be advisable will depend on both theoretical interest and available resources.

LOUIS HARTZ
The Problem of Political Ideas

I

THE POINT I want to make in this paper is that the study of ideas as a creative factor in political development deserves greater consideration than it has received and I want to support this view with a few observations concerning American politics. The relationship between ideas and institutions is admittedly an ancient source of argument generating the familiar battle between Marxian social determinism and Hegelian idealism. If one had to take sides in the battle now, it would be hard to see what of novelty might be said. Actually, however, this argument is concerned with an issue of ultimate causality of the hen-and-egg variety (which comes first: ideas or institutions?) that has obscured many vital issues which, if smaller in scope, are at any rate susceptible of more fruitful analysis. What I have to say might be accepted, it seems to me, at least with a certain stretching of premises, by any one of the school of thought which quarrel over the final question as to whether ideas reflect events or events reflect ideas. One can leave to the social theologian an explication of the text of Genesis and proceed as a social scientist to a study of the later time.

And yet there can be no doubt that the minimizing of the significance of ideology as an effective datum of politics in recent times has been largely produced by the influence of Marx who, as we know, turned Hegel upside down. The very term "ideology" and the very use of the term by many non-Marxists is eloquent testimony of this. For "ideology" means the intellectual rationalization of prior social interest and hence, as with Freud, shifts our attention away from the substance of thought to ulterior reasons behind it. Nor are Marx and Freud the only formal thinkers who have to be considered here. Sociologists of knowledge such as Mannheim, heavily under their influence, inspire essentially the same approach; and Progressive "economic determinists" such as Beard, who disclaim Marx and choose Madison as their father instead, produce only a cruder version of the same orientation to ideas in politics. We may not care to inquire into the metaphysical issue of origins, but if we are concerned with stressing the significance of ideas as a factor in politics, we cannot fail to observe that the metaphysicians have caused us a lot of trouble.

It is of course true that as against an arid idealism the Marxian approach, and that of the looser economic determinists, produced many results that were historically laudable. Even recognizing the fact that many idealisms

78

are not as arid as we have been led to believe (Hegel's, for example, where the student free of preconceptions will find an amazing quantity of empirical insight ranging from a class struggle proposition to a Turnerian view of the American frontier), it is still true that the revolt against sheer intellectualism in the study of politics opened up avenues of objective study in the connections between ideas and social forces that have been investigated with profit. There is now a body of socially oriented research in intellectual history for which any student of politics must be grateful. But as is often the case with progress made as a result of passionate distortion, the effort to hold on to the progress makes us live with the distortion out of a fear of moving backward. We labor under a kind of Robespierrian tension in scholarship. But surely it is time to give up this mood with respect to political ideas. We can relax now. If we affirm that ideas may be more than the automatic reflex of an immediate struggle of social interests, that they may contain a complexity of ramification which this view of reflex obscures completely, the Platonists will not arise from the grave and take over the world once more. It is safe to say that even Dunning will not come back.

What I am contending for, thus, is not a theory but an attitude which can accompany many theories: a willingness to explore the intrinsic structure of ideas because, as an empirical matter, they may have creative impact upon the political process. The degree to which this view can be accommodated even to a radical materialism is demonstrated by those recent developments in Marxism, beginning at least with Plekhanov, which stress ideological "superstructure." This is a concept weighted, to be sure, by definition on the side of material causality, but its recent use has been in fact to modify that emphasis. For it is designed to argue that ideas which are manifestations of anterior social forces can exercise a reciprocal influence upon those forces so as to condition them significantly if not to control them ultimately. When the Marxist admits as much as this he admits a lot, probably as much as anyone, given a specific problem, would require him to admit. "Sophisticated Marxism," as it is sometimes called, is dangerously close to common sense. Indeed it is so close to it that it will in the end undermine many of the millennial claims of Marx which are grounded analytically on fairly simple theories of material cause and class development. Whether or not you consider this a loss depends of course on your scale of values and your faith in man. Personally I am glad to exchange the withering away of the state for even a minor improvement in the understanding of political ideas.

II

The liberal idea in America illustrated excellently the degree to which an age of social "realism" can neglect ideal forces in politics. It is worth examining this case in some detail, since my point here is one of emphasis rather than novel method, and it is only in terms of concrete instances that it can be established. We have had, of course, a number of interpretations of American politics centering around essentially material or interest issues: the frontier, with Turner; sections and sectional needs, with Holcombe; pressure groups, with Bentley and Herring; and of course the Progressive interpretation with Beard. The student of American politics scarcely looks at an idea before he has, by a kind of automatic instinct, pinned it down to some issue of interest. But let us adopt for a moment another premise: that the basic character of American politics has been determined by the Lockean intellectual apparatus functioning without the feudal heritage it would have had to fight in Europe.[1] This premise is itself, of course, associated with certain material factors. One of them is the simple fact of new space, a new area not cluttered up by the feudal institutions of the Old World. Another is a set of predominantly middle-class settlers abstracted from Europe and imbued with liberal purposes. A third may even be the richness of resources and the abundance of land in America which made the individualistic pattern of Locke flourish easily. But after all of these have been named the ideal element turns out to be, especially in connection with certain familiar problems, of startlingly large significance. Consider one of these problems: the failure of American socialism. Marx intrudes again upon our analysis here, which cannot be helped, since it is in the nature of his massive impact upon our age that he influenced not only the method of social science but the social movements to which the method was to be applied.

About half a century ago Werner Sombard, that ardent student of European socialisms, raised the query as to why a comparable movement did not flourish in America. Since that time the crystallization of an objective proletariat in the country has proceeded apace, we have gone through a tremendous "capitalist crisis," and yet the query is as relevant as ever. Indeed practically all the material criteria for the emergence of a socialistic movement that Marx and Engels stressed have been met in America, so that we are confronted, willy-nilly, with the problem of reconsidering those criteria themselves. Of course one can adopt a rather subtle twist here which will save the day: one can affirm that the memory of material abundance has hung over into the modern time, that there is "lag," and hence that not enough time has elapsed for the "objective" conditions behind socialism to make themselves felt in the United States. Give the American worker another depression, heightened proletarian experience, and he will blossom forth as a class-conscious socialist in European terms. There is, of course, no way of finally answering this argument, since it is all projected into future time. But in light of the evidence it can hardly be more than a shaky reliance. One recalls that John Spargo used to hum this tune, not without a certain inner anxiety, as far back as the Progressive era.

When we stress the peculiar nature of the American liberal idea, we move much closer to sensed realities. In a forgotten essay Georges Sorel once remarked that "all notion of class, having its origin in feudalism, is inconceivable to the American." [2] And is not this a convincing insight? Is it accidental that the only Western nation which lacks a feudal background turns out also to be the only nation lacking a socialist movement? One sees in this interpretation certain obvious points: that feudal institutions generate the original concept of class, and if one reflects a bit, that it is the attempt to smash remaining elements of feudalism, rather than any battle against capitalist society, which in Europe inspires very considerably the socialist movement. If the latter is true in England, as certain students have suggested, how much truer is it in a place like Germany where not only the feudal ethos but significant phases of the feudal institutional structure persisted for a long time? We have to realize that Marx as well as Locke has had a hand in the battle against Filmer. But what is even more significant as regards socialism, however, is the distinction between a liberal theory fashioned in the struggle against feudalism and one not so fashioned. Marx is involved with Filmer, but he is even more involved, or as the American experience suggests, not involved, with Locke.

For where feudalism prevails, of course, liberalism also is class oriented, which is the central lesson we ought to draw from the insight of Sorel I have cited. Americans are so deeply involved in their own subjective experience that when they think of "class-consciousness" they usually think of a European proletariat they happily do not have, overlooking the major fact that it is the European middle class which originated this experience. The frustrations of Rousseau are antecedent to those of Harold Laski, which is what Marx meant when he said that the bourgeoisie was the great teacher of the proletariat. In an immediate sense the concept of class comes to the workers from the capitalists, as it were, and the important thing about the American capitalist is that, without an aristocratic structure to hem him in, he had no reason to develop it. The classless nature of the liberal ideology killed the socialist germ at its roots, regardless of economic development. All of the factories in the world, all of the surplus value, could not alter this.

In the American Revolution, one of the three great "liberal revolutions," why did we not have a socialist offshoot on the left, as with Winstanley and Babeuf in the Puritan and French episodes? The virtue of this instance is that it shows us not only the significance of the class concept in liberal ideology but other concepts as well. Now there are many issues involved in this comparison, but if we study the Babeuviste movement in France,[3] we see at once that it inherited most of its ideology from the revolutionary liberalism of the French Enlightenment. Looked at in terms of the class idea, it was of course only a step from the Tiers Etat emphasized by the liberals to the Pence emphasized by the Babeuvistes. But was it very far also from the

Final Epoch in human history envisaged by Condorcet to the Final Epoch envisaged by the embittered leftists? Was it very far from the liberal notion of Enlightened despotism to the socialist notion? Obviously, liberal thought fighting against feudalism is the matrix of socialist thought fighting against liberalism. But in the American case, where the feudal structure was not involved, these very ideas in European liberal thought so crucial to the manufacture of socialist attitudes are missing. The liberal revolutionary doctrine of James Otis and John Adams lacks a sense of class, it has no millennial dreams of social transformation, and the notion of concentrated political power is abhorrent to it. Is it any wonder that American radicalism, even at its height in Daniel Shays, was confined to the liberal code itself?

Shays was the forerunner of Jackson, and Jackson the forerunner of Wilson and Roosevelt, which reminds us how lasting this ideological barrier to socialism has been. This does not mean, of course, that we have not had a lot of "empirical collectivism" such as the New Deal most significantly initiated, but that kind of collectivism is itself an indication of the psychological issue involved. We say of the New Deal that as distinguished from European collectivist movements it was "pragmatic," but if we mean by this that it had no ideal commitments in any sense, we mislead ourselves very badly indeed. For the ad hoc character of New Deal action was actually made possible by a moral settlement of the Lockean type so powerful and so pervasive that even fundamental problems appeared in the eyes of the men who cherished it as problems of technique. The TVA is "socialism," or at any rate "collectivism" in a land where men dare intellectually to go beyond the liberal formula; but in America, where they do not, it is simply the "solution to a problem." Hence the presence of this kind of institutional drift does not alter the fact that Americans are hostile to the socialist work for ideal reasons: it confirms it.

There is another facet of the same problem which has recently been appearing on our television sets: McCarthyism. For the paradox that stares us in the face as a result of this analysis is that while America has fewer socialists and Communists than any other Western nation the hysteria against them is much vaster here than anywhere else. But the analysis itself shows us that this is only a superficial puzzle. If the grip of Locke in an originally liberal land lies in the fact that he becomes the limit of valid ethical experience, the boundary of the intelligible and the meaningful, the very mechanism which excludes the Marxist obviously will inspire an irrational hysteria against him. He rarely appears, because he represents religious heresy rather than philosophic deviation, so that when he does appear he is pursued with the passion afforded not the philosopher but the heretic. The dualism is logical. But again: will the student learn most about this by examining the size of American factories or the nature of the liberal idea as it has unfolded in America's nonfeudal setting?

Now one can anticipate certain criticisms of the analysis I have just sketched, quite apart from the material factors I conceded to begin with as relevant to it. It can be argued: granted that the Lockean idea has assumed a powerful religious significance in the American setting, offsetting the "objective" basis for socialism, producing irrational responses to it, you still do not disprove the proposition that that idea originally arose to rationalize the interests of a specific social group in Europe. All that is done here is to push the interest explanation back a stage, and one can still accept Harold Laski's interpretation of the rise of modern liberalism. Now without going into the Laski interpretation, concerning which one can entertain strong doubt, it is possible to accept for purposes of argument this whole criticism. I am not concerned here with ultimate cause: pushing the interest explanation back a stage is precisely my purpose. If the interest analyst accepts these propositions, arguing that they merely demonstrate the curious power of ideological "superstructure," then though we may have ultimate differences we are for immediate purposes on common ground. It is enough if we have seen, in a situation where traditional interpretations have been based almost exclusively on social interest, the neglected power of an ideal force.

This is not the only situation of its kind. By indirection the very remarks that we have made concerning America indicate comparable situations abroad, as regards, for example, socialism itself. What is involved here might be described in terms of the concepts of time and space. There is often a much larger "distance" that we have to travel with the idea after the social correlation has been made than we normally travel with it. There is often a longer "time" that we have to wait before making the interest link. The effect of modern "realism" in the study of ideas has been to shorten both the space and the time in which ideas are viewed as functioning in any creative way in the political process. Since this has become in many quarters a mechanical habit rather than a conscious position, it is no wonder that we often hear the complaint that the study of political ideas is empirically fruitless. It is hard to appreciate the significance of a factor one declines at the outset to consider.

III

In the field of political science today the traditional study of political theory has come under heavy attack. Some of that criticism is undoubtedly justified. Certainly to the extent that we pursue a purely genealogical enterprise in the study of ideas, tracing the text of natural law from Hooker to Condorcet, or the text of sovereignty from Bodin to Austin, the fertility of our insight is bound to be small. It is no disparagement of the work of scholars like Gierke to say that traveling again the ground that they traversed is a fairly thankless task. Nor can we deny that political science could use more of purely analytic theory such as current students of "political behavior," heavily under the influence still of Bentley, seek to formulate. But after all of this has been said, certain large statements remain to be made. One is that the analysis of political ethics, the inquiry into the Aristotelian good life, which has historically preoccupied so much of our political theory work, can never become outdated. I have not been concerned with a defense of that here, but in the light of the current criticism of political theory, and in light of its inevitable relevance to my own concern also, a word should be said about it.

In our own time the need for new ethical definitions in certain areas has become so compelling that there is something markedly incongruous in the demand that they be eliminated from political study in behalf of "scientific" endeavor. The ardent positivist who assails the ethical study of politics at a social studies conference will debate with a passion at dinner afterwards the question of whether an individual ought to inform on associates before a Congressional Committee. He is a "scientist" one hour, a moralist the next. Of course, it can be argued that this dualism is as it should be, that analysis and ethics ought never to meet, but after a century in which the Comtean fallacy has been exposed it should be unnecessary to expose it now again. Willy-nilly the ethical judgments of men creep into their empirical endeavor, if only to condition their selection of data and problems, so that at the very least a confession of those judgments is necessary. But why should we be satisfied with the very least here? Granted that all of our studies ought not to be directed toward this end, is anything gained by excluding from consideration those crucial ethical questions we cannot resist discussing? There seems to be the feeling among some that when a field embraces two problems the elimination of one will guarantee superior work on the other. But this is false optimism. Throw your ethical analysts out of a department of politics, and your empirical analysts may well remain at the same level of excellence, if not indeed decline somewhat in performance because of the inherent interplay between value and fact in any sort of scholarly work.

But this is negative argument, and more, a good deal more, is involved. If professional students of politics will not concern themselves with the ethical plight of the individual before the Congressional Committee, who will? The truth is, there is an obligation on professional students of politics, as in some sense guardians of an ancient tradition of Western libertarian norms, to redefine those norms in terms of the issues of the age in which they live. Of course these students are not the only guardians of that tradition: properly every citizen is as well. But the curious thing about the ethical issue of the present time, which the Congressional Committee case itself suggests, is that it tends to involve a challenge by the mass of the citizenry of the principles historically governing the integrity of private relationships. It tends to involve questions which we have conveniently lumped under the terms "mass state" and "mass democracy." If these seem to be new in America, they are old in Europe, and even in America they have in the past been more asleep than absent.

Now I believe it can be reasonably argued that under such circumstances a peculiar obligation holds upon the professional student of our ethical heritage in politics. As a specialist, he is placed at the outset in a position differentiated from the mass of the citizenry and what they forget he is bound, by the nature of his calling, to remember. There is nothing undemocratic about this view, nothing Platonic in it. It is one thing to say that an intellectual elite must govern because it alone understands the meaning of justice, it is another to say that the professional student has a duty to remind a citizenry of principles which, because of the nature of an historic situation, it is likely to ignore. This does not, of course, deal with the pressures of that same situation on the theorist himself: they exist, often powerfully, raising familiar questions of academic freedom. But whatever might be said about these difficulties, the norm implicit in the job of the theory student is not touched by them. In an age peculiarly characterized by what Tocqueville called the "tyranny of opinion" that student, if he responds to the special nature of his experience, can hardly escape something of the mood of Tocqueville himself.

But this side of the study of ideas has not of course been my main preoccupation in this paper. What I have been pleading for is something even the most ardent positivist can accept, for there is nothing in the positivist creed, however interpreted, which excludes the beliefs of men from the proper data of political study. Actually this latter point, which should be evident enough, often gets lost in the shuffle of argument. The study of political theory is identified with ethics, the study of fact is identified with interest, and the study of theory as fact is left hanging in limbo. This confusion, which is warranted by no respectable methodology I know of, is even more pernicious than oversimplified theories of social determinism. It does not minimize the empirical role of ideas, it abolishes it. There is no use flaying it here, since it obviously cannot withstand analysis. But anyone who has listened to argument among political scientists will be able to recall many instances in which, at a certain indefinable point, the issue boiled down to a choice between Plato and the Smoot-Hawley tariff. Somewhere along the line the very factual nature of political thought was lost from sight.

A final question might be asked: what would be the general effect of a wider appreciation of the empirical role of ideal forces in politics? It is very hard to answer such a query. Since we are dealing with a matter of emphasis, since the emphasis will produce newer results in certain cases than in others, the whole enterprise has a piecemeal quality about it. There is never anything millennially romantic about a plea to curb the excesses of an earlier approach. All of the romance lies with the excesses, and all of the sweeping promise too. But, in the last analysis, how do we test a general method if not in terms of the illumination to which it leads in specific cases? What is the virtue of the grand methodological explosion if not that it shakes loose neglected insights for individual scholars working on individual topics? On this count the American case that we have examined suggests that wider consideration of the creative power of ideas is no insignificant matter. In many places it could well add a new dimension to our political understanding.

FOSTER H. SHERWOOD

The Role of Public Law in Political Science

IT HAS BEEN frequently noted [1] that political science emerged as a distinct discipline in the final decade of the last century largely in the writings of Burgess and Goodenow. Sired by a European (particularly German) view of government, its early characteristics included a preoccupation with public law and public administration. As these were conceived at the time, the emphasis was formal, structural, and utilitarian. The reasons are not difficult to understand. It is only a microcosmic representation of a general tendency in the whole of philosophy throughout the nineteenth century which evidenced materialism, mechanism, and positivism. [2] As applied to law, the nineteenth century controversy over codification in western Europe had caused a preoccupation with the written law. [3] For the English-speaking world the same movement was represented by the writings of John Austin. Austin's work assumed significance for two reasons. In the first place he was concerned to attempt to introduce some order and symmetry into the chaotic and fiction-ridden common law as he found it. To this task he brought the tools of conceptualization and a belief that the remedy lay in the newly democratized legislature. Secondly, he sought to mark out the field of the law as the "science of jurisprudence" which would function in splendid isolation from the neighboring disciplines of the "science of legislation" and the study of morals. As all know the latter was to be accomplished through the employment of the concept of sovereignty. This concept, as has frequently been noted, is not a dynamic but a static one, and so resulted in the treatment of law on the false analogy with the concepts of force or energy in natural science. The conclusion reached was that the job of reform in the law was one capable of solution by a properly guided legislature once and for all, once the lawyers had made apparent the underlying nature of the materials of their field and had organized them according to the "necessary" concepts of the law.

As transmitted across the Atlantic to the United States this approach was modified only slightly. Here the natural law tradition of the legal profession and its conservative bent resulted in the attempt to refer all differences of opinion over legal matters to provisions of written constitutions. The point was that even though these constitutions became markedly longer and more detailed following the Civil War, as a reflection of the conservative distrust of democratized legislative bodies, they were framed in the light of a belief in laissez-faire and they were expressions of written law—of sovereign will —to both of which Austinianism was entirely congenial. Thus the D. D. Field controversy over codification in New York lost much of its meaning, since the constitutions of the states embodied most of the virtues of a code, and what was lacking could be discovered through the method of deduction from Austinian principles. Thus also, the problems of legal theory were solved—only the details needed to be worked out—so that law became a technical study carried on in law schools divorced from academic disciplines and more general problems of philosophy by the case method which was conceived to be the method of the natural sciences applied to its materials.[4]

In American political science, a similar formalism is apparent. It was compounded of utilitarian positivism and Hegelian idealism and was reflected in the focused attention given by the profession to abstract concepts such as sovereignty, legal personality, and the state and its emphasis on formal structure of government and positive law.[5] The evidence is too bulky to include here. As one example, however, witness the approach taken as late as the 1930's by the profession to the discovery of the processes of administrative regulation. The textbooks in American government were filled with factual descriptions of government structure, together with brief definitions of some theoretical abstractions like checks and balances or federalism. The first and for many years the continuing reaction to the discovery was to attempt to force this process into the concept of the separation of powers, which latter concept had been abstracted out of all historical or functional recognition. Similarly much of the current debate over state vs. national regulation of public utilities is being conducted on a level of abstract concepts and in terms of formal government structure without any (or at most, inadequate) knowledge of the nature of the regulatory process and the limits of its effectiveness at state and national levels.

Meanwhile public law all but disappeared as a recognized object of study for political science. The distrust of conceptualization resulted in a reaction of fact gathering for its own sake. Books on government in the 1920's and 1930's became progressively longer and longer and included more and more detail. At the same time the intellectual bankruptcy of the legal profession hardly encouraged borrowing or cross fertilization. The latter group became exclusively concerned with variations on the theme by Austin which produced the kind of "logic-chopping" so characteristic of the writings of a W. N. Hohfeld, which though no doubt of great interest and value to the professional attorney, are of only marginal, if any, interest to the political scientist. The result was that American legal theory consisted of a body of values inherited from the American Revolution and not since re-examined, combined with the employment of various logical devices designed to systematize the unmanageable volume of case law and the rules derived therefrom.[6] For it was in the decisions and opinions of judges that the American legal theorist ended his search for the Austinian sovereign. Small wonder that the political scientist found little interest or guidance in so narrowly conceived a discipline.

Nonetheless, legal facts *are* political facts and continued to find a role, though a subordinate one, in the study of political science. They became a kind of preliminary necessity for the political scientist who, as Easton has shown, developed an obsession with the notion of power.[7] Each of the conventional courses in political science—comparative government, local government, public administration, political parties—felt called upon to begin the discussion of any topic with a genuflection in the direction of law which usually took the form of a recitation of the principal constitutional or statutory provisions of most apparent relevance before getting down to the business at hand. Such information had a bad tendency to be both inaccurate and incomplete. Its inaccuracy may perhaps be judged by the controversy now going on in the pages of the *American Political Science Review* between a professor of law and a professor of public administration. Its incompleteness is evident in the treatment accorded by political scientists to the President's Court Reorganization proposals of 1937, and the lack of attention given by the same group to the various proposals for the reform of administrative procedure and their aftermath in the last ten years.

II

This raises the question: What should be the nature of the relationship between political science and law? As is perhaps inevitable in inquiries of this kind, we can begin by indicating what it should not be.

First, it should not be a formal or structural prerequisite to the study of power relations, political processes, or other functional analysis. The failure to recognize this is at the heart of much of the traditional friction between departments of political science and law school faculties. Few political scientists would deny the importance of legal materials to their discipline, however defined, but it is seldom treated as a body of data to be subjected to the same method or methods of treatment as other bodies of relevant political data. Rather, it is taken from the hands of the lawyer of a bygone generation as a kind of bench-mark with relation to which political vari-

ables may be considered. As such, the legal materials tend to be obsolete
and fragmentary as pointed out above. No matter how one defines the
discipline of political science, whether he emphasizes its subject matter or
its method, law is among its materials and represents a characteristic and
homogeneous function. As such, it is within political science, and not at its
borders.

Secondly, the law with which the political scientist is, or should be concerned, is not lawyers' law. It is both more and less than the latter's field
of interest. The lawyers' law is concerned primarily with the nature of
those advantages conferred and relations established which operate to create,
protect, or limit those interests on which society has formally taken a position. The political scientist, however, is primarily concerned with the interests
themselves, how and why they acquire the standing of government policy,
and how effective the law is in the accomplishment of its objectives. For example, in an hypothetical society, the "law" in the sense of a statute, constitution, or judicially enunciated principle, may be said to protect the integrity of the family. This is a conclusion of and problem for political science.
Or it may be said to establish a relationship whereby under certain circumstances a husband may have an action in damages against a corespond-
ent in a divorce action, or where adultery becomes a criminal offense. The
truth of the latter and the circumstances under which it is true is the scope
of lawyers' law. This is roughly equivalent to Savigny's distinction between
the political and technical element in his concept of the *Volksgeist*. In
modern society, he argued, the legal profession becomes the agent of the
volksgeist in accommodating the law in the technical sense to the felt needs
and demands of the particular society. The same technical element as the
lawyers' prerogative is described by Cardozo and has been institutionalized
in many states through the judicial council movement. It is clear from the
foregoing example that the old dichotomy between public and private law
is at best only a rough approximation of the distinction made here. As generally explained, the former is based upon subject-matter differences which
upon closer examination simply do not exist. In the Anglo-American legal
system the extent of public interests involved in justiciable disputes is obscured by the form which such disputes usually take—adversary actions between private litigants. In fact, one of the most troublesome problems of political science is the determination of what interests have or ought to have
achieved the status of governmental policy. This problem is frequently but
wrongly phrased as the balance between public and individual interests—
as if individual interests are something separate from those of the public.
Thus we are inclined to speak of the public interest in order as opposed to
the individual interest in freedom of expression in controversies over regulation of freedom of speech and press, thereby ignoring the fact that the
public interest in order can only be meaningfully balanced against the *public*

interest in freedom of expression and that there is a public interest in the latter. By the same token, the individual's interest in freedom of expression can only be balanced against the individual's interest in privacy or order.

This is not to say, however, that there will not be a substantial identity of materials which the lawyer and the political scientist will find relevant. Case materials are essential to both, and both will find much of value from their respective points of view in a book like *The Growth of American Law,*[8] or the writings of Roscoe Pound. The point is that these materials will be used for different purposes and from different points of view. Enough has been said thus far to indicate the lawyers' point of view. It is now necessary to turn to that of the political scientist, which involves consideration of the nature of the discipline in its relation to legal materials.

III

In the last few years much energy and ability has been devoted by the profession to attempting to define the nature of political science—so much that it would be bold indeed for this writer to attempt to reconcile the different views so far presented or to attempt a new and better definition. Further it is not necessary for the purpose at hand to settle upon a single definition.

The definitions thus far submitted seem to fall into several well-defined types. There are those who define the field institutionally as being concerned with government, or the state; those who define it in terms of its subject matter, power or public policy; and those who define it functionally as the authoritative allocation of values, decision making, or the control relationship of wills. While each definition and type of definition has its own strengths and weaknesses, it is clear that each includes law among its materials. What appears to have happened is that as the older institutional definitions have given way before the newer subject matter and functional definitions law has been largely abandoned on the assumption that it is inseparable from the institutional approach. It becomes increasingly only a survival of the false assumption of the stability of power relationships which the institutional approach once assumed. What has more recently been assumed is that whether political science be defined subject-wise or functionally, legal materials have only such relevance as they may deserve considered from one or another points of view. Thus they have lost their identity as a semi-autonomous part of the discipline. That this is a false assumption regarding the nature of public law hardly needs saying, yet political scientists as a group are almost completely unaware of the very important contributions to their field made by legal theory in the last three quarters of a century. These contributions for the most part have emerged in European circles where law has been considered a part, and an integral part, of the social sciences in general and the study of government in particular—a part of academic and not vocational education. The same has been true in Britain where and to the extent that it is likewise considered a part of university education—one thinks of Sir Henry Maine, and more recently, of C. K. Allen. In this country, the vacuum created by the obsolescence of the older institutional approach remains unfilled except by an occasional law school like that of Yale University which attempts to fill it, frequently at the expense of more vocationally oriented studies, which penalizes the student seeking to qualify in the profession. One thinks here of the studies of Underhill Moore.

What is lacking in political science is an integral study of law as a part, but a distinct part, of the political process. As such, it pervades the whole field to some degree. Recognition of its integral character emphasizes the interdependence of other parts which too often have a tendency to attempt complete separation from political science. Thus one of the principal available tools for maintaining the unity of political science and international relations is international law just as administrative law serves to demonstrate the homogeneity of interests of political science and public administration. However, this leaves unanswered two questions which must next be considered: What is the law that the political scientist must consider; and how may it best be considered—as an adjunct to other major points of emphasis or as an integral part of political science?

IV

Legal materials can best and most fruitfully be considered in this writer's view as one among several instruments of social control. As such, most of these instruments, but particularly law, require consideration from the political point of view. This consideration may be from the institutional, the subject matter, or the functional point of view. The institutional distinction with all its strengths and weaknesses is sufficiently familiar to need no elaboration. It involves directly or indirectly official or governmental policy. In the choice between alternatives where government has not sought to cast into the balance some advantage or disadvantage favoring one or some lines of conduct over others, we have nonlegal behavior which may be of a political nature. The subject-matter definitions concentrate their attention on the variety and the nature of the determinants of human social action. Again, among these must be included types or categories of such determinants, and one such is the law where for psychological and cultural reasons it appears as "the most specialized and highly finished of the means of control employed by men in society." [9] Similarly, from the functional point of view, law must be classified as one among several methods for resolving differences among men, distinguishable from robbery, war, bribery, and so on, both with respect to the greater likelihood of permanence and acceptability of its solutions as well as with respect to the form in which the controversy and the solution are presented.

It is true that this approach puts law at the heart of political science and implies the danger that all political phenomena may be viewed as potential or actual legal phenomena, that political data which fails to achieve legal formulation will be treated as insignificant. But this is a danger largely inherent in the older institutional approach. It is minimized to the extent that the law is recognized as not inseparable from governmental institutions —particularly courts—and that such institutions play widely varying roles in legal formulation. Thus legal solutions of both civil and criminal disputes are to a major degree determined outside the courtroom and in fact frequently with no governmental institutional interference. Sometimes the role of the court in the individual case is limited to recording the result arrived at by other institutions or the parties themselves, and sometimes the judicial or other formulation of a solution represents only a stage, and an inconclusive one, in the resolution of the controversy. All this demonstrates is that the political scientist must be on his guard not to treat the law and governmental institutions as convertible terms, or to think of legal materials exclusively in institutional terms. Failure to do so resulted in the assumption of the older social scientists that institutions were things capable of treatment by analogy to human beings, and possessed of the attributes of natural persons. This served to divide the real natural person up into as many fractions as there were institutions to which it could be seen he was related and the whole human was lost sight of. Thus church-state relations, or state-family relations were treated as if there were no underlying identity, as if the institution were the lowest common denominator of political or social activity. Also failure to recognize the phenomena of law apart from its institutional manifestation failed to give adequate emphasis to the law in the process of becoming and ceasing to be—legal change. That these errors can be avoided is well illustrated in the works of von Ihering and Eugene Ehrlich.[10]

There is, further, the danger that law considered as one among several instruments of social control may become a subdivision at best of a larger discipline called sociology which will ignore the distinctiveness of political phenomena which is the justification for political science. In fact this is what appears to be proposed in the recent writings of Parsons, Lewin, and Lasswell. Both law and political science from these respective points of view disappear as integral studies, and political and legal data become subsumed under their defined categories of psychology and sociology. What this seems to prove is that if political science is to retain its separate existence, it will be most easily defended by reference to the distinctiveness of its legal materials, although the defense need not and should not rest there. This brings me to the last question, what is this distinctiveness and what relation does it have to the teaching of political science?

V

Assuming the autonomy of political science as a field of study, its subdivision should be organized in the light of several considerations. First of all, any rational subdivision of political science should take into consideration the nature of the data which will fall within its limits. This data should, so far as possible, be homogeneous in both form and content. That is, the specialist and non-specialist both should have minimum difficulty in the preliminary classification of materials prior to study. This is not to say that such a subdivision of the field can or should result in no areas of overlapping interests or concern, that each piece of data can belong to one and only one part of the discipline. Rather, what is required is some fairly pragmatic and obvious classification of materials as they come to hand which will minimize difficulties inherent in specialization. That legal materials meet this qualification is clear. Whether one takes the decision making political institutions, the process of making decisions, or the decision itself, materials group themselves rapidly in terms of the proximateness they bear to the focus of attention. The whole of the data and each stage of relevance presents a kind of homogeneity very much to be desired. By virtue of its form, it is distinguishable from, for instance, decisions made on the legislative or policy level, since it usually appears as subordinate, concrete and specific, rather than general. It is distinguishable in content since it usually requires explicitly or implicitly a rationale relative to the source of its derived authority.

Second, a subsection of political science should be constructed with a view to the concepts which it seeks to use in the management of its materials. Some concepts will be common to all of political science; others will emerge from and become the tools of its subordinate parts. Wherever the conceptual stock is sufficiently large to enable the classification and management of materials recognized as political in some meaningful way, there is reason to recognize the existence of a sub-field. This need not imply the necessity of a separate technique for each sub-field. The same data may yield new results when subjected to new methods of study, and old techniques may produce new results when applied to unfamiliar materials. But the mere appearance of the same data or methodology in more than one subdivision of the field is no evidence of the inadequacy of the classification. Thus legal materials have been subjected to the historical, analytical, synthetic, and deductive techniques among others, without losing their identity because the primary emphasis is that of a normative science. It is concerned with human behavior and its consequences where the consequences are linked with the behavior by the intervention of an official or publicly recognized act or institution. As such, the system may be regarded from the point of view of its internal consistency, its coincidence with socially accepted values, and its methods of creation and operation.[11] Its concepts, such as rights, duty, person, norm, have been reasonably well worked out on these abstract levels and have been applied with useful results.

Third, a sub-field of political science should have as a focus of attention such problems as occur in experience. That is to say abstractions and concepts should be framed with a view to the understanding or solution of practical problems. Again, the law meets this criterion, not because we are trying to produce successful practitioners, which we are not, but because one of the characteristic forms (and in the United States the most characteristic form) in which political problems arise in fact is in the legal one. The legal formulation of a dispute is, whether rightly or wrongly need not concern us, regarded as a meaningful stage in its resolution.

Finally, the subdivisions of political science should reflect the fact that they are just that—subdivisions. They should be constructed with the point of view in mind that they represent different foci of attention, or platforms from which all of political science and of social science generally may be viewed. One hears a good deal these days about the evils of overspecialization and much of the criticism is valid. It breeds intellectual astigmatism, it fails to take account of the essential unity of human life, it casts a mesh of such uneven screen as to allow some of the most important problems of life to escape attention entirely, it prevents communication between those who have something but less than a complete solution to offer, and so on. In their enthusiasm for the attack, such critics frequently are carried by the logic of their criticism to the illogical conclusion that specialization is bad *per se*. What we need to do, it has been suggested, is to destroy all barriers, to produce political scientists, or better yet social scientists, or best of all philosophers. This loses sight of the fact that the target at which the criticisms are directed is overspecialization. It is also based upon assumptions as to the homogeneity of materials and technique in the social sciences generally which are, to say the least, unproved. And it suggests a simplicity in the nature of human behavior which experience denies. The simple fact is that in the present state of the social sciences it is premature to attempt to reorganize on the basis of discoveries yet to be made, particularly when our common sense tells us that social behavior is a complex phenomenon. There is no reason to believe we will come to an understanding of the whole more quickly or easily than to an understanding of its parts. Futhermore, those who have chosen to specialize in generalizations have thus far been forced to depend upon the painstaking collection of data by specialists. If all were to become generalists, the source of their data would soon dry up. This is why most integrative theories of social science methodology must assume a static nature of society which experience gives reason to doubt.

What should be sought is that form of specialization which permits the meaningful accumulation of data and production and verification of hypotheses with reference to the political problem under view, while at the same time keeping in the forefront of attention the interrelationships of field to field and problem to problem. Again, law meets this criterion. Law by its very nature is involved in almost all of the conceivable subjects of social science. Its study necessitates a breadth of integration of social science data which is unique in the sense that such integration is required not for its own sake, but as a practical prerequisite to the processing of legal materials. As such it represents a degree of specialization and generalization which serves both to protect the integrity of political science and direct the attention of political scientists to contributions of other fields which may have use there. It is submitted that no organization of political science which fails to grant a semi-autonomous role to the law meets these criteria so well.

In addition, the recognition of the separateness of the law serves other purposes which its integration into other methods of organizing the discipline fail to accomplish. For one thing it makes available a body of materials of relevance to the political scientist which is unequaled either in span of time or in geographical coverage. Some of the earliest as well as the most complete evidence of the settlement of human disputes appears in judicial records of primitive societies. In fact, such remains tell us more about societies in the political sense than do the anthropologists' and archeologists' artifacts. Taking these facts as they occur in "nature" involves the minimization of error due to the observer's selection of what is to be considered. This does not involve an assumption that all relevant facts invariably find their way into court records. Actually, sometimes the most significant and revealing facts are those which occur outside the formal decision-making process in which this process appears as only one of a number of forces at work or objectives in view. Nonetheless, the existence of the formal record constitutes a useful point of reference around which other data may be grouped for an understanding of the nature of the process itself. The subdivision of these materials in other ways which serve to deny the unity of the recorded data involve the risk that one point of impact of social policy, political institutions, or decision-making technique on human behavior will be lost sight of. In a word what becomes everybody's business tends to become nobody's.

Further, two thousand or more years of experience which is classified under the heading of law has allowed, if not necessitated, the development of a special vocabulary and methods of dealing with these materials conceptually and in terms of techniques of reference, indexes, and so on. These are matters which assume a form unfamiliar to most other parts of political science. This is likely to remain true due to the close relation of political science and legal technology. Vocabulary, concepts, and technical research methods will have to do double duty and to this extent will never reflect only the needs of the political scientist.

Finally, there are pedagogical reasons for the preservation of the integrity of the field. Experience is showing the value of the case method of dealing with political phenomena. The recent adaptation of this method to public administration [12] indicates that its utility is by no means exhausted in the law field. Its use, the limitations of its effectiveness, and the purposes to which it can be adopted will be most open to study if the area in which it has made its most notable contribution and where it has had use over the longest period of time is treated as a unit.

It may be argued that larger categories, more inclusive concepts, and different techniques are needed. To this I would generally agree. But it does not follow that such results will be produced by longing. They will emerge when the thorough mastery of the tools and materials now at our disposal permit wider and more inclusive generalizations. But as of this writing the law shows every sign of remaining a useful and realistic constant.

DWIGHT WALDO

"Values" in the Political Science Curriculum

THE TEACHING of political science in the United States appears from the evidence to have three main objectives. In order of their importance to the teachers these objectives are:

1) Education for citizenship;
2) Preparation for public employment;
3) Training for research in political science.

These are not, to be sure, mutually exclusive objectives; and the means employed in pursuing one may serve another as well. Back of them also—or perhaps it is above or beside them—is an objective which many teachers would place first: that of helping to produce "educated" or "civilized" individuals. It is the argument of this essay that conscious attention to "values" will enable the teacher better to achieve any and all of these objectives.

AUTHOR'S NOTE: It had been my intention after the conference at which this paper was read to make certain changes in the light of criticism directed toward it. These revisions were not made and present commitments foreclose the possibility of revision at this time. Indeed, I am not certain that the position stated in the essay is in every respect one with which I am now in full accord.

I

To begin with, I do not deem it open to serious argument whether a teacher should or should not teach values. I think it can be demonstrated that he inevitably does—if he teaches. The real questions are: What values? Why? How? The first two of these are value questions by definition, the third, as soon as it is explored, reveals value problems. If we are interested in directing our own lives, these questions should be consciously asked and answered with all the care and intelligence we can minister.

Apparently there are a substantial number of teachers of political science who feel it is not a proper task of the political scientist to inculcate values, and who believe moreover that they personally do not do so. The first task is to dispose of this fallacy. Fortunately, this is easily done.

Paradoxically, the demonstration that value-free teaching is a contradiction in terms has been made possible by positivistic-oriented empirical research, empirical research often spurred by the conviction that values are thereby being banished. The demonstration, or the basis for it, rests in several fields, and may be briefly indicated.

1) *Linguistics*. Students of linguistics assert that languages embody basic outlooks and attitudes, and that different languages embody different basic outlooks and attitudes. These different attitudes reach to the most fundamental physical and cultural categories.

2) *Anthropology*. The central concept of cultural anthropology is that of culture. The process of acculturation includes the inculcation of preferences. Where formal education exists it is a part of the acculturation process.

3) *Sociology*. Central in some important sociological models is the idea of a structure of norms. These norms become internalized in "actors" who play "roles." Teaching is instruction in role-playing.

Also, the so-called sociology of knowledge has "unmasked the unmaskers" and by revealing the socio-economic roots and historical relativity of all knowledge has cast a shadow upon even the most impressive claims to objectivity and universality. "Objective" science is in this view hardly above "self-evident" truths.

4) *Psychology*. All schools are in accord: The life-experiences of an individual prepare him to perceive or not perceive, to prefer or not prefer, to act or not act. Among these life experiences is formal education.

Before proceeding to point the moral it is well to deal with the question of definition: what is a "value?" The meaning which I ascribe here is "operational," not moral or metaphysical. In a recent publication appears this language: "The total of the strains within the individual resulting from his genetic imput and variations in the imput from his environment is often referred to as his values. The relative urgency of reducing these individual strains determines his hierarchy of values." [1] This is patently—even blatantly —the language of empiricism, not of morality, and I will not be accused of stacking the cards if I accept it for present purposes. Roughly speaking, then, a "value" is a preference, positive or negative. The language of "motor-affective attitudes," "drive tensions," and "consummatory satisfactions" is acceptable, but probably little more precise.

With our definition in mind, let us return to the above encapsulated empirical theories:

1) Much, perhaps most, of the teaching of political science might be described as instruction in the vocabulary or language of political science. Learning this language means receiving and accepting preferences. Probably there is little question as to this point with regard to such "emotional" words as democracy or nazism. It is much less obvious but no less true with respect to the "vocabulary" of mathematics or careful empirical research. New-born infants are not only ignorant of, they are neutral with respect to, differential equations. Adults who experience them may remain ignorant, but they are never neutral.

Preferences of political scientists obviously vary. Students will receive verbal, visual, and aural evidence of, and often accept as their own, quite different preferences on such matters as federalism or pluralism, depending upon the instructor who faces them. But this does not affect the point that some preference is being expounded or expressed on the one hand and changed or confirmed on the other.

2) In our culture a significant part of the acculturation with respect to the political aspects of life is done by teachers of political science. This is obvious, of course, with respect to the teaching of citizenship. Most political science teachers place preparation for citizenship first among their objectives, and this objective probably weighs heaviest in the minds of those who give financial support to political science teaching. Preparation for public employment usually means comparatively greater emphasis upon skills and techniques, but I should argue that no skill or technique is value-neutral. Position classification, for example, is not merely a technique of personnel administration. It is a reflection and enforcement of values built deep into American culture. It has both causes and effects in the realm of values. And anyone who deals with personnel technicians had better realize it is also valued for its own sake!

The values and techniques of science are also a part of our culture. When students are being trained for research in politics, they are undergoing an acculturation process. They are being taught to place a high value on scientific research in general, and to place particular values upon particular means or techniques of study or research.

3) From one of the perspectives of sociology, we may say that students of political science are "actors" being taught to play various political roles in our culture. These roles are various, but the initial three-fold classification would cover most of them. As "citizens" they are being taught (according to the values of the teacher) to "analyze issues," "provide practical political leadership," "appreciate democratic values," and so forth. As "public servants" they are being coached in the preferences to feel (or simulate) in this role, as well as in the necessary knowledge and skills. As researchers in politics they are being taught the values thought appropriate to this role —including sometimes the value of eliminating all value considerations from research and perhaps even a deep distaste for any discussion of values except as data in research.

This instruction in role-playing is not of course by precept alone. Much of it is by example; the student is shown, in flesh or in books, the "heroes" he should emulate and "villains" he must abjure. The teacher himself inevitably becomes something of an actor to be understudied—citizen, statesman, scientist or teacher—in this role of learning. I confess that I was a "sedulous ape" when I began my own teaching career, trying my best to reproduce the techniques and tricks and even the emotional effects of my own favorite teachers. The high incidence of pipe smoking in certain academic circles is presumably not a simple result of the "genetic imput" of the smokers.

4) The teacher of political science is responsible for some of the life-experience of the student, and inevitably participates in giving structure and meaning to the student's sense perceptions. The student's cognitive field and emotional responses are affected in direct relation to the effectiveness of the teaching. The student will "see" and "value" political phenomena differently the rest of his life.

Perhaps this rather elaborate argument that teachers inevitably teach values has been unnecessary. To some, certainly, it is a rehearsal of the obvious. But to repeat, the evidence indicates that there are many who think that the teacher (of political science, at least) ought not to teach values, and who earnestly try not to do so themselves. There are even many of this persuasion whose primary academic assignment (as apart from personal objective) is to teach citizenship. Let us consider such a case.

Let us suppose that this teacher finds the very idea of teaching citizenship abhorrent. Perhaps his own value-structure is highly positivist. "Values" are unverifiable and unscientific, he feels, and to purvey them under the label political science is a dishonest enterprise; even though his own value-structure includes firm preferences for democratic values, he knows that this personal set of "strains" is merely the result of genetic and environment imput, and he feels (here a "strain" becomes a conscious ethical principle) that he has no license to try to produce similar "strains" in his students.

What are the results of this situation in terms of teaching? One natural result is a concern with "facts," which are deemed to be value-neutral. The phylogeny, anatomy and physiology of democratic political institutions can be presented "impartially." The comparative approach may even be used, so that the student can "make up his own mind." Another common response of the teacher is to emphasize "analysis." Students should be taught how to analyze political matters so that they will know what is involved and how to implement their own values, whatever they are. Still another teaching response is "muscular" citizenship; students are engaged in various sorts of visiting and apprenticeship projects so that they will know "how things really work." Now there is much usefulness in all these teaching responses, and I have not listed them in deprecation. I list them rather to demonstrate —if the above analysis is essentially correct—that even such a teacher is teaching values in spite of himself. I will also observe that in some of the "muscular" or "motor activity" projects there is a strange meeting of the crudest empiricism with the most naive concepts of citizenship.

It is clear upon analysis of such responses and activities that the teacher has not succeeded in avoiding the teaching of values. He will not be able to avoid making explicit evaluations occasionally, which will have their effect even if he introduces them with an apology as his "personal" opinion. Even if he were able to avoid this sort of statement he must select what facts are to be presented and what projects students are to engage in; and by demeanor and voice he will be conveying and affecting value-responses. Teaching of values is done in many ways besides the setting forth of ethical precepts. Indeed, this may well be the least important means.

Several teaching techniques appear to go about as far as it is possible to go toward avoidance of value-direction. One is "non-directive" teaching, the Quaker-meeting approach. Another is the descriptive or problem "case" that is "open-ended" and merely a taking-off point for student response. Another is the technique of a teacher of political philosophy who presents his students with one central question: What do you have to believe in order to accept this conceptual system, this method of analysis, these recommended political institutions and practices? But the teaching of values is not absent even in such cases. Nor is it in fact usually intended to be. What is sought to be conveyed in the first case is the value of "democratic participation" or "group thinking"; in the second case the value of "objective" analysis; and in the last case the value of the deepest intellectual inquiry and the freest intellectual activity.

II

Since the demonstration that the teacher inevitably teaches values is so simple how are we to account for the present situation in which:

1) Some teachers of political science believe that values should not be taught, that the only legitimate concern of political scientists is with science, *i.e.* empirical or causal theory.

2) Some teachers of political science believe that they personally do not teach values.

3) Some teachers of political science recognize that values must inevitably be taught but that the political scientist (as a political scientist, at least) can have no legitimate concern with what values, by whom, etc.

4) Some teachers of political science believe that the political scientist should teach values but are unable to present a "respectable" justification for this position in general, or for the particular values, such as those of "democracy" or "freedom," which are part of their own value-system?

Probably most teachers of political science fall into one (or more) of these four groups (and since there are other classifications these four groups are not the full measure of the present complexity and opportunities for confusion). Since *teachers inevitably teach values,* how did this situation arise? What problems does this situation present? What steps may be taken to solve these problems?

A rounded discussion of the origins of the present situation would include a treatment of major intellectual currents and historical events through many generations. I must be content with noting a few prominent aspects.

Certainly some of the main roots of the social sciences lie in the Enlightenment.[2] The two dominant philosophies of the Enlightenment, Natural Law and Utilitarianism, were the soil from which the social sciences grew into their modern self-conscious and differentiated forms.

In neither Natural Law or Utilitarianism was there a distinction between social theory and social policy, fact and value, *is* and *ought.* In the case of Natural Law there was fusion of the *is* and *ought* in the concept of "natural." In the case of Utilitarianism the union of *is* and *ought* is hardly less clear: "happiness" or "utility" is the only rational motive. In the words of Bentham's Introduction to his *Principles of Morals and Legislation,* "Nature has placed mankind under the guidance of two sovereign masters, *pain* and *pleasure.* It is for them alone to point out what we ought to do, as well as to determine what we shall do."

From Natural Law and Utilitarianism the social sciences absorbed not only an initial philosophical orientation but some "very radical policy premises," which were the substantive or "public policy" part of these currents of thought. These radical premises included the idea of human equality, the idea of the moral superiority of labor as a title to property, the idea that the human material is highly plastic and subject to change and improvement through changes in environment, and the idea that freedom is the "natural" condition of man and productive of his happiness.

In short we may say that in their beginnings the modern social sciences were not aware of what we call the "value problem." "According to the philosophies which formed the seed-bed for the social sciences, there were objective values which, like other social facts, could be ascertained by reasoning or by observation and calculation. Rational policy conclusions could be drawn in terms of what was 'natural' or, later, of what led to the maximum 'general welfare.' " [3]

In broadest perspective, what has happened in the past one hundred years is that the original philosophical orientation of the social sciences has been largely eroded and replaced by fundamentally different beliefs, whereas the original "radical premises" have continued on down to the present hardly undiminished, indeed perhaps in even greater force. Since the new philosophical creeds of the social sciences deny the validity or "objectivity" of the old radical premises at the same time that these premises have been carried forward as preferences or "strains" the opportunities for confusion, frustration, and mental dishonesty are great indeed.

The current fashion in the social sciences is of course the sharp distinction rather than the fusion of fact and value, means and ends, causal theory and social policy. This fashion, while now as compulsory in some circles as the wearing of trousers, is comparatively recent, and it is little wonder that "all our thoughtways are still saturated with the old value metaphysics." [4] Nineteenth-century positivism, as represented in the first half of the century by Comte and the second half by Spencer, committed the "naturalistic fallacy" of assuming that *oughts* could be derived from *is's*. On the other side, nineteenth century idealism as represented by Hegel was also distinguished by this identification: "The real is the rational, and the rational is the real." Left-wing Hegelianism, as represented in Marx, made the same identification, whatever the validity to its claim of materialism. Pragmatism likewise is distinguished as a philosophy by an "organic" joining of fact and value, means and ends. It is in such sources as well as in Natural Law and Utilitarianism that American political science is rooted.

The sharp distinction of the *is* and *ought* goes back at least to David Hume. However, American political science, for reasons just suggested in part, was not much inclined to make this distinction a conscious and sharp one until rather recently. From the date of the formation of the American Political *Science* Association there was to be sure a commitment to science, and there was gradual movement of research and vocabulary in the direction of the fact-value antithesis, but—perhaps it was the popularity of prag-matism—until recently the general interpretation of science has not been one which exposed the "value problem."

Within political science one can rather easily discern some of the key in-fluences leading toward the present "hard" or "narrow" interpretation of science: Charles E. Merriam's stimulus to and leadership in more rigorous empirical studies; Arthur F. Bentley's reception and influence on the study of "realistic" politics; Harold Lasswell's hard and sustained drive for more, and more rigorous, empiricism; George Sabine's exposition of the Humean analysis and his demonstration of its efficacy in dealing with natural law and utilitarianism. A thorough treatment would trace the influence by osmosis of currents of thought from the other social sciences—which generally have been ahead of political science in this development.

Whatever the "native" sources and the "natural" tendency of American political science toward the fact-value dichotomy, the present main source and the most rigorous statement and defense of the position is the school of philosophy usually known as logical positivism. Logical positivism follows the classical positivist position in claiming escape from metaphysics (per-haps even from "philosophy"), placing reliance upon the empirical, and pressing a claim to alliance with science in outlook and method. It departs from classical positivism in making a sharp distinction between the categories of "fact" and "value" and in a disposition toward extensive logical and lin-guistic analyses.

Logical positivism holds that a proposition of fact is distinguished by hav-ing existential referents and empirical verifiability. Of it, one can say it is true or false. Of an "ethical judgment," contrariwise, one cannot say it is true or false. "Sentences which simply express moral judgments do not say anything. They are pure expressions of feeling and as such do not come under the cate-gory of truth and falsehood." [5] Ethical judgments cannot be verified; as science deals only with the verifiable, they are outside the pale of science. Whether a man prefers fascism to communism is a factual question which can be veri-fied; it is a proper matter for scientific inquiry. Whether fascism is "better" or "worse" than communism is unverifiable; the question that is presented is not one amenable to science.

On principle and in no event can a genuine factual proposition be de-rived from (though it may be made *about*) an expression of value; nor can a moral imperative be derived solely from a factual proposition. In our ordi-nary language and even in the language of applied science fact and value element are comingled. But the logical separability of the two is in principle always possible.

Meanwhile, the thinking of those interested primarily in "value" as against "fact" has tended to move in concert with the logical positivists. Some—though not all—protagonists of a natural law position have depreciated the empirical or "natural" aspect of natural law; with them, natural law retreats into the spiritual realm, becoming there a standard of value by which the empirical may be measured.

Idealism as a philosophical position has also taken new directions; some idealists have been shrilly insistent that it is impossible to derive moral imperatives from empirical data. A sharp line between fact and value has been found, indeed, to be useful to many on either side of the line. By reducing the world to managable size and dimensions the division solves some psychological as well as logical problems. There are some too who solve their problems by a public resolution to divide their time between the two sides of the line: in their professional lives they profess to be scientists dealing only with facts, in their private lives they confess a religious—or other —faith.

I suggest a general similarity between the entire movement of thought now and in the later Middle Ages, when the Thomist synthesis was being torn apart, faith being separated from reason, and will from knowledge. The interests, goals and tactics of the logical positivists have striking similarities to those of Marsilio of Padua and William of Occam. If this comparison has any validity parties to the present developments may find it valuable to review the previous struggle of ideas—and its sequels in history.

If the foregoing analysis is in general correct, we have now taken the gross, outside dimensions of the "value problem" in the teaching of political science. In general terms we are in a situation in which we cannot avoid teaching values, in which all (yes, all) have values that they wish to teach, but in which there is not for many what they regard as an "intellectually respectable" basis for these values. In the value system of all, or practically all, of us Reason has an honored place. Yet the dominant philosophical trends and conventions of our day seem to make it impossible to bring our values within the scope of Reason. Fate has prepared for us a bed of neurosis.

III

I turn now to try to measure some of the "inside" dimensions of the value problem in political science. What are the limitations and risks of the logical positivist separation of fact and value in educating for citizenship, preparing for public employment, and training for research?

In making logical positivism the center of a critical inquiry I am revealing—or is the word reducing?—a strain in my own value system. This is obvious and freely admitted. I do not like logical positivism, perhaps for "real" reasons that might interest a psychologist. After my arguments (or rationalizations) have been assessed it is fair to place me upon the analyst's couch—fair, that is, if equality of treatment is practiced.

Actually, logical positivism did not *cause* what appear to me to be present ills and dangers in the social studies. These ills and dangers characterize any philosophy or methodology which fails to come to grips realistically (as I see it) with the value problem; and as I indicated above the social sciences had moved in this direction independently. It is rather that logical positivism as an especially dogmatic and intolerant evasion of ethical problems accentuates these ills and dangers. I should add, too, that recent statements of "modified" logical positivism move a significant distance away from the early arrogance and dogmatism; but it is inevitably the early versions which will be known and influential in the social sciences for some time to come.

The strongest case for the truth or usefulness of logical positivism centers upon research; for it claims above all to be allied with science and to open the only door to genuine scientific work in the social sciences. I shall therefore concentrate upon what I regard as its methodological deficiencies in its chosen area.

The methodological deficiencies of logical positivism arise from its destruction of ethics as separate or meaningful fields of inquiry, and I would begin by re-emphasizing this point. All ethical statements or positions are alike in being incapable of empirical verification; all ethical judgments are alike in that they are "emotive," that is to say "used to express feeling about certain objects but not to make any assertion about them." Like the mooing of a cow, to which they are essentially equivalent, they can be investigated scientifically; depending on the science, they become phenomena in psychology, chemistry, mammalogy, and so forth. But ethical inquiry, the traditional inquiry into what is "better" or "worse" in human affairs, becomes in this view radically meaningless.

The first methodological deficiency of logical positivism is that by its harsh exile of values (except as data) from science (as defined by them and with which alone they then overtly concern themselves) it tends to obscure the inevitable role of values in selecting, guiding and interpreting empirical research. The logical distinction between a question of fact and a question of value quickly becomes not simply a useful methodological tool but a fetish which operates to obscure the many close and "organic" relationships between fact and value "in fact," *i.e.* in empirical reality. I regard it as adequately demonstrated by empirical inquiry (for example, by the sociology of knowledge) that human values guide the selection of matters for research and the interpretation of the results in "social science" (and many would say in physical science as well). If this is true, then the methodological tenet of at least some logical positivism that their findings are value free in the sense that they can be used equally to realize any scheme of values "efficiently" is a delusion—or rather half-delusion. The finding may "accidentally" (and there is a great deal of this "accident" in the history of science) serve values other than those sought, but if there is a means-end connection of research to problems posed, the findings serve the ends sought; they are answers to questions asked only because they were of "value" to the askers.

Thus—it seems to me—logical positivism is placed in an uncomfortable paradoxical position. By its original definition of terms and its dismissal of ethics as not suited to rational inquiry, what is hawked as the higher rationalism is placed at the mercy of the irrational. It leaves the definition of what is to be done in social science to emotion unguided by reason (except as reason guides instrumentally in attainment of meaningless ends) or to chance.

My second objection to the methodological impetus of logical positivism is that, by obscuring the role of values in selecting, guiding, and interpreting empirical research it leaves such research open to the biases of elitism or "passivism." Both of these biases have been prominent in those parts of social science most overtly intent upon being "scientific," elitism for example in industrial sociology, and "passivism" in certain areas of economics.

My point is not that there is any logical connection between logical positivism and the values of elitism or passivism. On its own terms logical positivism does not allow of identification with any set of values (except perhaps those of the "system" itself), and in fact some of its adherents (in their alter egoes) are prominently identified with values of freedom, equalitarianism, and reform. My point is rather that since "disinterested" social science is an illusion and "research" is an idea without form or content until particular values are added,[6] the way lies open for the dominant strata or persons of society to supply the values. Almost—though not quite—by definition, dominant strata or persons are interested in maintaining their superior position and find the status quo not unpleasing; and the almost—but not quite—inevitable result when the researchers wear a "for hire" sign is research which furthers the interests of the hirer. Obviously there need be no crude "buying," and the motives of "interest" on the part of research buyer and research seller may never rise to the conscious level. Equally obviously, unless your personal values are contrary to the results of this situation my point has no force.

My third objection to the methodological effect of logical positivism is that it has a special "passivist bent" in addition to the "vulnerability" just noted. My thesis here is that would-be value-free research has a tendency to minimize an important distinction between social and non-social phenomena. I refer to the well-known fact that the ideas of the actors in a social situation affects that situation, to what is usually designated by the phrase "self-fulfilling prophecy" or "self-realizing hypothesis." Thus, for example, widespread belief that the price of commodity x is due to rise may itself become the "cause" of the rise which was at first an "objective" prediction based on other data; or mere belief that ethnic group y is "inferior" may operate to keep members of that ethnic group in inferior positions.

Now among the ideas that affect the social behavior of people is what they are taught in and about "social science" itself. Thus there is general agreement that what people are taught about the "laws of economics" affects their economic (and for that matter their political) behavior; indeed there would be no point in teaching economics if it did not. It is my feeling (*i.e.* I think that sufficiently subtle empirical research could rigorously demonstrate) that an approach to social science which unduly emphasizes the objectivity and autonomy of the facts tends thereby to tip the social scale in the direction of the status quo—or at least in the direction of what the researchers believe the "facts" are. No doubt there are basic, limiting facts about human nature and human society, and it is the proper task of empirical research to try to discern these limits; but we are far from knowing what these are, and excessive emphasis upon the fact component in social science leads through the phenomena of the self-confirming hypothesis to acceptance and reiteration of the "facts" as momentarily interpreted and to restriction of the creative imagination. I believe it was Hobhouse who said that if we should discover an equivalent in the social realm of the phenomenon of gravity we should forthwith "fall flat on our faces."

I am aware that there are techniques such as theory of games and formulae of statistical probability which can be used to deal with self-confirming-hypothesis phenomena as a matter of empirical theory. My argument is not that there is an indeterminacy in social phenomena which makes them impossible of measurement and prediction in the mass in the same manner and degree as physical phenomena (although perhaps this remains to be convincingly demonstrated). My argument is primarily moral and rests simply upon the premise that people ought to control their own destinies to the maximum extent. The common sense intuition that what people believe are the social "facts" becomes itself a social fact with "causal" effects, is held to be valid in the most sophisticated empirical theory of the day. I argue therefore that a philosophy or methodology which tends not only to emphasize fact, but which hold that the only way in which values can enter into "pure" social science is as data—*i.e.*, facts—becomes itself a causal factor which operates to reduce the area of freedom or creativeness. By rendering ethically meaningless the choices both as to ends and means that confront us at every step these choices are made ethically blind. By obscuring the creative role of ideas the creative role of ideas is reduced. In closing the front door to the rational in human conduct the back door to the irrational is opened.

These arguments centered upon the effect or impact of logical positivism (or perhaps more narrowly upon some versions or interpretations thereof) need to be seen in a broader setting. Whatever validity they have is reinforced by certain long range, contemporary, and possible future developments. This perspective I can give most easily by reviewing the themes of three recent essays.

One of these is Reinhard Bendix' *Social Science and the Distrust of Reason.*[7] This a review of the modern development of the social sciences, which reveals a progressive abandonment of faith in reason and the substitution of the view that society is something "to be manipulated and mastered."

Modern social science began its growth in a climate of optimism. It was believed that society is in an important sense orderly, that its conditions or laws can be discovered by reason, and that this is the proper business of everyone: reform to create, liberate and utilize reason was a general program. "Everyone his own social scientist" is hardly too strong an expression for the early outlook. But under the progressive revelation of irrationalities and "biases" and the attempt to eliminate these from theory, social science became ever more narrow and esoteric, its devotees ever more specialized. They have tended to become, in fact, highly skilled technicians, willing to sell their knowledge about controlling human affairs. No moral qualms are felt in doing this, for there is a convenient rationalization: science is what sustains society, and science is even a good in itself; therefore whatever supports and makes use of it is good. Bendix has enumerated the tenets of this creed as follows:

1) The momentous problems existing in present-day society demonstrate the ineffectiveness of the traditional methods of solving them, such as diplomacy, parliamentary discussion, political pressure, and the like.

2) That ineffectiveness is due *in part* to defective knowledge of social facts; this knowledge the social sciences must supply. Without knowledge "human utility and power" are diminished; with knowledge they are enhanced to a degree, since knowledge is one of the synonyms of power. . . .

3) Our ability to produce the desired social effect increases with the accuracy of our knowledge; hence everything must be done to make the social sciences more scientific. On the success of that endeavor depends in considerable measure the survival of our civilization. . . .

4) To make the social sciences more scientific, social scientists must convince men of affairs of the promise which their work holds out for the exercise of greater power in the deliberate manipulation of social forces. They do this typically as follows:

a) On the basis of better knowledge of social facts you will be better able to do whatever you are now attempting to accomplish.

b) We need support in order to acquire such knowledge.

c) We shall never tell you what to aim at; we confine ourselves strictly to a study of the facts pertinent for an implementation of your policies; this includes a study of the consequences likely to follow from these policies (or alternatives.) [8]

The result or import of this outlook is that the social scientists are in an "ambivalent position which prompts them to modify their scientific inquiries to gain support and to persuade themselves that only those inquiries which gain such support are 'real' social science." [9]

Some similar themes are developed by Gunnar Myrdal in a recent essay on "The Relations Between Social Theory and Social Policy." Myrdal is concerned with what he believes is the ever-narrowing scope and freedom of social scientists in the twentieth century. There has been an increasing tendency to work for "hire," in the commercial sense. And beginning with the First World War there has been an increasingly large demand for social scientists as "technologists" in some aspect of government functions. As a result social scientists often work on what are not important problems from the viewpoint of the development of social science; significance is not defined by them but for them. Moreover, the conditions of war and cold war mean that the work is carried on under conditions of stress and secrecy. Many social scientists work under conditions of secrecy as rigorous as those surrounding atomic research. Present conditions threaten, he feels, not merely the growth of social science,[10] but more important, the traditional and important function of the social scientists, the "rich, full and free academic public discussion of the broad policy issues." [11] It is in this way that their science has influenced events in the past.

Other related themes are explored by Norman Jacobson in an essay title "Values and Science in Political Theory." It is paradoxical, Jacobson believes, that the most ardent advocates of a "coherent science of politics based upon a strict means-end separation" are also those who, in their "other" lives, have generally been firm believers in a subjectivist, individual-interest theory of value. For the science of politics for which they are striving, he believes, finds its natural correlation with a "closed" society in which there is enforced a belief in a definable, objective good. "It is perhaps only in the closed society that a *science* of politics, or, more properly speaking, of *manipulation,* is possible of achievement. For only in the closed society does there exist, or might there be induced the kind of public agreement on ends sufficient to the autonomous operation of science, agreement analogous to that which is so vital to the life of the physical sciences. A desire on the part of the rulers to convince the members of a closed society to accept the 'good' . . . without the frequent application of brute force, that is to say with the least amount of friction, renders a science of politics—in the sense of a body of systematically ordered axioms which constitute a reliable guide to the relative efficiency of manipulative technique under 'if—then' conditions—wholly desirable." [12] The goal of many social scientists is apparently the reduction of all "politics" to "administration."

It is not necessary to press the congruency of the themes of these essays. It is enough that they agree in general tenor. All three agree that there is a "bad" narrowing of focus in currently fashionable interpretations of the meaning or range of social science, all agree that there is a "dangerous" restriction in the area in which it is thought possible or desirable that "reason" should operate.

IV

To recapitulate and summarize:

The first task of the political science teacher is to teach citizenship. For most of us that means somehow teaching "democracy," or "American democracy" (the more precise meaning of which is likely to be given in the above "radical premises") to which we have an emotional commitment. But we are often in a position of being unable to make any sort of "intellectually respectable" defense of our preferences. We "believe" them, but everything we detest is also "believed." In a rather pathetic effort to find some sort of reasonable or convincing basis for their beliefs the "liberals" are nowadays—of all things—emulating Burke in an appeal to history and tradition.

The second task of the political science teacher is to prepare for public service. Here the task of the political scientist is both more and less difficult. It is more difficult because the public servant's value problems are greater; he plays a dual role of citizen and servant, and needs value responses or capacities proper to both. It is less difficult because the factual or skill component is greater; here the teacher's value problem can be avoided by the easy rationalization that all he is doing is "giving hands and feet to morality."

The third task of the political science teacher is to train for research. Some —many—would deny that any value problem is involved here, beyond the value of scientific method itself. But this is a viewpoint which will not withstand critical appraisal, probably not in any society, certainly not in our profession if we are serious about the "strains" which are in our radical premises.

What can be done which will improve the present situation? I have been practicing without proper licensing in trying to diagnose, from the viewpoint of what might be called political theory, the value-problem in contemporary political science teaching. I should be doubly guilty, and even more inadequate, if I should attempt the role of ethical creation or prescription. Perhaps, however, some procedural and peripheral suggestions may appropriately be set forth:

1) A first task is to convince political scientists that it is "sensible" or "fruitful" to discuss ethical questions. In view of the empirical temper of the day any effective appeal must be at the "empirical" level. The demon-

stration of the impossibility of avoiding ethical questions is a first step. The second step is the presentation or emphasis of the information that there are "hard boiled" schools of ethics, *i.e.* those that profess to make no appeal to the supernatural or the *a priori*. Those who find naturalistic ethics not to their complete satisfaction should, I think, be content with this procedure; better that ethical problems be brought within the area of respectable consideration than that they be completely avoided.

Incidentally, I recommend examination of Wayne A. R. Leys' *Ethics for Policy Decisions* in this connection. Here various points of view regarding ethics are briefly presented and applied—in sample form—to policy problems. It is some measure of our professional condition that—so far as I know—this is the only book of such a nature.

2) Political theorists should undertake "imaginative moral architecture," indulge their creative imaginations in utopia-building. Three currently popular interpretations of their role are: (*a*) study of the history of political ideas, (*b*) elaboration of empirical theory—model construction, and so forth; and (*c*) critical examination of ideas to determine their logical compatibility or incompatibility, *e.g.* "to make the student or citizen . . . aware of which beliefs and desires are and which are not coherent with the values which the student or citizen holds." I have no quarrel with these. I merely suggest another function be added. Whose function is it, if not the political theorist's, to project ways of organizing the political aspects of our lives? Who has—or should have—a better knowledge of the relevant empirical theory?

3) I should like to see it become a convention of the profession that all empirical or theoretical-empirical works be prefaced by a statement of the valuational structure on which they rest, in the author's opinion. (If in the author's opinion the work rests on no value structure, this should be stated and exposed to critical examination.) Such a convention will help keep the empirical and the valuational in balance and promote healthful reciprocal growth. Growth of empirical studies and theory apart from the needs or desires of society is cancerous growth, *i.e.* growth without function is the definition of cancer (to use a manner of analogy popular where the point has most relevance).

Perhaps we should go further. Perhaps we should, as David Easton has argued, require that research workers not merely "avow" their moral premises, but expose them in depth, engage in "genuine moral self-clarification." [13] As they are insistent that others not merely parrot a catecism, why should they be permitted to do so?

Enough.

The problems involved run beyond my competence and beyond political science. These problems cannot be solved short of basic moral and intellectual restructuring. I prefer to believe that this is possible. I know no reason to believe that man has run dry of ideas.

PART TWO

Political Theory

The significant part played by theory in the development of political thought and institutions is underscored by the essays in this section. The heavy debt owed to the classical writers in formulating basic political issues and concepts is stressed, as well as the role of contemporary political theorists in examining political problems and advocating solutions.

NORMAN JACOBSON

The Unity of Political Theory: Science, Morals, and Politics

EVERY SIGNIFICANT human enterprise gives rise to an extensive mythology centering round its goals, procedures, and achievements. Whether the enterprise be sports or war, business or science, there exists in the mind of the spectator an image, often oversimplified, of what the enterprise is all about. This does not always do a grave injustice to the activity involved. Frequently the image is the best single account the participant himself can offer to those on the outside looking in. But when the spectator wishes to enter into the activity, to become a part of the enterprise, such an account may be seriously misleading. The development of skills and sound judgment appropriate to the particular enterprise requires more than a superficial appreciation. It demands personal knowledge of the activity, knowledge best acquired by participating in it.

The image of the athlete only on the Saturdays of his glory is not an erroneous image, it is merely a partial one. The textbook view of the natural sciences, so neat and tidy and detached, is not altogether false. It merely omits from the account the years of passionate controversy which led to the formalization of consensus appearing in the texts as the agreement of theories and experiments. Where this image of science suffers is not in the answer it gives to the question "what is science?" but in its inability to tell us anything *about what the scientist does.*

In his admirable desire to strengthen his own discipline the student of political theory is impressed with the orderly image of science in contrast to the imprecision and chaos burdening his own undertaking. This has led him to compare two things not ultimately comparable: a textbook view of the exact sciences and a knowledge and experience, gained at firsthand, of the enterprise devoted to theorizing about politics. In striving for precision the student of political theory is increasingly tempted to apply methods and procedures he only dimly understands. Normally the sophisticated student of politics resists the imposition of institutions appropriate to one culture upon another culture where there appears little regard for the specific qualities of the second culture. Yet he does not hesitate to impose scientific institutions (methods and procedures) developed in one "culture," say physics, upon an entirely different "culture," political theory. I do not mean to reject the notion that there may be profit in infusing the corpus of one enterprise with the *spirit* of another. On the contrary, if the history of the acquisition of knowledge teaches anything,

115

it is that the one sure legacy of successful work in *any* of the disciplines is the spirit it imparts to *all* disciplines.[1]

I

By far the most interesting trend in contemporary political studies is the widespread determination to reduce politics to nonpolitical terms. Even the scholar whose genius it is to discover politics at work in the most out of the way places (churches, universities, business firms, even literary coteries), when it comes to politics itself, balks at the thought of discussing it in its own terms. It would seem that politics is psychology, or it is sociology, that it is moral philosophy or theology—that it is almost anything but politics.

Now if there is any single shortcoming from which academic thought in general has suffered most it is intellectual timidity. To those who are convinced that one provocative error is worthy of more respect than a hundred correct tautologies, it seems a pity that prudence should be permitted to play so important a role in undertakings where its value is most questionable. Were this trend of which I speak indicative, therefore, of an interest in drawing upon the best that other fields of inquiry have to offer for the purpose of making the study of politics more meaningful, few would find any cause to distrust it. The circularity of the scholarly disciplines, their mutual dependence, is never more apparent than when we seek to deepen the understanding of our own subject by bringing to it information, generalizations, and metaphors from outside. To the sociologist the society might call to mind some of the marvelous workings of the human organism; the biologist may see in the human organism certain resemblances to the smoothly functioning machine and be enlightened by his vision, and so forth from one discipline to the other. So long as there is no insistence that the society *is* an organism or that the individual *is* a machine, there can be no serious objection to such attempts by scholars to say something new about their overworked materials. It is unfortunate, then, that the current trend to reduce politics to nonpolitical terms rarely stems from a commitment to the study of politics in its own right.

At the same time, there is a growing dissatisfaction with political theory. There exists a belief that political theory is the victim of an irreconcilable tension within it, between its recent scientific development on the one hand and its traditional character as an ethical inquiry on the other. We are urged to factor the "scientific" out of political theory, leaving a worthless "ethical" residue; or we are told that political theory is really moral philosophy or theology, and that what will remain after the precious metals have been removed from the dross will not be worth bothering with, dull studies such as public administration or international organization. While these proposals are frequently advanced in the name of science, sometimes in the name of moral philosophy, their true sources are unmistakable. Surely this can be the attitude neither of science nor of moral philosophy, for whose researches the political theorist has traditionally had the greatest respect, and rightly so. But respect for science and moral philosophy need give rise to no obligation on the part of the political theorist to entertain the claims of scientism or of moralism, themselves as remote from science and moral philosophy as they are from political theory.

It is the purpose of this paper to suggest reasons why any attempt at atomizing political theory must have disastrous consequences for the study of politics itself. It might be well to bear in mind from the outset that it is *political* theory we are expounding. Whatever unity political theory may have it receives from its recognition of politics as a special kind of activity and a commitment to the study of politics as a special kind of undertaking. I can seldom escape the feeling that at the core of many of the tortured arguments for "scientific" political theory or for "ethical" political theory which grace the pages of the professional journals these days there lurks a hostility towards politics as an activity worthy of study in its own right. Although the central concern seems always to be the improvement of political theory itself, as students of political theory we are well aware that hostility towards an object often has a way of disguising itself behind a demand for its improvement. When we lack commitment to a thing we are capable not only of standing passively by while it is chopped to pieces, but even of reaching for the nearest axe ourselves. The wisdom of Solomon in its most celebrated example is perhaps less to be remembered for its anticipation of the normal reaction of the committed person than for its appreciation of the remarkable cruelty of the uncommitted.

The man who could write, for instance, that "Preoccupation with international rights and wrongs is a useful substitute activity, a vicarious discharge of emotional tension, the original source of which is infantile sadism," obviously has little use either for politics or for political theory. On the other side, there has not lived a moralist yet who did not rush to sacrifice politics before his own special gods.

The central mood of scientism and moralism is one of impatience. The impatience of scientism with politics is the impatience of precision with ambiguity. To scientism, politics—and political theory—symbolizes ignorance in the face of established scientific knowledge. The impatience of moralism with politics is the impatience of virtue with prodigality. To moralism, politics—and political theory—symbolizes the venality of man in the face of self-evident moral precepts. Scientism would take the politics out of politics. Moralism would destroy it if necessary as the enemy of virtue. In the unsophisticated view of both scientism and moralism, politics is literally a *means*. Scientism directs us to advise her of our ends so that she can devise the means to our ends, or in the words of a leading proponent of scientific political theory, so that she can calculate "the efficiency of the means for the attainment of specific ends" regardless of their morality. ("The sun of science, as that of God, shines on the just and on the unjust.") That, to scientism, is politics. Moralism sets forth our ends and is prepared to accept the notion, in the words of a leading theologian, that "the choice of means in fulfilling the (morally and rationally approved) purpose raises pragmatic issues" only, and not ethical ones. That, to moralism, is politics.

II

At first glance it might be thought strange that scientism and moralism, apparently stemming from different sources and oriented to contradictory aims, nevertheless seem to share similar attitudes on politics. But on further examination it will be seen that although they differ as to given sets of doctrine, their faith is a common one. They are motivated by a common urge, the passion for certitude. For the mortal enemy of one is the mortal enemy of the other: the stubborn persistence of complexities and ambiguities in human existence. That the passion for certitude is a faith unto itself is attested by the ease and frequency of passage from one of these denominations to the other. Frustration with the promise of scientism—itself a monstrous conception of the utility of science—often finds relief in the most vulgar sentimentalism. Disappointment with the results of an impossibly simple moralistic position can lead to an equally simple scientific one. These are not abnormal occurrences. Numerous examples may be found in our contemporary political scene as well as in our universities.

Those who, typical of the uninitiate in any specialized field of study, exaggerate the utility of applying at any cost what they take to be the methods and attitudes of certain of the sciences, feel that not a moment must be lost in making political theory a "scientific" study. Those who despair utterly of the wisdom of any attempt to instill the study of politics with rationality wish political theory to avow frankly and unashamedly the primacy of the ethical or the theological. Were two equal and opposite errors to make one significant truth, our problem would be far less complicated than it is. Political theory can accept neither course, for its view of its subject matter demands something more of it. Political theory demands a sensitivity to the historic development of politics as an institution and to its unique role in caring for public concerns. That politics is a "means" in the sense of being the substitution of ballots for bullets is only partially true, and to regard it only in this way is to ignore its place in the varied life of man. It is as misleading to characterize politics in this fashion as it would be to proclaim that life is a means to death or that health is a substitute for disease. Such assertions hardly exhaust the alternatives in approaching life or health— or politics—as legitimate subjects of inquiry.

Thus when we examine the claims of scientism and of moralism to be political theory we should not expect to discover any deep commitment to the study of politics in its own right. They approach politics from a motivation and in a spirit different from those of political theory. The urge which their practitioners seek to satisfy is different from the urge of the political theorist or of the student of political theory.

By the term "in its own right" I do not mean to suggest that politics should be investigated apart from other significant activities of men and societies. This would be most unwise even if it were at all possible, which it is not. What concerns me is the current practice of regarding politics and political theory as solely the formal manifestations of informal processes and attitudes. That these processes and attitudes are enormously important and that behavioral (especially ideological) analyses can be enormously valuable I have no doubt. But the belief that these processes *are* politics and that these attitudes *are* political theory seems to me unfortunate.

There can be no serious objection to the fascination of science with politics. After all, the scientific frame of mind has long held an honorable place in the history of political thought. The objection arises from the kind of political theory scientism alone seems to respect. Its image of what science is and how science has developed has misled it from the start. While there can be little doubt that the exact sciences have provided the model, I have yet to read a proponent of scientific political theory who displays more than a primer stage acquaintance with the history and theory of a single field within the exact sciences or an appreciation of what the scientific spirit demands of its practitioners.

The image of science from the outside, as it were, is quite unacceptable. It is distorted beyond recognition. It stresses rules and procedures and techniques and testing and prediction. But it leaves out of the account the central ingredient in the development of all science, namely scientific discovery. This distortion deprives it of the capacity to explain a single scientific advance of the first order or to place itself within the going scientific enterprise.

For the purpose of illustrating the nature of scientism and its outlook on politics and political theory I propose to deal briefly with the perversion of a legitimate scientific ideal as it has found its way into the study of politics— the ideal of the precise vocabulary. As a scientific ideal it hardly seems open to challenge. One difficulty arises, however, when commitment to a scientific vocabulary is thought to extend beyond the terms in which an idea is clothed to the substance of almost any idea, however trivial or unexciting, provided it is dressed to the fancy of the scientist. Unfortunately the reverse is as often true. Let a sound idea be stated in "metaphysical" terms, and it is likely to be judged guilty by association with the vocabulary in which it is expressed. Understanding, let alone unity of vision, does not come easily to one who insists upon viewing everything with a sort of mental squint. The commitment to a scientific vocabulary at any price can have the effect of blinding the individual to the value of some of the most useful and illuminating statements in the history of political thinking.

It is still more to be regretted that under the growing influence of scientism language is fast becoming a weapon of authority in political theory rather than remaining a means of communication among equals. There are lessons to be learned from those discipline which have developed to the point where they are almost entirely technical and exclusive. As language becomes increasingly technical, a weapon of scientific authority—as these studies concern themselves less and less with a comprehensive view of their subject matter, one by one they are compelled to accept ethical and philosophical direction from the outside. To abdicate such a responsibility is to render it neither unnecessary nor inoperative. Should the disciples of scientism ever be wholly successful, their victory would be a Pyhrric one. For there would be scant ground left on which to argue that ethical and philosophical direction should not originate exclusively with those who are at the present time regarded with the utmost hostility by scientism—the moralists and metaphysicians. And such an infusion of "scientific" discoveries with the precepts of the moralists or the systems of the metaphysicians would be as grotesque a caricature of political theory as might be imagined. It is unthinkable that a political theory can be woven from materials untouched by a principal concern for the political.

Furthermore, the indiscriminate sterilization of language can easily have the corresponding effect of sterilizing thought as well. The substitution of passive for active modes of expression makes for the substitution of passive for active modes of thinking. The mind is prepared for the role of spectator only, and not for that of actor. Aside from the distortions this may produce in our intercourse with non-professionals—say, undergraduate students—it has serious consequences for the intellectual development of the political theorist. At first glance it might appear that it is precisely the role of spectator to which we as students of politics should aspire, with all the world our laboratory and our words the words of the detached scholar. As I have pointed out, the physical scientist is most often visualized by the social scientist in this way, and it is certainly the picture uppermost in the minds of those who advocate the development of a "scientific" vocabulary for political theory. But unless he dare rethink God's thoughts, the physical scientist is not in the least dependent for his knowledge upon the skill with which he is able to imagine the motivation of a falling body or the sentiments of justice obstinately held by a gaseous element. On the other hand, the political theorist is enormously dependent for his knowledge upon self-awareness and introspection. We cannot hope to understand our fellows without seeking to understand ourselves. To perform relentless surgery on ourselves, to cut out the morally exciting and cramp the flow of the intellectually dramatic is to reduce the possibility that we will ever understand politics really well. We become like Montaigne's pendant who would not venture to say that he had an itchy backside before consulting his dictionary to discover the meaning of "itchy" and of "backside." It is doubtful whether such a man could ever appreciate the lengths to which other men are driven to rid themselves of this torment.

The sterilization of thought, were it desirable, is never entirely possible, however. Even the disciples of scientism cannot escape their humanity. For as Michael Polyani has put it: "Detachment in the rigorous sense of the word can only be achieved in a state of complete imbecility well below the normal animal's level." I used to believe that the moralist who, according to Weber, carries the "marshal's baton of the statesman or reformer in his knapsack," was more of a burden to political theory than the solemn "scientist." I am no longer so sure. If the moralist makes of the classroom a hustings, at least all are aware of the purpose of his dull harangues, including himself, although he is likely to have an exalted sense of his own purpose. But the advocate of scientism tends to communicate a state of complete abstraction, as though such a state actually existed. With his audience he is lulled into an unawareness of himself and of his preferences as those preferences are contained as elements in his thought. In an atmosphere presumably of science, the actual result often bears more resemblance to religious dogmatism than to science.

The alternative to scientism in theorizing about politics is most certainly not some brand of moralism. Moralism is no more a synonym for political theory than is scientism. Its relationship to moral philosophy is at least as tenuous as the relationship of scientism to science. For it is one of the chief characteristics of moralism to recoil from any involved discussion of practical morality. Unlike true moral philosophy, moralism treats morality simply, dogmatically, and almost always in the abstract. Where the contingency of politics is absent, however, the spirit of political theory can hardly be expected to thrive.

In my opinion there are two aspect of moralism which have from time to time managed to make some inroads into political theory. The first is perhaps best described as unctuous preaching. This is the attitude that the proper approach to the study of politics is a pious dissociation from the corrupting influence of politics itself. It assumes the pose of critic, but its suggestions rarely have anything to do with politics. It tends to propose easy solutions to the most complex questions, for it is quite above the battle. Its disciples think to gain the advantage of the political theorist by substituting their own infallible doctrines for the rigorous discipline of political theory. Yet its transparent simple-mindedness proves to be its own worst enemy. For only the most credulous could possibly be convinced that they are in fact listening to political theory.

More subtle, perhaps, but equally obnoxious to the best traditions of political theory, is the notion that all political theorists should be classified as political theorists on the basis of their ethical systems. Any such attempt must fail as utterly as the attempt to classify political theorists on the basis of whether or not, and if so to what extent, their vocabularies are "scientific." A recent effort to reduce political theory to ethical theory might serve as a case in point. In the scheme of its perpetrator, authors of such widely divergent political theories as Hobbes and Rousseau ultimately wind up in the same category. And how many writers are there whose most distinguished service has been to demonstrate the kinship of Liberalism with Communism or of Conservatism with Fascism by subordinating the political and the consequential to the "ethical" and the "theological"? Disrespect for striking differences in the consequences of theories is a mark, not of moral philosophy, but of moralism. Perhaps it is ethics—at least as understood and manipulated by the moralist—and not politics after all, which makes strange bedfellows.

III

It has been the central point so far that without commitment to the study of politics in its own right there may be scientism or there may be moralism, but not political theory. The idea is elementary, to be sure. Yet while we do not normally entrust the future of medical science to a society of misanthropes, love of subject has not been so apparent as a qualification for political theory.

Political theory is neither scientism nor moralism, whether viewed separately or taken together. They do not share its central concern. The central concern of political theory is with the search for political wisdom.

At the present time the persons most interested in bringing about a change in the standards of scholarship for the study of political theory are those whose desire it is to bring about a change in the very purpose of political theory itself. Their deepest commitment is not to the search for political wisdom, but to the idea of system, with the consequent stress upon methodology. The system-builders are men of great faith. They believe in the duty—and what is more, in the possibility—of producing political theorists in the universities. They believe that this can be accomplished through prescribed courses of instruction. For it is their conviction that there actually exists a political system, whose discovery has been made possible by recent advances in social scientific techniques and knowledge and in symbolic logic and mathematics. This faith, this belief in the possibility of achieving for the first time in history a "true" political theory, is as naive in its way as the belief of a certain contemporary scientific philosopher that "philosophy has risen from error to truth" almost entirely within his own lifetime. Such an attitude does more justice to the tender maid who, having just been introduced to the ecstasies of love, credits her inexperienced young lover with the invention of the game.

Where scientific political theory has "risen from error to truth" it has generally done so at the expense of having something relevant and important to say. The attempt to offset the absence of political wisdom in the writings of a theorist by an appeal to the elegance of his system will not answer the ultimate purpose of political theory. For system is more the product of the ingenuity and the training of a thinker, than of his wisdom. The universities can produce political theorists only if it can be shown that technical proficiency alone is sufficient for the creation of ideas.

Nor can political wisdom be saved by a bureaucratic insistence upon rules. Political theory demands the sifting of important ideas through a discriminating intellect, not the endless consideration of the means for achieving knowledge. Within limits political theory is indifferent to the techniques utilized in the search for political wisdom. It is eager to embrace the results of scientific, ethical, or any other type of legitimate inquiry, for it is interested less in the accretion of knowledge than in the penetrating statement of the results such knowledge might yield. Its methods, then, can never be exclusive.

Not long ago I read a sly essay by Dwight MacDonald on the "how-to-do-it" mania currently sweeping the country. The fat catalogue of books of instruction dealing with almost every conceivable topic, from pottery making to peace of mind, was no doubt designed to confirm the sensitive reader in the realization that his is an age which values techniques ahead of knowledge and which stands less in awe of wisdom than of blueprints. I remember that at the time I could not help speculating as to how much of present-day professional political theory deserves the honor of a place on Mr. MacDonald's list. The subordination of knowledge to techniques and wisdom to blueprints in political theory has not lagged far behind the rest. This has had the effect that might be expected of it, a general leveling down of the standards for creativeness in the field. Where it was once thought that imagination, experience, judgment, and love of subject were indispensable qualifications for the political theorist, today what it takes is apparently the ability to master the procedures invented by lesser minds for the treatment of great themes. Given the situation, it is not surprising that our universities should boast few students of political theory, but hundreds of political theorists.

To me this raises a crucial point. Can there be a milieu for creative work without the capacity to recognize and the readiness to appreciate merit, past as well as present? Can we, with impunity to the standards of our discipline, judge the history of thought on the basis of the pedestrian tests we have established for the political theory we ourselves are prepared and qualified to produce? It is one thing to organize mediocrity for its most efficient performance. It is quite another to regard organized mediocrity as providing *the* standards by which to judge creativeness and originality in political theory.

Eric Hoffer attributes sustained creativeness not least of all to the capacity for judicious praise. He sees in the capacity for judicious praise "an indication of a diffused excellence," and he credits Pascal with the idea that the more intellect we ourselves possess, the more originality we are apt to discover in others. "Ordinary people find no difference between men." When we ask imagination to show her credentials, or request good taste to depress herself to our own level, we give an almost certain demonstration that these qualities are lacking in ourselves. It would be a pity if, owing to an emphasis upon system and methodology, the test of worth in political theory were gradually reduced to the test of technical brilliance. A new and oppressive orthodoxy, this time supported by the powerful magic evoked by the use of the term "science," would be likely to commandeer the field. It might be well to remember that the history of thought is in large measure a history of the refusal of good minds to be bound by the conventions and procedures of orthodox scholarship.

It is obvious that the gifted amateur with a genuine interest in politics, untutored though he may be in the mysteries of formal scholarship, as a political theorist remains miles ahead of the unimaginative, disinterested, or rule-book professional. In our more rational moments we are forced to concede that all our ground rules will not create for us a single political thinker of note, nor assure us immortality or even influence. What is needed most is the capacity to understand and appreciate quality of thought, in order that we may continue to honor standards for political theory appropriate to the significance of the undertaking. If we cannot by our own efforts produce original political thinkers, we can at least contribute to the training of wise and useful critics whose chief concern will be with the substance of political thought and with the solution of problems in political theory. It is interesting that no truly great thinker has ever felt it necessary to justify his thinking on important matters. Practices which add to the normal difficulty of knowing what it is most important to think about might be a credit to human ingenuity, but not to human judgment.

The search for political wisdom does not presuppose the existence of a political system or imply the possibility that politics can be explained once for all. It should not be confused with the passion for certitude. The quarry does not have to be grasped unequivocally or possessed exclusively to be enjoyed. Impatience with ambiguities and imprecision, as if these were the *only* adversaries of significant thought, is a characteristic of the small mind. There is no question that political theory can benefit greatly from the attitudes and practices of science or of moral philosophy. As a first step, however, I would suggest a revaluation of the *image* of science and of moral philosophy in order to prevent their perversion into scientism and moralism. Finally, I believe that not until political theory is once again regarded as a unique enterprise is there much hope for the production of political theory of any significance at all.

MULFORD Q. SIBLEY

The Place of Classical Political
Theory in the Study of Politics:
The Legitimate Spell of Plato

CLASSICAL POLITICAL THEORY'' can, in one
of its meanings, refer to the diverse thought systems developed in antiquity
from the sixth century B.C. to the time of St. Augustine in the fifth century A.D. It may also be used to designate merely the political philosophies
of Plato and Aristotle. For reasons of space and because some concentration
would seem to be desirable, this paper will center its attention on the relevance of Plato, with only incidental glances at Aristotle and only passing
references to other theorists.

In singling out Plato as the writer who best reflects the tendencies of "classical theory," there is no intention of minimizing the importance of Aristotle
and other thinkers. Nor, in dealing with Plato, shall we be concerned to defend his system at all points. Logicians have pointed out again and again his
logical defects; modern philosophers and scientists have questioned many aspects of his methodology; and political ideologists have attacked him as an
apologist for ancient Athenian aristocracy who attempted to conceal his class
bias under a blanket of fine words. Many of these criticisms are well
founded. The fact that this paper does not, for the most part, state explicitly where the writer differs from Plato is not to be interpreted to mean that
he does not disagree, and rather sharply, with many of the important Platonic propositions and conclusions. Despite these disagreements, and, in part,
because of them, however, the paper will hold that the study of classical
political theory, particularly as reflected in Plato, is an indispensable part of
any adequate curriculum in politics.

I

For a thinker who has been dead 2300 years, Plato manages to remain
very much alive. The harsh, not to say vitriolic, attacks on him by his many
recent critics only emphasiize the point; for when men like Popper,[1] Fite,[2]
Russel,[3] and Crossman [4] deprecate his virtues in ethics and politics, they do
so with the vigor and insistence of men taking to task contemporary political
antagonists. And when the Platonists counterattack, as, for example, in the

125

works of Wild[5] and Levinson,[6] they do so with a conviction and vitality which would imply that their very lives depend upon it (as perhaps they do, in an intellectual sense).

Both the attack and the defense are at all levels: metaphysical, religious, ethical, political. Plato is attacked (and defended) for his alleged lack of appreciation of modern "scientific" method; for his naive theological notions; for his alleged identification of "ethical" with "political" problems; for his "organic" conception of state and society. He is made a fourth century B.C. Fascist; an advocate of militarism; and, by some of his defenders (notably Wild), a true advocate of "democracy." As in the case of Marx, the treatises purporting to explain "what Plato really meant" are legion; and on many important issues the interpreters seem to reach diametrically opposite conclusions.

A very high proportion of the attacks on Plato center their comments on those aspects of his thought which could be termed "political." That this is true is not surprising, in view of the fact that at least forty per cent of all Plato's writings make politics their central concern; while in the remainder political references or implications are often of more than passing interest. Even an avowed enemy of Platonism in politics has to admit that "For ten years or more past I have been giving an annual course in political philosophy and I have learned that, for me at least, it would not be possible to make political philosophy intelligible without a daily reference to the Republic."[7] Considerable homage to come from a stout opponent!

But when we say that a high proportion of current interest in Plato is concentrated on his politics, what, precisely, do we mean? We mean, first, that Plato has, whether rightly or wrongly, been identified with certain contemporary and hotly contested viewpoints—he has been interpreted as being essentially "Fascist" or "anti-democratic" or "democratic." Many make him, as it were, the progenitor or spiritual godfather of schools or parties whom the critics admire or repudiate. But secondly, current interest in Plato may be said to stem from a concern about the method or mode of thought by which he endeavored to understand "political reality."

On the whole, it is very difficult, with any legitimacy, to identify Plato with any contemporary "political" viewpoint. It is, by and large, easy to agree with Leo Strauss when he says:

> Plato composed his writings in such a way as to prevent for all time their use as authoritative texts. His dialogues supply us not so much with an answer to the riddle of being as with a most articulate imitation of that riddle. . . . In particular, no social order and no party which ever existed or which ever will exist can rightfully claim Plato as its patron.[8]

If, then, one accepts this judgment on the politics of the dialogues, one will be concerned not so much to identify Plato with a particular political credo as to inquire into the general spirit of his approach to the world of politics. His political proposals do, indeed, have affinities with the beliefs of certain historical groups but they can never be simply equated with them. Plato is thus both an "ideologist" and an analyst; and in discussing him one should always be careful to distinguish between the two, particularly when it is suggested that he can be thought of as the founder of this or that "school" of thought.

Now the value of classical political theory, as of any system or systems of thought, is twofold. It is, first, a phase of the history of ideas and institutions and, therefore, important in an *historical* sense. Secondly, it constitutes a set of principles or possible system of hypotheses about politics conceived as a universal aspect and experience of life—and is, consequently, significant *analytically*.

Let us now proceed to examine the contributions of classical theory in each of these realms.

II

Turning, then, to the first facet of the classical contribution, we may lay it down at the outset that "politics" involves the formulation, execution, and evaluation of "public policy" and the distribution of power in a human society. There is a "political" aspect of all human organization, whether the organization be family, church, trade union, or society for the prevention of cruelty to animals. The study of "politics" will necessarily involve all facets of human life and thought which have a bearing on or relate to the central concern. Thus, insofar as religious beliefs explain attitudes to the political world, they are of concern to students of politics; and the systems of value preferences held in a given society must necessarily be studied if we are to understand the formulation and implementation of policy and the distribution of power. Policy and power distribution involve, among other things, the effectuation of value hierarchies in the institutional world. Then, too, the study of politics, as of any other aspect of life, will always occur within the framework of a world-view of some kind. To comprehend politics, therefore, the student must keep in mind and be aware of the general framework of thought which characterizes the scientific and philosophical outlook of a given age.

True, politics is an aspect of life and constitutes an experience common to all ages of history—power distribution and public policy are problems in all historical communities; but, as Collingwood argues (albeit hyperbolically, many of us would agree), to speak of the State of the Greeks and the State of seventeenth-century England as the same, either in terms of empirical or of ideal polities, is illegitimate.[9] This does not mean that there are not principles, both in terms of goals, institutions, and methods, and in terms of explanations of "reality," that are applicable in every age, but rather that these common principles occur within the context of significant variations which depend upon the time and culture.

When, therefore, we speak of "understanding politics," we cannot exclude the "historical" dimension. Contrary to what some appear to argue,[10] the student of politics is necessarily interested, not merely in the "present" (whatever that is), but also in the political "reality" of all times "past." He must be interested, if only because "past" cannot be sharply differentiated from "present" (assuming for the moment that his major interest is in "contemporary" politics).[11] A full comprehension of "political phenomena" would, therefore, embrace an understanding of the way in which men in all ages and cultures have actually formulated and implemented public policy, as well as of the goals which they achieved, thought they were achieving, or thought they ought to achieve. The historical and cultural variations would, of course, be considerable; while at the same time the assumption of this paper is that, aside from all historical and cultural variation, the student of politics is also endeavoring to discover uniformities—not merely the kind of uniformities implied in the statement "if x, y, z, then $q, m, n,$ and $o,$" but also general common patterns which appear to underlie political phenomena under all historical conditions, and whatever the philosophical and scientific assumptions obtaining in a given generation might be.[12]

Hence, if we are talking of politics generically we are, it would seem, speaking of *all* politics, both in its diversities and in its uniformities; alike in its "appearances" and in its postulated "forms" or underlying patterns.

What, then, do we mean by the significance of classical political theory for an historical understanding of politics and the study of politics? Several dimensions of that historical significance may be discerned:

1) *The First Systematic Political Discussion.* Plato was the first writer (whose writings are extant, at least) who reflected systematically on politics at all. Before him, it is true, there had been those who concerned themselves with political questions—in Egypt, for example, and in ancient Israel. But Plato was the first to make political questions the center of his attention and to ask the epistemological, metaphysical, and ethical questions that must arise in any political inquiry. Assuming the institutional *polis* as in some sense the imperfect reflection of a metaphysically "real" *polis,* and making *practical* questions (that is, ethical and political) the center of his discussion, he then proceeds to examine what the *polis* as a type of political institution is trying to become. If the student of politics is intrinsically interested in his study—if he views the study as one of the "liberal arts and sci-

ences"—he cannot ignore either Plato or Aristotle, for they initiated the attempt to study politics both scientifically and philosophically.

2) *The Illumination of Greek Politics.* Both Plato and Aristotle are significant because of what they tell us about the political structure, organization, problems, assumptions, and goals of Greek institutions. Just as one naturally turns to a textbook on American Government for a comprehensive treatment of American political institutions, so one turns to the *Republic, Politicus, Laws,* and other Platonic dialogues and to Aristotle's *Ethics* and *Politics* for the light they might cast on the theory and practice of politics in the Greece of the fourth century B.C. To the student of comparative politics the *Laws* and the *Politics* are particularly valuable for this purpose, but the *Republic* can in no wise be excluded, as is sometimes assumed. We learn from Aristotle, for example, much about the then current utopian political speculation and something of the political history of both Sparta and Athens (not only in the *Politics,* of course, but also in the *Constitution of Athens.*) If Greek City States are significant examples of ways in which men have been organized politically, then the classical political theorists certainly give us important clues as to their development and functioning.

It is true, of course, that both Plato and Aristotle need to be read critically and with due regard for other contemporary and near-contemporary sources of information—including the dramas of Aristophanes, the histories of Herodotus and Thucydides, and others. But this fact does not minimize the importance of the classical theorists in this respect. After all, if we are concerned with American politics in the twentieth century, we would, if scientists and scholars, not take at face value even the best textbook in American Government and Politics but would supplement and compare it with many other varied sources. At least two reasons would lead us to do this: (*a*) The textbook writers all have biases and all are writing within the framework of certain assumptions about the world and about method and it is in the light of these biases and assumptions that they select the "facts" which they then organize into textbooks on American Government and Politics; similarly, Plato and Aristotle are working within the limits of their biases—class and cultural—and assumptions and should not be taken to represent a complete or adequate view of political phenomena. (*b*) Formal scientific or philosophical treatises by their nature often find it difficult to reflect the *spirit* of institutions. Poetry and art seek to go "beyond" analysis and attempt to see things as "wholes."

In some respects the *Republic* itself is an example of poetry, and it is significant that Plato, while distrustful of poets and such like, found it impossible to describe either his political ends or existing political institutions without resorting to what we should call poetical imagery and the figures of speech which are indispensable to pure "literature." Likewise, the observer

of American politics, if he is interested in American politics in all its ramifications and dimensions, would have to study twentieth-century poetry, literature, the cinema, and drama, before he could pronounce with any authority on the springs and goals of politics in twentieth century United States.

While we do not get, in the political treatises of Plato and Aristotle, any
complete or systematic discussion of Greek politics in all its dimensions, it
remains true, nevertheless, that those works provide us with valuable clues.
To students of comparative politics, both in the historical and in the "contemporary" sense of that term, this is no small contribution.

3) *Classical Theory and Scientific Method.* Plato and Aristotle were the
first to lay down the very notion of "scientific" method in politics. They
were, in other words, the great pioneers in suggesting that the apparently
multifarious phenomena of political life are "tied together" by underlying
patterns or principles and that men can, through rationality and observation,
know those patterns. We may disagree with the notion that these patterns
have a metaphysical "reality," but whether we agree or disagree with the
Platonic-Aristotelian assertions in this realm, it would be difficult to deny
that, from the viewpoint of the history of thought about politics, and, therefore, for an understanding of politics, this is a fact of greatest significance.

4) *Classical Theory and the Shaping of Institutions and Ideas.* But perhaps the greatest significance of Plato and Aristotle for an understanding
of politics historically lies in the enormous influence they have had on the
way in which institutions have actually developed and the even greater impact they have had on the manner in which men have thought of politics.
In its broadest sense, "understanding politics" means not only the comprehension, through whatever tools are available, of the actual way in which
men have conducted themselves politically but also an understanding of
how they explained "reality" and *what* they thought of as desirable goals.
It is assumed, of course, that explanations of "reality" and explicit formulations of goals do in some sense actually affect conduct.[13]

Now by this standard, classical political theory and classical political theorists have been, and are, of immeasurable significance. They are not dead,
but have remained very much alive. Thus, in the medieval period, when ec-
clesiastical political theory wrestled with the problem of reconciling the primitive Christian hostility to the State with the apparent permanence of the
State as an institution, Plato to some extent became a tool with which
writers sought to justify the idea that, while private property can be defended as an institution justified by relative natural law, communism is ideal.
Hence, Gratian, the great codifier of the canon law, supports the ideal of
communism by reference not only to the practice of the primitive Church
at Jerusalem but also on the authority of Plato. "In Plato," he avers, "that
State is said to be ordered most justly, in which each member is ignorant of

any private affections": "it was one of the wisest of the Greeks who said that the goods of friends should be in common." [14]

One might also note that, while there is no simple "cause-and-effect" relationship, more of the institutional structure of medieval life, and certainly much of its justification, is essentially Platonic. Thus, the prohibition of clerical marriage after Gregory VII is largely from motives which animated Plato in the construction of his ruling class: ties of family would interfere with the priest's function as a guide and ruler. The medieval estates of *oratores, bellatores,* and *laboratores* correspond somewhat to Plato's noetic, political, and economic classes.[15] Not that all this was in any sense due to the direct inspiration of the *Republic,* which, as a matter of fact, was lost between the fifth and fifteenth centuries.[16] But it is not improbable that indirectly, at least, through Augustine (who obtained his verson of the *Republic* through Cicero's work of the same name), Platonic political notions helped in some respects to condition not only medieval thought, but medieval institutions as well. It is certain that the medieval notion of Universals owed much to the *Timaeus,* which was preserved continuously from antiquity; and thus the "realistic" notions of politics, as of other realms, were in a sense part of the Platonic tradition.

With the rediscovery of the complete text of the *Republic* in the fifteenth century, the comprehensive Plato re-emerges and has remained very much alive ever since. He apparently constituted an important inspiration for Sir Thomas More, even though More's analysis in the *Utopia* differs in many profound respects from that of the *Republic.* More interprets Plato as advocating communism for all: he agrees "with Plato, and nothing marvels that he would make no laws for them that refused those laws whereby *all* men should have and enjoy equal portions of wealth and commodities, which is not possible to be observed where every man's goods are proper and peculiar to himself." [17] And several of More's specific legislative proposals are copied almost verbatim from the *Laws.*

It is hardly necessary to note the great impact of Platonism on late eighteenth- and early nineteenth-century thought, since it is so well understood by students of intellectual history. The paradoxical Rousseau, for example, is not only the last of the three great "Social Contract" theorists but also the first of the modern political quasi-Platonists; and through Rousseau, as well as directly, Hegel and Hegelians (including, if you will, Bosanquet and Bradley) continue analyses of Society and State which in many respects are inspired by Plato, even though specific statements may owe little or nothing to him. And writers like George Herbert Mead, in their reaction to much of the Anglo-American tradition in political thought, embrace Hegel and, in some measure, Plato.

It is always amazing to note that analysts who, in their substantive proposals, often differ widely from Plato, are nevertheless deeply indebted to him and often take their points of departure from him. There would seem to be two reasons for this phenomenon. The first is the rather revolutionary quality and assumptions of both the *Republic* and the *Laws*—the notion, in other words, that men can, by analysis and thought, change the fundamental institutions of society. The second might be termed the challenging methodological and substantive analyses of the great political dialogues—analyses which are so sharply stated and at points so uncompromising that men are compelled to come to grips with them, one way or another.

Among modern political writers who have been profoundly impressed by the revolutionary spirit of the Republic and the Laws one might mention the late H. G. Wells. In his autobiography [18] he tells us that Plato has been a major influence on his political thinking. In the development of his political conceptions, Wells was confronted by an empirical political situation in some respects radically different from that within the context of which Plato wrote; and Wells' basic assumptions about human nature and his political conclusions diverged sharply from those of the Greek thinker. Yet despite divergence on substantive proposals and basic differences in framework of thought (the notion of a Universal State, rather than a *polis,* for example), it is evident, both on the testimony of Wells, and from an examination of their contents, that Plato lives again in both *A Modern Utopia* and in *Men Like Gods.* The first is a rather "authoritarian" socialist scheme, the latter an "anarchist" political order. That Plato could help inspire both socialist and anarchist ideals is not surprising, if one remembers that one of his greatest contributions to subsequent generations was his creation of a "model" for political speculation—a pattern for the imaginary political integration of life, which, as we shall argue in the next section, is an important tool for the understanding of "empirical" as well as "ideal" politics.

Among writers who have been challenged by the sharpness and vigor of Plato's presentation, one might mention politicians like R. H. S. Crossman and severe antagonists of Plato like Warner Fite and Karl Popper. It would seem obvious, for example, that Karl Popper [19] is a kind of inverse Platonist. He professes to be concerned, of course, about the nefarious influence of Plato on successive generations of presumably intelligent men and this, he suggests, is the occasion for the writing of his book. Yet his very concern with Plato, and the pains to which he goes in his stimulating volume to refute the stubborn Greek indicate the degree to which classical theory has contributed to his system of thought. Plato furnishes the thesis to which Popper becomes the antithesis, with the synthesis yet to be written. In other words, Popper in taking issue with Plato exemplifies the Socratic and Hegelian dialectic and how essential a modern logician and political philosopher finds Plato to his own development in the twentieth century. The classical theorists, whatever else they may have been or contributed, have in fact given us many theses, without which many of our antitheses would have been impossible.

III

The particularities of any system of political thought may be associated with what we might call "historical politics"—they frequently are simply the reflections of the cultural conditions of the times and in turn will give us clues to those conditions. Thus, Plato's "three class" system, the scheme of religious persecution suggested in the *Laws* (Book X), the seeming endorsement of homosexual love in the *Republic* (and its repudiation in the *Laws*), the details of the educational system in both the *Republic* and the *Laws,* the military training of both great dialogues, the Aristotelian defense of slavery and repudiation of usury, and many of the details of Aristotle's ideal system, are "dated" and belong to historical politics. This does not mean that they are not important—indeed, as noted before, the student of politics cannot ignore them if he would understand the many attempts of men to comprehend the "political" problem and its diverse solutions. In terms of the problem with which he is attempting to deal, that of an alleged necessity for some basic uniform belief system, one can, for example, view with considerable sympathy even Plato's ventures into censorship and a theory of religious persecution; and one can endeavor to understand why, in fourth-century Athens, he should raise such issues.

Moreover, the particularities or details of classical political theory are important for another reason, divorced from historical politics. For in many instances those details still constitute possible answers to certain seemingly perennial problems of politics—problems with which we are still wrestling with but a modicum of success. For example, many of the modern critics of Plato have charged (with much justification), that his systems of education in both the *Republic* and the *Laws* are in considerable degree schemes for what we today call "propaganda" or "indoctrination." This is made the basis of a serious indictment of the classical view of politics. "Progressive" educators particularly tend, on this ground, to be hostile to Platonic proposals. Yet it is notorious that in practice all modern educational schemes, and particularly public education, have at their base many elements of "propaganda," and that they use myth, fable, and distortion to support particular political and social orders; and this is true of "totalitarian" and "democratic" systems alike. Nor is all this confined to practice. Books advocating "education for democracy," which usually means "indoctrination for democracy," are legion; and their use in public education is often defended by those concerned with the civic aspects of education.

Even those who honestly oppose prescribing fundamental beliefs will often turn "Platonic" a few pages later. Thus, a very able political thinker, Professor C. J. Friedrich, avers that even the most basic beliefs should not be imposed by "education." Yet in the same volume he argues that "education is concerned with shaping human beings in the light of a believed-in ideal" and thinks that it is "essential that the schools . . . step in . . . to mould as many young people . . . as possible" into the form required for the "conduct of civic affairs." [20]

William H. Kilpatrick, who has written widely on educational theory and who can hardly be termed a Platonist, contends that the basic function of American education is "to furnish the character traits . . . necessary to support and implement the desired civilization." He asks for an educational system which will give us a "common outlook on life." [21]

Professor D. W. Brogan, moreover, infers, after studying American education for years, that the public educational system serves the primary function not of developing intellectual acumen and critical ability but of "Americantizing" children—fitting them into the mold of the American cultural and political tradition and leading them to the civic habit which (as both Plato and Aristotle argue) most men can acquire only by "indoctrination." [22]

In other words, the critics attack Plato and Aristotle for outlining a social order in which only the "few" have what Aristotle would call "intellectual virtue," which the "many" have at best only the virtues of "character." The criticism would seem to allege either that this is not true of modern democratic society or that, if it is true, it need not necessarily exist—that all men can potentially transcend the secondary "virtues of character" and develop reasoned bases of moral and political action. If Brogan's account, however, is correct (and it is difficult to dispute it), then the first proposition is simply not true, and critics must rely on the second. Now all men *may* be potentially capable of the "virtues of intellect" and therefore of transcending the myth-based habits which are inculcated in them by contemporary educational system, but it is by no means certain. What is certain, however, is that no historical educational system has equaled the ideal systems of Plato in terms of consistency and attention to detail.

Even in the particularities of their systems, therefore, Plato and Aristotle stand as a perpetual challenge to those concerned with perhaps the most basic problem of politics—that of the relationship between education and achievement of the consensus so essential for civic and social order. One may not agree with their answer, but one cannot ignore it. In educational theory as in political theory, Plato must remain at least a point of departure if not a destination.

We have thus suggested that there are two senses in which the "particularities" of classical political theory are of value to the student of politics. The fact that they are anchored in a particular period of time and culture helps us on the side of historical politics, which is one dimension of the study of politics. Secondly, the very particularities which may be historically anchored raise the question, at certain points, as to whether the answers they offer may not be relevant for other periods as well; especially when other epochs are none too clear themselves about what would seem to be similar issues. We have used the relation of education to the problem of social order as one illustration of such an issue, although classical theory affords many other examples as well.

It is always difficult to distinguish between the particularities of a system of thought and the more universal statements which seem to rise above the meshes of a limited cultural context or the details of application. Here, however, we attempt to do just that—to suggest propositions in classical theory which have escaped the ravages of time and circumstance and which remain viable propositions today to those searching for frameworks within which to analyze and understand "political" phenomena in general. We shall single out five such propositions for attention: (1) the analysis of personality and State; (2) the three factors in politics; (3) application of the three-factor analysis to organization; (4) the theory of disintegration in organization; and (5) the role of ideals in an understanding of politics.

1) *Personality and State*. The basic framework of classical theory is the conception of the "soul" in its relation to society and State. The "soul" is the essence or principle of life in a man [23] and a man is a man fully only in an organized—and, when complete, a rationally organized—society. The political characteristics of any given State spring from the characteristics of the souls of the men inhabiting it. The preponderant types of characters draw after them the others and give us the shape and main outlines of the constitution or ordering of the State.[24] Political constitutions do not initially *produce* the characteristics of the souls of citizens but constitute a clue to those characteristics. The "happiness" of a State has no meaning apart from the happiness of its citizens. True, there is nothing sacrosanct about any given individual or set of individuals; but it is possible, nevertheless, to discover a Good for the whole which is not the mere sum of individual welfares individually conceived. This good of the "whole" secures the maximum fulfillment or "happiness" of its "parts." As Joseph put it, this welfare of the group is "an identical factor in the welfares of many different citizens." [25]

As is well known, both Plato and Aristotle emphasize the element of purpose. The "State" is a body of persons united and cooperating from some common purpose—a purpose shared by men because they are living in a fellowship. Men are not men except in society and therefore the individual "soul" can achieve its *telos* or end only through sharing in the life of the group. Only in this sense is the individual subservient to the "State" or "absorbed" by the State or other organized groups. And it should be remembered that in both Plato and Aristotle the political Good of the State is strictly subordinate to the ultimate moral Good in which both States and souls participate and for which they are in constant search. Thus, not only is no particular "State" a complete State but no individual soul is a complete man until and unless he or it participates fully in the objectively "real" and discoverable moral Good. The State and social groups in general are, therefore, intermediaries between the soul and the Good—they are vehicles, as it were, through which souls are assisted to become just, by virtue of the fact that no soul is complete unless cooperating with other souls for ends which they have in common. The purpose of the State is the production of the "best possible" human beings; [26] and Plato at one point goes so far as to suggest that the citizen of any alleged State whose constitution is moving against the idea of the Good should "allow it to be revolutionized . . . rather than to change to a polity which naturally makes men worse." [27]

This is obviously one version of the so-called "organic" theory of groups and the State. Without for a moment denying the invalid elements in any analogy between "soul" and State, [28] Plato's account of the relationship between "individual" and "political" experience would seem to be as valid as most accounts and more valid than many. It avoids the naive biological analogies by men like Herbert Spencer, [29] whose analysis is also often called "organic"; while at the same time it cannot be identified—although some have mistakenly attempted to do so—with the "historicist" views of thinkers like Hegel and Marx, who seem to allege that they can derive moral and political "norms" from "history." At the same time, the Platonic hypothesis is far more carefully drawn and takes account of more of the relevant problems than, for example, statements of such "individualists" as Jefferson, Bentham, or John Stuart Mill.

2) *The Three "Factors" in Politics.* The second hypothesis of Plato may be said to offer an explanation of the meaning of "order and disorder" in State and personality. Admitting always the limitations of his analogizing, this explanation would yet seem to be at least one possible framework within which students of politics could work fruitfully today. In an age such as ours, when a Lasswell can stress the interrelationships of "personality and politics" and "psychopathology and politics," the Platonic statement has a familiar ring, although it is not, of course, to be equated with any other view.

Political activity, both Plato and Aristotle held, is purposeful activity and can therefore be most characteristically understood in terms of its end or goal. It is also characteristic of Plato and Aristotle that they think of politics as incorporeal, just as the soul is incorporeal. Hence, politics is best explained, not in terms of mechanism, but rather in terms of "nonmechanistic" wholes which are not merely "pushed from behind," as it were, but guided by ends not yet in "existence." [30] Both State and soul are such "wholes," when rationally organized, and both, in turn, find their over-riding end in the idea of the Good or Righteousness. The Idea of the State, therefore, is the idea of the rationally organized community of souls "integrated" (to use a popular modern term) by the Good. Historical "States" and historical "souls" are to be thought of as imperfectly integrated entities; and the "scientific" study of politics is to be conceived as the endeavor, by the discovery of patterns of unity behind the apparently great diversity of political phenomena, to integrate communities about the Good. Such communities when so integrated would exemplify rational "order."

Both Aristotle and Plato contend that in this quest, the "rational" aspect of man can discover both the patterns or unities behind the great diversity of "facts" and the patterns or unities underlying men's diverse "opinions" about the contents of "justice" or value. Political science is, then, both "scientific" (in the sense that it systematically studies "facts" and the "laws" behind them) and "normative." The rational faculty operates at both levels—for it, the alleged difference between "fact" and "value" fades; thus justice itself is simply another comprehensive "fact." But initially, at least, the rational faculty discovers the good by analyzing implicit tendencies in phenomena [31] and understands empirical "facts" by controlled experimentation, critical analysis of materials using the canons of logic, observation, and generalization.

But the rational factor is not always uppermost, and, indeed, is usually not. The State and the soul alike are always on the point of greater or lesser disintegration or departure from rationality. Conflicting particular passions or "appetites" are in a state of uneasy balance within the soul and within the State, or politics, as well: hunger is at war with lust, desire for gain with desire to procreate. Or the tendency of the soul to *do* without taking thought (thus integrating its appetites solely on the plane of action), while it involves some rationality, is yet primitive and uncomprehensive in its scope—it can fight or burst with anger or "righteous indignation" but it has lost or has never found the relation of its action to the action of the soul as a whole or to the action of the world of souls.[32] The dominance of the desire *to have* Plato identifies with the first kind of irrationally governed soul and State and the supremacy of the desire *to do* with the second. The first is the "appetitive," the second the "spirited."

It should be observed that the soul, in this analysis, acts as a whole: reason, spirit, and appetite are "factors" in it, and, as Joseph observes,[33] not parts. No soul is purely appetitive, or spirited, or rational. But some are dominated by reason, some by spirit, some by appetite. Plato is suggesting that men tend to be characterized by what the Greeks called *pleonexia*—limitless desires, either to have or to do; and that these limitless desires, because they involve, on the one hand, material goods, and on the other, the quest for power and honor, have somehow to be organized, controlled, and integrated, if the postulated Good—order and "fulfillment" of personality—is to be attained. This involves integration both at the level of the soul and, because souls are interrelated by Nature (*physis*), at the level of social organization as well.

Plato's whole discussion of the interrelationships of soul, culture, and politics anticipates, in many respects, elements of the Freudian analysis. Indeed, Werner Jaeger calls Plato the "father of psychoanalysis." [34] While we need not go that far, we do note the same awareness of the unconscious factors in human life and politics and an acute understanding of the role of the subconscious repression and consequent conflict with the soul.[35] Like Freud, at least in his later writings,[36] the major problem of politics and civilization is seen to be how to control rationally and consciously the aberrant desires which, left uncontrolled by conscious rationality, are sublimated or repressed in haphazard and inconsistent ways, thus leading to conflict, aggression, and the emergence of the inadequate spirited or appetitive factors as governing forces in both soul and politics.

Of course, we should recognize that there lies behind this statement of Plato a major value assumption—namely, that it is right that men seek the life of cities, rather than remain at the level of primitive decentralized tribal or village communities. It is their Nature, teleologically, to become "civilized," for only in the *polis* or *civitas* and its close-knit fellowship can they develop the characteristic which sets them apart from other life—their rationality and capacity to contemplate the Good as as end.

Plato's analysis of the problem of order and disorder reminds the modern student of politics of the necessity to make clear the premises within which he is working. He is also called upon by classical theory to bring his values out into the open, where they can be inspected; for classical theory is acutely aware that "value" and "fact" are first cousins. It understands that in selecting and organizing "facts" a value system is involved; and that "facts," in turn, affect the way we see our value schemes. Both Plato and Aristotle are keenly aware that a "fact" can be understood only within a logical framework of some kind and that simple gathering of "facts," in the absence of that framework, will never create a "science" of politics, either in the "natural science" sense of that term, or in a "normative" sense.

Much political discussion today, even by scholars, is lacking in that conceptual clarity which Plato so painfully sought, even though he did not achieve it. In the State of Minnesota, for example, political scientists today are often asked what their judgments are on the desirability of restoring "party designation" to the ballot in the election of what is now ostensibly a nonpartisan Legislature. Most of them have opinions, one way or another (mostly one way). Yet I suspect that very few of them have sat down and worked out with any care the reasons for their judgments—to do so would be to make explicit all their premises and would involve them not only in empirical investigations (which in this instance are relatively simple and for the most part have been done) but also in normative inquiry. The American Political Science Association report on "responsible parties" can be subjected to the same kind of criticism: "responsible" implies valuations—and valuations within a very broad context indeed. Or note another area: how many analysts of international relations really attempt to define "national interest"—a term which is central to their inquiries? [37] This is not to say that classical political theory completely succeeds in its quest for conceptual clarity. But at least it attempts to do so, and, in the process, by underscoring and dramatizing the complexity of the task, makes for understanding.

3) *Three-Factor Analysis of Organization.* The three-factor analysis of soul can be applied, according to Plato, to all organized purposeful human activity. Every organization is "political" in the sense that it must formulate, implement, and evaluate policies for itself. But it is "political" in another sense as well: for an organization built around a single purpose—like the Salvation Army or a trade union—can be understood fully only in relation to the organization which reflects men's common interests, whatever it may be called (whether state, polis, civitas, or church). "Political" for classical theory has much broader connotations than for much modern theory. This is not because classical theory is "totalitarian," as is sometimes alleged, but rather because Plato and Aristotle were so conscious of "politics" as the integrating factor of civilized life. In our own day, with enormously complex division of labor, we become increasingly aware that labor divided must be brought together again on the socio-political level. Life becomes "politicized," therefore, not because men agree to the process arbitrarily or because they are forced into it but because of the nature of complex organization itself.[38]

Plato's three-factor analysis helps us understand the basic requirements of any complex organization. Every organization—university, union, club, church—must have a factor of rationality which will understand its purpose and devise means to effect that purpose. At the same time, in addition to rationality, every organization must have embodied at some point in its structure the element of "spirit." This element, as Nettleship observes,[39] includes the "fighting" element which enables man to resist aggression (by whatever means, of which the military is only one), the capacity for "righteous indignation" at injustice, and that which enables man to compete and to be ambitious. Even the most pacific organization, by the nature of organization itself, must make provision for the "spirited"—churches, pacifist groups, economic organizations. A political movement like Gandhi's, pledged though it was to "nonviolence," must discover defensive techniques of some kind. Sects like the Mennonites, ostensibly "nonpolitical," when faced by the demand for a military service against their principles, have to discover schemes of protection: perhaps, as has been often true historically, by fleeing to another land.

Within any organization, too, the "spirited" element must be present, to preserve the distribution of values connected with its purpose and to make certain that limits established by that distribution are observed. Classical thought is almost obsessed by the "limits" which Nature presumably fixes for human conduct;[40] and this *sophrosyne,* as the ancients termed it, is central to the thought of both Plato and Aristotle. The rational element in organization must discover the limits; the spirited element support and sustain them, through executive action and "righteous indignation." The great issue for classical theory is whether *sophrosyne* is purely arbitrary, which is the position taken by Thrasymachus (and after him, fully developed by Hobbes) and which makes limits solely a matter of power; or whether there are universal and objectively "real" limits, which, of course is the position taken by both the *Republic* and the *Laws,* as well as by Aristotle's *Politics.* If there *are* no such real limits, then no theory of political obligation can be constructed and, logically, no political revolution can be initiated in the name of "right."

This theory of objective limits discoverable by reason, so stressed by classical theory, makes almost laughable the claim that Plato is a "totalitarian" or a "Fascist"; for if there is anything characteristic of Fascist doctrine in the twentieth century it is that there are no "limits" save those of "might." No stronger intellectual defense against the Fascist outlook can be found than in the notion of inherent limits to action laid down so emphatically by classical theory. Both the ethical and the legal distinction between legitimate "force" (whether physical or nonphysical) and illegitimate violence (or, as the Greeks called it, *hybris,* or outrage) owe much to the formulations of Plato and Aristotle. The basic conceptions of public law in the twentieth century would have been impossible without something like the classical theory; and the student of legal philosophy will always find Plato and Aristotle amazingly pertinent for problems of the twentieth century.

It was this classical emphasis on "limits" which was partly responsible for such doctrines as the traditional Roman Catholic doctrine of the "just war"; and those of us in the twentieth century who contend that no war today can possibly be "just" and therefore "legitimate" (whatever the alleged reason for the war) are in the spirit of the classical inquiry.

The "spirited" factor—or, as some would have it, the factor of will—is essential for any organization, both in its external and in its internal relations. Equally essential, of course, is the third factor in the Platonic analysis, the appetitive. Men die and must be replaced by other men, and for this the sex "instinct" is useful. Every organization—even those devoted primarily to spiritual concerns, like churches—has material needs. Thus every organization must by its public policy organize the appetitive factor, or at any rate take cognizance of it; for the competing appetites will inevitably affect for good or ill the manner in which the organization functions.

This does not mean, however, that from the viewpoint of the "individual," the organizational demand for material goods is exclusive. Men also need goods for their private wants. While Plato has often been charged with destroying the "private" domain, it is difficult to sustain the charge. True, there is much more snooping into private affairs than most of us today would tolerate; at the same time, however, even the rulers of the *Republic* whose political function is that of ruling, have the quasi-private end of contemplating the Good. Their material sustenance, meagre as it is, will support them not only in the first but also in the second. Likewise, while the "appetitive" group in the *Republic* must be responsible for material sustenance of the rulers, it will also share material goods for its own private ends—undoubtedly having a larger measure of material comfort than the rulers.

Now the ideal organization, in Plato's terms, is one in which rationality is in control, sustained by will and supplied by appetite. One can separate the basic statement of this ideal from the peculiar way in which Plato sought to implement it; but one can hardly deny that the analysis itself is a useful one for the student of politics—whether one is studying the politics of the American Medical Association or the structure and functioning of a political party or the politics of corporate reorganization. Here we have recalled only the skeleton of the Platonic analysis, but this should be sufficient to remind us of its universal utility.

4) *Theory of Disintegration in Organization.* As fruitful or even more fruitful is the Platonic notion of disintegration, which can likewise be applied to all organization.

If the less comprehensive element of the soul, the spirited, gains predominance in an organization and makes the more comprehensive factor (reason) its servant, we have the beginning of a "timocratic" organization or State. In such an organization, there will still be an element of rational integration, in the sense that "reason" will discover means for the implementation of "honor" and the original purpose of the organization will be somewhat recalled by the repetition of slogans. It will not, in other words, be purely arbitrary in its governance (as contrasted, for example, with tyranny); but since the binding tie is no longer complete reason but only an attenuated reason, as it were, the possibility of dividing the ruling class is opened up. Once the division in the ruling class occurs, oligarchic elements emerging from the appetitive aspect of organization usurp the functions of a now dispossessed reason. The churning appetites are still subjected to a kind of rule by the chief appetite of money-getting; but once reason is disowned the potentiality for complete "disorganization" or "disorder" is evident. That comes when there is no longer even a chief appetite in control. The control of oligarchy gives way to the principle of no principle. Conflict becomes perennial; agreement and co-ordination exceptional; integration rare and momentary.

This is the stage called by both Plato and Aristotle "democracy." Everything is at cross purposes and all doctrines of "limits" are forgotten. A skeletal organization indeed remains, but the central notion exhibited is now the struggle of contending factions, each integrated by its own particular appetite but having no central principle—even that of the attenuated rational principle, "honor" or "will,"—to unite them or relate themselves to one another. Out of this jumble emerges the tyrant who unites in his person the principle of no principle and who is the least free of any precisely because he has no principle.

Books VIII and IX of the *Republic,* which describe the process of disorganization or disordering, are among the most "empirical" of all Plato's dialogues—in the sense that they are obviously based on careful observation of actual polities. Yet the "States" described are not actual States. Plato here uses, after a fashion, a method associated in modern times with the name of Max Weber—on the basis of actual observation of the "impure" forms witnessed in the "empirical" world, he creates "ideal types" of timocracy, oligarchy, democracy, and tyranny. He is saying, in effect, "These systems have never existed, in pure form, on earth, any more than my pure Idea of the State. But by picturing them in this way, I shall provide points of departure and frames for the analysis of quasi-States and souls. In providing these ideal types of 'degeneracy' I am attempting to get at underlying patterns of organization, just as I endeavored to provide such patterns in my picture of the Ideal State." But Plato developed these pictures only after long and intimate empirical study. Aristotle's criticism that Plato did not describe the forms of "degeneracy" as they actually took place in Greek City States misses the point: this was not Plato's object. He is not writing a history of the rise and fall of States but is trying to understand the logical and psychological implications of certain *principles* of organization—a scientific task of first order, as must be admitted. At no point in the whole literature of classical political thought do we find a clearer union of the "empirical" approach and the "rational." At no point are the principles enunciated more universally in their application and more suggestive of further research.

Nettleship puts it well when he observes: [41]

> Our first impulse on a superficial reading of the *Republic* is to say that Plato altogether ignores what we call observation and experiment, and writes as if we could construct laws of nature simply by thinking out certain axioms to their consequences. We think so because, coming to Plato with certain expectations, derived from what we know of the methods of modern science, and with a certain modern phraseology in our minds, we apply these to him. Really he says nothing which has not been practically confirmed in *i*ts spirit by modern science . . . The most real facts are those which contain most, the widest and deepest; the most superficial facts, mere "empirical" facts, are those which contain least . . . My fact of observation of the sun's position tells me very little about the sun; but the fact of observation is not denied or ignored by the greatest astronomer, it is used along with a great deal

more. There is no hard-and-fast line between empirical facts and ultimate laws; a fact is empirical so far as it is isolated.

The classical portrayal of the tyrant has never been excelled in all political literature, including that of modern times. It is as topical as this morning's newspaper and as relevant in its interpretation as anything from the pen of Max Weber, Harold Lasswell, or Charles Merriam. Because it is based not only upon observation but also upon thought it is far more helpful in an understanding of contemporary politics (and far more permanent in its contribution to political science) than many a current treatise which remains at the merely "empirical" or descriptive level.

5) *Ideals and the Understanding of Politics.* Both Plato and Aristotle are interested in explaining existing politics and at the same time in outlining the form of the Ideal State. Both endeavor to generalize on the basis of observation and, almost simultaneously, to suggest the form of the political good (and evil). This, perhaps, is a stumbling block for those in the twentieth century who think of "realistic" politics as an analysis of the alleged *is,* with a rigid eschewal of the *ideal.* The first, it may be said, is "science," while the second is not.

Here it will be argued, primarily on the basis of Plato's method (the great model of "utopian" speculation), that, whatever the ethical and utopian method may be called (whether "science" or not is immaterial to the argument), it is relevant for the politics of existence; and that the latter cannot be fully understood except in the context of ideal "forms." Secondly, it will be suggested, the utopian notion is indispensable from a *practical* point of view, in that it provides a stimulus for social development and at the same time a guide to that development.

But initially let us note what Plato is actually doing and what he is not doing. Assuming always the "reality" of an objective moral order and assuming, moreover, that all things are endeavoring, in a measure, to implement it in the world of "existence," Plato takes actual tendencies in empirical "States" which resemble or remind him of the "real" moral order, projects those tendencies to the limit of his capacities, and constructs the ideal State. Thus, in the process, he emits tendencies in empirical "States" which seemingly contradict the ideal—tendencies which are just as "real" as those in the direction of the "Good" which he abstracts. As Barker puts it, "The ideal of the *Republic* . . . is not ideal in the sense that it is divorced from actuality . . . : it is ideal in the sense that it is an exhibition of what actual States would be, if they conformed with those fundamental laws of the constitution of human nature on which, even as they stand, they are based, but of which, in greater or less degree, they fall short." [42]

It will be noted, too, that in this way Plato feels free not only to change what we should call law but also to create his own religion and customs and to abstract and project tendencies in contemporary human beings and fit them into his ideal structure. Utopias necessarily involve a manipulation of institutions and men. Moreover, the ideal State is a whole—not an ideal police system, or series of courts, taken as separate institutions, but a web of institutions interrelated to one another with ostensible consistency. Indeed, this *wholeness* is made a leading point of attack for such critics as Popper, who profess to see in the very notion of a whole utopia (as contrasted with piecemeal utopias) a "totalitarian" technique.

Plato's method is, as we remarked before, to use something like Max Weber's *ideal type* abstraction. But it is never, for him, merely an ideal type; for he professes to be able to differentiate between good and bad types in the process. We might suggest, therefore, that the Platonic method is one of the ideal types plus open identification with a scheme of moral values.

Plato is not, in projecting his ideal State, attempting to resurrect a presumably stable *historical* order—a hypothetical State which existed in the past and through the resurrection of which he hopes to cut off all change. Despite Popper's vitriolic charges to this effect, it is impossible to sustain them if one takes into account the Platonic dialogues as a whole. There is too much of novelty in both the *Republic* and the *Laws* to make any such allegations plausible, as Levinson points out.[43] And Cassirer demonstrates fully that, rejecting both pure tradition and, obviously, pure "power" as bases for the ideal State, Plato instead relies on rationality: "To break the power of the 'eternal yesterday' became one of the first and principal tasks of Plato's political theory." [44] Instead, Plato thinks of reason as possessing the capacity to discriminate between the morally valuable and morally valueless element of any actual situation or system of politics: the former afford him clues, we might say, as to what the ideally good would be if fully realized; the latter, equally, give him hints as to what the ideally evil would be if ever achieved. He may misinterpret the clues or hints—certainly Aristotle, among many other, thinks that at certain points he does—but this does not detract from whatever merit the method itself may have.

The ideally evil would be literally a "non-State." His picture of tyranny may be identified with this complete falling away from the idea of the rationally organized community. Some have suggested that any such picturization of an ideally "evil" community might be called an "inverse utopia." Whatever it may be called, however, is always closely connected with some aspects of "actuality," after the same manner as the ideally good State. In our own day one of the best examples of an inverse utopia is obviously George Orwell's *1984,* which few would deny takes its point of departure from, and in a sense returns to, the empirically "real,"—though not, to be sure, to *all* the "real."

Now what is the relevance of a Platonic utopia for the understanding of politics? We should remember, at the outset, that Plato thinks of politics and the State as primarily the product of the soul. Now "soul" involves a capacity for acting with purpose and cannot be explained as one would explain mechanism: the "movements" of soul are as much "caused" by purposes and ideas which may never be achieved as by antecedent "events" or "facts" which are "real." The "final cause," as Aristotle would put it, of an athlete's running in the arena is the "idea of victory." The final cause is not the particular juxtaposition of muscles, movements of legs, stance of the body, history of the athlete's family, and environmental background which might be studied before or during the race. Victory may never be achieved, and certainly during the race itself is "existentially" unreal—yet, despite the "unreality" of victory it is the best explanation of the movements we witness in the arena. Plato, accustomed to think in terms of mathematical analogies, preferred to compare the process of creating the ideal State to a mathematician's abstracting the "form" of a triangle from the inevitable "matter" in which it is always involved. As Ernest Barker points out, there is no line ". . . of only one dimension *in rerum natura;* and there is no ideal State. But Euclid postulates the one, and Plato and Aristotle postulate the other, as the condition of sciences which are none the less sciences because they proceed on the assumption of something 'unreal,' and indeed are only sciences because they proceed on such an assumption." [45]

True, one must gather facts and conduct controlled experiments (where possible) as an indispensable prerequisite for an understanding of political phenomena; but unless one can go beyond this and from the observations thus made *project* the tendencies into the "unreal," the significance of the existential phenomena, and, from one point of view, the "cause" of those phenomena, cannot be discerned. Who will deny, for example, that Orwell's *1984* teaches us things, both about current "democracy" and about contemporary "totalitarianism," which could not be taught by even the most thorough "factual" study of contemporary British, Russian, and American politics? No pure system of "doublethink" exists anywhere. Yet who can contend that the scheme of "doublethink" in *1984* is merely a fairy tale; and who can deny that it helps us understand mass communications, censorship, and governmental practices today? [46]

Turning from inverse utopias to the *Republic* and the *Laws,* when Plato outlines in the former the ideal of government by wise men, without the intermediation of laws, he helps us understand both the function of law and the limitations of law. He is telling us what the pure idea of righteousness and equity based on reason would imply and in the process helping us comprehend the significance of equity and righteousness in all political systems. On the other hand, in the *Laws,* where he postulates the absence of pure philosopher-kings, he examines what the ideal of the Law-State might mean. Now every existing "State," he is suggesting, is a mixture of the arbitrary, or power-laden; the legal; and the righteous and wise—now one, now another quality is dominant. If we imagine what the Law-State would be, in which power is subordinate to law, and yet supreme wisdom is rare, a flood of illumination is cast on the legal elements of existing culture.

But a well-wrought utopia does more than illuminate isolated and separated aspects of actual politics. It attempts to relate the aspects to one another and thus to create a pattern which by its contrast with the actual will help us understand the latter as a whole. Just as the intimate study of another culture will heighten one's understanding of one's own, so the patterning of a utopia will assist in the more adequate visualization, through perspective and emphasis, of the general or over-all structure of an "existential" polity.[47] Moreover, complicated social and political relations can sometimes best be seen in all their ramifications through the mythological and quasi-mythological devices sometimes used in utopian works, as, for example, in Book X of the *Republic* and elsewhere.

In sum, as Barker argues, utopias, "by showing us what the State would be if its immanent principles were fully realized . . . show us the real significance of the State as it is. It is only in such an ideal aspect that the State can be understood; for if the mere phenomena of its actual working were alone considered, we should be able indeed to collect a number of facts about the State, but not to grasp the reasons for its being or the significance of its functions." [48]

But Plato-like utopias have a second important role to play: they do and can provide a standard for social reform and a dynamic for social change. Or, as Plato himself tells us, "The inquiry into the nature of absolute justice is for the sake of attaining an ideal, in order that men may judge of their actual condition according to the standard which that ideal exhibits and the degree in which their condition resembles it." [49] This is made a matter of reproach by Popper, who accuses Plato of the nefarious intention of "utopian" or "wholesale" social engineering. What we need, argues Popper, is "piecemeal" engineering.

But if we admit the interrelation of institutions and the seamless web of community, as it seems to me we must (and as was certainly recognized by Plato), "piecemeal" social engineering would appear to be dependent on some picturization of a complex of relationships; for to propose a utopian plumbing system without some idea of how its existence will impinge on electricity, sewage, the habits of housewives, and the extent of natural resources looks on the face of it rather foolhardy. If, for example, one takes the "traffic problem," so-called, of any large city, and attempts to formulate the notion of an "ideal traffic system," one will find oneself engaged before long in the writing of a general "utopia" of some kind. And, indeed, this is precisely what Plato is arguing. Given a complex society of minute division of labor, the "solution" of any one practical problem is dependent, he is saying, on an understanding of the whole and of the whole that ought to be; and the complex of relationships that ought to be will at one and the same time give us a clue as to the whole that is and how to attain the "ought." Moreover, the attainment of the complex "ought" will always limit and condition, in some degree, the attainment of any particular "ought." Popper is, of course, fearful that the mere projection of a whole utopian ideal will mean an attempt to impose its pattern on the world by force; and he even attempts to show, unsuccessfully, that Plato wished to impose his particular utopia by violence.

A utopia, however, is primarily, from the practical point of view, a guide— useful and indispensable for rational action, but not to be translated from its "heaven" to "earth" in face of the actual conditions of the world. Thus, there is no real contradiction between the *Republic* and the *Laws:* in the one, Plato projects the ideal as far as his rationality will take him; in the other he stops short of the ideal, restores law, and re-establishes ordinary citizen participation. But the *Republic* furnishes the model for the *Laws,* as he argues it must furnish the model which existing polities should emulate.

Plato in his "utopian" method thus recognizes the two great functions of ideal States: to complete our understanding of the existentially real and to act as a guide for social reform and revolution and for "piecemeal" engineering. Both functions imply the exercise of rationality and both assert that men make, or at least potentially make, their own institutions. No political theorist is so aware of the significance of "politics"—that "politics" implies man's emancipation from the gods, on the one hand, and from the beasts, on the other; and that this very emancipation means that man must create his own order, by the only method available to him, reason, and unassisted either by the arrangements of the heavenly choir or by the instinctual patterns of the beasts.

IV

Having suggested a few of the contributions of classical political theory to the study of politics, it might be well to emphasize in conclusion the limitations of any one system of political thought. No one scheme embraces all "reality," either in physics or in politics; and this is true whether one is speaking of the "nonnormative" or the "normative" aspects of political theory. Thus, while Plato and Aristotle have made their contribution, both historically and analytically, so have the other great systematizers, including those, like Hobbes, who differ sharply with classical theory. An attempt to understand politics will necessarily involve an examination of the propositions of all of them and an endeavor to test those propositions by whatever means are appropriate and available.

In the process of relating "theory" to "politics" the theorist is under a heavy obligation to remember that, however schematic and abstract he becomes, he is still purportedly talking about human relations. On the other hand, the "non-theorist" is under an equally great obligation to remember that the goal of his activity is, after all, the development, extension, and testing of theory. The two activities are not, or at least should not be, mutually exclusive. While this may be obvious, it is often forgotten.

FREDERICK M. WATKINS
Political Theory as a Datum of Political Science

WHETHER WE like it or not, the existence of political theory is a fact. Ever since the beginnings of history, and perhaps even from the days of prehistory, men have been speculating about the nature and justification of political authority. A large mass of written documents survive to record a substantial part of this speculation. Are these documents relevant to the purposes of political science? And if so, by what methods can they best be studied for the furthering of these purposes?

The traditional curriculum of political science has a clear answer of its own to both of these questions. Acquaintance with the writings of outstanding political theorists has normally been regarded as a legitimate and useful, sometimes even as the one quite indispensable element in the equipment of fully qualified political scientists. It has also been generally, though less universally, accepted that the proper means of studying these theorists was to adopt the criteria and methods of sound historical scholarship. The establishment of reliable texts, the tracing of borrowings and influences, the investigation of personal and environmental factors in the creation and trasmission of political theories—such are the problems that have constituted the traditional areas of research in the field of political theory. The standards of verification have been essentially the same as those applied in any other branch of historical research.

Time-hallowed though it may be, however, this traditional approach to political theory is open to serious question. There can be no doubt that the writings of political theorists provide the material for a legitimate and interesting specialty within the general field of intellectual history. It is much less obvious why this specialty should be a matter of concern to political scientists, and not simply left to the historians. Political science purports to be a discipline devoted to the study of political behavior, however that may be defined. Its immediate purpose is not to throw light on the past, but to contribute toward the understanding of the present and future. Although a study of the life and works of political theorists may provide some clues to the ways in which political theorists as a class are likely to develop their own particular modes of thought and action, the number of people belonging to this class is so small as to constitute an almost wholly negligible fraction of the total population. Unless it can be shown that this handful of individuals, including even those long since dead, have something very special to contribute to our understanding of current political behavior, the attention customarily bestowed on them is hard to justify.

There is, to be sure, one aspect of the writings of the great political thinkers of the past which is clearly of importance to modern students of politics. Political problems have often engaged the attention of great minds. Although the primary interest of many of these outstanding men was to investigate and justify the purposes of government, they were also forced, since the normative can never be wholly divorced from the possible, to consider the problem of means. Their works are therefore full of observations and generalizations about the actual behavior of men. Since many of the problems of political behavior are constantly recurring, it is natural that many of these findings should prove, in some measure at least, to be generally valid. Even when, as in the case of Hobbes' theory of the ruthlessly competitive state of nature, or Godwin's theory of the rational harmony of interests, the generalizations are obviously idiosyncratic and wrong, they may still be valuable as logically developed limiting cases or working models, which may help in the analysis and study of certain genuinely significant aspects of normal political behavior. Many of the more promising concepts and hypotheses which current political scientists are trying to test and refine were in fact derived from the preliminary insights of great political thinkers of the past. And even though it has long been worked, the mine is rich, and there is no reason to think that it has yet been exhausted.

The fact that early writings have contributed, and may still contribute, to the scientific analysis of political behavior is not, however, in itself enough to justify political scientists in devoting any considerable amount of attention to the history of political thought. The analogy of the natural sciences would seem in this respect to be quite decisive. Modern chemists and physicists also make use of concepts and hypotheses which were first developed by great men of the past. Sometimes, in the elementary textbooks, these figures are even awarded the graceful tribute of a footnote. The value of their discoveries does not in the least depend, however, on the historical circumstances under which they were made; it is simply a question of the light they can contribute toward the solution of current problems. Newton's mind may or may not have been jolted into action by the fall of an apple; what matters is not the truth or falsity of the anecdote, but the law of gravitation. For those interested not in natural science as such, but in the history of the process whereby scientific discoveries have come into being,

Newton's apple may be a serious issue. But the physicists are well content
to leave it to those scientifically very submarginal people, the historians of
science. If the historians of political thought have no more than this to contribute, political scientists could well be forgiven for relegating them to an
equally submarginal obscurity.

But is this really all the historians have to contribute? It has long been
recognized that the analogy between the social and natural sciences breaks
down in one important particular: the world of nature has no awareness
of what is going on in the minds of men, and is therefore uninfluenced in
its behavior by the theories of natural scientists; the world of society, being
composed of men, is capable of sharing in and reacting to the ideas of
other men, including social scientists and philosophers. This means that political thought is at least theoretically capable of influencing the political
behavior not merely of political theorists, but also of society as a whole.
A society is, moreover, a system of communications which extends not only
over space but also over time. Behavior patterns once established tend to
be handed down from generation to generation. Thus the human mind is
in part a palimpsest on which are recorded the impressions left by a succession of past generations, including generations of political thinkers. Why
then should not the history of political thought, by establishing the character
and interrelationships of these successive layers of impressions, be expected
to throw light on the political behavior of contemporary men?

The clearest prima facie support for the affirmative is to be found in
the case of those low-grade and derivative political theories known as ideologies. There can be no doubt that ideological factors have always played
a significant part in political events. Catholics can, in many respects, be
relied on to act unlike Calvinists; laissez-faire liberals and social democrats have their predictable points of disagreement. For anyone interested
in the analysis and prediction of political behavior, the identification of
these ideologies, and the charting of their probable course of future development and influence, are matters of high importance. Many ideologies, like
Marxism and Calvinism, proclaim allegiance by their very names to the
doctrines of easily identifiable historical figures; even when, as in the case
of laissez-faire liberalism or anarchism, there is no comparable association
with any single forerunner, the ideology is usually connected in the minds
of its followers with some well-known group of founding fathers. As an
ideology develops, moreover, and begins to encounter new conditions and
new problems, the resulting stresses and modifications of the original doctrine are reflected and recorded in the controversial literature of the movement. Thus in order to understand the nature and strength of the belief
systems which, whether true or false, are likely to have an important effect
on the course of political action at any given time and place, the obvious
first step would seem to be to study the available literature in the fullness

of its historical context. This has been the method traditionally pursued by students of political thought.

On closer examination, unfortunately, the value of this approach is rather less obvious. The difficulty is that the writings of the leading political thinkers, as befits the products of uncommonly distinguished and enquiring minds, tend to be complex and subtle, while ideologies, being adapted to the comprehension of ordinary men, are crude and over-simplified. Although there is certainly some connection between ideas and ideologies, the distance between them is so great, and the connection so remote and tenuous, that it is impossible to bridge the gap with any sort of assurance. Rousseau, for example, is rightly said to have left his mark on a wide variety of contemporary ideologies. Yet the difficulty of interpreting the *Social Contract* is so great that generations of competent specialists have argued about "What Rousseau really meant" without, as of the present writing, reaching a firm consensus. How then can our reading of Rousseau throw light on the political behavior of modern voters, the vast majority of whom have never even heard of the man? Or does a thorough acquaintance with *Das Kapital* help us to foresee with any degree of certainty the vagaries of the Party Line? It is not impossible to trace the influence of Rousseau on Kant, or of Marx on Bernstein, and to show the extent to which each of the later thinks was led to adapt or modify the ideas of his predecessor. Political thinkers, for all their disagreements, are engaged in the same realm of discourse, and the historian of ideas is thus in a position to establish reasonably certain links between them. But by the time ideas have found their way into the politically efficacious world of ideologies, they are simplified and distorted, and so inextricably entangled with extraneous elements, that it would take more than human skill to demonstrate the nature and extent of their influence.

Because of the difficulty of establishing the direct behavioral consequences of political thought, there has been an increasing tendency among current political scientists to by-pass the problem entirely. The argument in favor of such an approach is easily understood. The basic concern of the political scientists is to understand the political behavior of men. The historian, whose business is to interpret a past which lives only in its surviving records, is necessarily forced, in the absence of other evidence, to use the writings of political thinkers as a clue to the political attitudes prevalent in the period with which he is dealing. But the political scientist suffers from no such limitation. The people with whose political behavior he is primarily concerned are not dead but living. Their activities are a currently observable fact, and it is possible, by methods of controlled observation and experiment, to isolate and measure many of the factors, including the ideological, which enter into their political decisions. Why bother to speculate about the possible influence of *Das Kapital* on the attitudes of contemporary Communists, when the attitudes themselves are subject to direct investigation? Why cross the long and hazardous bridge which leads from Marx to present-day Marxism, when we ourselves are already standing on the other shore? For many political scientists the answer to these questions is obvious. The devising of new methods for the analysis and measurement of political attitudes has accordingly tended to replace the older historical methods as the most vigorously prosecuted, and subsidized, area of contemporary research in the field of political thought.

Although the results so far yielded by these methods are often disappointingly commonplace, there can be no doubt that this is a useful and promising approach to the problem of politics. It must in all candor be observed, however, that it has a long way to go before it can hope to offer anything like a general explanation of the role of ideology in the total political process. The respective strengths and weaknesses of the historical and the behavioral approaches are, indeed, curiously complementary. The strength of the historical approach is that its results are synthetic and dynamic. By studying political thought as an integral part of a total historic context, it sets ideologies in meaningful relationship to all the other political and social forces operating at a given time and place. By placing these events in a moving stream of historical developments, it provides the basis for an estimate of the possibilities of future change. The weakness of all this is, of course, that the results are by no means rigorous or objective, being derived in large measure from historical intuition, which is just another name for informed guesswork. The behavioral approach, on the other hand, is inspired by the highest standards of objectivity and rigor. This is its greatest strength and promise. The corresponding limitation is that its conclusions tend to be merely analytical and static. In deference to its scientific standards, it is forced to break each total problem down into manageable components, deferring any more synthetic treatment to the long hoped for but still distant day when the components shall all have been satisfactorily identified and measured, and their complex quantitative interrelationships established. With its emphasis on what can be observed in the here and now, moreover, the behavioral approach also lends itself more readily to the construction of static models than to the explanation of dynamic processes. Such limitations may be overcome in the long run. This does not alter the fact that political scientists will have to reckon with these limitations for a very long time to come.

Now political science, because of the nature of the problems with which it deals, can hardly afford to dispense, however temporarily and in the interests of a future however promising, with methods of investigation which are capable of yielding dynamic and synthetic results. It is perhaps significant that the social sciences, such as social psychology and anthropology, which have taken the lead in developing the behavioral approach are disciplines whose primary concern has been with social situations of a relatively simple and static character. The primitive tribes on which the anthropologists first sharpened their wits are small and relatively uncomplicated social units. Since little or nothing in the way of historic records is available in preliterate societies, the investigators made a virtue of necessity, and worked out the current patterns of belief and behavior in their chosen tribes by methods of direct observation. Like procedures have also served the purposes of sociologists and social psychologists in their attempts to deal with other comparatively limited groups. But the situation of the political scientist is rather different. The group with which he has always been centrally concerned is the territorial state, the largest and most complex unit of social integration yet devised by the ingenuity of man. Since the characteristic purpose of the governmental process is to maintain a workable balance between all the various social, economic and other forces operating in modern society, the process itself loses meaning unless it is considered in relation to the whole social context. Since these forces are constantly shifting, moreover, the problem of government must be considered as a process of dynamic adjustment over time. Political ideologies, which reflect and mold the attitudes of men in relation to this problem, must likewise be viewed as dynamic and synthetic wholes, rather than as assemblages of isolated and momentary attitudes. Valuable as they may be in other connections, any methods of investigation which emphasize the static and the analytical are by their very nature precluded from dealing with these central issues of political science.

For the student of political thought, the conclusions to be drawn from all this would seem at first glance to be extremely discouraging. The historical method makes it possible to view ideologies as meaningfully interrelated systems of ideas which evolve in a dynamic social context, but offers no rigorously scientific assurance that the resulting picture bears any close relationship to the realities of political behavior. The behavioral method rigorously analyzes and measures specific attitudes, but provides no means of showing how attitudes evolve and merge into effective ideologies. Faced with such an uninviting pair of alternatives, a man might well be forgiven for abandoning the whole thing as a bad job.

That this state of affairs is not necessarily a discouraging or unhealthy one is suggested, however, by the strikingly parallel situation of another academic discipline, psychology. The psychologists have long been living with the problem of working on both sides of a gulf which cannot as yet be bridged from either direction. In fact, their plight is even more complicated than that of political scientists, for their field of interest is divided not only by one gulf but by two. At the one extreme are the physiologists who, knowing that mental phenomena are largely and perhaps wholly an expression of the physical constitution and functions of the human body, especially the brain, are busily engaged in investigating the physical and chemical operations involved in mental acts. The results have been considerable, often brilliant, but as yet they are far from having proceeded to the point where it is possible to explain so much as a single mental act in purely physiological terms. Without waiting for this particular bridge to be built, however, the experimental psychologists are content to work on the opposite shore. Taking the single mental act as their as yet unexplained and unexplainable starting point, they have made substantial progress toward an understanding of the laws which govern many different types of mental activity, such as the process of learning. But just as the individual mental act is too complex a unit to be explained by the laws of physiology, an individual human personality is in turn too complex a unit to be explained purely in terms of the presently available laws of experimental psychology. The result is another gulf and another specialization, psychiatry, which tries by the tracing of case histories to throw light on the particular idiosyncrasies and problems of individual human beings. Each movement along this sequence from physiology to psychiatry is marked by a progressive increase in the complexity of the subject matter of the discipline in question; a single mental act is a synthesis of countless physiological events, while a single human personality is a synthesis of countless mental acts. With each increase in the complexity of the subject matter goes a corresponding drop in the rigor and objectivity of the methods used; physiologists insist on all the refinements of an advanced laboratory science, experimental psychologists run largely to questionnaires and statistical correlations, while the pronouncements of psychiatrists are often pure poetry. But this does not prevent the three specializations from existing side by side, and contributing each in its own way to our knowledge of the human mind.

In political science the position of the historians of political thought is comparable to that of the psychiatrists in the field of psychology. Social groups, like individuals, have histories and traumatic experiences which greatly affect, for good or for ill, their ability to perceive and to cope with current realities. The anticlerical passion which has done so much to complicate the political recovery of postwar France is a classic case of neurotic behavior with causes deep-rooted in the past. The function of the student of ideologies, like that of the experienced psychiatrist, is to throw light on the present idiosyncrasies of the patient by unraveling the intricacies of his personal history. Just as the psychiatrist must proceed from the fragmentary and deceptive verbalizations of his patient's conscious mind to the more complex levels of subconscious experience, so must his political confrere use the potentially misleading but indispensable statements of political theorists, whose awareness of political matters is uncommonly acute, as a clue to the less fully articulate experiences and reactions of ordinary men. The dangers of the psychiatric method, with its heavy reliance on tact and intuitive insight, are obvious, and it is undoubtedly true that a psychoanalysis may reveal more about the analyst than about the subject. The historical approach to problems of political ideology is equally perilous. In both cases, however, the results achieved by competent practitioners throw genuine light on the nature of genuine problems. In the absence of any more effective technique for the handling of such problems, the psychiatric method has perforce to be accepted as an indispensable resource of modern psychology. The historical method must occupy a position of like importance for all those who are interested in the problem of political thought.

But if political scientists are condemned for the foreseeable future to divide their attention between historical and behavioral studies, there is no reason why this should not, in a real rather than in a cold-war sense, be a case of peaceful coexistence. Here again the example of psychology can be helpful. There was a time not so very long ago when experimental psychologists and psychiatrists were consumed by mutual animosities, and disdained to learn anything from each other. This attitude has been largely dissipated of late, and psychiatrists in particular are increasingly aware of the fact that physiologists and experimental psychologists, though unable as yet to construct a clinically useful picture of a single human personality, have many important things to contribute toward that end. The situation in political science is essentially the same. To develop a corresponding degree of mutual understanding should be a prime objective of all those who are trying, each in his own way, to throw light on the ideological components of political behavior.

ROBERT G. MC CLOSKEY

American Political Thought and the Study of Politics

THE TITLE of this essay poses not one vexing issue but two, and each of them sharply challenges the student of American political thought. To begin with, the title presents us with what might be called the common problem of political theory—the question of its relevance to the institutional facts of life. How, it is asked, can the analysis of political ideas help to illuminate our understanding of political action? Can theory lead us to a surer knowledge of why government and electorates behave as they do? Can it help us to diagnose and prescribe? Or is the study of theory, on the contrary, justified simply on the ground that the words of Plato and Hobbes and Locke are part of what Matthew Arnold called culture: "the best that has been thought or known in the world"? This is, I take it, a problem universal among students of political thought, whether they choose America, Europe, or China as their realm; and it lends itself to no easy answers.

When the realm is America, however, a second issue is presented—what may be described as the special problem of American political thought—and surely no reflective student of the subject has been untroubled by it. The difficulty, to be downright, is that American political thinkers have not often produced works that rank with the best that has been thought or known in the world's intellectual history. The scholar in the European field can hedge the question of relevance by arguing that the *Republic* is worth reading and pondering for its own sake, and that it is no more necessary to seek some utilitarian justification for doing so than it is to justify reading *Othello*. Or he may, even better, insist that Plato is both relevant to an understanding of ancient and modern politics *and* intrinsically self-warranting; and he may thus rest his case with two feet firmly planted. Such a course of argument is not really open to the student of American political thinking. He must stand on the leg of relevance if he is to stand at all.

The implied depreciation of American political thought may seem a little strong, but it is actually no more than extension of the commonplace that we have not as a people been much given to philosophizing about government. We have talked about it a great deal; we have even, in a certain sense, done a lot of thinking about it. But it has not been characteristic of Americans to concern themselves with the stratosphere of political speculation, and the result among others is that our soil has bred no Hobbes, no Locke, no Marx, no Rousseau. The *Federalist* has been much praised both at home and abroad, and it is surely a wise book; but can it really be arrayed with the great political literature of the western world? If so, it is strange that the secondary work concerned with it has been so scanty, that no book *about* the *Federalist* has, as far as I know, been published. Jefferson is surely the patron saint of the American political tradition; we start from Jefferson as the medievals started from Aristotle. But sage and eloquent though he often was, Jefferson could hardly be called a great political philosopher. It is no accident that he never wrote a systematic book about his political ideas (the *Notes on Virginia* certainly cannot so qualify) and that the valiant attempt by Wiltse to piece together a philosophy of government from Jefferson's scattered writing is unsatisfying.[1] Calhoun has been rediscovered in comparatively recent times and decked out in a philosopher's regalia, but the fit is not a very happy one at best. Lay his *Disquisition* beside any of the indubitably great works of Western political thought, and its glitter fades at once.

It is probably considerations like these that help explain the inchoate quality of American political thought when it is viewed as a branch of the political scientist's discipline. Good books have been written in the area, but many are weakened by the paradox that they attempt to deal with political philosophy in a field where there are no political philosophers. They endeavor to transmute able statesmen and learned judges into something else; they try to focus the lenses appropriate to the study of European political theory on a subject whose dimensions are quite different. The result is not only to distort the subject, but in a way to trivialize it. If we approach Jefferson with the same frame of reference we apply to Rousseau, we are missing the point of both Jefferson in particular and American political thought in general. Moreover, we are inviting an unmerited disparagement of Jefferson and his importance. We are encouraging the judgment, common enough among students of European theory, that American political thought is a "peripheral" subject.

This pronouncement is surely in error. But it is equally certain that the dilemma presented in the foregoing paragraphs is real. We cannot argue that the justification for studying American political thought is self-evident, like the truths in the Declaration of Independence. If the conventionally convenient man from Mars were in search of examples of human thought at its most profound, one could hardly recommend that he spend as much time on Hamilton and Madison as he spent on Plato and Hegel. One would certainly not send him to Andrew Jackson instead of Cicero, unless there were reasons for persuading him that humanity's political thinking remained on a surprisingly rudimentary level even at its best and even after some 3000 years of recorded practice.

But if he wanted to understand the government of the United States as it has been and is, that might be quite another matter. For these men and others like them made the American government both with their thoughts and with their hands. Hamilton not only laid down a conceptual base for American nationalism in such papers as his opinion on the Bank of the United States; he deftly maneuvered in the battleground of practical politics to make that conception a reality. Madison not only propounded a theory of American political behavior in the famous Federalist Paper Number 10; he played a crucial role in setting a pattern for the way the domestic political animal does behave. Jackson not only gave voice to the dreams and prejudices of a burgeoning democratic movement; he also gave the movement shrewd and skillful political leadership. Profound philosophers they were not; but they were something perhaps equally vital—they were architects of American political institutions and of the American political mind.

However, the significance of such men does not rise wholly from this creative part they played in history. They also performed an important "reflective" function. Thus they provide us with a double clue to the compre-

hension of American political mores, since they mirrored the thought of the
nation as well as helping to guide it. And they reflected the mind of America
all the more faithfully precisely because they were not giants of western
intellectual history, because they did not stand too far above the level of
their times. Franklin, John Adams, Jefferson, Madison, Marshall, Jackson,
Calhoun, Lincoln, Theodore Roosevelt, Woodrow Wilson—these were all
extraordinary men by any standard, but no one of them was exceptional in
such a way as to be out of touch with the American grain. All shared
to a considerable extent the prevailing ideas and prejudices that could be
found as common coin among their less articulate countrymen. They were
leaders and writers, but they were also reasonable facsimiles of the American
political man.

Some of them, of course, fill this bill more neatly than others. Jefferson,
for all his brilliant versatility, in spite of his certified membership card in
the heavenly city of the *philosophes,* was so American that a catalog of his
qualities is itself a political history of the nation. Even his ambiguity and in-
consistency, so troublesome to his greatest admirers, were archtypical; for
the nation, like Jefferson, has never quite been able to make up its mind
about the major problems of political philosophy. Hamilton and Calhoun
were somewhat more special perhaps, but neither was really esoteric; and
they both represented important elements in the stream of national political
doctrine. As for Roosevelt and Wilson—the strenuous colonel and the as-
tringent professor—they were, each in his own way, as indigenous as a
revival meeting.

I would not be understood as suggesting that we can learn about a nation
only from those who approximate its norm. Henry Adams was a *rara avis*
in the American scene; so was Veblen; so was Irving Babbitt. Yet their
insights have helped us to comprehend ourselves. Indeed it is probably
safe to say that no one has contributed as much to our political self-knowl-
edge as two foreign observers, Tocqueville and Lord Bryce. Moreover, it
is of course true that a full understanding of America must involve an
understanding of the rest of the world as well. "What know they of England
who only England know?" Mr. Kipling once asked; and the query is no less
pertinent when applied to America.

But I do agrue that our more conventional thinkers can lead us to a level
of understanding about our political character that no other source could
duplicate, partly as has been said because they helped create that character
and partly because they reflected it in their own words and deeds. It would
be a great mistake to imagine that a grasp of Louis Armstrong is equivalent
to a full understanding of American music, but it would be similar nonsense
to believe that he and others like him could be left out of account or to deny
that they had something unique to tell us. Milton teaches us something
about America that cannot be found in Mark Twain; but it is also true that

Huckleberry Finn catches an essence that we would seek in vain in the pages of *Paradise Lost*.

All this may smack of turning a necessity into a virtue. The student of American political thought is confronted with the obstinate fact that its spokesmen are not immortal philosophers. He is therefore thrust into a position which requires him to discover in these spokesmen some significance beyond themselves, some relevance to another range of inquiry. And he finds by a happy coincidence that their very inadequacy as philosophers is a left-handed attribute, that although they can teach him less about absolute truth, they can teach him more about America. Specifically, they can lead him towards an understanding of the operative political mind of America and of the governmental institutions which that mind has created.

The answer is that seeming faults do sometimes turn out, upon examination, to be virtues and that it is the part of wisdom to assay every vein of ore most carefully before abandoning it as unpromising. Yet it is not enough to say what has so far been said. One may feel that it is important to uncover the operative ideals of American politics and that the words of the nation's statesmen will furnish an important guidepost to that objective. One may also feel that these operative ideals, once understood, will augment our perception of how America is governed. But nothing is more familiar and more dissatisfying in the social studies than the vague feeling that there is a relationship between two sets of facts if we could only recognize the bridge that connects them. We are sometimes told, for example, that the insights of modern psychology can greatly enlighten the field of political science, and this may be quite true. But the excursions across the lines of these two disciplines have not yet, so far as I can see, irradiated much except the obvious; and even those who take a more generous view of the matter will probably agree that the map of the route is still somewhat primitive.

The point is not to belittle cross-disciplinary ventures as such but to emphasize the fact that such projects are not self-executing. It is not enough to suggest that there may be a road from Ghent to Aix; the road must be found before the good news can be delivered. To revert to the matter in hand, the student of American political thought needs not only a belief in its relevance to practical politics; he needs a method, an approach, which will help him to establish what the relevancies are. And surely this sought-for approach must disclose something more subtle than the obvious cause-effect relationships of intellectual history. A Madison composes the Virginia Resolutions; his composition gives comfort in the future to the proponents of both nullification and secession. There is patently a connection here, and it is important to know about it; but this is only the surface layer of analysis, the starting-point rather than the conclusion of the inquiry. Does the fact that Madison, who wrote the Virginia Resolutions, also helped author the

Federalist tell us anything about the nature of American political opinion? Do the Virginia Resolutions and their reception help explain the general American attitude towards national-state relations? Can we integrate the Resolutions, not only with the Civil War, but with the phenomenon of modern federalism? If so, the study of them has a plain bearing on the problems of modern politics. If not, their significance remains largely anti-quarian.

The approach to the subject here proposed is doubtless only one of the several modes of entry, yet it is one that seems most likely to develop the potential relevancies of the material, to narrow the gap between the "political scientist" strictly so-called and the student of political ideas. Compendiously stated, the suggestion is that the study of American political thought would be more meaningful if it were rooted in the study of existent American political institutions, that such a blending of ideas and things would bring us closer to an understanding of both. Daniel Boorstin, with a somewhat different objective in mind, comes very close to what is meant here when he speaks of bringing to the surface the ideas about democracy which are "latent" in the institutions by which we have actually lived.[2] Inherent in these institutions, he argues, we can see the operative political ideas that make up the American political ethos. The present suggestion, to go a step farther, is that the idea thus delineated will in turn help to clarify the nature of the institutions, and that the study of American political thought can thereby become an important step in the process of political analysis.

Now, of course, there is nothing either startling or original in the bald recommendation that institutions and theory should be studied concurrently, and indeed the pious hope that they will be so studied lies behind almost every Ph.D. curriculum in the political science field. But it is hoped that the approach here advocated can carry a little beyond such standard optimism and open up the possibility that the marriage may actually take place. Such an aspiration requires that the notion be spelled out a little more particularly and that its implications be examined with some care.

In the first place, it must be noted that the proposal conceals a premise—that American political institutions do, in a general way, reflect the American political mind, that we can come close to discovering the concensus of the American community by pondering her governmental forms. Of course, in a broad sense this is true of any nation; institutions seldom if ever spring full-panoplied from the head of some master legislator, and we can always learn something about a people from the way they are governed. But the suggestion is that the correspondence between political arrangements and national presuppositions is especially striking in the case of America. If we attempted to find the dominant political concepts of Germany embodied in her political institutions, for example, we might be puzzled by the discrepancies between the Weimar Republic and the Nazi dictatorship, even though we were at the same time enlightened by certain threads of consistency that might be observed. But America, as Boorstin has also perceived, is a horse of another color. It is, paradoxically in the light of its supposed revolutionary origins, one of the most "Burkean" of nations. At least since 1789, its major institutions of government have undergone no sudden or radical changes, but rather have adapted gradually to new circumstances and new attitudes as the occasions might require. The presidency, the Congress, the Supreme Court, the party system, the pattern of national-state-relationships have all been altered by time in varying degrees; but the shifts have been slow and evolutionary, not abrupt. Even the Civil War, which seemed to tear the nation apart, worked surprisingly little instant transfiguration of America's basic political forms. In most ways the modification produced was less startling than that produced in English politics by the passage of the Reform Bill; and it cannot be remotely compared to the cataclysmic upheavals that history recognizes as truly revolutionary.

It must be emphasized, moreover, that these gradual developments in American politics have been the product of organic growth and not deliberate contrivance. Again the results of the Civil War are in point. Some of those who framed the "war amendments" to the Constitution undoubtedly hoped that with one stroke they would destroy the old system of intergovernmental relations and substitute a new doctrine of national supervision. But the failure of that ambition is notorious, and it was ultimately not the Joint Committee on Reconstruction but history that determined how the nation and the states would live together. Similarly, the development of the presidency since its low point of prestige under Johnson has been not a purposeful advance but a series of *ad hoc* adjustments to circumstances as they arose. In short, our political institutions, like many other features of our nation, have been shaped in that "pragmatic" spirit which has so often been described as characteristically American. And exactly because we have been a pragmatic people, because our political alterations have been piecemeal and contingent, it is reasonable to argue that the institutions so produced bear a close correspondence to the actual American mind. Had we been a more philosophical nation, had it been in our nature to commit ourselves to abstract principles, the result might have been quite different. For principles often have a self-propelling quality. They generate, so to speak, a mind of their own. In America, unburdened by such semi-independent variables, it has been possible for political forms to fit themselves more faithfully to the contours of national opinion.

In the second place, the approach here advocated does imply on the other hand that political ideas have institutional consequences, that what Americans have thought about politics has played a significant part in determining what politics would be. The questions that might be begged by this assumption are too many and complex to be argued in detail in a paper of this kind. But it should be pointed out that the contention, taken in the broad sense, requires no very great act of faith on the part of the reader. That ideas on some level help account for the nature and composition of such an institution as the American Congress would seem a truism beyond serious dispute. Whether those ideas are the mere reflex of interest calculations; which of them, if any, have the tensile strength to persist in the face of adversity; whether they are explicitly or tacitly held; whether they are shared generally or cherished only by an influential majority—these are problems whose answers might be found at the end of the suggested inquiry, rather than at its beginning. For the present it is only necessary to assert that our institutions have in some way been moulded by the ideas we have had.

In the third place, it should be observed that the argument so far advanced does not preclude the idea that institutions have a certain persistence value, that once established they tend to survive, enjoying a degree of autonomous existence in spite of shifting currents of opinion. This familiar truth is, however, in the nature of a signpost, warning the student to be alert against the error of mistaking yesterday's mind for today's. It does not vitiate the assertion that operative ideals shaped our institutions in their inception and are continually reshaping them as the course of history proceeds. Only the most sterile analysis could rest content with the notion that the institution of judicial review, for example, is accounted for by the circumstances of its origination in a horse-and-buggy age and its perpetuation through inertia ever since. If the Supreme Court had not reflected a vital and continuing element in American thought, it could not have survived the vicissitudes of the Marshall period, much less the Dred Scott decision, the self-inflicted wounds of the 1895 term, and the agonizing reappraisal of the New Deal era. Whether judicial review as we know it today is the creation of ourselves or our fathers is another matter; but it is surely not wholly the creation of our remote ancestors. Its own corporate will-to-survive has helped to preserve the Court; but it has also been protected and nurtured by the climate of American opinion.

Finally, it must be understood that while this approach is asserted to be broadly and generally valid, no more than that is claimed. The idea is not that going institutions always and exactly and automatically reflect the mind of America, either past or present, but that they can provide an extremely important clue to a comprehension of that mind. A multitude of scholarly problems involving discriminatory judgments will still remain. Room must be made in any analysis for anomalies and anachronisms. Some institutions—the "no establishment of religion clause" of the First Amendment before 1947 might be a fair example—can hardly tell us much about modern American thought for the sufficient reason that almost no one has, for a

long time, done any thinking about them. Each purported relationship between institution and idea must be evaluated with care before it can be
regarded as established. Neither is it suggested that the true relationship is
always, or even often, the obvious one. A naive application of this approach
might, for instance, lead to the conclusion that Americans in general are
passionately devoted to bicameralism as a political idea, because of the
prevalence of two-house legislatures in the United States. A more searching
inquiry might reveal that bicameralism is merely the fortuitous expression of
a vaguer and deeper political premise—perhaps the idea that two cooks
make better broth than one; perhaps the idea that both geography and numbers deserve representation; perhaps the simple but by no means insignificant
idea that traditional forms are best in the absence of overwhelming evidence to the contrary. In short, the proposal to unite the study of American
theory and the study of American institutions probably brings up as many
questions as it answers; but it may at least insure that the questions asked
are pertinent and real.

Among several possible objections that might be raised to the approach
here prescribed, two may warrant special attention. For one thing, it might
be asked why it is worthwhile to study individual thinkers at all. That is,
if the political mind of America is latent in its institutions, why not focus
on the institutions, draw the appropriate inferences from them, and leave
Jefferson, Hamilton, and Company to those who are concerned with intellectual history *per se?* The answer is that individual thinkers may articulate the latent prejudices and ideas that govern American politics, thus helping to give them form and making them easier for the student to identify.
The historian of the future, for example, may well be grateful to a modern
Secretary of Defense for some off-hand remarks he made in the 1954 campaign about various kinds of dogs. Without his statement a scholar in the
year 2000 might imagine that American political thought in the 1950's was
quite devoid of the "rugged individualist" bias that so captivated the nation
in earlier days, that both parties and all shades of opinion were united in
their admiration for the workingman in the service state. Or, to take a somewhat more serious example, Lincoln's expressed opinion that it was more
important to save the Union than to free the slaves or punish the South
confirms the belief that a moderate pro-Unionist sentiment underlay the
extremism of conflicting factions in the Civil War and helps explain the
modus vivendi that was worked out when Reconstruction Era fevers had
cooled. Without an understanding of men like Lincoln and Alexander Ste-
phens an observer might gain the impression that the nation's conflicts
were utterly irreconcilable, and the famous "deal" of 1876 would have
seemed impossible. Again, Jackson's veto message on the Bank Renewal
Bill helps explain that curious blend of mistrust towards great wealth and
tolerance of its inevitability that is documented in the American regulatory

system. The paradoxes of that system are no doubt implicit in its structure, but knowledge of Jackson's attitude toward capitalism is an aid in recognizing and understanding them.

Another question that might be posed is whether the suggested approach to American political thought involves the ignoring or rejecting of ethical considerations as an aspect of political theory. Does it presuppose that whatever is is right, by postulating a sort of American general will which ratifies and thus justifies all existing institutional arrangements? The question is not entirely rhetorical. If it is assumed that the American mind has created American governmental forms, then it might seem to follow that those forms were best calculated to express what the American people needed and desired. A suggestion to change them might appear both futile and undemocratic.

But of course it is always open to argue that the popular will has erred, even when it has spoken unmistakably. Moreover, there is plenty of room for hoping that cogent argument can succeed in working changes both in the American mind and in American institutions by stimulating the revaluation of ill-considered convictions. The proposition here advanced is that American political institutions are shaped by the American mind, but not that the mind itself is a changeless entity. New circumstances may require new applications of old premises or alteration of the premises themselves. It would be hard to argue, for example, that American opinion has yet worked out a viable attitude towards political interest groups and that the modern "polity of pressure groups," as Lippmann has called our contemporary institutional setup, reflects exactly what America wants. The truth may well be that America does not yet know what it wants in the area of group political representation, and much ink might be usefully spilled in realistic public analysis of the problem. In this, as in a multitude of other fields, the American political mind is in flux, and the question of "ought" may be just as important as the question of "is." On the other hand, the realization that political institutions do bear an organic relationship to American thought may help to guarantee that prescriptions for change strike somewhere near the boundaries of probability, will serve to remind us that there is a "given" ideological factor which must be taken into account and that problems in political science are not analogous to problems in engineering. Some of the proposals for constitutional reform that sprinkled the literature of the field a few years ago might have been more helpful, if less spectacular, had they recognized the necessity of coping with the rooted political convictions of the nation.

This brings us back, almost squarely, to the point at which this paper began. Suppose, for the sake of argument, that all the propositions thus far set forth are acceptable. Concede that American political thinkers have not been great philosophers, but that they have performed both a creative and a reflective function in the history of American politics. Concede that American political institutions have been formed by an entity which has been loosely called the American political mind and that the lineaments of that mind can thus be traced through the study of institutions. Concede that it does therefore make sense to approach the field of American political thought in these terms—to seek out, as Boorstin puts it, the ideas latent in the institutions. How, it may still be asked, does this answer the question of relevancy as it was originally propounded? What are the implications of the approach, not only for the better understanding of American thought, but for the better understanding of empirical institutions? Can the insights the approach makes available help us to comprehend and even predict the course of contemporary political behavior? Is the method which is valuable to the intellectual historian also of use to the political scientist?

The reply to these questions is already fairly plain. The study proposed, if successful, should enrich political analysis by widening its horizons and giving them a surer contour. The more deeply we comprehend the forces that shape our institutions, the better we should be equipped to describe their present nature and forecast future development. To take a currently familiar example: Much of the criticism of President Eisenhower during his first years in office centered around the charge that he had failed to provide strong executive leadership, *i.e.* that he had not gathered the reins of administration firmly into his hands, that he had not attempted to dominate and direct Congress. With the merits of this criticism we are not here concerned, and it may or may not be true that the President's assumption of a comparatively passive role cost America a heavy price. But what does seem true is that the indictment is almost meaningless as a political lever for his opponents. There is good reason to believe that a study of the presidency as an institution would reveal a strong popular conviction that the president *should* don just such a robe of grandfatherly benignity under conditions like those Mr. Eisenhower faced, and that those who would unseat him had better look for other tools. Whether this judgment is right or wrong, the illustration does indicate the importance of knowing what Americans in general, rather than the Committee on Administrative Management, have thought the presidency should be. Such knowledge is a matter of direct and practical political significance.

Yet—the question naturally presents itself—is not the task here described already performed for political science with full adequacy? Is it not proposed to substitute a conjectural and intuitive method for evaluating the public mind in place of the highly developed and relatively precise techniques of opinion analysis that have been evolved in recent years? The answer is that no pretense is made to usurp the role of opinion measurement, which will of course continue to provide the political scientist with irreplaceable data. But it is contended that the suggested approach can supply important corroborative and supplemental insights and thus enlarge the range of political understanding. Polling methods cannot by their very nature tell us much about what Americans *have* thought; *i.e.* they cannot often separate the traditional from the transitory in American opinion. And it may be very important to identify our ideologic constancies if we are to estimate the intensity of public convictions. Moreover, polling always faces the difficulty that it is asking men to analyze their own attitudes and to predict their own course of conduct. It is a commonplace that there may be a great difference between how and why men think they will behave and how and why they actually do behave. Thus the inquiry here suggested may tell us something about the "real will" of America which is only partially discoverable by other means.

The variety and scope of the analytic possibilities inherent in this approach to the study of American political thought are nearly endless, and it could serve no very useful purpose to list them. However, it may be worth while to attempt a couple of experimental forays into the field in order to see how the method might be handled and to determine what light it can shed on the problems of political action. Those ventures must of course be suggestive rather than definitive, so as to avoid extending unduly the confines of this paper, but they may illustrate better than abstract exposition can the nature of the proposal.

Let us consider, for a start, the concept of due procedure in American constitutional law; or more specifically the "due process clause" of the Federal Constitution. What can the contemplation of this institutional phenomenon tell us about the attributes of the American mind, about the latent premises of American political theory? To recapitulate here the long and familiar "due process" chapter in American history would be both wearisome and gratuitious, but certain features of the tale deserve to be underlined. For one thing, it is noteworthy that the most effective and far-reaching substantive check on governmental power yet devised in our legal system—the due process clause of the Fifth and Fourteenth Amendments—entered the Constitution through a door marked "procedure" and that a certain confusion as to whether it was concerned with substantive or procedural liberty has persisted from first to last. Indeed a careful examination of legal decisions in the heyday of the due process clause suggests that what students have called "substantive due process" was in the minds of the judges more like a widened concept of procedure. Surely they almost never admitted frankly that they were weighing the objectives of governmental policy rather than the manner of its accomplishment, and they tirelessly probed challenged legislation to discover elements which would smack of procedural irregularity.

Another point worth observing is that when the Supreme Court was finally persuaded in the 1930's to abandon due process as a substantive limit on economic legislation, it nevertheless still continued to maintain procedural guaranties in the economic field and so maintains them to this day. Still a third significant fact is that modern American legislation aimed at restricting substantive liberty is often peppered with so many procedural safeguards as to raise a serious question that the laws can accomplish their repressive purpose. A prime example is the Internal Security Act of 1950, the so-called McCarran Act, which in spite of its author's indubitable hostility toward communism and related menaces, reads like a parody of the law's delays. And finally there is the circumstance that the Court's recent doctrinal path in connection with that same problem of internal subversion has been distinguished by a uniform acquiescence to governmental power where substantive freedom was concerned but by a tendency to hold the line more firmly when procedural rights were in question. One of the latest manifestations of this judicial viewpoint is to be found in Mr. Justice Frank-furter's majority opinion in *Galvan v. Press* which holds that the substantive power of Congress to deal with aliens is virtually unlimited, although in enforcing the law "the Executive Branch of the Government must respect the procedural safeguards of due process." [3] Indeed, the opinions of this Justice constitute in themselves an impressive documentation of the point here being made, for they disclose a pervasive concern for procedural niceties coupled with broad tolerance of substantive inhibitions on freedom.

The foregoing generalizations provide us of course with only the sketchiest description of due process as an American institution, and the dissection would have to be carried much farther if we hoped to arrive at secure results. However, the outlines that are revealed may be plain enough to warrant a tentative judgment or two about the nature of the political mind that gave this institution its being.

What the description may suggest is that the American concern for pro-cedural rights runs deeper and steadier than the concern for substantive liberty. Indeed, so far as it goes the evidence implies that freedom in the obvious sense of liberty to think and speak and act unhindered holds no very favored place in the American hierarchy of political values. Naturally, Americans like everyone else are in favor of such liberty for themselves (*i.e.* the corner grocer is opposed to price control for corner grocers) and even for others if there are no important chips on the table. But when the stakes become fairly high—in times of stress—we seem remarkably quick to master our quenchless thirst for liberty. On the other hand, we tend to cling to the concept of procedural regularity a good deal more obstinately.

It is not for a moment intimated that there is something trivial or ignoble in this American preoccupation with process as contrasted with substance. As Mr. Justice Jackson has said:

Only the untaught layman or the charlatan lawyer can answer that procedures matter not. Procedural fairness and regularity are of the indispensable essence of liberty. Severe substantive laws can be endured if they are fairly and impartially applied. Indeed, if put to the choice, one might well prefer to live under Soviet substantive law applied in good faith by our common-law procedures than under our substantive law enforced by Soviet procedural practices.[4]

At its best due procedure is synonymous with the bright ideal of fair play, and it lies very close to the heart of the rule of law. But it is important to note what procedural fastidiousness is not as well as what it is. It is not a manifestation of the kind of spirit that makes revolutions or libertarian crusades. It is the attribute of an essentially conservative, order-loving character. The procedural-minded individual is likely to be drawn to the usual, the respectable, the orthodox in human behavior; and to be repelled by the eccentric, the fervent, the extreme.

Now if this is, as I believe, a reasonably accurate estimate of one aspect of American political belief, what practical conclusions might it lead to? Possible inferences crowd to mind at once. Might it not be surmised, for example, that those who would check the repressive tendencies which have been popularly called "McCarthyist" are more likely to succeed if they focus on guarding procedural right than if they rest their case on the pure ground of freedom of opinion? The observation was commonly heard during his heyday that it was not the objectives of the Wisconsin Senator, but his methods, that deserved censure, and one suspects that this judgment, infuriating though it might be to some, largely accounts for the lapse in his fortunes. A related point has to do with the predictable behavior of the American judiciary and the public reaction to that behavior. Can we not hazard the guess that our courts will in times of stress bow to the legislature on substantive issues and limit their supervisory activities to the procedural field, and that this discrimination between the two kinds of rights will be supported by public opinion?

A fuller comprehension of the American obsession with procedure might also be useful to those who are interested in the problem of administrative action and judicial review. A few years ago there was much enthusiasm for the project of minimizing judicial control of administration, and its advocates often appeared both surprised and aggrieved that the tradition of court supervision was so tenacious. Its tenacity can be partly explained by the procedural bias that has been noted here, and both labor and disappointment might have been spared if policy formulators had realized how deeply rooted this bias is in the American political temperament. Rightly or wrongly, Americans tend to think of courts as the symbols of procedural fairness, and any proposal to define administrative-judicial relationships must reckon with this conviction.

The same conviction helps account for the first serious political setback of Franklin Roosevelt's presidency, and again it can be argued that the contretemps might have been foreseen and forestalled if those responsible had seriously considered the implications of American legal history. The court-packing plan of 1937 seemed to be based on the assumption that the doctrine of judicial control was an illogical carry-over from a simpler age and the Supreme Court's conflict with the indisputably popular New Deal had destroyed its prestige in the eyes of the nation. The outcome of the controversy demonstrated, however, that American attachment to the institution was more fundamental than many had suspected; and it may be suggested that this detachment was due in no small part to the general feeling that the court is the champion of orderly procedure in a chaotic world. Here was an instance then when knowledge of the premises of American political thought might have been a matter of immediate practical relevance.

ANOTHER AMERICAN institution which could be profitably considered in these terms is federalism, a particularly appropriate choice, first, because it represents perhaps the most ambiguous of American political ideas; and, second, because it provides us with a good example of how the study of individual political thinkers can aid the understanding of a contemporary political form. One of the most impressive facts about this institution in America is its incoherency. Any attempt to describe in general terms the pattern of national-state relations is foredoomed to collapse in the face of stubborn contradictions. Not even the modest generalization that nationally significant functions are assigned to national control can survive examination of the practical reality. American federalism is a patchwork quilt in which logic and uniformity seem to be largely ignored, a complex of *ad hoc* relationships replete with apparent inconsistencies.

This is also a fair enough description of federalism when we view it historically. In spite of his temperamental devotion to the nationalist principle, John Marshall bequeathed a commerce clause doctrine whose essence seemed to be that some matters should be handled by the nation and some by the states, an unexceptionable but not very enlightening conclusion. The Court under Taney made some effort to clarify this ambiguity, but the tortuous history of the so-called "Cooley Rule" suggests that it accomplished little more than to substitute one equivocation for another. Meanwhile the enigmatic character of federalism in legal terms was matched by federalism in practice. The national government would sometimes assume certain functions, but at the same time analogous matters would be left undisturbed in the hands of the states. Even more baffling to the logician, the very functions undertaken by the nation would often be handled by the states *concur-*

rently and without much discernible concern on either side for drawing a palpable line of distinction. The result was a vast confusion, but it was also —and the point is important—a *modus operandi*.

The ideological assumptions that can be inferred from this perplexing network of relationships are themselves inevitably ambiguous, but they are no less instructive for that. The evidence suggests that the American attitude towards federalism consists of the rather vague and certainly nondogmatic idea that it is best to maintain a fair balance between central and local authorities and that this balance is a value in its own right. However, the evidence also seems to imply that this value, though real, is far from absolute, and that it is traversed and modified by the concomitant notion that the distribution of powers is a practical arrangement for getting things done. That these two premises are ultimately contradictory has never seemed to disturb Americans unduly, and it should not greatly disturb us. In fact it is just in connection with this point that the study of individual thinkers becomes illuminating. Writing at the time of the Civil War, Lord Acton observed that the American federal system was not founded on principles but on "momentary suspensions of war between opposite principles, neither of which could prevail." [5] It followed, he thought, that the development of the nation would deepen tensions and that the resulting conflicts would unavoidably destroy the Union. What he failed to reckon with was the American capacity to assimilate inconsistencies and live with them.

This capacity was never more admirably illustrated than in the career and thought of Thomas Jefferson, and his attitude towards federalism goes far to explain the attitude that has been characteristic of his countrymen. The circumstances of political life in his times made it inevitable that most of his pronouncements on the issue of federalism would have a states' right flavor. But his actions when President, as for example in connection with the Louisiana Purchase and Embargo, frequently seemed to contravene these stated principles and certainly revealed that his devotion to them was by no means doctrinaire. The disaffection of "Pure Republicans" such as Randolph and John Taylor was summarized by Randolph's charge that the President simply spelled Federalist backwards; to such men Jefferson's ambivalence looked like hypocrisy.

However, the truth was that for Jefferson the states' rights ideal enjoyed that equivocal status in which most Americans seem to have held it throughout our history; that is, for him, as for Americans generally, it was a contingent and tentative doctrine which could be readily modified by practical considerations. But the important point is that these modifications did not mean that the doctrine itself was abandoned, as strict logic might appear to require. After his nationalist apostasies while President, Jefferson could with perfect equanimity retire to Monticello and from that vantage point proceed to hurl thunderbolts against the minions of nationalism. By the same token,

Americans in the 150 years that followed were able to support accretions of national power on pragmatic grounds while continuing to cherish the concept of federal balance. The practical result has been a national government whose powers are reasonably commensurate with its tasks, but whose assertions of power have had to overcome a presumption against them. Acknowledging exceptions, this nevertheless seems to have proved a pretty effective way to cope with the problems of a federal republic.

Of the numerous practical inferences that might be drawn from this institutional and ideological material, it is perhaps especially worth dwelling on one or two which have to do with America's participation in world affairs. The story of American federalism gives us a basis for suggesting, for example, that perfervid statements about the sacred principle of sovereignty need not be taken overseriously in themselves, so long as they are not backed by a well-grounded appeal to concrete interests. A closely related point is that we should be especially careful in this field of mistaking what Americans say for what they do. It was neither Hamilton nor John Taylor of Carolina but Jefferson who became the American President and whose ambiguous federalism was stamped with the approval of his generation. It follows that those who seek to bring about America's participation in projects for international control and even world government would be well-advised to settle for a vague commitment at the outset and to trust history to define the reality. It seems very unlikely indeed that the American Constitution would have been ratified if it had been clear that the national government enjoyed the powers claimed for it by Marshall in *McCulloch v. Maryland*. Yet that decision came only thirty years after ratification, and in spite of the furor from Virginia and neighboring points it was soon the law of the land. A nation which can thus pragmatically drift towards centralism may similarly drift towards world government. But it would be a serious error to try at first to impose a rigidly logical formula upon a nation whose very life principle has been ambiguity.

THE FOREGOING paragraphs are meant only to illustrate in a tentative way the kind of insights that might be discoverable through the approach to American political thought that has been proposed. Unquestionably the inquiries should be driven much deeper and quite possibly the conclusions drawn from the material are subject to doubt. Nevertheless, I hope that they do point the direction one might follow in order to find more reliable answers, and that they go a little way towards resolving the issue with which this paper has been chiefly concerned. The study of American political thought, as was said earlier, must find its major justification in relevancy. An approach which takes its starting point in living political institutions may help insure that objective will never be lost to view.

CARL J. FRIEDRICH

Political Philosophy and the Science of Politics[1]

THE DISCUSSION of the relation between political philosophy and political science has, especially among political scientists themselves, been confused with the problem of what might or might not be the contributions of older political philosophies to the study, presumably scientific, of politics. Lasswell, quoting Laski, observes that historically "such doctrines have chiefly served to justify the political philosopher's own preferences (and of course of the groups with which he identifies himself). Witness for instance Hegel's appraisal of the Prussian state as the highest embodiment of universal Reason."[2] Leaving aside both the question as to how accurate a description of Hegel's view this might be and just how representative Hegel is of political philosophy altogether, the view of Lasswell can be taken as fairly characteristic of a substantial section of present-day opinion in this matter.[3]

Political philosophy is seen as essentially the sequence of master expositions of political ideologies, rationalizations as it were of preconceived class or other interests. The two-barreled attack is leveled against political philosophy as at once normative and composed of outworn norms; its place is to be taken by nonnormative, value-free science. There can be no question that the history of political philosophy is, among other things what it is thus alleged to be: highfalutin propaganda;[4] but this undeniable fact does not preclude the possibility that it is also a record of various approximations to the truth, that is to say the true and within reason verifiable generalizations concerning established matters of fact. Plato may be wrong about many propositions he sets forth in the *Republic,* the *Statesman,* and the *Laws,* but is he wrong in insisting that the question of law and right is one which every political community faces, and that that question inevitably raises the issue of justice which in turn opens up the problems of what is a norm and what is a virtue?[5] Dissatisfaction with the answers Plato gave need not prevent us from recognizing that these problems are genuine or that the solutions Plato suggested contain at least partial truths.

But I do not in this paper wish to address myself to the question of the value of the history of political thought to political science (and to political philosophy). Let me just mention in passing that in arguing the value of

172

such past work on politics by philosophers and others, I would stress the continuous re-evaluation that the increase in historical knowledge brings. This need in no sense be a "great books" approach treating these labors of the past as something to be handled as a "given" akin to Biblical revelation.[6] What I am interested in is the nuggets of insight that can be gathered through the study of government and politics which such earlier works open up, as an antidote to the frog's perspective that a preoccupation with contemporary situations is likely to engender.

But political philosophy, truly speaking, is something else than the history of past political philosophies. It is that branch of philosophy and political science, in my understanding, by which the two are linked; it brings the main knowledge, both facts and generalizations, of political science into philosophy; and it brings the relevant aspects of philosophy to bear upon this knowledge.

A very important and ancient branch of political philosophy is legal philosophy. Indeed, at certain times, such as the Middle Ages and the eighteenth century, when central importance was attached to law, the two tended to merge into a doctrine of "natural law." These doctrines are universally acknowledged to be an important part of the history of political thought.[7] Hence, the bearing of philosophy upon law is germane to our subject. The relevance of general philosophy for legal science has been the subject of extended discussion among jurists during the last generation; names such as Duguit, del Vecchio, and Stammler at once conjure up the "revival of natural law" which is involved in this argument.[8] But in spite of the striking parallels between this discussion and our own topic, I shall abstain in the following pages from tracing the jurisprudential argument about the relation between legal science and legal philosophy further.

It is evident that a discussion of the relationship between political philosophy and the science of politics is dependent upon an understanding among the discussants about philosophy as well as about science. To raise this point is to plunge into the quagmire of highly controversial, indeed hopelessly controversial issues. For, to start with philosophy, there are so many philosophies, past and present, that any attempt at reaching agreement among even a small group of philosophers is out of the question. But if agreement on the kind of philosophy to adopt seems unlikely, perhaps there could be a measure of agreement on what philosophy is. But no sooner do we explore this possibility than we find that philosophers are sharply divided on this issue as well. If we go to the dictionaries where common usage is reported, as contemporary logicians tend to do, we find that "philosophy is the study or science of the truths or principles underlying all knowledge and being (or reality)" and also that it is "the study or science of the principles of a particular branch or subject of knowledge."[9] Another dictionary tells us that philosophy is "love of wisdom or knowledge, especially that which deals with ulti-

mate reality, or with the most general causes and principles of things." [10]
There are some important divergencies here; one speaks of study and
science, the other of knowledge and wisdom, but ultimate reality and the
principles of such reality are involved in both; philosophy appears to be
knowledge of a very general kind.

Can we leave it at that, or must we try to settle the issue? If we turn
to a survey of contemporary philosophy, such as Morton White's *The Age of
Analysis* (1955), we find the philosophers there reviewed to be diverging
widely on their definitions of philosophy. Thus, G. E. Moore suggested that
what philosophers have tried to do is "to give a general description of the
whole Universe." Onto this he tacked logic and ethics, as somehow also
being part of the universe. Russell, on the other hand, thought that "philosophy, throughout its history, has consisted of two parts, inharmoniously
blended: on the one hand a theory as to the nature of the world, on the
other an ethical or political doctrine as to the best way of living." If these
and similar characterizations are compared to the dictionary definitions
quoted above, it becomes clear that an empirical view of what philosophy is
would presuppose an answer to the question: how have philosophers be-
haved over the centuries, what have they done, written, said, in carrying on
whatever it was they were doing or thought they were doing? My own conclusion from such a review of past philosophizing, as an activity, is that they
have asked the most general questions which the prevailing state of knowledge permitted them to ask, and that some have done this by sticking to the
prevailing state of knowledge, while others went beyond it, asking "metaphysical" questions and trying to give answers to them either on rational or
on mystical-intuitional grounds.

Now it may be asserted that I should state my own conception of philosophy. That this is essential, in order to determine whether there is any real
distinction between philosophy and science, though arguable, seems to me
not at all clear. They certainly *have* been in the past, are at present, and
show every sign of being treated as distinct in the future. Would anyone confuse Merriam and Dewey, or Laski and Russell? Whether philosophy is defined in terms of an exploration of "ultimate reality" conceived as meta-
reality, or as the non-phenomenal world, or whether it be believed to be
occupied with methodological problems, that is to say the theory of theory
and related matters, it seems to me obviously distinct from, though by no
means unrelated to, the empirical realm of government and politics. But
what is science? If we turn to the dictionary once again, we find that science
is "a branch of knowledge or study dealing with a body of facts or truths
systematically arranged and showing the operation of general laws" or more
generally "knowledge, as of facts or principles, gained by systematic study,"
"a branch or body of organized knowledge." I believe that these latter definitions, while general enough, omit two very important aspects of all

sciences, namely (*a*) the agreement on method, and (*b*) the training of the human beings engaged in scientific work. I therefore submit to you that it would be more appropriate to define a science as "a body of ordered knowledge, known to and progressively enlarged by the specialists in that field of knowledge through the use of methods which they as a group accept as workable ways for arriving at that particular kind of knowledge." [11] It is this agreed-upon use of particular methods which distinguishes the scientist-scholar from the layman (and the charlatan) and which renders scientific statements capable of validation by other scholars. The methods, the ways of arriving at the result, allow all members of the fellowship of this particular science to retrace the steps which led to the statement, to re-examine the reported facts and to test the generalizations based upon them. It is this process which gives order and coherence to the progress of science and scholarship, indeed makes it possible. It is the *new* evidence, or the *new* generalization which occupies the fellowship of scholars in the particular field, receives detailed criticism and either wins out or is discarded. A scholar who challenges a well-established fact or a generally accepted theory (generalization) will accompany his proposition by evidence which fulfills the standards of accuracy and relevancy established in that field of learning. This means, among other things, familiarity with the existing literature and knowledge of possible counter-arguments. These propositions hold for all scientific work. They show that the agreement on methods of work is as symptomatic for a "science" as the "body of facts or truths" or "of principles"—that this agreement on methods is at the very core of what is meant when the definitions speak of a body of "organized" knowledge; it is organized, because it is given logical coherence to a degree as a result of the consistency of the methods employed in the gathering of the particular knowledge of that science. It is clear from these observations, or ought to be, that the different sciences are also distinguished from each other by their method, and that any suggestion that the method of one *should* be employed by another is suspect, until extensively tested and until shown to have produced significant results. While experiment may be the method in one, documentation in another, case analysis in a third, the results as assessed by the fellowship of the workers in the field remains the ultimate test.

All this is probably familiar enough, but I felt the need of establishing a firm basis of common understanding of "science" in general, before entering upon a discussion of the relationship between political philosophy and political science which is, of course, part of the more general problem of the relationship between philosophy and science. Indeed, something more needs to be said by way of clarification, as far as political science is concerned. I refer to the degree of generalization possible and the importance of it in scientific work. The striking successes which modern physics and chemistry achieved with quantitative methods have led a considerable number of people to feel (and philosophers to say) that these methods are "better" and "more scientific" and that generalizations based upon them and called "laws" are the real test of "scientific" work. Actually, the value of these methods and the remarkable results achieved with them are due to the very nature of the subject matter of these fields. Their particular generalizations are on a high level of abstraction. But it would be an error to think that the level of abstraction in itself is the acid test of "scientific-ness." Astronomy, for example, operates on a much lower level of generalization than physics; much of its most striking work is in fact concerned with individual description of such things as "the corona of the sun." Yet, there is no good philosophical ground for preferring physics to astronomy on this score. It may be replied, however, that both are operating with precise quantitative data. Regarding that argument and to reinforce what was already remarked upon, not only accuracy, but also relevancy and adequacy of the results are valid tests of scientific-ness. Human anatomy is no less a science than chemistry. What is more, the progress toward more scientific history in the last few generations is almost totally unrelated to quantification. Here the critique of sources and the critical use of other types of evidence [12] constituted the progress in method, and made the latter "more scientific" than its predecessors had been. In short, neither the degree of generalization, nor the degree of quantification are in themselves "absolute" criteria of scientific progress, but must be evaluated in relation to the material in hand and to be assessed. Aristotle put it very nicely: "It is the mark of an educated man to look for precision in each class of things just so far as the nature of the subject admits." [13] This holds not only as between science and various kinds of practical skills, but also as between sciences. To put it more pointedly, every scientific statement, no matter what its degree of generality, is an hypothetical description of what are believed to be observed phenomena; the more recurrent the phenomena, the more general the description can be. That is the reason for calling generalizations "descriptive formulae." But the degree of recurrency of the phenomena does not determine their degree of relevancy: for in the center of all efforts at knowing stands man, and the degree of relevancy is determined by the extent to which the observed phenomena are related to man in the universal chain of being.

We do not have to go as far as Immanuel Kant's metaphysic of the "thing-in-itself" [14] though a word may be said regarding it. Kant's statement of the matter suffers from the positing of an entity behind and beyond and wholly separate from what we observe, so that this thing-in-itself is presumed to stay forever wholly outside our knowledge. Hegel's bitter critique that this implies a denial of all rational knowledge of reality is justified, but he goes to the opposite extreme. It would seem more in keeping with scientific progress and its metaphysical implications to assume that the human understanding is progressively appropriating the real world and the things in it (for how else could one explain successful engineering action based upon such scientific knowledge), but at the same time to recognize that this process is never complete, and that there are always aspects, phases, in short parts of the things we study which lie as yet outside our knowledge. There are formulations in Kant which in fact support this view. We political scientists have every reason to be grateful to him for having established once and for all that human experience is conditioned by what human minds are like, and that even the most abstract and general law is conditioned by the "forms of thought" which the human mind brings to all description of observation. In short, we are never really describing facts, but observations of these presumed facts. This means, in the large area of historico-political facts with which political science is concerned, that we are dealing with reports about events, not with events themselves directly. The evaluation of reports must therefore be in the center of our interest, and our "methods" will be shaped by such evaluation. To illustrate, a hundred reports about a hundred interviews with a hundred escapees from the Soviet Union are not inherently more "scientific" (*i.e.,* relevant) than one report about one speech of Stalin (nor less "scientific" either). It all depends upon what happens to be the subject under discussion. If it is the role of "ideology" in the Soviet Union, the latter may be far more weighty and significant as evidence for the proposition that ideology continues to be a significant factor.[15]

When we speak of verification and validation, we mean that the description, of whatever degree of generality, and whether quantitative or qualitative, is capable of being tested by whoever possesses the requisite training in the methods appropriate to the field of observation involved. This presupposes that the description must correspond to the phenomena covered by them, whether general or particular, and therefore if new discoveries of hitherto unobserved facts are made, the description or descriptive generalization must be accordingly revised if the new facts do not accord with it. This general rule has very serious implications for such sciences as political science in which new facts present themselves continuously, as political practices and institutions and the thought corresponding to them evolves. Thus, the emergence of totalitarian dictatorships in our time—congeries of facts unprecedented in the history of political systems [16]—presents the political scientist with numerous novel problems, but so did the emergence of modern constitutionalism. Not only the evolution in the actual world of politics, but likewise the rapid accumulation of politically significant data by such fields as prehistory, history, ethnology, anthropology, and psychology confronts the political scientist with new issues that imperiously demand adequate correlation and systematization. But our more immediate concern with contemporary government, and more specially American and European government, has impeded the progress of political science, and more especially political theory, and has left us with any number of propositions that probably will turn out to be outworn and untenable when properly tested by the available "facts."

It should be noted in passing that political science, because of the nature of its subject matter and problems, is obliged to employ and combine effectively the methods of a number of related sciences. The documentary method of history, the analytical and case method of legal studies, and the statistical and interview methods are all of importance in studying that core phenomenon of human society which is its government. The argument, heard at times, that any "true" science is characterized by *one* particular method, unsound when considered in the light of the history of science, proves entirely untenable as far as political science is concerned.

We are here interested primarily in clarifying what this slowly progressing science has to do with political philosophy. Some of the preceding remarks presumably have, by their evident philosophical implications, already served to illustrate the connection. But it is necessary to elaborate this connection and to show its vital significance for the science of politics. To recall the dictionary definition offered above, philosophy appears to be concerned with ultimate reality and the principles thereof, and therefore with the principles of a particular branch of reality. It would be possible to develop this further by showing how the science of politics, as expounded by Aristotle, is related to and depends upon Aristotle's general philosophy. But such an exercise would not carry much weight with those who would readily admit that this was very true for the time of Aristotle, but that just as in physics so in political science we have now come to detach ourselves from such teleological views, and that a non-normative and non-philosophical, strictly "positive" science of politics is both feasible and useful.[17] I am not going to argue the problem in terms of the proposition that positivism itself is a "philosophy." For all positivists would presumably readily admit that if that is all that is meant by philosophy, some kind of philosophy is involved in political science. Rather do I propose to show how and why philosophy in a wider sense, and more especially through its political branch, is relevant to and cannot be bracketed out of political science, except for limited and specified purposes. In other words, I propose to block the retreat often adopted by positivists of saying that "in any set of definitions some terms must be left undefined on pain of circularity. The chain of definitions must have a starting point . . ."[18] For while this observation is true enough, it does not absolve us from concern with what these basic terms refer to. It will be found that definitions (characterizations) of political science usually include the word "power," and sometimes include the words "justice" or "value," as well as "action," "person," "sentiment," "symbol" and "group" or related terms. Thus Lasswell-Kaplan define political science as a "policy science" which "studies influence and power as instruments of the integration of values realized by and embodied in interpersonal relations" (*op. cit.*, p. xii).

These words, or some of them, if left undefined, presumably possess referents resulting from the experience of some groups of human beings (college professors, for example, or American, or English-speaking persons, or English-speaking American college professors). The crux of the argument involves the potential change in these referents, resulting from changes in word usage that are consequent upon philosophical argument and discussion, that is to say, changes in the view of being or reality, and the principles and truths regarding it, which are defined as the province of philosophy. Philosophers who thus "shape our thought" are actually themselves responding to widely felt experiences that may be associated with political, economic, artistic or technical change and evolution.

In order to develop this argument, I propose to take three very recent writings in the field of philosophy, and more particularly related to political philosophy, briefly characterize them and then ask: what, if any, implications have the concepts and arguments of these philosophers for three key areas of political inquiry in which descriptive generalizations are available that can be reappraised in light of these philosophies; constitutionalism, totalitarianism and the general problem of power? The three philosophical positions I propose to examine are (1) that of Leo Strauss, as put forward in his *Natural Right and History;* (2) that of the existentialists, and more especially Paul Tillich, on the subject of power; and (3) a new approach to the problem of freedom as advanced by Maurice Cranston, in his study *Freedom; A New Analysis.*

Leo Strauss' work [19] is, by implication, a repudiation of the entire corpus of political philosophy stemming from Hobbes and Locke. He argues that their thought is closely related, that Locke is, in fact, a Hobbesian, at least on the subject of natural right which he places in the very center of all reflections on law and government. It constitutes a repudiation of classic natural right doctrines, as found in Plato and Aristotle, according to Strauss, who maintains that this classic doctrine was sound. I do not here wish to go into Strauss' exposition of the classic doctrine, except to observe in passing that he tends to interpret Plato in terms of Aristotle which seems highly questionable, and to impute to both of them a view of the constitution (*politeia*) as meaning "the factual distribution of power within the community" calling it the "regime." [20] Upon this (in my view rather doubtful) proposition, Strauss builds his view of classic natural right as follows: (1) natural right teaching culminates in a twofold answer to the question of the best regime: the simply best regime would be the absolute rule of the wise; the practically best regime is the rule, under law, of gentlemen, or the mixed regime (*ibid.,* 142–3), and (2) there is a universally valid hierarchy of ends, but there are no universally valid rules of action (*ibid.,* 162). With this must be contrasted modern natural right teaching, more particularly as found in Hobbes and Locke. Strauss develops his argument in terms of an interpretation of

Hobbes which is familiar from his earlier study.[21] Hobbes is the political rationalizer of the acquisitive middle class, of the bourgeois gentleman of "impeccable manners" as Veblen was later to sneer, and his individualism as well as his adulation of power must be understood in this way. He argues that in Hobbes' teaching, the supremacy of authority as distinguished from reason [22] follows from an extraordinary extension of the natural right of the individual, any individual. Hence, the central role assigned to "power." "Opposing the 'utopianism' of the classics, Hobbes was concerned with a social order whose actualization is probable and even certain," and therefore Hobbes reduced virtue to the political virtue of peaceableness (p. 187). The fear of violent death becomes the central motivation of man, and this insight is not "hypothetical" but absolute and certain. This certain knowledge leads to a recognition of right as power. Locke followed this lead, according to Strauss, who quotes with considerable emphasis Locke's dictum that "the first and strongest desire God planted in men, and wrought into the very principles of their nature, is that of self-preservation." After exploring Locke's emphasis on property, which he considers the most characteristic part of his political philosophy, Strauss concludes that it leads to the identification of self-preservation with the preservation of one's property (p. 245); he adds that "Locke's thought is perfectly expressed by Madison's statement: 'The protection of (different and unequal faculties of acquiring property) is the first object of government.' " [23] Locke says in effect, Strauss asserts, that the greatest happiness consists in the greatest power. Hence Locke's teaching on property, and on natural right, are revolutionary with regard to the philosophic tradition of natural right (as well as the Biblical one).

It should be evident by now that if these propositions are correct the implications for political theory and science are considerable. Conventional constitutional theory, in the Anglo-American tradition, thinks of constitutionalism in a variety of ways, but the protection of the individual's rights is central to most of them. It has been argued by a number of authors, since Jellinek stressed the English origin of the Bill of Rights, that the American constitutional order rests upon the Lockean pattern of thought. This is a question which bears directly upon the interpretation of American government and of the behavior of the human beings involved. Although it may not be the intention of Strauss, Western constitutionalism is devalued, and a search for an hierarchy of values is called for. A government of laws and not of men is not only impossible, but philosophically undesirable. To struggle to maintain constitutionalism and the rights of man is to lose sight of the "basic truths or principles" of political science. The current treatments of American government and politics are unsound and hence misleading. I am purposely confounding the theoretical and practical consequences, because to the extent to which Strauss' views might prevail, their consequences will be of both types. (I am omitting here the more generalized type of systematic political science; the other two philosophies relate more clearly to them.)

Now it might be argued that all this philosophy of Strauss is of no consequence, that political science can just go merrily on its way, paying no attention to the profound challenge that has been issued to its underlying assumptions. But on what ground is such an assertion based? If on the ground that Strauss' position is unsound, then surely it is the task of political theorists to set forth this ground which presumably results from their understanding of the issues involved. I am not here going to undertake this kind of demonstration. But I would like to state that I consider Strauss' argument vulnerable both in terms of the history of political thought, in terms of the political generalizations involved, and in terms of the scholarly apparatus employed. And I submit that the discussion of this issue is a vital concern of political scientists (theorists) and that their methods must be broad enough to cover this dimension of political discourse.[24]

But let us turn to a range of political philosophy that is not historical, even in the materials it handles, but strictly contemporary. It is a striking fact that existentialist philosophers since Kierkegaard and Nietzsche have been much preoccupied with the problem of power. Karl Jaspers takes up power at length in several places, for example his great systematic treatise on truth.[25] Jean-Paul Sartre, exploring the clash of man and man, has recurrently dealt with the problem of power.[26] Martin Heidegger, in *Sein und Zeit* as well as more recently [27] has shown a central concern with the same problem. But perhaps it would be most useful to turn to a study by a leading theologian-philosopher, Paul Tillich. His thought is moulded to some extent by a central concern with Marxism and its challenge.[28] But in these lectures, he addresses himself to what he considers the basic ontological problem, namely the root meaning of being, the "never-ending task of describing the texture of being-as-being." Within this context (which I shall forbear critically evaluating here), he identifies three dimensions of the meaning of being: love, power, and justice. After exploring the meaning of love as "the drive towards reunion of the separated" (p. 28) which he believes to be the common aspect of its different modes, such as *libido,* friendship, *eros* (creative impulse), and charity, he turns to being as the power of being. It turns out to be the central concept, for "the concept I suggest for a fundamental description of being-as-being is . . . the concept of power" (p. 35). He recalls Nietzsche's will to power (and Heidegger's interpretation of it) and terms it "the dynamic self-affirmation of life." What this means is that "power is the possibility of self-affirmation in spite of internal and external negation." And he adds that human power is "the possibility (capacity?) of man to overcome non-being infinitely" (p. 40). From this it follows that power is real only in its actualization, in the encounter with other bearers of power and in the everchanging balance which is the result of these encounters. "Life includes continuous decisions, not necessarily conscious decisions, but decisions which occur in the encounter between power and power." Tillich gives as an example that Toynbee's interpretation of history is essentially cast in terms of such power relations and decisions resulting from the encounters of power. Challenge, response, and the like are categories derived from the encounter of power and power. He speaks of the power of man as centered, and asserts that such centeredness results in a hierarchy of powers. "Even the egalitarian societies have centers of power and decision . . . these centers are strengthened . . . in emergency situations" (p. 45). In a rather murky discussion, Tillich explores the relation of power to compulsion, claiming that power while actualizing itself through force and compulsion, is not identical with either. "Power needs compulsion, but compulsion needs the criterion which is implied in the actual power situation" (p. 48). What Tillich means is that it all depends upon what the power is being used for. Can love be united with power? Tillich thinks it can, and he develops this thought in terms of justice which is "the form in which power of being actualizes itself in the encounter of power with power." And he adds that only that compulsion is unjust "which destroys the object of compulsion instead of working towards its fulfillment." To students of the history of political thought it will occur that we are back at Rousseau's famous proposition that it is right for the general will to force the reluctant citizen to be free.

But let us stay with Tillich's propositions regarding power. What is their bearing on political science? Lasswell, following Merriam, defines, as we have seen, political science as concerned with the study of influence and power as instruments of value integration.[29] Hence his definition of power as "participation in the making of decisions" may be adduced here. It bears a clear relation to Tillich's concept; for life is by Tillich interpreted as decision-making, and these decisions result from the encounter of power with power and the struggle to overcome non-being. For Lasswell, a decision is "a policy involving severe sanctions." These sanctions result from the necessity of overcoming opposition, and they are "severe" in terms of the values prevailing in a particular culture. It is evident, then, that Tillich's existentialist philosophy is sufficiently clearly involved in the base line hypotheses of Lasswell (as embodied in his definitions) to provide a general perspective. The exaltation of power as the essence of being goes hand in hand with a deprecation of authority which for Lasswell is merely "formal power," or "power of low weight" (pp. 133–34).[30] The implications for an interpretation of totalitarianism are significant, to cite a concrete aspect. While Tillich summarily describes the dictator as "ultimate authority in a totalitarian system" (p. 89), Lasswell-Kaplan more discriminatingly observe that "naked power," which they define as "nonauthoritative power openly exercised," "tends to be formalized as it increases in weight, scope, and domain" (p. 140). As far as empirical evidence is concerned, it may be observed that what we now know about the Hitlerian dictatorship does not support this proposition; it is a hotly debated subject of controversy among Soviet experts, whether the evidence regarding the USSR falls into this pattern or not.[31] This example shows, as could many others, that the kind of philosophical argument which is attempted by Tillich, and is implied, if not admitted by Lasswell-Kaplan, has basic importance for the interpretation of so central a concern of political science as totalitarianism, because the "models" or "patterns" which provide the framework for an exploration of empirical reality and a systematic ordering of observation and documentary evidence, are shaped by these philosophical discussions. At the same time, such theorems as those advanced by Tillich are, from the viewpoint of empirical science as well as ontological, concerned with ultimate reality subject to the data of experience (in the broad sense). Without arguing the point here, I might say in passing that Tillich's propositions concerning power are most questionable in light of what we know about it as a result of genuinely scientific inquiry in our field. The stress on self and the related emphasis on compulsion and force, while significant features of power, inadequately express the predominantly relational aspect of power which is stressed by Lasswell-Kaplan and others, including myself. The whole range of cooperative power positions which result from a sharing of objectives and purposes is inadequately handled in the propositions of Tillich which claim to be ontological, but fail to get to the root of being.[32] I hope that this second illustration has again, and perhaps more poignantly, shown that political philosophy has a bearing upon political science, and that in turn political science has a bearing upon political philosophy and thereby in turn upon philosophy as a whole.

The third philosophical enterprise I wish to examine is Maurice Cranston's *Freedom; A New Analysis.* It calls itself a book "about the meaning of freedom." But while starting with linguistic analysis, it does not stop there, but seeks to contribute to a restatement of this vital issue. Besides the linguistic analysis in the manner of Wittgenstein and his school, the book considers liberalism and the issue of the freedom of the will—surely readily recognized as subjects which have not only been debated over the centuries in political theory and philosophy, but which have also had a bearing on such immensely practical or empirical matters as constitutionalism and totalitarianism and the kind of government and politics carried on under these labels.

What do we find in this rather significant study? The first part, containing the linguistic analysis, is entitled "the meaning of freedom," and deals with words, meanings, theories, definitions and finally "persuasion." These chapters are pert, and they are apt. They do in a brief compass what a group of American researchers did in a very comprehensive and ponderous fashion (Mortimer Adler and Associates, *Research on Freedom*—unpublished MS., ca. 1954). The absence of any real difference between "freedom" and "lib-

erty" (in spite of Herbert Read's argument to the contrary) is part of this review of past and present usage. Cranston more particularly shows that besides the lexicographical definition ("lexicographical" is a definition which
"reports what words mean conventionally, what people commonly mean
when they use them") of freedom which seems to be related to "the absence
of constraint, compulsion, impediments, burdens," and to be more "emotive"
than "descriptive," though some of both, there are numerous "stipulative"
definitions. The most celebrated philosophical meanings, namely those of
"rational" and "compulsory rational" freedom, are persuasive definitions.
Such appeals to the feelings of men work with the "emotive" definition or
meaning of words. Thus the existentialists are shown to be concerned with
shifting the emotive significance of freedom, to make it a pejorative term,
a "dread word." Yet beyond all this linguistic analysis, Cranston rightly insists that freedom is not "just a word," but a real condition of real people.

Such conditions of real people are to an extent adumbrated in the several
ideologies that go under the name of "liberalism." In a remarkably skillful
analysis of its English, French, German, and American versions, Cranston
clearly differentiates a Lockean strand which favors the "minimal state,"
and a Rousseauistic strand which he calls "étatiste." He also notes the
wishy-washy American connotations, with their progressive and democratic
ingredients.[33] His analysis of liberalism though very brief is very much to the
point; his comments on Laski, Hallowell, and de Ruggiero very apt.[34] He
rightly praises the last one for having elaborated the national differences in
liberalism. The different strands of liberalism are evidently related to the
divergent conceptions of liberty or freedom; the unhappy consequences of
Hegel's dialectic combination of opposites and the resulting notion of a "compulsory rational freedom" are duly delineated, though perhaps not sufficiently qualified.

Any discussion of freedom and of liberalism must, if it takes its argument
seriously, confront the issue of "freedom of the will." Cranston does so, and
for the effectively argued reason that this issue is not a pseudo-problem, as
is at times asserted. He does not care about either the word "freedom" or
the word "will" as long as it is recognized that the real question is: "Are
human choices and actions wholly predictable?" The argument about inde-
terminism in modern physics aside, he shows that the weight of the argument seems to be on the side of the negative answer. He freely admits, as
do most sensible libertarians, that many such human actions are predictable,
but he is unwilling to grant that therefore, if knowledge were sufficient, all
of them would be. This unpredictability is particularly evident in the case
of creative activity and invention. Here the predictor himself would have to
be the inventor, in order to be able to predict the invention. Yet, there remain lingering doubts; for to establish the case for the proposition: "I could
have acted differently" one would have to argue in terms of "contrafactual

propositions." Hence the strong case against determinism remains the mainstay of the belief in liberty. The author concludes on a cautious note: "Our inquiry has afforded some grounds for belief and some for doubt. Without grounds for doubt the subject would not be philosophy; and without grounds for belief there would be no point in writing."

It seems hardly necessary to labor the point that these propositions have a bearing upon the work of political science. Since modern constitutions provide for "freedom" in various respects, since the degree of freedom of such entities as the press, labor unions, even of the academic profession itself [35] are subjects of continuous inquiry, any significant contribution to an understanding of the basic questions involved would clearly be of value. But again there is also the reverse aspect: what criticism might the scientific inquiries of political science afford regarding these propositions? How satisfied can we be with negative statements such as that which defines freedom as the absence of constraints? Is not the capacity for effective participation in the political life of the community equally important, not merely as a matter of definition, whether lexicographical, stipulative or persuasive, but as a matter of behavioral fact? An affirmative answer to this question seems also rather clearly implied in Cranston's final conclusions about the freedom of the will, or rather about the ability of man to engage in unpredictable actions and choices.

If one consults the descriptive, generalizing accounts of political behavior, he might not find a general discussion of freedom, but he will find what various groups are doing in a free society.[36] These descriptive accounts show further that the problem of freedom is not an absolute one (as Cranston's own discussion of liberalism does also), but that in concrete, scientific terms the problem is one of more or less freedom. A free society is one in which individual freedom is maximized, that is to say, in which more men are more free, in the sense not only of absence of constraint, but also in that of capacity for creative and inventive, including self-perfecting and civilizing, activity.

In all this there are clearly "ideological" issues involved, for the issue of ideology is quite central to the discussion of political philosophy and the science of politics. It is well-known that Marx and Engels in terms of their particular materialistic interpretation of society and history suggested that all ideas were mere superstructure. As representative of many passages, let me quote the famous phrase from the *Capital:* "the ideal world is nothing else than the material world reflected by the human mind." And further that "the ruling ideas of each age have ever been the ideas of its ruling class." [37] As contrasted with such ideologies, Marx looked upon his own ideas as "scientific" and "positive," and that view has ever since remained the Marxist position. Naturally, it has been contested both in theory and in fact by any number of acute minds (*e.g.,* Pareto, Max Weber, and Max Scheler), but Karl

Mannheim faced the challenge more explicitly.[38] He considered that Karl Marx had in mind a "phenomenon of collective thinking" which he called "ideology." Discarding the negative value-judgment which Marx-Engels' discussion had implied, he defined "total" ideology as "the outlook inevitably associated with a given historical and political situation, and the *Weltanschauung* and style of thought bound up with it." He differentiated it from particular ideologies which "includes all those utterances the falsity of which is due to an intentional or unintentional, conscious, semiconscious, or unconscious, deluding of one's self or of others, . . . structurally resembling lies." But he eventually tries to "avoid" using the term "ideology" for what he had termed "total ideology" and speaks of such things as "perspectives" of a thinker or group. We are therefore left with a terminological uncertainty in which the particular ideology is pretty nearly what Marx had understood by "ideology," which since it "structurally resembles lies" presupposes on the part of the scientific analyst a knowledge of the truth. Now Lasswell-Kaplan build upon Mannheim, though significantly changing the basis.[39] They define "ideology" as "the political myth functioning to preserve the social structure" while an "utopia" is a similar myth, but functioning to supplant the existent social structure. Lasswell-Kaplan reject all notions that any standard of evaluation is involved. They consider their definitions as functional characterizations, not related to content. But can the function of ideology be considered without relation to content? Let us take once more the issue of constitutionalism versus totalitarianism. Is the role (or function) of ideology going to be unaffected by the "total" content which makes it an important instrument of compulsive control? To ask these questions is to suggest the answer.

But I should like to go one step further and suggest that the meaning of the term ideology, from a political science standpoint, ought not to be so broadly conceived as is implied in the concept of myth. Mythology and ideology are quite distinct; they are related to very divergent social and political phenomena, namely to myth in the one case, and to ideas in the other. As is already clear in Plato's writing, the myth begins where the ideas stop, to put it very crudely. It seems to me that we have to face the fact that ideas, whether they may at times serve as parts of myths, are independently subject to the standard of truth, but how they fare when subjected to this standard of evaluation, is not necessarily related either positively or negatively to their serviceability in the role of ideology. I am inclined to suggest that "ideology" is characteristically a system of ideas concerning the existing social order, and at the same time concerning actions to be taken regarding it. An ideology provides a critique of the existing society and a program of desirable change. A totalitarian ideology, then, is a total rejection of an existent society and a program of total reconstruction. The totality of the rejection implies of necessity the use of force or violence. Thus, to put it the other way around: a totalitarian ideology is a reasonably coherent body of ideas (belief) concerning practical means of how totally to change a society, by force or violence, based upon an all-inclusive (total) criticism of what is wrong with the pre-existing society. Whether and to what extent the ideology, that is to say such a set of ideas is "true" will always be not only of great urgency to those who accept it, but as well as to those who reject it, in whole or in part. It is therefore no valid ground for objecting to the relevance of political philosophy to political science to argue that such political philosophy, or some of its tenets, are part of an ideology. It may well be true (and I believe it is) that Plato's ideas were related to the ideology of the aristocratic party in Athens. If true, it would not thereby be proved that they are in error, in whole or in part. The fact that any set of ideas may become part of an ideology must be considered inherent in their very nature. Lasswell-Kaplan's ideas are no different from other ideas in this respect, nor do they become a myth on this account, nor do they therefore "structurally resemble lies," as Mannheim insisted. From all this it follows that the ideological potential, generally admitted, does not detract, but rather heightens the significance of political philosophy for political science (in the sense defined above).

The problem of truth calls for a few more words on the subject of authority. Authority is not a species of power, low power or formal power, as I have remarked before, but another dimension of social relationships altogether. Jaspers, in his work on truth, gives fairly detailed attention to the issues involved. He shows authority to be a configuration of truth, but its inner dialectic springs from the tension between the truth that is known and the truth that is in the process of being discovered. Authority has a psychic and sociological dimension, but this is surface. True authority is implicated in the never-ending search for truth. What may be true at one time, ceases to be true as new insights develop. Philosophically, one can understand authority as the marginal configuration of truth, since beyond each truth there is still another truth, a new horizon, which renders it partial. Hence, philosophy, in spite of all its questioning of authority, yet always at a certain point (the point of farthest reach) must accept something as unanalyzable, that is to say, on the basis of "authority." Even for the philosopher (as indeed for the scientist) there is a point at which the meaning of authority is related to power—the power of truth that is "beyond understanding." At this point authority may be said to be a configuration of truth which is accepted in reverence and faith, though not yet rationally comprehended, though the act of acceptance itself is a kind of rational comprehension, namely that comprehension of the inherent and ineluctable need of authority itself.[40]

But this need of the truth-seeker to recognize the finiteness of all found truth,—as contrasted with the infinity of all truth to be found—does not oblige him to consider the problem of truth as resolvable in terms of mere relativity, as is suggested by the notion of ideology as a designation for all philosophy and more particularly political philosophy. Even if one argues: *sum, ergo cogito,* rather than *cogito, ergo sum,* there are statements to be made about the workings of politics (*e.g.,* Athenian democracy or democracy in general), that are more true than others. The standard of true or false, involved in all scientific work, links in the last analysis, through its relationship to what are authoritative statements, political science with political philosophy, as indeed it does all sciences with all philosophy. This issue cannot be avoided by talking about a pragmatic or operational test, that is to say, about whether something works or not, because (*a*) since politics deal with contingent matters we cannot know whether something will work, because it has worked, and (*b*) such pragmatic or operational test is in turn subject to the test of true or false.

To conclude, then, we have tried to show that political science and political philosophy are intimately tied, that the one cannot be usefully pursued without the other, and that political science in this respect is not at all different from other sciences which likewise are linked to philosophy. We have argued this not only generally, but also with reference to certain specific issues, by showing how the work of three contemporary philosophers, dealing with political matters, or aspects of them, impinge upon the work of political scientists; they deal with the problems that stand in the very center of all scientific and philosophical effort: power, law, freedom, authority, and the rest. When you consider the controversy in relation to these cases, you incidentally discover that the argument against the role of philosophy in political science resembles the argument against theory in political (and other) science. In fact, we have a recurrent pattern in which he who knows something particular argues against him who knows both more and less by knowing less about a larger class of things. The practitioner of politics, the politician, holds the scientist in low esteem, questioning his work as mere "theory," by which he means something unsubstantial and essentially false. The specialist in some particular phase of descriptive political science doubts the value of "theory," calling it "generalities" which he considers misleading and essentially false. The theorist who cherishes the notion of a general systematic political science in turn objects to the political philosopher as a man concerned with "ideological" questions, with value judgments which he considers subjective and essentially false. They are all, however, talking in terms of truth, and the question: what is truth? which they presumably must be able to answer in order to vindicate their claims, practitioner, specialist, theorist, and philosopher alike, is the most fundamental and philosophical question there is.

LINDSAY ROGERS

Political Philosophy in the Twentieth Century: An Appraisal of its Contribution to the Study of Politics

THE INVITATION that I participate in this symposium did not, I feel confident, result from any illusions about my competence or interests. So far as political philosophy is concerned, I cannot pretend to speak with authority, and I am perhaps rash in hoping to speak as a scribe. Indeed I am reminded of an appointment to the British Secretaryship of State for Foreign Affairs during the nineteenth century. The Noble Lord, said the French, will be an admirable Foreign Secretary, "parce que les affaires lui seront étrangéres."

My participation in this symposium, I take it, results from your knowledge of the fact that I have had rather extended experience of graduate students and have once or twice expressed some opinions on their proper care and feeding. Hence, before and after dealing briefly with the subject assigned to me, I shall wander from twentieth century political theory into gardens which, following Candide's advice, I have sought to cultivate.

But first a word about terms of reference. The titles for two of the six papers contain the phrase "the study of politics." I take this to mean the study of politics by graduate students in graduate schools, or by amateurs who want to be better informed on a subject that Aristotle called "architectonic." Hence I am supposed to enumerate the twentieth-century political theorists that I think a student, seeking to fill gaps in his information, should not overlook. I reject another possible meaning: how in or out of the light of the "contributions" of twentieth-century theorists we can strive to make politics a "more rigorous discipline" or suggest new methods of dealing with political phenomena—methods in the large and unconnected with a problem that seems difficult or an idea that appears to warrant exploration. Some twentieth-century writers on government have been much more realistic, informing, and influential than their nineteenth-century predecessors, but the advances have been achievements that individuals made on their own and not because some one gave them a new formula. I am allergic to giving other people advice of this kind.

There is an old story of an irate playwright who turned on a severe dra-

189

matic critic and taunted him by saying that he could not write a play himself.
"That is true," the critic replied: "I cannot lay an egg, but I am a better
judge of an omelette than any hen in London." All of us can judge omelettes,
but should we give admonitions on how omelettes should be made? Rather
should we not try out our own formulas, make excellent omelettes ourselves,
have them approved by those who eat them, and hope that subsequent omelette makers will do even better? That, learned natural science friends assure me, is roughly the way in which the great developments have come in
the subjects they know.

I state the case rather bluntly because I remember a pre-World War II
apostasy. For some years I was on the "Problems and Policy Committee" of
the Social Science Research Council. There we attempted to be Mr. Micaw-
ber in reverse and waited for something to turn down—that is, if the proposal did not seem to be novel. Then we were all agog, and did not ask
ourselves whether the one who proposed to break the sound barrier knew
how to pilot a plane or what kind of a crate he would fly. Later, when Walter
Millis remarked that only the clergy were more sensitive to the winds of
novelty than professors I could not challenge him, but at the time I frequently thought of the complaint that Macaulay had made a century before.
"So great is the taste for oddity that men who have no recommendation but
oddity hold a high place in the vulgar estimation." We set up other committees and charged them with the task of defining the undefinable and un-
screwing the inscrutable. These committees then employed men who employed other men who employed secretaries, research assistants, and field
workers. There must have been thousands of these committee meetings since
I ceased attending a dozen years ago. "Addiction to meetings" as my colleague Jacques Barzun has written, "is the teachers' professional disease.
One can see why. The weakness comes from the nervous strain of teaching coupled with the burden of a professional (he does not say professorial)
conscience." When one's own work cannot be done because "freshness and
inspiration are lacking," a committee provides the satisfaction of seeming to
do something.

And what have been the results of all this committee activity? I do not
think I am digressing in asking this question or being more specific and asking whether any Foundation has been responsible for discoveries or insights
that enable us to study political phenomena more successfully, or to state
our conclusions more convincingly than was possible for the men under
whom we studied? What Foundation-sponsored undertaking has changed
our thinking or has prevented us from continuing to propagate errors? Of
course some interesting and important work has been made possible, that
without financial support would have had to be postponed: the monographs
and case studies fathered by the S.S.R.C.'s Committee on Public Administration; the Cornell books on civil liberties; the valuable analysis of the

make up of the 1952 Party Conventions, and the recently announced inquiries into Communist influence in different areas of our national life. But in respect of making politics a "more exact science" is it unfair to recall Dr. Johnson's boast that he could repeat a complete chapter of the Natural History of Iceland? It was Chapter LXXII: "Concerning Snakes," which in Johnson's words went as follows: "There are no snakes to be met with throughout the whole island." Some historian of thought, writing, say, in "1984," may pay his respects to the desire of the Foundations to find sires for political snakes during the second quarter of the twentieth century and may hint that perhaps the abortive efforts they subsidized kept the would-be sires from making a more profitable use of their energies in cultivating their own gardens and working with graduate students.

ODDLY ENOUGH, the only course on political theory that I ever gave dealt with Twentieth Century Writers—once at Harvard and once at Columbia. What are the names that come back? G. E. Moore, to whom Bertrand Russell and Keynes have paid such glowing tributes, and whose *Principia Ethica* the Cambridge University Press has recently republished. This was too strong meat, but I could not overlook Bradley's essay, *My Station and its Duties,* or Bosanquet's *The Philosophical Theory of the State*. At the time I thought I was able to understand Bosanquet's famous third chapter entitled "The Paradox of Self-Government." I would not attempt again to understand it. Life is too short, and I do not know why any student who is not himself setting up as a political theorist should be asked to try to understand it. Bradley was relatively easy to read, but Bosanquet was obscure. As someone has remarked, if they had said the same things, you would willingly have read the former and shunned the latter.

So far as I remember, the great debate over whether Rousseau had given the totalitarians light and leading had barely begun because there were no totalitarians save in the Soviet Union; that, militarily, was powerless, and so seemed a thing apart. But Leonard Hobhouse, embittered by the experience of his son in the First World War, had written a tract that he called "The Metaphysical Theory of the State." What kind of a tract would it have been if the son had been in Hitler's instead of the Kaiser's War! At the time of my temerarious venture, pluralism was in the air; certain political philosophers wanted to do good to the world and to have political, economic, and social institutions remade in the light of the theories they were expounding —and to have the remaking take place rather promptly.

So among my principal pigeons were the pluralists—the Guild Socialists —who were spewing out books at a great rate. I suspected at the time that all this was pretty ephemeral, but the attention that the Guild Socialists commanded was not completely wasted. There were the works of J. N. Figgis (*e.g., From Gerson to Grotius*), and Maitland's magnificent introduction to Gierke which I should think will make Gierke enjoy more frequently than would otherwise be the case, what William James called "the immortality of footnotes."

The Pope of the Guild Socialists was G. D. H. Cole, who (with his wife) wrote better detective stories than political philosophy. There were Hobson, A. J. Penty, and Orage and others whom I have forgotten. They wanted a brave new world on modified syndicalist lines. Still we must say one thing for the pluralists: their philosophy had a factual content. They discussed the institutions they wanted to remold, and did more than argue about verbal definitions. The world they wanted seemed to me likely to be pretty grim but I was reassured when a year or two later I met Cole and he said that if Great Britain ever faced an experiment with Guild Socialism he would try to be on the first ship that carried emigrants. He did not rule out the United States as a haven because he then did not have the phobia on our country that he now has. Unhappily he and his wife have ceased to produce who-done-its.

But twenty or so years ago, he delivered some literate and provocative lectures on "Literature and Politics" (I do not recall seeing them referred to in any American publication). Latterly Mr. Cole has been the historian of the British Labor Party and its Socialist progenitors, and is currently preaching that the cure for the ills of the British Welfare State is more socialism— as a stimulant and not as an antibiotic. Since his Guild Socialist adventures, Mr. Cole has probably been more prolific than any other academic writer in our field.

Even more prolific was the *enfant terrible* who, as he acquired years, required that admirers and critics stipulate what period they meant when they discussed his writings. I refer, of course, to Harold Laski. His footnote sempiternality is assured. He is immortal also in the law of libel: the costs assessed on him in his unsuccessful suit amounted to $60,000—a sum that gives him a permanent eminence among professorial angels. My guess is that, with the possible exception of his fattest book to be mentioned later, future students of politics will be able to study him adequately enough in a monograph by my colleague Herbert Deane.

But if I rule out all these writers as now being of scant importance, what twentieth-century thinkers should loom large in the future study of politics? One would have no claim for attention if in the spring of 1917, Ludendorf had not given him a sealed train to pass through Germany on his way from Switzerland to Petrograd. Ludendorf did not know he was transporting a future political theorist; he only hoped that the passenger could add to the weakness on the Russian home front. I refer to Vladimir Ilyich Ulganov, better known as Lenin.

Mr. A. J. P. Taylor has recently written: "Marxism has many excellent qualities as a religion. It demands total adherence from its victims."

> It alone is right; all other creeds or philosophies are wrong. It has its own vocabulary or clap-trap—the proletariat, the dialectic, the negation of the negation, and so on. The works of the founders are admirably obscure—mostly works of occasional journalism, some gibberish, many concerned with issues long dead. The gospel has to be pursued through out-of-date tracts and pieced together from fragmentary hints, often in private correspondence. Then regard the early fathers; what a splendid and cantankerous lot, quite up to the standard of Athanasius. Kautsky, the first Pope—as rigid as could be one day and bolting from the consequences of Marxism the next. The revisionists, watering the primitive religion down to a set of harmless commonplaces. Then comes Lenin with his puritan revival; and Stalin, perhaps following in Lenin's footsteps, perhaps not.[1] Throw in confessions and witch-hunts, crusades and excommunications. What religion could be nicer? It will make wonderful material for a Gibbon one day—as farcical a chapter of human history as any devised. But, as the example of Gibbon shows, the successful historian of a religion must not care about it one way or the other.[2]

I hope Mr. Taylor is correct when he says "as farcical a chapter of human history as any devised." When this comes to be true, Lenin's "puritan revival" may have only an antiquarian interest. For the time being the chapter is a tragedy and no one knows how many acts remain to be played. Hence, until the curtain falls and a different play begins, and perhaps after that, students of politics will not be able to ignore Ludendorf's passenger.

Only four other twentieth century theorists seems to me important—one American and three Englishmen. The American, Reinhold Niebuhr, I am not competent to discuss. I include him on the advice of learned friends.

Collingwood, I suggest, demands the attention and respect of every student of Politics, for so much of our writing is historical even though the events with which we deal are quite recent and contemporary or even in the future. Sir Robert Peel's decision to repeal the Corn Laws; Great Britain's entry into the War of 1914, and Lend-Lease are matters belonging to history. Franklin Roosevelt's decisions or indecisions at Yalta and Mr. Eisenhower's refusal to authorize the use of carrier based airplanes in the Indo-China fighting are matters of history also, but they figure in much that is now being written on current and future foreign policy. The tactics of the congressional Democratic majorities in Congress and the success or failure of the pressure groups that will battle against less protectionism are discussed now by students of politics and will interest future historians. The task of the political analyst is almost precisely the same as the task of the historian and both will better understand what they are doing if they know Colling-wood. Incidentally, the recent Report of the Committee on Historiography of the Social Science Research Council ("The Social Sciences in Historical Study," Bulletin 64) achieves the remarkable feat of failing to mention Col-lingwood even in a footnote. For that matter, the report fails to mention Croce, but after reading Collingwood, I concluded that I need not bother any more with Croce at first hand.[3]

In an able paper read at the last meeting of the American Political Science Association, my colleague Thomas P. Peardon explained why he thought Michael Oakeshott important. I shall refrain from attempting to restate and even from quoting Mr. Peardon's reasons. Suffice it to say that Oakeshott deserves continuing attention apart from (perhaps despite) his inaugural lecture which told us that "in political activity" we "sail a boundless and bottomless sea; there is neither harbour for shelter nor floor for anchorage, neither starting place nor appointed destination." Our endeavor should be no more than "to keep afloat on an even keel; the sea is both friend and enemy; and the seamanship consists in using the resources of a traditional manner of behavior to make a friend of every inimical occasion." All this, or only this, in a world which "is the best of all possible worlds, and everything in it is a *necessary* evil."

Of George Orwell one should read more than his brilliant satires, *Animal Farm* and *1984*. Some of his essays and certain passages in his novels are ventures in political philosophy. And as for his satires? What other political philosopher has had one of his tracts made into an excellent movie, and the other broadcast by the B.B.C. with a response that showed the audience to have been terrified and also, as sober critics pointed out, was itself terrifying.

The four men I have listed constitute my hard core. I prefaced them with Lenin; I add to them an economist, and then, before I get to my cultivated fields, shall mention some writers who, although not at the time pretending to be political philosophers, dealt with government so illuminatingly that they should have a run for their money before they appear only in footnotes.

The English essayist G. M. Young, who is not as widely read in this coun-try as he deserves, once described Frederick William Maitland as "the royal intellect" of the Victorian Era. I would nominate John Maynard Keynes as a "royal intellect" of the Georgian Era. His *Essays in Persuasion* (*Essays in Prophecy* also) were such brilliant performances that he could bring them together for book publication without resorting to *l'espirit d'escalier*. How many other writers have been able to do that when their subjects had not been pretty well relegated to the past? The essays demonstrate how well Keynes had acquired the ability that Matthew Arnold thought so important —of letting the mind "play freely about the facts."

For graduate students studying politics—for those of us attempting to teach graduate students—examples of achievements well beyond our attainment are worthy of study on Browning's belief that a man's reach should always exceed his grasp (Paracelsus).

BAGEHOT ONCE remarked that when you set yourself to describe any form of popular government, you would have to conclude that it seemed ridiculous. A battle for stockholders' proxies every two years; the designation of a president who is opposed by nearly half of the stockholders; the majority of the directors at once beginning to quarrel publicly; the minority directors agreeing on little more than a desire to become the majority in the next proxy fight, and conducting regular and guerrilla warfare against it (in Great Britain a salary is paid the leader of Her Majesty's Opposition so that he will be vigilant and vigorous); managers chosen on grounds that frequently make ability a minor consideration; decisions taken or avoided because of pressures of groups of stockholders; morning and afternoon newspapers and radio commentators assailing the stockholders, and giving them and other customers news and rumors and views of what is right and wrong—if any great industrial enterprise, bank, university, or trade union were run in such a way, early bankruptcy or collapse would be inevitable. Is this an unfair picture of what representative government is? If my analogy became more detailed the description would seem more ridiculous. It becomes grotesque when one adds that the stockholders (the people) do not want to govern themselves: *vide* nonvoting and lack of interest in referendum proposals; they want no more than to be well governed and not to be pushed around. And in a democracy who is charged with the business of looking after the Public?

When Bagehot made his impish proposal—much like his saying that the cure for admiring the House of Lords was to go and look at it—the suffrage in Great Britain was far from universal. The nursery, in Bismarck's phrase, had not yet begun to govern the household. There was no penny press; the hustings were still important as a means of political education, and government had not become a great Leviathan.

But whether or no certain of its practices seem ridiculous, representative government commands the allegiance of the western peoples. The danger is that the allegiance is tepid; support seems too often to be *faute de mieux*. As an acute English writer has said:

> What liberal democracy seems to lack today is inspiration. The torch which it carried a century since has passed to Communism; that is now the creed which spurs men on to enthusiasm and sacrifice. Of course enthusiasm is difficult to maintain for causes which are supposed to have achieved their object. The promises made on their be-

half inevitably prove to have been exaggerated, and the disillusioned blame the leaders for having promised too much rather than themselves for having believed the promise. As Dumbey says in Lady Windemere's Fan, "In this world there are only two tragedies. One is not getting what one wants and the other is getting it." Or in the less sparkling words of the Psalmist, "He gave them their desires: and sent leanness into their souls withal." Yet before liberal democracy is reproached for failure, it should be given the credit for having emerged successful from two world wars, while North America provides the most amazing success story yet known to mankind.[4]

This gives some comfort, but the greatest test may come next week, next month, or next year—if there is atomic warfare. If enough bombs are exploded, scientists seem to be divided on the question of whether or no climates will be changed, fertile lands will become deserts, and mankind will be able to survive. A few weeks ago *The Manchester Guardian* found some comfort in the belief that

> The balance of advantage in air power, with atomic weapons, is heavily on our side and is likely to remain so. Although the layman cannot know with any certainty, there seems reason to suppose that the main American air bases are too numerous and too remote to be reached from Russian territory, whereas the Russian bases are vulnerable. In cold reckoning the Communist Governments cannot expect to cripple the means of retaliation at one blow, or even to injure it seriously. That is their disadvantage and our safeguard—unless our nerves fail.

This is thinking in narrow physical terms. Mathematical calculations of advantages can be comforting, but "We need more than cold strategy inside us, more than mere fear of being blown to bits, more than national self interest." Justification for being ready to fight must be based on the "belief that the Western form of society respects men as individual human beings in a way that no other society has yet achieved. That belief is the foundation of Western morality." Democracy, as a form of government, "is not important so much for itself as for its success in making for the fulfilment of individual human lives"; and as "the early Christians were ready to face death if necessary for their faith, we too should have that strength." But, as I have said, although the flesh is strong, the spirit is not dedicated, and will not be until a new prophet comes along and rallies followers to his gospel. Meanwhile, is there anything that can be done by the hewers of wood and the drawers of water—those of us who discuss western political institutions and current problems of public policy?

IN THE September, 1953, *Political Science Quarterly,* Alfred Cobban had what seemed to me a rather striking article called "The Decline of Political Theory." Mr. Cobban's argument is based on learning that he bears lightly, and he never fails to give the reader concrete examples of what he means—a practice, as I shall say later, that many American students seem to endeavor to avoid.

In the past, Mr. Cobban tells us, political theory was essentially practical, and the theorist, "in his way, was a party man." John Stuart Mill "lived in an age when new social problems called for measures of state action which conflicted with established ideals of individual liberty." Bentham sought to establish "a theoretical basis for the legislative and administrative reforms that were urgently needed in *his* day." Burke, confronting challenges "to the existing bases of political allegiance, attempted to provide an alternative to the new democratic principle of the sovereignty of the people." Faced with the "moral collapse of divine right monarchy," Rousseau "offered a new justification for the rightful powers of government." Earlier, Montesquieu "had seen the defects of absolute monarchy but his alternative . . . was the limitation of all power by law." Locke provided the political philosophy "for a generation which had overthrown divine right and established parliamentary government." Hobbes and Spinoza wrote "in an age of civil wars" and maintained that sovereignty meant all or nothing. "So," says Mr. Cobban, "we might continue till we reached in the end—or rather the beginning—Plato and Aristotle, attempting to prescribe the remedies for the diseases of the city-state." In Mr. Cobban's opinion of recent writers on politics perhaps only one followed the traditional pattern, accepted the problems presented by his age, and devoted himself to the attempt to find an answer to them." He was Harold Laski. Although Mr. Cobban did not agree with Laski's analysis or conclusions, he thought "that he was trying to do the right thing."

I do, too, and I therefore suggest the continued study of that fat book to which I referred earlier—*A Grammar of Politics.* Turgid as some of the passages were and repetitious though the book was—the principles of the grammar were discussed, with some anticipation of the parts of speech; then there was a detailed consideration of the parts of speech followed by an iteration of the principles—Laski's *Grammar* should not be forgotten, even if it is used only as an ancient model whose merits for its time are an incentive for greater merits at a later day. It was the first attempt since Professor Henry Sidgwick's *The Elements of Politics* (1891) to discuss political institutions (and in Laski's case some economic institutions as well) not only as they were but as they should be. Magistral though it is, Lord Bryce's

Modern Democracies is not in the same class. Bryce was primarily descriptive; he was more interested, that is to say, in political anatomy than in political physiology and pathology. Nevertheless his observations on institutions at work were extensive and valuable and no perceptive reader laid down the volumes with his faith in democratic government having failed to become a little more intense. Of the writers of texts currently in use, who, save Mr. Friedrich, attempt to follow in the steps of Sidgwick, and Bryce and Laski and (methods are different) assist their readers to pass judgment on what they think they have learned?

"For a century and a half," writes Mr. Cobban, "the Western democracies have been living on the stock of basic political ideas that were last restated toward the end of the nineteenth century. That is a long time. The nineteenth century did pretty well on them, but provided no restatement for its successors. The gap thus formed between political facts and political ideas has steadily widened." Perhaps it can be somewhat narrowed if those who start with political facts cease being so careful to keep their ideas to themselves.

There are a few other twentieth-century writers who I think should not be forgotten. Lord Morley's *Politics and History* contains some gems worth pondering. Occasionally a critic goes to such extremes that he stirs his readers to violent revolt and strengthens them in the convictions he is attempting to destroy. Hayek has, I suppose, accomplished this. So, to my mind, has Emile Faguet with his *The Cult of Incompetence* and the more penetrating . . . *"et l'horreur des responsabilités,"* which may not have been translated. Since the excessive specialization of the courses that we now give in graduate schools may let certain writers be overlooked, I venture to mention Graham Wallas: not only his *Human Nature in Politics* but also *Our Social Heritage*. I conclude with F. S. Oliver's volumes, *The Endless Adventure* of governing men. They are a mine of political wisdom.

I hope no one is noting and lamenting my omission of George Gallup and his *The Pulse of Democracy,* if that was its title. At the time of its publication Dr. Gallup had a good many academic accolytes and some of them thought—or at least said—that Gallup had something: one of Gallup's samples would enable the whole electorate to function as a town meeting. We would be able to have Direct Democracy. One academic altar boy wondered whether a sample could not show electoral preferences more accurately than the use of ballots and voting machines: forgetfulness, illness, weather, ennui, would keep voters from the polls. This oddity was for a time not without esteem in certain academic quarters. But to be more serious and to follow Candide's advice.

Wнат I have to say about future graduate instruction I divide into several parts and trust that my endeavor to be brief will not make me seem more dogmatic than I want to be.

I. (*a*) We must face the fact that, with some notable exceptions, the best of college graduates who are interested in the political world rather than the sciences, business, or the humanities, go to law schools and do not desire careers in teaching or in the public service. If you think I am overstating I suggest that you sit down with a bound volume of the *Harvard Law Review* or any other first class law review and compare it with a bound volume of the *American Political Science Review*. In the law reviews the intellectual temperature, the literacy, and the clearness with which points are made, do not compare unfavorably with what appears in our house organ; and this even though the law reviews are edited and largely written by *students*. I add that by and large the days and nights of law students are far more laborious than the nights and days of graduate students in the social sciences and that the case method is a good instrument for sharpening minds.

(*b*) We face a second fact. Each generation of graduate students, save those who have gone to private schools and first-class Liberal Arts Colleges, and have had home advantages as well, is less well educated than the previous generation.

Not long ago Professor Douglas Bush of Harvard attributed this development to an acceptance of "principles extracted from John Dewey's philosophy of barbarism." He had in mind "Dewey's hostility to what he regarded as leisure-class studies; his anti-historical attitude; his desire—intensified in his followers—to immerse students in the contemporary and immediate, and his denial of a hierarchy of studies; his doctrine that all kinds of experience are equally or uniquely valuable; and it would not be irrelevant to add his notoriously inept writing." Whether this is the complete or even a principal explanation is a question I do not pause to discuss. The fact is there. As the French would say, *Je constate,* and I do so confidently.

The lessened literacy of graduate students becomes evident in two forms:

(i) When I was a student most of us could write tolerable English. At least we could make ourselves clear and some of us even paid attention to niceties. For some time now, so far as my experience goes, many graduate students are unable to explain what if anything they have in their minds. I gain support for this dim view from authoritative evidence coming from that august body, the Council for Research in the Social Sciences. A year or so ago the Council awarded some fellowships to college juniors so that they could undertake research projects during their summer vacations. The

wisdom of interrupting an education for a college junior to engage in research is a matter that I am sorry I cannot now discuss. The Council found
that very few of the persons to whom fellowships had been awarded—and
they were the cream of the junior crop—could explain clearly the project
that they wished to undertake or write intelligibly about their hopes or their
accomplishments. Given these results, would it not be sensible for the Council to drop its experiment but to continue to award fellowships to juniors
interested in the Social Sciences and to tell them that they were being subsidized to improve their knowledge of English? The Council would doubtless
reply that it had been set up to encourage research and was not concerned
with literacy or education. This may well be true, but the Council could
alibi itself by asserting that the English language is a tool, and that it was
therefore justified in subsidizing students to perfect themselves in its use,
just as it subsidizes students to perfect themselves in the use of statistical
tools.

I do not think that I overestimate English deficiencies as a handicap to
the future study of Politics. Our counterparts in French and English Universities do not have to worry with graduate students who cannot handle
their mother tongues. To a large extent this is still true of Canada, although
in this case geographical proximity increases vulnerability. For many years
I have told my students that Fowler's *A Dictionary of Modern English
Usage* should be more highly prized by them than any single treatise on
any branch of Political Science. Moreover, Fowler is good bedtime reading.

(ii) Of Macaulay's essays, Mark Pattison once said that they "are not
merely instructive as history; they are like Milton's blank verse, freighted
with the spoils of the ages." Few students now seem to have read Macaulay,
but I let the illustration stand. Fewer still have read Maitland, who, as
Herbert Fisher said, was not allusive "from ostentation, but from absorption,
and from a tendency common to learned and modest men to credit the
general reader with more knowledge than he is likely to possess." Both
Macaulay and Maitland would floor most graduate students. In lectures and
in seminars all of us have been brought up short by finding that allusions
which were once familiar to every person with a smattering of education
have fallen flat. I suppose the trouble goes back to the home where, frequently, education is thought chiefly valuable because it may permit some
assistance in homework; to mechanical aids for the use of leisure; to high
schools that put the intellectual temperature at the lowest common denominator; to colleges that struggle unsuccessfully to help students catch up.
Whatever the causes, each year college and graduate students are less well
read and as yet comics and television are too young to have taken their
full toll. Crossword puzzles have too few addicts to permit the hope that
there will be general familiarity with ancient gods and goddesses. I have
no doubt that one of our students or a student of our students will someday

refer to the Sermon on the Mount and will find that he has no comprehending hearers.

II. Ortega y Gasset has warned us that "if each generation accumulates printed material at the rate of recent ones, the culture which liberated man from the jungle will thrust him anew into a jungle of books." When something over a century ago Sir George Cornewall Lewis wrote his two volumes, *On the Methods of Observation and Reasoning in Politics,* he could be familiar with everything—even trivial things—that all his predecessors had written in several languages. When Freeman lectured at the Johns Hopkins in the eighties and President Gilman asked him where he had written his *History of the Norman Conquest,* Freeman replied with some surprise: "Why, in my own library, of course." When Messrs. Langer and Gleason get around to chronicling the influence of the Joint Chiefs of Staff in political matters from 1941 on, they will want to use a motorcycle; the files with the documents extend for miles.

The students of our students, when they are at the height of their powers, and if they happen to be at Yale (for whose library estimates have been made), will have access to 200 million volumes resting on 6,000 miles of shelves. These volumes will be catalogued in 750,000 drawers, which will occupy eight acres of floor space. (*Circum* 2040 A.D.) Someone whose identity I have forgotten made it a rule never to read a new book until he had reread an old one. The rule is still a good rule, but it has long since been impossible to adhere to it. The books currently published and purporting to deal with some phase of political life could occupy the entire reading time of a student of politics. Twenty years ago the crop of doctoral dissertations amounted to 2,630 annually. In 1953–54 there were 9,000 dissertations of which 2,745—more than the 1933 total—were in the Social Sciences. The annual output of Congress and the state Legislatures runs to 30,000 pages; each year the administrative regulations of the Federal Government are a dozen times the size of the Bible. What we can do about this I do not know but it is a factor that will more and more condition the future study of Politics.

III. In one of his essays G. M. Young says that one morning, when he and William Temple were students, they walked away from an Oxford lecture together. His friend, a future Archbishop of Canterbury, remarked: "After all, the only things we learn at Oxford are the things we say to one another between lectures."

"That observation," Young goes on, "having germinated in my mind for some time, produced at last the definition of a University to which I have since adhered. 'A University is a place where young men and women educate one another by conversation, under the guidance of people a little older and more often than they might imagine, somewhat wiser than themselves.'"

Graduate professors of Politics do too much lecturing. We force too many of our auditors to endure what a Trollope character described as the "verdure and malleability of pupildom." I would like to see a graduate school organized on the principle that there would be lectures only when the lecturers were sure that they had something to say. That students realize we may have nothing to say results in the absenteeism that we condone, but unfortunately students cannot know in advance whether they will be bored, moderately interested, or (in a rare case) thrilled.

I am fond of quoting Alfred North Whitehead's conviction, "based on no confusing research (*sic*), that as a training in political imagination the Harvard School of Politics and Government cannot hold a candle to the old-fashioned English classical education of half a century ago." Whitehead expressed himself at greater length in *The Aims of Education,* which Mentors' books brought out in a cheap edition a few years ago. Here is what he said:

> The primary reason for the existence of universities is not to be found either in the mere knowledge conveyed to the students or in the mere opportunities for research afforded to the members of the faculty.
>
> Both these functions could be performed at a cheaper rate, apart from these very expensive institutions. Books are cheap, and the system of apprenticeship is well understood. So far as the mere imparting of information is concerned, no university has had any justification for existence since the popularisation of printing in the fifteenth century. Yet the chief impetus to the foundation of universities came after that date, and in more recent times has even increased.
>
> The justification for a university is that it preserves the connection between knowledge and the zest of life, by uniting the young and the old in the imaginative consideration of learning. The university imparts information, but it imparts it imaginatively. At least, this is the function which it should perform for society. A university which fails in this respect has no reason for existence. This atmosphere of excitement, arising from imaginative consideration, transforms knowledge. A fact is no longer a burden on the memory: it is energising as the poet of our dreams, and as the architect of our purposes. . . .

What is the justification for a graduate school offering a course in every subject about which a student might like to learn something? On the other hand, I suspect that in many quarters there is neglect of subjects broad in scope on which perhaps courses should be offered. The reason for the neglect is, I think, that each of us wants to pursue his own will-o'-the-wisp. We inflict on students our lucubrations on specialties which we want to study further or on which we want to write. (Sometimes we continue to repeat orally little or no more than we have already put into print.) Graduate students are handicapped in their studies of Politics because their teachers have vested interests and refuse to abandon the satrapies that they claim as their own.

In sum, if I could make a curriculum to my liking, I would be mindful of Napoleon's definition of the ideal Constitution: "It should," he said, "be short and obscure." And its elements would have much more generality than many curricula have today. My students would have to listen to me only when I thought I had something to say; the resulting hours of leisure they would, I trust, spend in what Mr. Justice Holmes called "improving the mind"—an operation which in his nineties he told Charles Beard gave him somewhat less of a thrill than it had when he was in his eighties. The increased leisure that I enjoyed I would devote to ascertaining how the students had spent *their* leisure.

And I would make much greater use of a device that I have spasmodically employed in seminars. "History," Macaulay once said, "can often be best studied in works that are not professedly historical." This I think applies to the study of politics as well. Only one illustration: if a student is interested in dictators, instead of reading some confused and confusing monograph by a psychoanalyst, say, he had far better study or—this would be rare—restudy *Coriolanus*. The theme, the conflict between authoritarian and popular government; and in the play, common folk, ordinary citizens and soldiers, talk much more wisely than their elders or their officers on the significance of the events of the day. "Peace," says a serving man, "makes men hate one another." Another serving man replies: "Reason, because they need one another less in peace than war." What textbooks have said this as well? But I hope that no student of mine would go so far as to agree completely with Hazlitt, who said that anyone who studies *Coriolanus,* "may save himself the trouble of reading Burke's 'Reflections,' Paines' 'Rights of Man' or the Debates in both Houses of Parliament since the French Revolution. The arguments for and against aristocracy or democracy; on the privileges of the few and the claims of the many; on liberty and slavery, power and the abuse of it, peace and war, are here very ably handled with the spirit of a poet and the acuteness of a philosopher."

Yet, as John Palmer points out, the politics are incidental. Shakespeare, whether he writes of Brutus, or Henry, or Coriolanus, is interested "in a human character who also happens to be a politician. There are more politics to be found in his plays than in those of any other dramatic writer. We invariably find, however, that his theme as it takes shape and moves to a climax is not essentially a political problem but the adventure of a human spirit." Rather than arguments for or against aristocracy and democracy, there are arguments between aristocrats and democrats. Power and the abuse of it? "There is no discussion of this problem," Mr. Palmer remarks.

"There is only a proud man who assumes the right to despise persons of a lesser breed." [5]

I do not apologize for the degression for the matter is so important that I glory in belaboring it at length. Let me cite some authorities. Who will deny that our schools of political science are becoming more and more like technical schools? "At a technical school," said William James, "a man may grow into a first-rate instrument for doing a certain job, but he may miss all the graciousness of mind suggested by the term 'liberal culture.' He may remain a cad, and not a gentleman, intellectually pinned down to his one narrow subject, literal, unable to suppose anything different from what he has seen, without imagination, atmosphere, or mental perspective." "Don't teach my boy poetry; he is going to be a grocer," an English mother wrote to her son's teacher. Some American schools of public administration run no risk of receiving such a missive.

Or take international relations—training for teaching or for the foreign service. "This is my plea," writes George Kennan, and than he can there be a greater authority?

> Let those students who want to prepare themselves for work in the international field read their Bible and their Shakespeare, their Plutarch and their Gibbon, perhaps even their Latin and their Greek . . . Let them guard that code of behavior which means that men learn to act toward each other with honor and truthfulness and loyalty, to bestow confidence where confidence is asked, and to build within themselves those qualities of self-discipline and self-restraint on which the integrity of a public service must be founded.
>
> "If these things are clung to and cultivated, then our colleges will be doing what is most important to prepare their sons to confront the problems of international life, whether as citizens or as public servants. *Whatever else can be taught them about the contemporary facts of international life will be a useful superstructure—but only that.*[6]

Take next the judicial profession. In an address before the American Philosophical Society a year or so ago Felix Frankfurter discussed what should go into the making of a great judge. He said (I have to quote from memory) that in addition to being learned in the law, he should know his Montaigne, his Shakespeare, his Montesquieu, and his Burke (whom Gladstone reread every year but I have not been able to see what good it did him; Macaulay also reread Burke, and to much more advantage). Greater judges than Frankfurter had expressed the same opinion before: Holmes, Cardozo, and Learned Hand. Indeed Frankfurter may have been quoting from Hand for the latter somewhere is specific about Montaigne. A man who had read and pondered him, will, as Goethe said of a man who had been "under the palms," never be the same again. If the prescription is good for judges, it is good for those who discuss political institutions and tell their readers how they should choose between alternative public policies or, as is more likely, what compromise is a tolerable substitute for victory by neither side.

And Learned Hand himself tells us that a "law" of any kind—constitution, statute, or rule—or any political decision "is at once prophecy and choice." Prophecies as to the consequences of a law are but slightly aided by formulas or statistics. "They can rest upon no more than enlightened guesses; but those are likely to be successful as they are made by those whose horizons have been widened, and whose outlook has been clarified, by knowledge of what men have striven to do, and how far their hopes and fears have been realized. There is no substitute for an open mind, enriched by reading and the arts."

Take, finally, a great essayist, G. M. Young, who in *Victorian England: Portrait of an Age,* p. 160, writes as follows:

> The common residual intelligence is becoming impoverished for the benefit of the specialist, the technician, and the aesthete: we leave behind us the world of historical ironmasters and banker historians, geological divines and scholar tobacconists, with its genial watchword: to know something of everything and everything of something: and through the gateway of the Competitive Examination we go out into the Waste Land of Experts, each knowing so much about so little that he can neither be contradicted nor is worth contradicting.

This I fear is what we are attempting to do, or at least not attempting to prevent, in our graduate schools of politics or political science. God knows, I do not claim to have been a successful practitioner of what I have long preached, but no one of my students has ever doubted that I would prefer him to have some knowledge of the Elizabethan House of Commons (about which Professor J. E. Neale has so eloquently written) rather than exact information on closure by compartment; that I would prefer that he be able to tell me why, when Metternich sneezed, Europe caught cold, and why Lord Acton called Talleyrand the "wonder of European politics" than that he be able to discuss the drafting niceties or ambiguities of the Charter of the United Nations. If he needs to know about these, he can look them up. And my students have long known that if they were reduced to reading only one magazine I would prefer it to be the *New Yorker* rather than the *American Political Science Review,* or even the *Harvard Law Review.*

Reading, we are told, maketh a full man. (Given what I have said above, I add that writing maketh an exact man.) I can think of no writer on politics who now deserves to be reread, who was not a full man. The study of Politics will not advance—indeed it will go back—if those who study it are not full men. It seems to me that it is a duty of graduate schools to attempt to do away with the emptiness that is now so general. What we can do in the way of sharpening the mind *à la* the case method I do not know. Great stretches of our subject are far more misty than the law, crepuscular as this sometimes is. And mistiness, as Cardinal Newman told us, is "the mother of safety"—safety from being found out.

IV. Since foundations have seemed hard put to it to find ways of spending money—have they forgotten that some great libraries are impoverished and that some fine Liberal Arts Colleges have difficulty in keeping their heads above the water?—there has been a great deal of time and energy devoted to trying to discover ways and means of making political science more scientific. It is futile to argue whether the subject we profess is a science or an art; it is something of the former, and more of the latter. When we refine too much on this theme we descend to logodaedely and logomachy. Whatever we say must conform to the facts: so far we may be scientific. But when we elaborate on the facts? The House of Representatives has 435 members. Is it too large or too small? The average age is x, and twenty per cent of the members are over $x + y$. Good or bad? Lawyers are the dominant occupational group. Welcome or regrettable? John L. Lewis and Douglas MacArthur are in their seventies. Ruled out for the Presidency?

I do not think we should bother graduate students with the schemes of those who think they have found ways of making political science more scientific. In the past some brave souls have sought for the Elixir of Life and for the Philosopher's Stone. As Bertrand Russell has remarked, if men could have found them they would no doubt "have conferred great benefits upon mankind; but as it was, their lives were wasted." We should not waste the lives of graduate students. But perhaps the warning is not necessary. When I read some of those who in my opinion are liable to waste their lives, I wonder whether they write as they do in order to avoid a summons to appear before a Senate's Committee. Hazlitt once declared that Bentham could "wrap up high treason in one of his inextricable periods" and it would never be discovered. I do not suspect treason, but one can say with the Frenchman quoted by Jacques Barzun: "These words must be greatly astonished to find themselves together for assuredly they had never met before." Examples of what I mean will occur to all of you.

"It is the fashion of youth," wrote Hegel, "to dash about in abstractions: but the man who has learnt to know life steers clear of the abstract and adheres to the concrete." To my mind, Hegel remained something of a boy, but if we are boys too frequently we will keep our students from growing up.

In a recent lecture, *Philosophical Style* (University of Manchester Press), a Yale philosopher, Mr. Blanshard, says that "most men's minds are so constituted that they have to think by means of examples; if you do not supply these, they will supply them for themselves, and if you leave it wholly to them, they will do it badly. On the other hand, if you start from familiar things, they are very quick to make the necessary generalizations." In other words, unless you can point to an event or situation and say: "Now you see what I mean," there is no meaning in what you have said. Or, as T. H. Huxley once put it, "There is nothing like a brutal fact to kill a fine theory."

With many graduate students I find that the teaching (or lack of it) they have had ignored the bit of pedagogical theory that I have just stated. The language the students use to me seems designed to make the simple seem intricate and the obvious obscure. They make me recall the lines from *Patience:*

> *The meaning doesn't matter if it's only idle chatter*
> *of a transcendental kind*
> *And every one will say*
> *As you walk your mystic way*
> *"Why if this young man expresses himself in words*
> *too deep for me*
> *What a singularly deep young man, this deep young*
> *man must be."*

For William James and for others, it has been "a peculiarly stubborn effort to think clearly" but how can we be confident of our success or failure unless we can explain to others the results of our effort? How can politics be studied profitably unless those who try to study it can understand each other? Yet they do not and many of them don't seem to care. Since my youth I have been hipped on this matter. Five or six years ago I hammered the point again in a *Political Science Quarterly* article called "Notes on the Language of Politics." I do not repeat anything I said there. My concrete cases are more recent and if they fail to impress you, I beg of you that you will ponder the Cromwellian injunction, "Conceive it possible, in the bowels of Christ, that you may be mistaken."

Mr. Blanshard, to whom I have already referred, quotes Macaulay's familiar diary entry anent a translation of Kant's *Critique:* "I tried to read it, but found it utterly unintelligible, just as if it had been written in Sanscrit. Not one word of it gave me anything like an idea except a Latin quotation from Persius." Mr. Blanshard gives examples of what floored Macaulay and pays his respect to philosophers other than Kant who did and did not make themselves understood. But there is something more. A mathematician writing on the binominal theory may be excused for not caring whether his readers respond to his ideas. A writer on philosophy (and I add on Politics) has a different responsibility. "On the great issues of philosophy (politics)," Mr. Blanshard says, "many of men's hopes and fears do hang, and plain men feel that their philosopher should be alive to this and show it. It is not that they want him to give up his intellectual rigour and scrupulousness—at least they do not think that it is; it is rather that when men are dealing with themes of human importance, they should not deal with them as if nothing but their heads, and somewhat dessicated heads at that, were involved."

In this passage Mr. Blanshard's own rhetoric may leave something to be desired but his point is well taken. Years ago before the professors of rhetoric were purged (save for the titles of endowed chairs) we strove for "clearness, force and ease" (A. S. Hill). "Academic tradition," Mr. Blanshard thinks, "does not require clearness." On the contrary, "there seems to be a presumption that anyone who writes in such a way as to be understood of the many is debasing the coinage of scholarship. But plain men do not see why this should be true and, being one of them, neither do I." I am a plain man also and neither do I. The study of Politics will not be advanced unless we think it an architectonic duty (Aristotle applied the adjective to the subject we profess) to attempt to establish for ourselves and our students the standard that Napoleon demanded of his Code. Not only such clearness that the well intentioned can understand but such clearness that the ill-intentioned cannot maintain that they fail to understand. The French have a saying, *"La clarté et politesse"*—we should do more than just not be impolite.

V. Since I was rash enough to accept the invitation to participate in this symposium I have encountered several former students and have polled a couple of others by mail. I put to them this question: "Do you think that you missed much when you were at Columbia by not being compelled to take a course in methodology? It is true that these gentlemen (and a lady) knew the answer that I would like. But even when they were students they were delighted to be able to give me the answer that I would dislike if they could support it by good arguments. There was no intimation of regret that methodology had not been crammed down their throats.

When "experts on education" insist on courses on methods of teaching, and on the duties of janitors, to the subordination to further work in Sciences or Humanities; and when they seek changes in—the deterioration of—high school and college curricula so that second- or third-raters will not feel that they are out-shone by the first-raters, the taunt has been made that these experts in Education want everyone else to remain as ignorant as they are. I sometimes suspect that at least occasionally the insistence on training in research methods before a student has anything in mind to research upon;

on field work, and on training in the use of techniques comes from persons who are themselves not too well informed on anything else. Let me for a moment expatiate on "method." What I write comes from two learned friends—a physicist and a chemist.

When the picture drawn of science is one of triumphant method, the picture is greatly distorted. Philosophers from Bacon to John Stuart Mill have fooled the lay public, and in this group fall the social scientists. Bacon drew a picture of a research institution so carefully planned along methodological lines that even a congressman could have discovered laws of nature. His contemporary, the great Harvey, commented on this scheme that "his ideas of science were such as might be expected of a Lord Chancellor." Mill's Canons of Induction have long been taught to unsuspecting seniors as the last word in scientific method. Physicists say that they may be applicable to such a problem as finding a leak in a vacuum pump, but challenge anyone to adduce a single important law which has been discovered by their aid. The reason for this sterility is due in the first place to the fact that no method exists for formulating problems, and secondly to the fact that a problem for whose solution a known method is available is essentially trivial. This is from the point of view of the would-be scholar: an elementary problem may have great practical importance, but its solution contributes little to the development of a science.

The one requirement for real progress in a science is insight, which is a creative activity of the mind. To ask a really pertinent question is an attribute of genius. Huxley quotes Newton as saying that he solved his problems by "intending" his mind on them, and adds "but twenty lesser could have intended their minds till they cracked, without a like result." It was Huxley also who remarked that though there might be wisdom in a multitude of counselors, it was only in one or two of them. These two quotations are a sufficient commentary on all schemes for effecting miracles in science by weight of numbers, by co-operation of second rate minds, achieving first rate results. Institutes of Human Relations are about as effective as a horse race or Mothers Day for putting money into circulation without leaving any permanent effect. Science is in its own way the most marvellously co-operative enterprise ever undertaken by man. But that way is not the way of committees. A Pasteur, a Newton, or a Darwin can put a generation to work filling in the details of one great synthetic idea, and in this process method plays a large part. It provides jobs for the lesser minds. But these jobs would not have existed otherwise, and here I think we touch the fundamental defect of most social science. It has had no Newton to give it a great vision, and until such a man appears, there are no real tasks for the second- and third-rate minds. This in itself would not be so bad; the real trouble is that while there is as yet no science of sociology, there are professors of sociology; that the bunk is so elaborately organized, with such large funds at its disposal. Economics and Government have a few great names to show, a few clear concepts to serve as a foundation, but the sociologist has only a technical vocabulary to cover his intellectual nakedness. Today we spend millions, and with some effect, on the problems of disease. How much, think you, would those millions have accomplished before Pasteur? And the worst of it is that when the Pasteur of social science arises, he will almost certainly not be a professor of sociology, and will met with their united opposition, just as Pasteur had to fight the medical profession in his day. (The pen is mine but the words are those of a physicist.)

Next the question of pooh-pooh. It is undoubtedly true that men of genius have had to face ridicule, and prophecy of failure, but it does not follow that committees which we think are making ridiculous proposals or the evangelists of method to whom we refuse to listen will turn out to be geniuses.

If as Lord Halifax once said (the quotation is mine and does not come from my physicist), "The struggling for Knowledge has a pleasure in it, like that of wrestling with a fine woman," who is rash enough to suggest a method for making the wrestling successful? And, if it is sometimes true that "Experience maketh more Prophets than Revelation," it is not experience with method. Scientific method, as the Nobel Prize winner P. W. Bridgman said, is no more than doing your damndest "with no holds barred." That, I think, is the gospel we should preach to graduate students. And we should not forget Mr. Justice Holmes' belief that what we frequently need is better understanding of the obvious rather than further investigation of the obscure.

The core of truth here is not affected by Jacob Viner's

Let unlearned laymen not be too sure
That what seems simple is not obscure.

Yes. But then the need may be for further explanation and not for investigation.

VI. One matter has disturbed me ever since the days when I was a graduate student and I am ashamed to say that, as a graduate professor, I never tried to do anything about it.

When I left the Johns Hopkins University, I was struck by the fact that the professor under whom I had studied used warm terms in recommending me as a teacher when he did not have the faintest idea whether I could handle myself in front of a class of undergraduates. He knew me as an irregular listener to his lectures, as a member of his seminar, as the possessor of a certain number of facts, and as the author of some articles that had appeared in American and English reviews and of a dissertation that was almost ready for the printer.

I was so impressed by his indifference to my jejuneness that I wrote a short article entitled "A Neglected Aspect of Graduate Instruction" (*The Nation*, Sept. 9, 1915). I pointed out that medical schools gave clinical training; that law schools had moot courts; and that at divinity schools the "seminoles" practiced the preparation of manuscripts which would be kept in a barrel. I boldly announced that "this analogy is closest, for both the clergyman and the teacher give the public not what it demands but what is good for it." I suggested that in the graduate school there should be some practice in "oral and extemporaneous discussion of elementary problems" so that the professors might discover "whether the student is able to teach," and his fellow students might report on whether they profited or suffered. I bolstered this proposal by quoting from a recent report by Nicholas Murray Butler to the Trustees of Columbia University: "The youngest of instructors," he said, "is shut up in the classroom with a company of students and left to his own devices. The damage he may do in learning what teaching is all about is frequently irreparable but no older or more experienced head is at hand to counsel and direct him." So far as I know Nicholas Murray Butler never tried to do anything about this. Nor did any of his graduate departments.

What I have just said comes in part from some comments that I made on the 1951 report, *Goals for Political Science*. That report told us that there were five thousand persons "teaching in Political Science in the United States." When I recall my tyrociny and when I reflect on those whom we have speeded from the Faculty of Political Science at Columbia—some very good, and now in the faculties of major league Universities and Colleges and in the government service; some good, and doing useful work in the minor leagues; and some lost in the sticks—my feelings range from pride to uneasiness. When I ponder the figure of five thousand—it must be larger now—I am inclined to shudder. After he had reviewed some new recruits for the British Army, the Duke of Wellington once remarked: "I don't know if they will scare the enemy; but by God they scare me."

I should like to see some graduate department of political science tear a leaf out of the book of the law school or the theological seminary.

VII. An addendum to what I have said above:

In his provocative lectures, *On Understanding Science,* Mr. Conant proposed an interesting test of whether or no an area of inquiry is a science. He asked whether, if early pioneers in certain fields could be brought to life again, they would be enormously impressed by the great advances that had been made in their specialities. He answered that Galileo, Newton, Harvey and others would be astounded. That, he said, would not be the case with the painters or the poets or the philosophers. Plato, Machiavelli, Gibbon, and Burke would be unimpressed by what they found people saying and doing about the political and social world in which we live.

The test is one with which I do not quarrel, nor do I dissent from Mr. Conant's conclusion. But there is a matter that he does not mention. It is germane to what I have been trying to say, and it will be true in "1984." Conant's galaxy of scientific pioneers would return to a physical world which is substantially the same as the one they left. There have been various Acts of God—earthquakes, floods, soil erosion (insufficiently checked by man)—but these have not presented the astronomer or the geologist or the physicist with any new problem.[7]

But what changes there have been in the political and social world!

Had the Roman Emperors returned to earth in Bolingbroke's age—in the days of Walpole, the first English Prime Minister—the contrasts they found would not have surprised them as much as the developments since then would surprise Bolingbroke and Walpole. Seventeen centuries wrought less than have the last two centuries. The data of the natural scientist have remained constant. The data of the writer on politics have increased enormously. And, as Mr. Weldon tells us, "the questions of political philosophy unlike those of science are eternal questions which every generation of men must propound and answer anew."

Mr. Conant says none of these things, and perhaps there is no reason why he should have said them. With a poise that is unusual in these days when some natural scientists are profuse with orgiastic opinions on what the world must do to be saved from the atomic bomb, Mr. Conant remarks that "the very subjects which fall outside my definition of accumulative knowledge far outrank the others," and asks two questions: "How often in our daily lives are we influenced in important decisions by the results of the scientific inquiries of modern times? How often do we act without reflecting the influence of the philosophy and poetry which we have consciously and unconsciously imbibed over many years?" and he adds: "A dictator wishing to mold the thoughts and actions of a literate people could afford to leave the scientists and scholars alone, but he must win over to his side or destroy the philosophers, the writers, and the artists."

Two centuries and a half ago Andrew Fletcher of Saltoun wrote: "I knew a very wise man [Selden?] who believed that if a man were permitted to make all the ballads, he need not care who should make the laws of a nation. And we find that most of the ancient legislators thought they could not well reform the manners of any city without the help of a lyric, and sometimes of a dramatic poet." Perhaps there is someone in our guild who will eschew turgid prose and write poetry.

VIII. For a good many of us who labor in universities the chief hope of achieving a measure of transient academic immortality lies in the discovery of choice spirits among students and in the influences we can bring to bear on them. Unfortunately, however, we have no formula for anticipating results. We cannot be sure that we have separated the sheep from the goats or the bright from the dull. We cannot forecast achievements, for students not infrequently are chameleons rather than leopards. We cannot guess the accidental influences and stimuli that will make for moderate or even great ability.

I take it that no one would say that the founder of the Faculty of Political Science at Columbia University, John W. Burgess, is a scholar in the field of history or public law who should be consulted. Yet he had one claim to greatness: the students whom he encouraged and perhaps inspired, even though in their mature years they were inclined to laugh at him. I have wondered whether they laughed as students when they heard him say, "Now, sound political science teaches that. . . ."

Among the students to whom he lectured there was talent greater than the talents that he possessed. There were the seeds of unwritten books that were abler and more influential than those that he wrote. I doubt whether he sensed this, but we should in the case of ourselves, and, alas, there is no philosopher's stone; there is no *vade mecum* for achieving the results that we desire. There is no formula that enables us to avoid offering either swaddling clothes or mental straightjackets.

There is, however, one distinction that we should always insist upon. The function of a university, as I have said, is not primarily to inculcate knowledge. The teaching of wisdom may not be possible, but a university is a place where it can be learned. There is a Chinese saying: "What one knows: to know that one knows it. What one does not know: to know that one does not know it. That is true wisdom." In another sense the distinction has been put plainly and felicitously in some lines of Cowper:

> *Knowledge and wisdom, far from being one*
> *Have ofttimes no connection.*
> *Knowledge dwells*
> *In heads replete with thoughts of other men;*
> *Wisdom in minds attentive to their own.*
> *Knowledge is proud that he has learned so much;*
> *Wisdom is humble that he knows no more.*

This says better than I have been able to much of what I have been attempting to say; and I therefore say no more myself. I conclude with, as Ed. Murrow would put it, a thought for today, and good many tomorrows. The thought is from *The Education of Henry Adams:*

A parent gives life, but as parent, gives no more. A murderer takes life, but his deed stops there. A teacher affects eternity; he can never tell where his influence stops. A teacher is expected to teach truth, and may perhaps flatter himself that he does so, if he stops with the alphabet or the multiplication table, as a mother teaches truth by making her child eat with a spoon; but morals are quite another truth and philosophy is more complex still. A teacher must either treat history as a catalogue, a record, a romance, or as an evolution; and whether he affirms or denies evolution, he falls into all the burning faggots of the pit. He makes of his scholars either priests or atheists, plutocrats or socialists, judges or anarchists, almost in spite of himself. In essence incoherent and immoral, history had either to be taught as such—or falsified.

Henry Adams wrote "history;" you and I, professing what we do, can write "politics."

PART THREE

Analytic Systems

The essays of this section describe the methods used by several behaviorally oriented systems of analysis, including learning theory, communications theory, small-group theory, and action theory. The possible applicability of these analytic systems for the study of political relationships is considered in some of the essays.

CHARLES E. OSGOOD [1]

Behavior Theory and the Social Sciences

PSYCHOLOGY HAS a rather unique position among the sciences. It is at once the most social of the biological sciences and the most biological of the social sciences. As the science of behavior—particularly human behavior—it claims and maintains active interest in much of what is equally the domain of neurology and physiology and is much of what is equally the domain of sociology and anthropology. And its practitioners reflect this Janus-faced orientation; some of us are quite indistinguishable from neurophysiologists, and indeed prefer their meetings to our own; others of us consort almost exclusively with cultural anthropologists, and a few, like myself, seem to contain Janus within themselves—on the one hand I am an experimental psychologist specializing in learning theory and on the other I do research on human communication, meaning, and psycholinguistics. Despite fractionation of both the field and the individual, this duality of interest may have certain advantages; whereas principles of human behavior may aid our understanding of problems in the social sciences, so may the nature of these problems impel reanalysis and modification of behavior theory. This paper will, I hope, illustrate both effects.

CERTAIN RELATIONS BETWEEN THE BEHAVIORAL SCIENCES

One indication of the validity of a principle is the vigor and persistence with which it is opposed. I think this holds for the rather old-fashioned notion of the hierarchy of sciences—that the principles of chemistry are reducible to physics, that the principles of biology are reducible to physiochemistry, and so on. There is today very strong resistance to this sort of reductionism, particularly among social scientists, and they may be right, but I find it a fruitful point of view. Fruitful, that is, as a guide in theorizing, not as a restriction on such activity.

Let us look for a moment at theory in psychology from this viewpoint. The psychologist, when he is functioning as a psychologist, is limited to observing what goes into the organism (which he calls *stimuli*) and what comes out (which he calls *responses*). Between these two observation points lies a no-man's-land of speculation; this region is the nervous system, also referred to these days as "the little black box." Now the psychologist's task is to explain and predict relations between and among his two sets of observables, stimuli and responses, and to do this he must make certain assumptions about what goes on in the little black box. In other words, psychological *theory,* as contrasted with psychological observation, is made up of hunches about how the nervous system operates. This is true for every psychological principle, whether it be a simple association postulate by the behaviorist or a field of interaction postulate by the gestaltist. These assumptions about the nervous system may be explicit or may remain implicit, but they are being made nevertheless. One criterion of psychological theory, then, is compatability with what is known about neurophysiology; other things equal, a theory that is consistent with such knowledge is better than one that is not—but this is only one criterion.

I like to think that the same logic holds for the relation between psychology and the more social sciences. In this case, behavioral principles become the great unknown, the little black box about which the economist, sociologist, or political scientist necessarily makes assumptions when he postulates general principles or laws operating at his own level, explaining and predicting relations among *his* observables. When the economist states laws, for example, he is setting up some kind of "economic man," who perhaps behaves rationally and is motivated by self-interest. When the linguist describes certain general laws governing language change over space and time, he is making assumptions about how individual language users learn and modify the myriad habits of hearing and speaking. When the sociologist generalizes about status and role in a society, surely he is also assuming something about how individual human beings perceive, learn, are motivated, and come in conflict. And, without knowing anything about it, really, I nevertheless expect that when the political scientist interprets repeatable relations among *his* observables he is also making certain assumptions about human behavior.

For the most part, as in psychological theorizing, I imagine that these assumptions about the principles of behavior, the more molecular science in this case, remain implicit. In fact, the social scientist is sometimes quite shocked at the inappropriateness of his assumptions when they are made explicit—as when labor-management people discovered that economic self-interest was by no means the only, or even strongest, motivation of workers. It would seem useful to make the assumptions of social science theory as explicit as possible so that their compatability with what *is* known about human behavior can be examined. The greater this compatability—again, we must stress "other things equal"—the better the theory. And let me hasten to add that this does not mean that theories at a molar level must be limited to what is known at the more molecular level. Quite to the contrary—just as the psychologist is always far beyond the neurophysiologist in the assumptions that he must make about the nervous system, so is the social scientist far beyond the psychologist in the assumptions *he* must make about human behavior. Only when molar assumptions prove to be flatly contrary to what is known molecularly does the molar principle lose tenability. And, as a matter of fact, what seem to be necessary assumptions for psychological science often provide an impetus and direction to the research of neurophysiologists, and I'm sure this holds for the impact of the other social sciences upon psychology as well.

BEHAVIOR THEORY—AN OVERVIEW

As I have already said, behavior theory in the broadest sense is made up of hunches about how the nervous system operates to generate the lawful relations we observe among and between stimuli and responses. Over the past century we can trace a gradual refinement in the rules of procedure whereby psychologists make and test these hunches, and this trend toward increased rigor in theorizing has been paralleled by similar development in other social sciences.

In nineteenth-century psychology the characteristic procedure in theorizing was to simply postulate a new entity or mechanism whenever some new regularity was discovered. Whenever something needed explaining, a new explanatory device was stuck inside the little black box, and it rapidly became chock-full of ill-assorted and ill-digested demons. For every nameable phenomenon of human behavior a different "faculty" would be posited to explain it; for every nameable motive, a different "instinct" would be listed as its explanation. And, at least for communicating with patients, Freud had big, flat-footed Super-egos stomping around on red, slippery Ids, while cleverly anxious little Egos tried to arbitrate. Thus, as suggested in Figure 1 (below), the little black box was filled with a wonderously diverse collection of explanatory devices, just about as many as there were things to be explained. This could fairly be called "junk-shop psychology." While it had the advantage of free exercise of often brilliant intuition, it had the disadvantage of complete lack of parsimony and consequent confusion.

FIGURE 1.

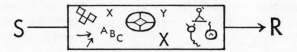

In direct revulsion against this brand of theorizing, a group of American behaviorists around the turn of the century went to the other extreme, claiming that the psychologist was better off if he made no assumptions whatsoever about what went on in the little black box. The group included Weiss, Kantor, Watson, and somewhat later, Skinner. This viewpoint toward theory has come to be known as "empty organism psychology." According to this view, as shown below in diagrammatic fashion, there is absolutely nothing in the region between S and R, and what *is* there is none of the psychologist's business! This objective viewpoint was a healthy antidote for the loose mentalism which had preceded it, and it came to characterize American psychology. It led to increased emphasis on the details of accurately measuring stimuli and recording responses, to the establishment of dependable empirical laws relating input and output events, and to a general suspicion of unobservable explanatory devices, like "ideas," "purposes," and "feelings." But it also led psychologists to limit their interest to problems that could be handled in this simple mold—which automatically eliminated most phenomena of peculiarly human significance. The rat replaced the human as the standard subject in psychological research.

FIGURE 2.

Most contemporary behaviorists could be characterized as "frustrated empty-boxers." Armed with a minimum but effective set of principles—really a set of empirical generalizations gleaned from systematic observations of S-R functions—they set out to explain and predict behavior in general. It soon became obvious, even with rats as subjects, that something had to be put back into the little black box, that some intervening variables had to be postulated between S and R in order to explain our observations. But the contemporary behaviorist was more sophisticated about theory construction than his nineteenth-century forebearer and, furthermore, he was under constant critical pressure from his objectively oriented colleagues. Therefore [1] he tried to put as little back into the box as possible, *e.g.*, postulate as few intervening variables as possible, and [2] he tried to anchor these hypothesized constructs to antecedent and subsequent observables as firmly as he could. What he has done, in effect, is to postulate an intervening response-like process which produces self-stimulation, *e.g., a two-stage mediation process,* as shown below. In other words, "mediation psychology" sets up within the

FIGURE 3.

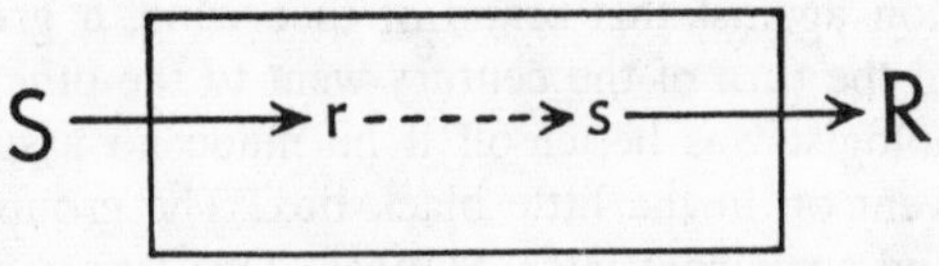

$$S \longrightarrow r \text{-----} s \longrightarrow R$$

organism a replica of the S-R model, and it assumes that the same laws governing single-stage S-R processes apply to both stages of the mediation model. This is the essence of Hull's "pure-stimulus-act," a response whose sole function is to provide the organism with distinctive self-stimulation (and which Hull identified, interestingly enough, with symbolic processes); it is the ubiquitous "movement-produced-stimulus" of the mechanist, Guthrie, with which he extricates himself from most tight empirical corners; and Tolman's "expectancy" or "hypothesis" in rats can, I think, be shown to be functionally the same process. Later I shall try to show how the postulation of a mediation process makes possible a tremendous expansion of the explanatory power of learning theory.

Although the gestalt psychologists have been more concerned with perception than with learning, at the level of higher mental processes like problem solving, insight, and concept formation they have certainly come into competition with the behavioristically inclined people. Using principles of organization developed in connection with perceptual studies, they have tried to interpret processes like insight as sudden restructurings of the perceptual field of the organism. This kind of behavior theory, since it seems to involve interactions among sensory processes, has been called "S-S psychology" and might be diagramed as below. Some writers have put Tolman's kind of theory in this category, because he deals with associations between signs (S_1) and

FIGURE 4.

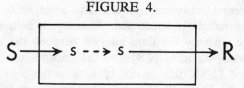

their significates (S_2), but I think his view is essentially a variant of S-R behaviorism. In passing it should be noted that behavioristic S-R conceptions have had practically nothing to say about perception itself, and this is certainly an important part of behavior-in-general.

Under the pressure of trying to handle language phenomena, I have found it necessary to put something else back into the little black box. Along with symbolic, representational processes (which I think can be handled with the two-stage mediation model), language behavior also includes the most complex integrations of both perceptual processes and motor skill processes. On both input (decoding) and output (encoding) sides of the equation as shown in the diagram below, I think we must postulate *central integration* among neural events. We need something of this kind to handle standard perceptual

FIGURE 5.

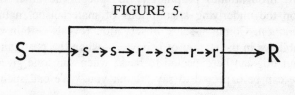

phenomena like closure as well as standard motor phenomena like the execution of skilled movements at a rate far greater than could be explained by S-R feedback mechanisms. We might call this model "integration-mediation psychology." But we have been leaping ahead much too quickly here; let's back-track to the simple "empty organism" model and see what basic principles appear to govern S-R relations.

BASIC PRINCIPLES OF S-R BEHAVIOR THEORY

Although learning theorists disagree among themselves somewhat as to the language to be used, and occasionally as to the necessity of certain postulations, the basic principles described below would find pretty wide acceptance. They all deal in one way or another with the formation of *associations* among input and output events by organisms and thus reflect our heritage from philosophical Associationism—except that the events associated are stimuli and responses rather than ideas. They all may also be viewed as fundamental assumptions we psychologists make about how the nervous system both organizes and is organized by behavioral experience.

(1) *Contiguity. In general, the closer in time the occurrence of a stimulus event and a response event, the greater the increment in their association.* It is the time interval between a stimulus and a response, not two stimuli, with which this principle is concerned. Although it is true that in *conditioning* procedure we vary the time interval between the to-be-conditioned (or to-be-associated) stimulus (CS) and the unconditioned (or already-associated) stimulus (US), this is simply to guarantee sufficient contiguity between CS and the R which US controls. Some such principle as this is necessary on common-sense grounds—all events that occur in a lifetime are not associated indiscriminately. Its operation is also clearly evident in all experimental data on learning; the more we separate in time the S-R events to be associated, the more difficult it becomes to form the association, *e.g.,* to get this S to elicit this R predictably. Degree of associativeness is probably a negatively accelerated decreasing function of time interval and limited to short time periods in the pure case. A number of assumptions about the nervous system are implicit in this psychological principle: (*a*) that the neural correlates of motor events are capable of becoming dependent on those of sensory events; (*b*) that these neural correlates must persist or reverberate over at least short intervals of time; and (*c*) that to become 'associated,' the sensory and motor correlates must be simultaneously active and somehow brought into propinquity in space. The latter notion really depends upon the underlying assumptions of materialistic, natural science.

(2) *Summation.* Common-sense observation reveals certain consistencies and predictabilities in the stream of behavior—when the postman approaches the door, your dog can be expected to bark; when someone gives your child a present, he can be expected to say "thank you." We call such predictable

regularities *habits*. We also note that these habits can vary in *strength*—which we index by observing the probability with which R follows S, the amplitude of R given S, and the latency or speed with which R follows S. Futhermore, this *habit-strength* seems to increase with repetition or practice. As a general principle we may state that *successive increments in the association of a stimulus event with a response event summate to yield habit strength.* It seems reasonable that the strength of any habit should have a limit or asymptote, and empirical data do show that with large numbers of repetitions the increments per trial become imperceptible. Habit strength is an increasing negatively accelerated function of the number of repetitions. Here again the psychologist makes assumptions about neurophysiology—perhaps that at the synapses linking the neural correlates of sensory and motor events certain progressive and cumulative changes in conductivity can occur.

(3) *Generalization.* Now, it is one of the very fortunate things about behavior as we observe it that having learned to make a particular response in a particular situation we do not have to completely relearn this habit if the situation changes slightly, nor do we have to accomplish the behavior with precisely the original movement. Having learned to say "thank you" in the home, your child is likely to employ the same bit of social grace elsewhere; having learned to walk normally, we can usually hobble about pretty well with a sore ankle. It appears that habits spread or generalize among similar stimuli and similar responses. There is also a logical necessity for postulating a generalization principle—our habit principle says that successive increments in the association of a stimulus and a response summate, yet if there is one thing we know about behavior it is that precisely the same stimulus and response are never repeated. How, then, can there be summation among unique events? The following principle takes account of common-sense observation and the apparent paradox: *the habit-strength generated between a stimulus event and a response event generalizes to other stimulus and other response events, the amount of such generalized habit strength being a function of (a) the similarity between directly associated events and non-associated events and (b) the strength of the original association.* Laboratory evidence is consistent with such a principle; if we train a rat to jump in the air to a 1000-cycle tone, by pairing this tone repeatedly with shock, and then test with other tones of varying frequency, results like those shown in Figure 6 are typically obtained—the more similar the test tone to the conditioning tone, the greater the amplitude (speed, probability) of generalized jumping. This principle assumes that, in both sensory and motor nervous systems, the neural correlates of similar events are closer together than those of less similar events, and the organization of both sensory and motor projection systems does seem to display just such an organization.

(4) *Motivation.* The mere fact that a set of associations or habits have been learned does not guarantee that they will be utilized. Place a satiated

rat at the starting point of a well-learned maze and he will probably groom himself or go to sleep rather than running; place a highly motivated worker on the job and he will usually produce more than a poorly motivated worker. Learning theorists phrase this general law of behavior somewhat as follows: *motivation combines multiplicatively with habit-strength to yield performance.* In other words, if either the motivation level or the learned habit-strength is zero, the probability of the behavior in question becomes zero; and further, this implies that within limits, at least, we can trade or exchange drive for learning and maintain a constant output—a highly motivated student with poor training may equal in performance a poorly motivated student with good training. In the laboratory we usually index drive level operationally by the number of hours deprivation of food or water in the case of hunger and thirst drives, by physical intensity of shock in pain drive, by the measured amount of testosterone in the blood in sex drive, and so on; with human subjects we usually depend upon such indirect indices

FIGURE 6.

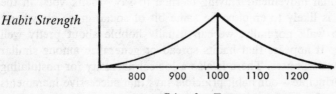

Stimulus Frequency

as the subject's verbal statements—what he tells us about himself—or even, quite circularly, upon how energetically he performs.

(5) *Reinforcement.* It is commonplace in the home as well as in the animal laboratory that subjects learn better when they are rewarded than when they are not. In fact, in the laboratory as well as outside of it, unrewarded or unreinforced associations tend to get weaker despite repetition— a process we call *extinction.* Some psychologists—so called "effect" theorists like Thorndike and Hull—have incorporated this basic empirical fact about behavior in a postulate; others accept the phenomenon but think it can be derived from other principles—for example, a sheer contiguity theorist like Guthrie. Since this paper is not the place for arguing fine points of theory— and, indeed, the amount of evidence that would have to be evaluated is prohibitive—I shall merely state the reinforcement principle in its usual form: *the size of the increment in association between a stimulus event and a response event varies inversely with the time interval between association and a reinforcing state of affairs and directly with the amount of reinforcement.* If a rat is learning to press a bar in order to obtain food pellets, (*a*) the greater the delay in receiving pellets the more trials it takes to reach

a criterion of performance and (*b*) the smaller the size of the pellet the longer it will take. What actually constitutes this "reinforcing state of affairs"? Some theorists, like Hull, specify reduction in the intensity of a drive (hunger, thirst, pain, anxiety, and so on) as the essential condition. A possible neurophysiological correlate of reinforcement has appeared in some recent experiments at Montreal—when performance was accompanied by electrical stimulation of a certain brain region in animal subjects, learning occurred; when stimulation of this region was eliminated, learning failed to take place and old habits were extinguished. What relation this may bear physiologically to drive states and their reduction I do not know. I should also add that I have only read a newspaper account of this work, and newspaper accounts of scientific work are notoriously unreliable.

(6) *Inhibition.* Now, let me describe two paradoxes. The first, already mentioned briefly, is *extinction.* Suppose a rat has already learned to press a bar to obtain food pellets that roll down into a cup in what we call a Skinner Box; suddenly, without the rat's knowledge, we shut off the supply of pellets. For some period of time, the rat will persist in pressing the bar because he has both a learned habit and is hungry; but the rate of pressing will gradually go down until he fails to press the bar for some criterion interval, say 5 minutes, and we say he has extinguished. This in itself is paradoxical, because there is nothing in our principles so far to account for this behavior—a motivated organism is reacting to a stimulus (pressing the bar) repeatedly, S is being followed by R, yet the habit seems to be getting weaker. Why, you may ask, do we not simply postulate that unreinforced associations are weakened by repetition? If we do this, we run into another paradox, called *spontaneous recovery.* Let us now take our extinguished rat out of the Skinner Box and let him rest overnight in his home cage; the next morning we put him back in the Skinner Box again and, Lo and Behold!, he is busily pressing the bar again—if we claimed that the habit had been lost during the previous extinction, then it would appear that a habit could be learned spontaneously without reinforced repetitions, which would be contrary to all of our principles! These paradoxical phenomena are well-documented, and it is situations like these that 'put the pressure' on theorists.

To handle this type of situation we may postulate an inhibition principle: *the execution of any response produces an increment of inhibition toward making that response, such inhibition increasing with the effortfulness of the response and dissipating spontaneously with rest.* During learning the effects of reinforcement conteract this work-produced decrements, unless the rate of responding is too great, but as soon as reinforcements cease to be given, inhibitory tendencies mount to a point where the animal stops responding, *e.g.,* extinction. During rest in his home cage, the work-produced inhibition dissipates and in the morning the learned habit appears again spontaneously. Q.E.D. But haven't we explained too much and gotten ourselves into another paradox? If what we have said were literally true, animals would never be able to unlearn habits, and this doesn't jibe with facts—the recovery from successive extinctions actually becomes less and less. As a matter of fact, we can handle this without any new principles. Since the fatigue sensations accompanying work-produced inhibition constitute an unpleasant drive state, and since rest involves spontaneous reduction in this drive state, we have the necessary reinforcement conditions for new learning. During the later stages of extinction, whenever the subject stops reacting and rests while still in the situation, he is actually learning *not* to press the bar and this response-of-not-responding is being reinforced by fatigue-drive reduction. This inhibitory habit subtracts directly from the previous excitatory one and constitutes the permanent unlearning produced by extinction operations.

(7) *Selection.* We are all familiar with situations involving response conflict. Approaching a divided staircase, we experience a momentary ambivalence as to turning left or right; warned not to touch the freshly baked and frosted cake, but seeing it right there before our eyes, we can remember oscillating between approach and avoidance. In general, *whenever two or more responses have been associated with the same stimulus, the reaction having the momentarily strongest habit strength will occur.* If the reactions in question are compatible, of course (like smiling and shaking hands), then both may occur simultaneously. When a number of incompatible reactions are associated with a common stimulus, we speak of a *divergent hierarchy;* this is a response competition situation, and probabilities of alternatives depend on contextual factors and the strengths of motives associated with each. When a number of stimuli are associated with a common reaction, we speak of a *convergent hierarchy;* this is a facilitative, transfer situation and follows the principle of generalization already discussed.

These seven principles are by no means exhaustive, and they are not worded precisely as any particular theorist might state them, and they are not the exact assumptions made by any particular theorist, but they do represent, I think, a set of basic notions which are common in one form or another to most phychologists who deal with learning. To give you a better idea of how learning theorists operate with principles like these, we may analyse a few standard learning situations.

Maze Learning. The maze is one instance of a general category we refer to as *instrumental learning;* the subject must make the correct series of responses before reinforcement is given, and hence the correct responses are "instrumental" in obtaining reward. Figure 7 diagrams a multiple-T maze, where *S* is the starting point, *G* is the goal box where a food reward is found, and the encircled numbers refer to successive choice points. At each such choice point we have a stimulus situation and two alternative reactions, turning left or right. We shall assume that our subjects are highly motivated. Now we may ask a series of questions of Nature and predict from theory what her answer will be. (1) *What will be the order of eliminating errors?* Prediction: other things equal, errors will be eliminated first at the choice point nearest the goal and work back progressively toward the starting point. Why? The closer an S-R association to the point of reinforcement, the greater the increment in habit-strength. Although the animal always gets to the goal, any wrong response necessarily causes a longer delay in obtaining reward, and hence the ratio always favors the correct choice. (2) *How will increasing the physical similarity between choice points 3 and 4 affect errors at choice point 3?* Prediction: increased similarity will increase errors at choice point 3. Why? In (1) above we have deduced that the right-turning response at 4 will tend to be learned earlier than the left-turning

FIGURE 7.

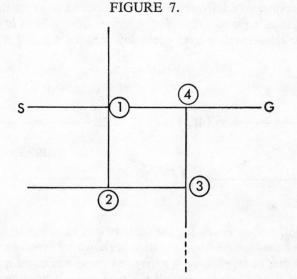

response at 3; the greater the similarity of choice points 3 and 4, the greater will be the generalization of the right-turning response from 4 back to 3, where it is an error. Since this "error" is also followed by reinforcement, it will be strengthened and compete more successfully with the correct reaction at 3. (3) *What effect upon errors at choice point 3 will lengthening the blind alley there have?* Prediction: the longer the blind, the more quickly it will be eliminated. Why? Two principles combine to yield this prediction: in the first place, the longer the blind the greater the delay in reinforcement and hence the more favorable the ratio of strengthening for the correct reaction; in the second place, running a long blind produces more extinctive inhibition, which would be used to explain the fact that the rat runs less and less far into the blind as trials continue.

Classical Conditioning. Pavlov studied a learning situation in which one stimulus which was not originally capable of eliciting a response became gradually capable of doing so if it was paired with another stimulus which regularly and reliably produced this response. Figure 8 diagrams the relations assumed in conditioning in two ways—first descriptively (A) and then interpretively (B) according to the principles we have been discussing. A typical case would be that in which a dog subject learns to salivate to a tone (CS), food-powder blown into the mouth being the unconditioned stimulus (US) and amount of saliva secreted being the reaction measured (R). The model given as *A* makes it appear as if this were a different "kind" of learning, simple substitution of one stimulus for another. The model given as *B* assumes that the dog must be hungry (motivated) in order to be conditioned and that the US (food-powder) has a dual function, both in reliably eliciting the correct response of salivating (an unconditioned reflex in this case) and in providing reinforcement (reduction in hunger drive). Thus in conditioning, according to this view, we have contiguity between CS and R, motivation,

FIGURE 8.

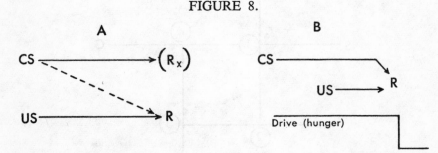

reinforcement, and evidence for summation into habit-strength, in that the probability of the tone eliciting salivation is shown by experiment to increase with the number of repetitions. We may ask some additional questions: (1) *Does ease of conditioning vary with the time interval between CS and US?* Prediction: from some optimal interval (about .5 sec., presumably dependent on nervous system functioning), ease of conditioning will decrease as interval between CS and US (and hence interval between CS and R) increases. This phenomenon is regularly observed. (2) *What will happen as the pitch of the tone is varied?* Prediction: the less similar in frequency any test tone from the tone used during conditioning, the less will be the amount of saliva secreted. This phenomenon is regularly observed. (3) *What occurs if the US is discontinued?* Prediction: since reinforcement is no longer given, but the reaction keeps occurring, inhibition develops and the magnitude of the salivary reaction will decrease. This is known as extinction of a conditioned reaction.

Discrimination. Now, suppose that in the situation we have just been describing one tone is always associated with the giving of food-powder (SA) and another tone is always associated with the withholding of food-powder (SB). As shown in the diagram below, the habit-strength associated with the positive stimulus must generalize along the pitch continuum. Similarly, we assume that the inhibitory tendency associated with the negative stimulus must generalize (e.g., generalization of a response of not-responding). If we apply principle 7 (selection among competing R's according to momentary habit-strength) to each point along the continuum, we in effect plot the resolution of these two gradients (dashed line). Wherever the resolution is above the base-line, there will be that degree of excitatory tendency; wherever the resolution is below the base-line, there will be that degree of inhibitory tendency. What this operation does in effect is to narrow the range of generalization, e.g., produce discrimination. As can be seen, it could be predicted that the more similar the two tones, the more difficult it should be to obtain dis-

FIGURE 9.

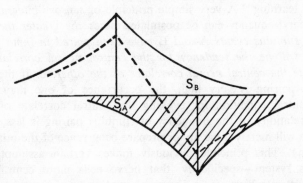

crimination, and this is precisely what is observed. To climb out into the world of everyday affairs again, it would be predicted, for example, that a man hired to reject unpainted plaques in an assembly line would have a harder job if the paint were white than if it were red.

Insufficiency of the Single-Stage S-R Model

Employed with ingenuity, even such a minimal set of tools as these can be effective in predicting and interpreting over a considerable range of behavioral phenomena. But there are some gross insufficiencies with this single-stage S-R model, particularly when one tries to handle typically human activities. For one thing, the entire problem of *perceptual organization* seems to be omitted, since it involves relations among input events, S-S integrations; for another, the development and use of *motor skills* is omitted, to the extent that such behavioral phenomena involved R-R integrations; and finally, in its unextended form, the single-stage S-R model is incapable of handling *symbolic processes,* which are so characteristic of human behavior. The reader should keep in mind, however, that in pointing out these insufficiencies of the S-R model I am not claiming that its basic principles are thereby invalid—to the contrary, in dealing with the symbolic processes, at least, the same general principles will be assumed to operate.

Perceptual Organization. Our sensory, receiving systems are so planned by Nature that points on the receptor surface (*e.g.,* the retina of the eye) are mapped in more or less point-for-point correspondence onto the sensory cortex in the brain. In other words, activity in certain sensory portions of the brain is isomorphic with the stimulus events affecting our receptors. This first stage in reception is called *projection.* Furthermore, the transmission characteristics of this projection system have been shown to be unaffected by experience, *e.g.,* unmodifiable through learning. But it has also been shown that beyond this first projection level, point-for-point correspondence breaks down, and organization on the basis of learning replaces organization on the basis of innate "wired in" isomorphism. What is the nature of this "perceptual learning"? A very simple principle of *sensory integration* on the basis of sheer frequency can be postulated here: *the greater the frequency with which stimulus events A and B have been paired in input experience, the greater will be the tendency for the central neural correlates of one,* a, *to activate the central neural correlates of the other,* b. If the frequency of stimulus pairing is very high, the occurrence of one may become a sufficient central condition for evoking the central correlate of the other (evocative relation); if the frequency of stimulus pairing is less, the occurrence of one will merely 'tune up' or prepare occurrence of the other (predictive relation). This principle obviously makes certain assumptions about the nervous system—specifically, that nerve cells more central than the projection system which are in fibrous contact and are caused to be simultaneously active somehow increase their capacity to fire one another.

One behavioral manifestation of the working of this sensory integration principle can be seen in the very well-documented phenomena of *closure.* We typically inspect our environment with rapid samplings and the sensory information must be sketchy, yet we perceive wholistic, complete forms; experimentally, an incomplete circle can be flashed on a screen briefly and most observers will report seeing the completed form—the given signals are sufficient to evoke the central correlates of those which are missing in a familiar form. Similar effects have been observed in language decoding: when printed words are flashed briefly on a screen, a highly regular inverse relation is found between the duration of the flash necessary for perception of a word and its frequency-of usage in printed materials like magazines and books; the same relation is found for the auditory intelligibility of spoken words. In general, on the sensory side of behavior, it appears that the original chaos of sensations which William James postulated for the newborn infant is gradually molded into a world of perceived forms on the basis of sheer frequency of stimulus pairing in experience.

Motor Skill. On the final output side of behavior we also find a "wired in" isomorphic projection system between motor cortex and muscle elements; this motor projection system is also unmodifiable through experience. But just as in the sensory system, the nervous tissues in the motor cortex more central to the motor projection system seem capable of being organized on the basis of sheer frequency of response pairing and sequencing. We can formulate a principle of *motor integration* or programming: *the greater the frequency with which response events A and B have been paired in output experience, the greater will be the tendency for the central neural correlates of one, a, to activate the central neural correlates of the other, b.* Again, extremely high frequency of response pairing or sequencing will result in completely evocative units (like the syllables in spoken language) and lesser frequencies will result in merely predictive integrations (like the grammatical sets or expectancies in language). S-R behaviorists have usually tried to explain motor skills like shoe-tying, typing, and piano playing in terms of proprioceptive feedback—each muscle movement in a sequence produces proprioceptive self-stimulation which becomes the cue for the next response in the series—but measurements on the maximum rate of nerve fiber conduction show that there just simply isn't enough time for such control in rapidly executed skills like playing a cadenza.

The merely predictive sensory and motor integrations are interesting because they provide an experience-based stability in both decoding (receiving) and encoding (expressing) activities of the organism. Sight of a falling object is predictive of a certain striking noise; hearing Lowell Thomas say "So long . . ." is predictive of hearing ". . . until tommorow"; seeing a piece of ice and one's hand reaching toward it is predictive of cold sensations—and in all such cases one's shock of surprise is great when these predictions occasionally are not borne out. (Indeed, if the lack of confirmation is not clear and intense enough, we often misperceive in accordance with what is expected.) On the motor side, lighting a cigarette is predictive of blowing the match out; saying *"either he will . . . "* is predictive of saying *"or he . . ."*; unbuttoning one's shirt is predictive of peeling it off. (One is usually aware of a sense of incompletion when, for some reason, such integrated sequences are interrupted.) In other words, there is a syntax of preceiving and behaving just as there is for hearing and speaking a language, and this syntax seems to depend on the formation of S-S and R-R associations or integrations, as I have called them.

Symbolic processes. The unextended S-R model uses certain hypothetical constructs, like habit-strength and inhibition, to make possible summary statements about a wide range of phenomena, but it does not use intervening variables—its principles concern relations between external S and external R. There are many observations we make of stimulus-response relations, however, which require the postulation of intervening variables; these observations fall generally in the category of symbolic or representational processes and, although they are certainly more characteristic of human behavior, they can also be observed in primitive form in subhuman species. Before we try to extend our principles to cover such phenomena, let's review some of the evidence that seems to require such extension.

We may look first at some evidence in rat behavior. In the typical *avoidance training* situation a buzzer sounds a few seconds before a strong shock is delivered to the animal's foot-pads; in the course of reacting agitatedly to shock, the rat hits upon the correct response, perhaps turning a ratchet-wheel which eliminates the shock; after some number of trials, the rat will come to react to the *buzzer* in a way that takes account of the coming shock (*e.g.*, will turn the ratchet-wheel before the shock comes on). In an operational sense, we could say that the rat has foresight, that it anticipates the shock, that the buzzer has become a *sign* of shock. To demonstrate that the buzzer has indeed acquired a danger significance for the rat, we can now remove the ratchet-wheel and substitute a handing chain; without ever being shocked at all in this new situation, the rat can learn to pull the chain if that act turns off the buzzer—he will be galvanized into vigorous activity by the persisting buzzer (*acquired or symbolic drive*) and will learn the new act on the basis of eliminating this anxiety-producing sound (*acquired or symbolic reinforcement*). Perhaps more striking is this demonstration of "intelligent transfer" in the rat: Initially these animals are subjected to unavoidable shock in a little pen, the experimental group having a buzzer paired with the shock and the control group also hearing the buzzer but not paired with the shock—all they can do is freeze and crouch in this situation; then both groups are trained to escape a shock in a different apparatus by running and leaping over a barrier, until they do this immediately when they feel the shock come on; finally, both groups are tested by suddenly sounding the buzzer— the experimental animals immediately run and leap the barrier *to the buzzer* whereas the control animals do not. Since the buzzer-sound has never been single-stage associated with running and leaping, we must infer that the buzzer excites *some intervening process* which is associated with this response (*e.g.*, some shock-representing process). Many other sources of evidence from animal behavior could be cited—delayed reactions when cues are eliminated, problem-solving, learning from sheer observation, and so on—but this will have to suffice.

Nearly all of the phenomena we consider peculiarly human depend upon symbolic mechanisms. A simple but typical example is semantic generalization: a subject is shocked whenever the word JOY appears among lists of other words; some response, such as finger-flexion or electrodermal skin reaction, is recorded; then a list of test words is presented and we find that the subject makes a generalized reaction to words like GLEE and FUN, but not to words like BOY or TOY—and this despite the fact that the latter are physically more similar to JOY than the former. It is clear that some symbolic, meaningful process, common to JOY and GLEE but not to JOY and BOY, must be mediating the transfer of reaction. Another impressive demonstration of the necessity of postulating a two-stage process in human learning, when you think of it, is the simple fact that we humans can be tremendously modified in our attitudes and subsequent behavior by merely watching a TV program like the Army-McCarthy hearings—yet at the time S is given no observable R is made. Similarly, a man can spontaneously initiate complex instrumental responses—smiling, walking out of his study, talking about a thousand-and-one things—without any observable appropriate S being present. And needless to say, the entire structure of language behavior, upon which any adequate understanding of social science must be based, is quite incomprehensible when viewed within a singled-stage S-R framework—because within such a framework questions of significance, meaning, and intention can only be sidestepped.

REPRESENTATIONAL MEDIATION PROCESSES IN BEHAVIOR

We have come upon a number of facts about both animal and human behavior which cannot be handled with a single-stage S-R model. This means that we must make some additional assumptions about what goes on in the little black box. In keeping with the law of parsimony, we wish to make as few assumptions as possible, and yet be able to incorporate the relevant phenomena. In order to account for S-S relations (perceptual organization) and R-R relations (motor skill), it seemed possible to cover the ground by simply postulating neural integration among the central correlates of sensory and motor signals respectively on the basis of sheer frequency of input or output pairing. What's the least amount of additional baggage needed to handle symbolic processes? In effect, we shall break our single-stage process into two stages by postulating a learned, self-stimulating, response-like process as an intervening variable. The first stage, which we shall call *decoding,* will be the association of external stimuli with these internal, symbolic responses; the second stage, which we shall call *encoding,* will be the association of the self-stimulating (produced by these symbolic reactions) with external responses. The great advantage of this solution is that, since each stage is itself an S-R process, we can simply transfer all of the conceptual machinery of single-stage S-R psychology into this new model without new postulation. The critical problem, of course, is to anchor this intervening variable firmly to both antecedent and consequent observables, *e.g.,* objective stimulus and response variables.

Development of Representational Mediators. We start with the fact that certain stimulus patterns have a "wired in" connection with certain behavior patterns (unconditioned reflexes) and additional stimuli have acquired this capacity (conditioned reflexes). Food-powder in the mouth regularly and reliably elicits a complex pattern of food-taking reactions (including salivating, swallowing, and the like); a shock to the foot-pads regularly and reliably elicits a complex pattern of escape reactions (leaping, running, urinating, autonomic "fear" reactions, and the like). What I shall call a *significate,* then, is any stimulus which, in a given situation, regularly and reliably produces a predictable response pattern. For the naive organism, there are multitudes of stimuli which do *not* have such characteristics—a buzzer-sound does not reliably produce escape behavior like the shock does; the sound of a metronome does not reliably produce foodtaking behavior like food-powder-in-the-mouth does. And for the human infant, the visual image of its bottle or the breast does not initially produce sucking, salivating, and the like. Our problem really is this: how can neutral, meaningful stimuli like these become meaningful *signs* for the organisms affected by them?

A moment's thought convinces us that ordinary single-stage conditioning does not provide a satisfactory answer—the reactions made to signs of objects (CS) are almost never the same as those made to the objects themselves (US), even for the rat subject. When the buzzer sounds in the avoidance situation, the rat behaves in such a way as to take account of the shock, not as it would to the shock itself; when 'the human hears the word FIRE, he behaves in a way appropriate to the whole situation including this sign, not as he would to the object referred to. But if we look into the so-called conditioning situation more carefully, we can, I think, see an answer to our problem. Many experiments on the details of the conditioning process combine to support the following conclusion: not all components of the total unconditioned reaction are conditionable to, appear in, the conditioned reaction equally; rather, certain "light-weight" components, like autonomic reactions (changed heart-rate, glandular secretion, etc.) and minimal muscular and postural adjustments (tensing, lip-licking, etc.) tend to be elicited by the CS long before the "heavy-weight" components like paw-lifting, chewing, running and the like. Incidentally, this could have been predicted from single-stage principles—"heavy-weight" reactions will involve greater amounts of work-produced inhibition.

The diagram in Figure 10 represents the formation of a representational mediation process, which we may phrase as a principle in the following way: *Whenever a neutral stimulus is contiguous with a significate, and this occurs sufficiently close to a reinforcing state of affairs, the neutral stimulus will acquire an increment of association with some portion of the total behavior elicited by the significate as a representational mediation process.* This stimulus-producing response process (r_m) is *representational* be-

cause it is part of the very same behavior produced by the significate itself
(R_T)—thus the buzzer becomes a sign ($\boxed{S}$) of shock ($\dot{S}$) rather than a sign
of any of a multitude of other things. It is *mediational* because the self-stimulation (s_m) produced by making this intervening reaction can become associated with a variety of instrumental acts (R_X) which "take account of" the
object signified—the anxiety state generated by the buzzer may serve as a
cue for turning the ratchet which eliminates the shock.

Now, with this principle in mind, let us look back at some of the symbolic
phenomena which proved embarrassing to the single-stage conception. In
avoidance training, shock reliably produces total escape behavior; being
regularly paired with buzzer, or the traces of the buzzer sound, this initially
neutral stimulus acquires some distinctive portion of the total behavior to
shock (here, what we call an *anxiety reaction*); the self-stimulation from
this mediator also becomes associated with the instrumental act of ratchet-

FIGURE 10.

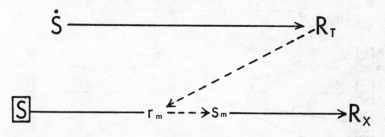

turning. That this mediator has an impelling danger significance (symbolic
punishment) is shown by the fact that a new instrumental act, like pulling the
hanging chain, can be learned simply on the basis of turning off this stimulus.
We could fairly say that this buzzer-sound has acquired a new *meaning* for
the rat, has become a sign of something other than itself. The learning of
meanings is central in human behavior, of course, so we look at semantic
generalization in terms of this model. Prior to the experiment itself, we assume
that our subject has learned the meanings of JOY, GLEE, BOY, and so
forth. JOY and GLEE, as arbitrary social signs, occurred in similar total
situations, in which intense pleasant reactions were taking place; therefore
these signs will be associated with representational portions of these reactions.
BOY will be associated with quite different mediation processes, we assume.
Now, since the quality of self-stimulation depends entirely upon the reactions
producing it, it follows that the s_m produced by JOY (and conditioned to a
new reaction in the experiment) must be more similar to that produced by
GLEE than that produced by BOY; therefore it follows from the generalization principle (applied to our stage 2, encoding) that the new reaction conditioned to JOY will transfer more to GLEE than to BOY.

As illustrated in this last analysis, the most important role of representational processes in behavior is as the common element in mediated generalization and transfer. It is this, I think, which gives the tremendous flexibility we observe in the behavior of higher animals, particularly humans. Figure 11 diagrams this mediating role. Whenever a set of stimuli are associated with the same significate, and hence with the same total behavior pattern, they must become a hierarchy of signs associated with the same representational process and hence have the same significance. Thus, for the rat, the sight and smell of the food pellet, the cup in which it is found, the click which announces its delivery, and so forth all become more or less equivalent signs of food reinforcement; thus, for the male human, a lace handkerchief, the smell of perfume, words like "pretty" and "nice" become partially equivalent signs of the feminine goal object. Similarly, on the other side of the behavioral equation,

FIGURE 11.

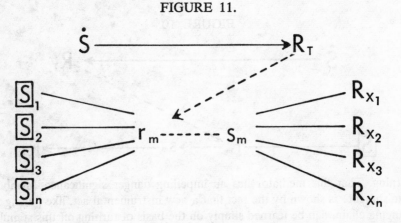

this common mediation process as a form of self-stimulation becomes associated with a hierarchy of overt instrumental acts. To situations which have in common a danger significance, the rat has learned to run, to crouch and freeze, to squeak, to turn a ratchet, and so on; in similar situations, the human has learned to run also, to plead verbally, to "talk his way out," and so forth. Selection among such a divergent hierarchy of responses depends upon both the absolute habit-strength of the alternatives and the contextual cues present (*e.g.*, the human is more likely to "talk his way out" when in a locked room than when in an open field). Note the remarkable increase in flexibility such a mechanism provides: Once a novel stimulus has been associated with an established mediator (*e.g.*, a flickering light is made a sign of shock), it immediately takes command over the entire hierarchy of instrumental acts already associated with this mediator (*e.g.*, the rat will operate the ratchet to turn off this flickering light without new training). Similarly, once a new instrumental act has been associated with an established mediator, it immediately becomes available to all members of the class of signs having the same significance.

This analysis leads one to draw a distinction between what might be called primary and secondary learning. *Primary learning* would involve the original formation of sensory integrations (perceptions), motor integrations (skills) and representational processes (meanings); such learning is the daily work and play of the growing child, and what evidence we have indicates that this primary learning is extremely time-consuming and laborious (albeit happily dealt with as natural "play" for the most part). *Secondary learning* would involve nothing more than associative reshuffling of signs with mediators and of mediators with instrumental acts. This kind of learning is characteristic, I think, of the mature or sophisticated organism. One type of secondary learning, as shown in Figure 12, is *change in significance* of a sign: Most so-called conditioning experiments are of this sort; a dog for whom a whistle has already

FIGURE 12.

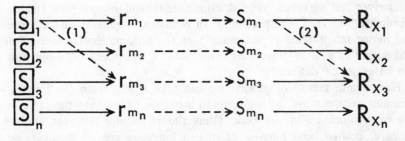

some significance (seldom investigated, actually) must come to associate this stimulus with a food-taking significance, indexed by salivation. A young lad for whom an officer's uniform has one significance, based on movie-going experience, comes to modify this significance somewhat after being drafted (in passing, note the relation of this analysis to status and role conceptions in sociological theory). Another type of secondary learning is *change in instrumentation*. As we have seen, the rat may be induced to modify its overt responses to a buzzer-sound (from running to ratchet-wheel turning) without changing the previously learned danger significance of this sound. The maturing human changes radically his instrumental responses to his mother and father, to his peers and superiors, as he shifts through childhood, adolescence and maturity, without necessarily changing the significance of these people to him; similarly, he learns to behave differently to danger signals, food signals, and so on; on the other hand, the changes in his behavior to females of his species probably involve simultaneous changes in both significance and instrumentation. What I am suggesting, in other words, is that the average mature individual (human or animal) engages in very little "new" learning, very little in the way of forming new perceptual integrations, new skills, or even new meanings—he has the familiar physical and social world pretty well organized with respect to himself—rather, what learning he does do is concerned with occasionally shuffling relations among established perceptions, meanings and skills, and most of us do precious little of this.

This leads rather directly into the problem of *psychological units*. As compared with the linguist, for example, the psychologist has done a very unsatisfactory job of defining his stimulus and response units on the purely descriptive level. Linguists agree among themselves quite well upon the identification of both the molecular units of messages (phonemes) and the molar units (morphemes), but it would be difficult to find two psychologists who, observing the same situation and activity, could agree on their identifications and classifications of stimuli and responses. I think we can take a hint from the linguist here—for, in actuality, he is dealing with a particular segment of the psychological domain, language, which is simultaneously both responses from one individual and stimuli for another. The linguist identifies two major levels of units: *phonemes* (which are meaningless in themselves but serve as basic discriminanda) and *morphemes* (which are meaningful units). Correspondingly, in behavior in general we have sensory and motor integrations ("phonemes") as the fine, molecular units of input and output as well as "situations" and "acts" ("morphemes")—but how are the latter to be defined?

Here again, methodologically, we can take a hint from the linguist—he classifies as "the same" all segments in messages which have the same *meaning* or significance in the code (thus the physically different endings of *walk-ed, add-ed,* and *play-ed* in spoken language are all members of the same past-tense morpheme), without inquiring into *what* this meaning may be per se. Now, I think the representational mediation process in behavior makes possible a similar definition of molar units in psychology. I would say that all members of the class of physically different stimuli which are associated with a common representational process (*e.g.,* have the same significance to the organism) are "the same" as molar situations; thus, "a welcoming smile," "Hi!," "Good to see you again," and the like are functionally equivalent situations in the social interaction matrix. Similarly, I would say that all members of the class of physically different instrumental acts which are mediated by a common representational process (*e.g.,* express the same intention for the organism) are "the same" as molar actions; thus, a tight-lipped glare, a muttered oath directed at someone, a clenched fist, and the like are functionally equivalent acts in the social interaction matrix.

This type of learning theory analysis places a premium on developing methods of indexing representational states, *e.g.,* measuring meaning, particularly in human organisms. My own research work over the past few years has been directed chiefly along these lines. Dealing with language responses themselves—which, after all, are supposed to be 'expressions of meaning'

—we have been trying to discover a limited number of basic factors or dimensions along which meaningful reactions vary and hence can be measured. Several fairly large-scale factor analyses have already been done, and the same first three factors have appeared in each case: an *evaluative* factor, a *potency* factor, and an *activity* factor. We have devised a number of semantic measuring instruments for specific problems on the basis of these factors, and these applications have been successful so far. We assume that these factors, derived in judgmental situations, are representative of at least some of the major ways in which representational mediation processes in human beings can vary. Since the present paper is concerned with learning theory, I shall say no more than this about semantic measurement.

ANALYSIS OF SOME BASIC SOCIAL MECHANISMS

It is a truism that the social behavior of human individuals is learned. The tremendous variation in personality and culture across the continent testifies to this fact. To the extent that the learning principles discovered by psychologists are valid, then, they should be operating in the complex matrix of social life, always conditioned, of course, by the particular situations of each culture. And if my analysis in the preceding few pages has been adequate, the most characteristic mode of learning at this level will be in terms of a two-stage process—learning of significances for signs and learning of instrumental acts which express intentions.

Assign Learning—Concepts, Stereotypes, and Symbols. In complex societies most signs representing categories and relationships are highly abstract, far removed from the earthy behaviors in which we presume meanings have their origins. We may refer to signs of this abstract sort as *assigns, e.g.,* their meanings are literally assigned through repeated association with simpler signs having direct behavioral reference. Let me illustrate with an experiment recently completed by one of my students. The problem was to demonstrate that the meaning acquired by a nonsense item, MEBLU, was predictable from the frequency of association of this item with simple adjectives, the meanings of the latter being measured with the Semantic Differential referred to earlier. Subjects read a brief article, presumably taken from the National Geographic Magazine, in which they saw references to "the brawny Meblu" several times," "the excitable Meblu" twice, and "the friendly Meblu" only once; other groups of subjects encountered this hypothetical Meblu tribe with other adjectives and with different frequencies of association. In all cases the measured meaning of MEBLU shifted from neutral meaninglessness in a direction and to an extent predictable from the meanings of the common adjectives with which it had been associated. Figure 13 diagrams the sign-learning process presumably involved—the representational mediation processes already associated with the first-level linguistic signs tend to transfer to the assign as a function of their frequency of association, the representational process finally characteristic of the assign being a compounding of those characteristic of the various signs. Suppose an individual is exposed repeatedly, and more or less exclusively, to a nationalistic newspaper: He experiences the initially meaningless stimulus ALIEN in such contexts as "Aliens are *not* to be *trusted*," "Our national life is being *poisoned by* alien ideologies," and "we should *deport* these *dangerous* aliens." The resulting connotation of ALIEN is predictable from the meaningful contexts in which it appears. The important thing to consider is that most of the linguistic signs with which we deal in the mass media—Eisenhower, Fixed Farm Supports, McCarthy, the U.N., the Fifth Amendment, and so ad infinitum—acquire their meanings as assigns rather than through direct behavioral experience.

FIGURE 13.

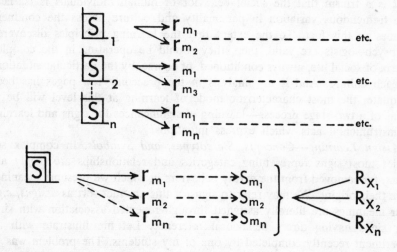

The notion of *stereotype* is that of a common meaning or significance attached to a class of people, not necessarily similar physically, this common significance serving to mediate a class of instrumental actions, variable with the total situation but all reflecting the common meaning of the class. Thus "stereotype" is a special case of the mediation model described in Figure 11. On the decoding side, the identification of a particular individual as a member of the stereotype (*e.g.*, the evocation of the appropriate mediation process) usually depends upon certain combinations of cues—skin color, shape of nose, certain gestures, certain dialectic deviations in speech, and so on—but the use of the appropriate linguistic label, in the newspaper, by someone else, is also sufficient to elicit the common mediation process. Since we all use stereotypes indeed, categorizing of this sort is the essence of concept formation or "coding" of our world—the real problem concerns the *nature* of the mediation process or meaning. Either based upon direct behaviors as shown in Figure 11 (*e.g.,* living in a race-conscious neighborhood where gang war-fare along national lines occurs), or more often based upon assign learning through the words used by parents, friends, and the media, as shown in Figure 13, we acquire such meanings—NEGROES may be conceived as friendly, kind, and submissive or as dangerous, cruel and aggressive depending upon such learning conditions. The classes of instrumental behaviors associated with stereotypes will necessarily reflect such significances, but will vary with the total situation in which the stereotype is experienced—Man A may hire a Negro for a menial job but avoid sitting next to him on the train, for exam-ple. The learning of such contextually dependent behaviors presumably de-pends upon the differential rewards and punishments delivered by those other individuals in the learner's environment (parents, superiors, etc.) who have prestige for him and with whom he identifies.

Abstract *symbols* play an important role in society. We have our V's for victory, our flags, our ceremonial robes, and our briefcase in the hand. The distinguishing characteristic of the symbol, I think, is that it is a stimulus pattern which, already having its own specific representational process, is used to signify something else. For example, perception of a briefcase in a man's hand, as a visual pattern, specifically signifies a container for papers and the like; but above and beyond this specific denotation is its symbolic significance of "professional man." I suspect that we are dealing here with a rather direct process of transfer of meaning through association. Let's look at the hypothetical development of *money* as a symbol: The young child early learns to recognize nickels, dimes and quarters, as well as paper bills, as objects having certain characteristics—round and rollable, hard and jingly, tearable and foldable and so on. But the nickel, let us say, is later used in exchange for an ice cream cone, and part of the ice cream cone significance (including its gratifying aspects) comes to occur in anticipatory fashion when nickels are held in the hand. If this were all that nickels were good for, they would presumably become a symbol of ice cream cones and nothing else. But later still another nickel is exchanged for candy, another for a ride on a bus, another for a pencil to write with, and even another to pay "protec-tion" from the local bully. What do all these situations have in common? About the only thing is generalized gratification—getting something desired at the moment. As a result of such a learning sequence, one would expect money to acquire a very general "pleasure" and "security" significance, *e.g.,* a very abstract symbol.

Imitation and Identification. Another basic problem for social science is the transmission of culture (*e.g.,* ways of perceiving and behaving in specified situations) from one generation to another. Deliberate training, of course, plays an important role, but much of the transmission is on a more informal, *imitative* basis. As Miller and Dollard describe it, the dependent individual, not knowing the critical cues himself, learns to match his behavior to that of a model, an individual who does know the critical cues. For example, the older of two brothers in a family knows that heavy footsteps on the stairs signifies the arrival of father (often with a little present of candy or toys); he runs to the door; the little toddler in the family happens to imitate the older brother, responding to his running behavior by doing the same thing; both are rewarded with candy gumdrops. After a number of rewarded experiences of this kind, the younger individual will develop a generalized imitative set, a readiness to match his overt behavior with others in situations where he does not know the significance of the cues. Note that the prestige of the model here determines the probability of imitation, but this prestige in turn presumably depends upon rewarding associations.

But in many cases—most cases in adult behavior—what we observe is not simple imitation of the overt behavior but rather "appropriate" behavior in terms of the interpreted attitudes or meanings of the model. The teen-age son does not imitate his father's behavior toward girls—not only has he had no opportunity to observe such behavior on his father's part, but times have changed and also courting customs—but rather he behaves "like his father might in this situation." When I see a person strike his thumb with a hammer, I do not behave like he does, but rather as I might behave in the same experienced situation—*e.g.,* I 'put myself in his shoes' and behave accordingly. We refer to this as identification of one person with another—but how does it operate?

Again we must use our two-stage model. Based on imitation of overt behaviors, *e.g.,* of parent by child, the dependent individual acquires meanings of situations, people, activities, etc. that are similar to those of the model. Given such similarities in the significance of cues, the dependent individual will then behave in ways that are equivalent to those of the model, *e.g.,* express the same intention, even though not identical and not based on direct imitation. Figure 14 illustrates the nature and development of such identifying behavior according to this type of theory. Subscript *a* refers to the model and subscript *b* to the dependent individual. Note that imitation refers to the identity of behavior to certain objects and identification to the similarity of meanings (representational processes) resulting. Thus, having imitated the authoritarian behavior of his father toward women in the family, the child develops a significance of women like that of his father, this condescending significance determining subsequent behaviors on his part to girls-in-general which, while not imitated from his father, are 'like what he might do in such situations.' The broader import of such an analysis is that when some individuals in a society (followers) identify with another (leader), they do so on the basis of shared meanings for situations and then proceed to interpret situations as the model does and hence behave in ways equivalent to those of the model, *e.g.,* quite literally 'putting oneself in the place of another (interpretatively) and behaving accordingly.'

Personality Traits and Culture Traits. Gordon Allport has defined a personality trait, in essence, as that which renders equivalent classes of situations and classes of behaviors for an individual. Thus, for a person with an "inferiority complex," any competitive situation signifies threat and he responds by avoidance, by "big talk," by compensating with some other activity in which he excells and so on, depending upon the particular context. Similarly, a person with a "stingy" trait perceives situations like requests for loans from him, sharing the tip at a meal, and spending money for presents in similar ways and behaves toward these situations in equivalent ways, *e.g.,* ways which have in common the avoidance of giving things up. Looking back at Figure 11 again, it can be seen that this mediated generalization and transfer model applies here as well; a class of signs have acquired a common significance to

FIGURE 14.

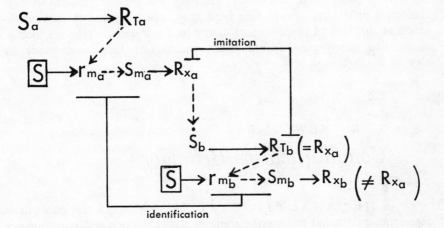

the individual and this common significance mediates a class of equivalent instrumental actions.

Now, when the members of a society *share,* as a result of common experience and training, a mediational mechanism such as shown in Figure 11, I think we may speak of a *culture trait.* If, for example, members of a given society agree in perceiving spirits in natural objects like trees and lakes and agree in behaving appropriately toward these objects by ceremonial avoidance of some, giving offerings to others, talking about them with animistic terms, and so on, we have a *shared significance which renders equivalent a class of stimulus situations and a class of behaviors,* and thus, in my terms, a culture trait. At a more molecular level, all of the lexical items of a language can be thought of as culture traits—the concept "red" is a common cognitive reaction to a class of functionally equivalent stimuli, as is the concept "dog," the concept "happy" and so on. I do not know whether this conception of a culture trait is consistent with sociological theory or not, but it does offer a hand-hold for analysis of the formation of such shared significances and behaviors.

SUMMARY

Starting quite frankly from the notion of the hierarchy of the sciences, this paper has tried to show how psychology, as a sort of Janus-faced discipline between the bilogical and social sciences, both implies certain neurophysiological conceptions and is implied by certain social science conceptions. The basic principles of simple S-R psychology were described and then shown to be insufficient (but not necessarily invalid) for an analysis of characteristically human behavior. A two-stage, mediational model was then suggested, a model which emphasizes both the decoding of situational significances and the encoding of intentions instrumentally. The implications of such a model for the observed flexibility of human behavior, for a distinction between "primary" and "secondary" learning, and for the problem of psychological units were drawn. Finally, a very superficial and sketchy application of this type of psychological theory to a few socially relevant mechanisms, like stereotyping, identification, and culture traits, was made by way of illustration.

T. M. NEWCOMB

Communicative Behavior

THE "ANALYTIC SYSTEM" with which this paper deals represents an attempt to describe some of the conditions and consequences of communication among humans. It aims to state, in terms of regular and orderly principles, certain states of affairs both within and among persons which give rise to various forms of communicative behavior; and also, in terms of congruent principles, the consequences of communication for relevant states of affairs within and among persons.

More specifically, I shall attempt to describe "states of affairs within and among persons" in terms of a set of hypothetically interdependent relationships (1) among two or more human entities (individual or collective) viewed as actual or potential communicators; and (2) between such communicators and the objects of their communication. Such interrelated "states of affairs," which under certain conditions are viewed both as giving rise to and as being modified by communicative behavior, will (for reasons noted later) be referred to as "systems of orientation."

I am particularly indebted, for essential theoretical components of the analytic system, to F. Heider and to L. Festinger, and for many research contributions to a host of colleagues, especially at the University of Michigan, and to many of my students there.

I. BASIC CONCEPTS

A few definitions are first in order—in the interests not of dogmatism but of clear communication.

1) *Communicative behavior*. For present purposes, communication can best be regarded, paraphrasing G. R. Miller (in *Language and Communication*) as the transmission of information from a human source to a human destination. Information, in turn, may be regarded as the occurrence of one out of a set of arbitrary symbols. In the simplest possible terms, then, communicative behavior refers to the sending and the receiving of symbols by humans. (The approach to communication via "information theory" was initiated and has been rather fully developed by telephone engineers, cyberneticians, etc. But, as we shall see, many additional assumptions and many additional complications are involved in the application of their formulations to communication among humans.)

2) *Orientation*. This term, more restricted than the deliberately inclusive "relationship," is loosely equivalent to "attitude," though I shall use the latter term in a specially restricted sense. An orientation (as its etymology suggests) connotes directionality and selectivity; in addition, it refers to some sort of "anticipatory set" or "readiness to respond" vis a vis that which is oriented to. It is, so to speak, a transitive concept: that is, there is no orientation without something to be oriented to. It is basically an individual concept, but it is meaningful to refer to the orientation of a group, in the sense of an orientation characteristic of many of its individual members.

Sooner or later I shall have to refer to various dimensions of orientations, but for the moment I want only to make a distinction based upon *objects* of orientations. Orientations toward co-communicators are different in some important respects from orientations toward objects of communication. I shall use the term "attraction" to refer to orientations toward co-communicators (actual or potential), and the term "attitude" for orientations toward objects of communications. (Both attraction and attitude may have either plus or minus values; that is, both communicating persons and the objects of their communication may be either positively or negatively valued. Both attraction and attitude, moreover, may have any degree of valence, or strength.) Thus the "hypothetically interdependent relationships" to which I referred at the outset include (though not exclusively, as we shall see), in the simplest possible case of two persons, four orientations: from each person to the other person and to the object of commuication. The system of orientations, as thus far outlined, might be pictured as follows (A and B represent the communicators, and X the object of communication):

FIGURE 1.

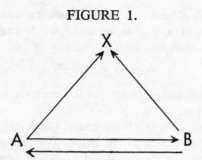

So far I have said nothing as to how these four orientations might constitute a system, in the sense of being characterized by interdependence. (I have in mind, of course, a "real system"—*i.e.*, empirically real—as distinguished from an analytic system. Henceforth I shall use the shorthand label "system" to refer to "real systems of orientations," and when I mean "analytic system" I shall say so.) As a matter of fact, these four orientations can constitute a system, but only under certain limited conditions. In order to make these conditions clear I must say something about the dynamics of systems of orientation, and in so doing I shall have to note one other essential feature of such systems.

When two persons (or two groups, for that matter) communicate with each other about something, X, they are (by definition) transmitting information. The symbols by which they do so refer, in a direct sense, only to X. But each of them is also informing the other about himself—specifically, about himself-in-relation-to-X. If, for example, A (a butcher) says to B (a customer), "This steak is very tender," it may be that the only information which B receives (in the sense of "accepting" it, noting and remembering it) concerns not the properties of the steak but the properties of the butcher—specifically his desire to sell the steak. The point of this illustration is simply that the consequences of communication in such instances (and, as I shall argue, in all instances), depend upon what kind of orientations are attributed by the receiver to the sender. I shall refer to these elements of the system as "perceived orientations." The "full system" (including perceived orientations, indicated by broken lines) may be pictured as shown on page 247.

II. SYSTEM PROPERTIES

It is often useful to regard related phenomena as constituting a system—a real system, that is—when it can be shown that certain of their properties or their inter-relationships (1) vary interdependently, and (2) vary within definable limits. When a given kind of influence is no longer countered by another influence in such manner as to maintain the limits of variation, the characteristic forms of interdependence disappear, and the system no longer exists. The justification of any such system thus depends upon evidence for interdependent influences as brought to bear when the limits are approached.

In its general form, the real system which is central to the present analytic system consists of orientations of two or more human entities to one another and to objects about which they communicated. It will be helpful at the outset, however, to distinguish psychological (or phenomenal) from social systems of orientation. The distinction is simply that the former includes only orientations as they exist for a single one of the communicating entities (a person or a group), whereas the latter includes all the orientations of all of the communicators.

FIGURE 2.

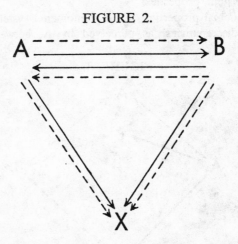

It is somewhat simpler to begin with phenomenal systems, which consist of A's orientations toward B and toward X (Figure 3) and of his perceptions of B's orientations toward himself and toward the same X. The first assumption involved in asserting that such a system may be deemed to exist is that whenever A simultaneously attends to (or co-orients to) B and X, psychological influences are aroused toward the perception of B as oriented to both A and X. If these influences are outweighed by counter-influences, the system does not exist. As to the influences which bring the system into being—that is, which induce A to perceive both himself and B as oriented to the same X—they are extremely varied, but it is easy to describe a large class of these conditions. Whenever A perceives X as instrumental to a desired state of affairs with respect to B, or B as similarly instrumental with respect to X, he is influenced toward co-orientation.

Given a situation which has induced co-orientation, the means by which the instrumentality of X for B, or of B for X, is ordinarily effected is communication. Perhaps some illustrations will be helpful. A child wants a cookie, but he cannot reach it without his mother's help; his mother is the instrumentality in this case, but the nature of the communication which he initiates will vary with her attitude toward him and toward the cookie, as he perceived those attitudes. Or, to illustrate the other variety of instrumentality, a student who is not very much interested in medieval history is very much interested in the professor's judgment of him, the student; so he asks questions about 13th-century Florence—questions carefully tempered to fit the professor's perceived orientations both toward history and toward the student himself. In short, the occurrence of communication, as well as its nature, are determined by the existing state of the system of orientation. But I am getting ahead of my story, since I have still said very little about its system properties.

One of the principal properties of the phenomenal system has to do with similarities and discrepancies, as perceived by A, between his own and

FIGURE 3.

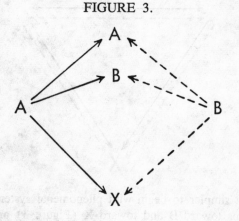

B's orientations. Since there are three objects toward which A can have orientations—B, X, and A himself—and toward which, also, A can attribute orientations to B, there are three possible loci of similarity-discrepancy in any phenomenal system. (The "full" phenomenal system is pictured in Figure 3.) Let me remind you again that A and/or B may be either individuals or groups. In the former case the perceived similarities and discrepancies are, in every-day language, between the attitudes of a person and comparable attitudes he attributes to another; in the latter case they are between collective attitudes, stereotypes, group norms, etc. on the part of some group and comparable attitudes, sterotypes and norms as commonly attributed by that group to some other group.

But one can't very well arrange similarities and discrepancies along a continuum unless one first answers the question: similarities and discrepancies with regard to what? What are viewed as the dimensions of orientations, with regard to which they can have much or little similarity? For present purposes I shall limit myself to two of them, to which I shall apply the psychological terms *cathexis* and *cognition*. Cathexis refers to the like-dislike, or pro-con dimension of orientations; cathexes can vary with respect to both sign (or direction) and valence (or strength). Cognitions cannot (at the present stage of development) be so easily dimensionalized. While there are interesting developments in the measurement of cognitive structuring, I shall deal with cognitions only in terms of discrete content—that is, in terms of properties attributed to objects of orientation. My present problem is not to make a complete analysis of cognitive processes, but to study degress of similarity (actual or attributed) between two or more cognizers of the same object. For my purposes, therefore, I need only to ascertain whether, or to make sure that, the cognitive orientations of two or more persons oriented to the same object include the same properties, as attributed to that object.

The relationship between cognitive and cathectic aspects of orientations can be briefly stated. An object is cathected only as it is cognized. Cathexis presupposes cognition; whether the latter is global or differentiated, what is cathected is the object as cognized. The usefulness of the cathectic-cognitive distinction for a theory of communication becomes obvious when one re-members that communicative difficulties often arise between two or more persons whose cathectic orientations (sign and valence) are more or less the same, but whose cognitive orientations differ sharply. What appears to be a case of their liking the same thing to the same degree turns out to be liking different things—*i.e.,* an object to which they give the same label but which, cognitively, is two different things.

III. SYSTEM DYNAMICS

How does a system of orientations come to be as it is at any given moment? How does it change? And what do the answers to these questions have to do with communication? The heart of a theory concerning any real system, and the test of its usefulness, lies in the hypothetical conditions under which change and stability occur. (This, by the way, is what I mean by dynamics —conditions of change and stability.)

Let me begin my dynamic analysis with a simple proposition—a plausible one, however verifiable it may later turn out to be. Following a communica-tion from A to B about X, the chances are that A's and B's orientation about X will be more similar than they were before. Every-day illustrations of this consequence of communication abound. You ask a friend what time it is. Assuming that he hears and understands, he immediately shares some-thing about your orientation to the hour of the day that he did not before— namely, the knowledge that you are curious about it; both of you now know that you are curious about the hour, whereas only one of you knew it before. Once he has answered you, you share still more—the knowledge of what time it is. These are instances, primarily, of increase in cognitive similarity following communication, and the proposition with which I have started holds fewer qualifications for purely cognitive than for cathectic orientations. But it is easy to cite illustrations of increase in cathectic similarity, too. A church deacon remarks to his wife, "I've just met the new preacher, and he stinks." My initial proposition merely states that—under some rather prevalent conditions—communications like this one tend to increase cathectic similarity between communicators; in this case, the wife's attitude toward the preacher is likely to be less favorable (*i.e.,* more like her husband's) just after than just before the communication.

Illustrations of this kind, as I have said, are plentiful—but so are illustrations to the contrary. Your friend of whom you ask the hour may conclude not that you are curious about the time, but that you wish he would leave you. When he replies, you may decide that he is lying. The deacon's wife may think her husband is teasing her, or she may have a profound mistrust of his judgment of people in general and of preachers in particular. Under any of these conditions we would not necessarily expect increased similarity of orientation, either cognitive or cathectic, following communication. Such considerations lead us to add a qualification to the initial proposition, to the general effect that the recipient of the communication must trust the transmitter of it, if the proposition is to hold true. In more formal terms, the probabilities of increased similarity following a communication vary with the degree of positive attraction on the part of the receiver toward the transmitter.

But attraction (*i.e.,* sign and strength of A's orientation toward B, or of B's toward A) is a highly complex phenomenon. You may like a person (plus attraction) and at the same time put no confidence at all—or even less than no confidence (minus attraction) in what he has to say about one or more particular topics. I shall have more to say later about some distinctions which it is necessary to make among varieties of attraction.

You have probably been thinking of other kinds of exceptions to the initial general proposition about communication and similarity of orientations. I assure you that there are others, but before taking note of them I want to state a kind of converse to the initial proposition, which had to do with consequences of communication. The same commonplace observations which might suggest that proposition also suggest another one concerning the preconditions of communication. It is this: a communication is more likely to occur between two persons if their orientations to the object of communication differ in some respect than if they do not. This one is less self-evident, but before you reject it outright let me first remind you that, like the initial proposition, it holds only under special conditions.

Let me also say something about the general rationale of the second general proposition. Given what psychologists think they know about the conditions under which behavior is modified (the principles of learning), if the first proposition is correct under certain conditions then the second is almost certain to be correct—on a probability basis, that is—under those same conditions. This is only to say that when behaviors pretty regularly have certain consequences, those consequences, if rewarding, come to be goals toward which behavior is directed. Or, put the other way around, if certain behaviors are repeated (when alternatives are available) their consequences are presumably rewarding. The evidence for either of these versions is pretty clear. I scarcely need to convince you that people do continue to communicate when they have the privilege of not doing so, and it is almost equally self-apparent that there are tremendous advantages in having similar orientations on the part of people who are concerned with common objects—co-workers about their machines, for example, or parents about their children. The whole fabric of society—its institutions, its subgroups, and its role structure—hinges upon the possibility of similar orientations to objects (including persons) of common concern. It is hardly to be doubted that—under certain conditions which are in fact very prevalent indeed—similarity of orientation is rewarding.

Summarizing the argument up to this point, within certain limiting conditions communication is most likely to occur when there is less rather than more similarity of orientation among potential communicators, and its consequences tend to be those of increasing similarity of orientation.

Now let me return to the qualifying proposition according to which the similarity-producing effects of communication vary with attraction among the communicators. This same qualification applies to the instigating conditions of communicative behavior, quite as obviously. If two or more potential communicators are indifferent to one another, or mistrust each others' motives, the mere fact of discrepancy of orientation among them will not necessarily lead to communication among them. It is most likely to occur if the bonds of attraction among them are strong and positive. More formally put, the probabilities of communication concerning a given object vary jointly with the discrepancy in orientation of the potential communicators and with the strength of positive attraction among them. The relationship between the two independent variables is a multiplicative one, above a certain threshold at least; that is, if either value is close to zero, the probabilities of communication are very low no matter how great the value of the other. There must be both some discrepancy and some positive attraction.

So far I have considered only objective similarities and discrepancies of orientation—that is, as observed or inferred by an outsider as distinct from the communicators themselves. I am sure it has occurred to you that it must make a good deal of difference how the communicators themselves look at things. Subjective (or, as I prefer to say, perceived) similarity and discrepancy is surely the more important of these two variables from the point of view of instigation to communicative behavior. If A's attraction toward B is moderately positive, then the probabilities of his initiating a communication to B will vary more closely with his perception of their discrepancy in orientation than with their actual discrepancy. This is simply to say that judgments of such discrepancies are rarely perfectly accurate, and that one's behavior in such situations (as in most others) is governed more directly by the manner in which one experiences the situation than by the "real" situation.

Mutatis mutandis, the same qualification applies to the individual consequences of communication as to its individual preconditions. There are always possibilities of misunderstanding a communication or of drawing unwarranted inferences from it. It follows that the general principle of increasing similarity of orientation following a communication should apply more directly to perceived than to objective similarity. That is, within the limiting conditions under which the principle applies, changes in orientation following a communication are more likely to be toward than away from the orientation which one attributes to the other (mistakenly or not). Perceived discrepancy of orientation, in short, becomes an indispensable variable, particularly in describing the individual preconditions and consequences of communication.

There is one other major qualification—that is, a set of limiting conditions—to the basic propositions about consequences and preconditions of communication. Degree of cathexis toward the object of communication, as well as toward the co-communicator, makes a good deal of difference. Given a perceived discrepancy between one's own orientation to a specific object and that of another person to whom one's bonds of attraction are strong, probabilities of being influenced toward greater similarity following communication about a specified X are greater if one cares about it than if one is indifferent to it. By the same token, the likelihood that, under the given conditions, a communication will ensue is greater if the cathexis is great than if it is weak. In sum, both the probabilities that a communication will occur and the probabilities that it will be followed by increasing similarity of orientation if it does occur, vary with strength of object cathexis, as well as with strength of attraction and with degree of perceived discrepancy.

This proposition has, I concede, an inherent implausibility—particularly as regarding the consequences of communicating. It would seem to make more sense to say that the more strongly one feels about something the *less* likely it is that one's opinion will be changed on discovering that another person disagrees. I agree that this makes sense—but it is not inconsistent with the proposition which I have offered because, so far, I have limited myself to an examination of a *single* A-B-X system—that is, to intra-system dynamics. In the "real world," of course, most of our strongly cathected orientations are anchored in many A-B-X systems involving many different Bs. If one feels strongly about a given X, and perceives similarity of orientation with one or more highly attractive Bs, then the present theory does not require that the discovery of discrepancy with a less attractive B result in a changed orientation to that X. In fact, the theory requires just the opposite.

The "inherent implausibility" of the proposition—to the effect that probability of attitude change following a communication varies with strength of cathexis—stems from a contrary-to-fact assumption that everything can be accounted for in terms of a single A-B-X system. Most "real" situations, of course, require simultaneous consideration of all of the A-B-X systems actually in effect, and if this requirement is met then I believe the proposition is defensible. I have so far limited myself to consideration of one A-B-X system at a time solely in the interests of simplicity. Even with this limitation I find that my difficulties of clear communication are considerable.

My present problem, let me remind you, is that of dynamics—that is, the conditions of change and stability. I have presented a single central principle of change, together with several limiting conditions. The central principle is that similarity of attitude tends to be both a consequence and a goal of communicative behavior. The limits within which the principle applies have to do with the properties of and the interrelationships among the relevant orientations of the communicators. That is to say, one property (similarity of orientations) of a "real system" of two or more persons varies interdependently with other properties of the system. This opens the way to an analysis of dynamics in terms of system properties, along lines already suggested.

Any real system presupposes both the interplay of forces (or forms of energy) and some form of communication among system parts. I shall make use only of psychological forces; without stopping to discuss the sources of their energy. I shall merely state that they are motivational in nature, and have to do with the invoking and with the selective directing of bodily energy. The parts of the system are orientations of persons. The means of communication in multi-person systems involve the behavioral apparatus by which symbols are emitted and the sensory apparatus by which they are received; the means of communication among the parts of a single-person (that is, phenomenal) system are less open to observation, and though they are no less "real," I shall not stop to discuss them.

Two kinds of forces are, hypothetically, brought to bear upon A-B-X systems. The first is purely intra-individual and psychological. For want of a better term I have referred to it as *co-orientation,* meaning that attention is simultaneously directed toward a fellow communicator (actual or potential) and toward an object of communication; the cognitive field is dominated by a *Gestalt* made up of self, other, and object of communication. There is nothing mysterious about such an hypothetical force; it is no more ethereal or non-material than the energy invoked in any other act of selective attention. I think it would be too much of a digression to stop to discuss the conditions under which such co-orientation occurs; suffice it is to say that they are not particularly mysterious, that they presuppose learning, and that they are very prevalent.

The other kind of hypothetical force is our (by now) old friend, a force (or strain) toward similarity of orientation. It too is psychological in nature —*i.e.,* intra-personal—but it can also be referred to as "at work" in a multi-person system; that is, such a force exists within a multi-person system if it exists within one or more of the persons. Henceforth I shall deal almost entirely with this second force; though it is logically necessary to postulate the force of co-orientation, its existence will hereafter be taken for granted in communicative situations.

There is only one remaining assumption which I shall make concerning system dynamics. This is that the system tends toward balance—that is, that certain states of the system represent equilibrium, and other states do not, and that influences whose effects are in the direction of disturbing equilibrium are likely to be countered by influences in the direction of restoring equilibrium. I have already presented the assumptions in terms of which a state of equilibrium can be defined. Given that a system exists—and this occurs whenever one or more persons co-orient toward another person and toward an object of communication—the most obvious state of equilibrium is one in which positive attraction is greater than zero and (for the phenomenal system) there is no perceived discrepancy of orientation. Under conditions of negative attraction (*i.e.,* dislike, contempt, mistrust, etc.), equilibrium may accompany either perceived similarity or perceived discrepancy of orientation, depending upon certain other conditions. For the present I shall concern myself only with changes from equilibrium to disequilibrium and vice versa, when positive attraction is greater than zero.

Suppose we have a phenomenal system characterized by positive attraction and by perceived discrepancy; that is, one attributes to a liked or respected person beliefs, feelings or evaluations about an object which are different from one's own. Such a system, according to hypothesis, is not in balance, but is characterized by what I shall call a strain toward similarity. Changes of any of the following kinds would in some degree reduce such a strain: (1) change in own orientation in the direction of the other's, as perceived; (2) perceived change in the other's orientation in one's own direction; (3) reduced attraction toward the other; or (4) reduced valence (concern, or importance) toward the object. These are the basic possibilities as theoretically predicted, to which the only alternatives are (1) tolerating the strain, or (2) "leaving the field"—*e.g.,* by forgetting it and turning to other matters—in which case the phenomenal system no longer exists. Interestingly enough, however, our research has recently turned up another alternative, as often happens when theories are sullied with empirical data. Many of our experimental subjects, when confronted with this kind of strain, chose none of these six alternatives, but instead increased the range of what they defined as similarity, or agreement. As a matter of fact, this proved to be the most frequent of all the alternatives with our student subjects, in an experiment dealing with politicians and political attitudes. With some difficulty I resist the digressive temptation to discuss some of the possible implications of this choice of alternatives.

The hypothesizing of these several alternatives leads immediately to several kinds of questions—most of them, fortunately, researchable. First, are they really alternatives? That is, does one *or* another of them tend to be chosen, rather than some combination which is no more strain-reducing than no change at all would have been? This is closely related to a second question: do changes (whether singly or in combination) following the experimental introduction of strain occur in such manner as to reduce strain? This is a way of asking whether observed changes can better be accounted for with than without the strain hypothesis. And thirdly—the most important question of all, assuming that the answers to the preceding questions are in general affirmative—under what conditions does one rather than others among the possible alternatives get chosen?

Because I want to attack the last of these questions, let me give only hurried answers to the first two. (Perhaps my preference for concentrating on the third question springs from the fact that, up to now, our research has provided much clearer answers to the first two.) A score or more of studies can be cited (not all from the University of Michigan) showing that almost all subjects prefer less to more strain, as here defined. When presented with information which is designed to be strain-inducing, they do something about it—including, under some experimental manipulations, the rejection of the proffered information. Perhaps I can best summarize this aspect of our research findings simply by saying that, among many hundreds of subjects under a wide variety of conditions, there is only a tiny minority who, following the experimental introduction of information designed to be strain-inducing, change their phenomenal systems in ways which increase the amount of pre-experimental strain. In view of the prevalent assumption among educators that new experiences, sometimes at least, really ought to produce some strain, at least pending the working out of a "reasonable" solution, I must again resist the temptation to digress.

Perhaps it is worth noting, in passing, that individuals seem to have characteristic limits within which they can tolerate the strain of perceived dissimilarity with attractive others, at least within a given topical area. We have no evidence, so far, as to how widely generalized such individual characteristics are.

In short, our research seems amply to justify our theoretical assumptions to the general effect that we can account for wide ranges of alternative reactions to conditions hypothetically stressful by the single notion that, within a system of interdependent parts, there are many alternative ways of "taking up the slack." One always feels encouraged when superficially disparate phenomena begin to take orderly places—and especially if they are predictable places—under a single theoretical tent.

Since our data are still in the process of analysis, I shall have to limit myself to statements of theoretical prediction as to the conditions under which one rather than any other alternative is most likely to be taken as a "solution" to strain. Let me briefly examine each of the major alternatives (for the moment ignoring the possibilities of tolerating strain and "leaving the field").

First, under what conditions is one most likely to change one's own orientation in the direction of the attractive other, as a way of reducing the strain of perceived dissimilarity? Two conditions immediately suggest themselves; the first is an object-orientation which might be described as "committed." There are many sources of committedness; perhaps the most important are immediacy of own, first-hand experience (especially sensory experience) and anchorage of the orientation in other A-B-X systems, especially if the bonds of attraction in these other systems are stronger than those in the system immediately under strain. Other things equal, one is most likely to choose the alternative of changing one's own orientation as a path to strain-reduction if it is an orientation of low committedness. This, of course, is a property of the A-X orientation.

The A-B orientation is equally important, and in the same way. The second condition has to do with attraction, and especially with that variety of it which has to do with expertness, or informedness, or knowledgeability (we have come to refer to this as "respect"). Positive attraction (and also negative attraction) is often widely generalized—as in the case of the proverbial small boy and his all-knowing father, for example. For most adults, however, such admiration has its limits, and the "respect" dimension of attraction, more or less specific to the particular X in question, is more directly related to the strain toward similarity than are the more generalized forms of attraction. Other things equal, then, the stronger the A-B attraction—especially its respect dimension—the greater the likelihood of changing one's own orientation as an alternative path to strain reduction.

These two, as I have said, are the two obvious conditions of change in our orientation. There is at least one other of whose importance I am quite certain, though I am not at all sure that I can be convincing about it. It is something which we have come to call "relevance," *i.e.,* joint or shared relevance of the common object to self and other. It refers not to the strength of either the A-X or the A-B orientation, but rather to the strength of the linkage between them. It is, quite literally, the strength of co-orientation. It might also be referred to, somewhat metaphorically, as the tightness of the phenomenal system by which a person views himself, another, and a common object as tied together. Relevance is most apt to be high, I concede, when either attraction or attitude is strong, but this is not necessarily the case. A strong A-B attraction may have little relevance for a strongly committed A-X orientation—as in the case, for example, of a business man's wife and an engrossing business deal. Or, contrariwise, situational demands may be such that relevance is high even though both attraction and attitude are weak—for example, two people who are quite indifferent to each other have a joint committee assignment about which both are very lukewarm. It is possible that the conditions which have led us to take note of what we call the relevance variable might be handled adequately by way of the "respect" variable, but as of now I doubt it. In any case, other things equal, one is most likely to choose the alternative of changing one's own orientation as a path to strain reduction if one's phenomenal system is characterized by high relevance, in the sense which I have tried to describe.

When is the second alternative—perception of change in the other's orientation—most likely to occur? Since such perception may have any degree of accuracy, or correctness, the answer to this question will vary with the degree of accuracy of perception of the other's orientation. Relatively accurate perceptions of change in B's orientation are most likely to occur if A's existing strain has, as already hypothesized, led to one or more communications from him to B, and if such communications have had the effect of making B's orientations more like A's. (Whether or not this does in fact occur depends upon the properties of B's phenomenal system, as already discussed.) Relatively inaccurate ("distorted") perceptions of change in B's orientation are most likely to occur under exactly opposite conditions—that is, in the absence of further opportunity for exchange of information with B. Given the absence of opportunity for either persuasion or reality-testing via communication, distortion is most likely to occur when strain toward similarity is greatest and when other alternatives are least welcome. For example, if A learns that a highly attractive B diverges radically from an orientation to which he himself is deeply committed, he may be able to convince himself, in the absence of any communication on the subject with B, that it was all a mistake, or at least greatly exaggerated—in short, that there really isn't any disagreement.

What about the third alternative, decreased attraction toward a person whose orientation is seen as divergent from one's own? Such a change may of course be either a generalized one (over-all liking for the person) or specific to the object of communication (respect). Several conditions already mentioned readily suggest themselves as favorable to this alternative. If committedness to one's existing orientation is strong; if the conditions making for distorted perception of the other's orientation are not present; if persuading the other to one's own point of view is ruled out; if relevance is so high that one cannot readily leave the field—under any of these conditions one would predict a greater likelihood of reduced attraction to the other. One other condition should also be mentioned: the number and strength of A-B bonds in other A-B-X systems. That is, if one is involved in many different phenomenal systems with different Xs but with the same B, the perception of dissimilarity with the B concerning a single X is not very likely to reduce general attraction to that B; it may, however, reduce respect (which is defined as X-specific), according to the other conditions already mentioned.

Perhaps this is as good a point as any other to point out that preferences for one or another of the several alternatives are to some degree dictated by personality characteristics. Some individuals seem to have a generalized preference for reducing attraction as a first alternative, others as one of the last. Our analyses, to date, seem to indicate that most college students, in the case of most of the issues we have studied, are surer of whom they like and dislike than of what they believe (if I may give a much over-simplified version of rather complex findings). Again, I forbear digressive comment.

The fourth among the major alternatives, reduced valence toward the object of communication, should perhaps be viewed as a sort of compromise solution to the problem of strain toward similarity. If all other alternatives are unwelcome, one can, without changing the nature of one's own orientation, convince oneself that it doesn't really matter so much. In the extreme case, one can even convince oneself that "these things are really matters of taste"—that is, that the object of communication is, like the amount of cream one takes in one's coffee, irrelevant; no reason exists why similarity should exist. This extreme case is tantamount, of course, to abandoning the system and, in a way, represents "leaving the field." It may be expected (though as yet I have no supporting data) that the alternative of reducing valence toward the object is apt to be associated with another alternative I have already mentioned, extend the range of what is considered to be "agreement."

One specific condition favorable to the selection of this alternative remains to be mentioned (as I have already noted). The same person finds himself involved in many overlapping A-B-X systems; if the same X is involved in many of these (with different Bs), and if valence toward the common X is strong in all or most of the other systems, then the alternative of reducing valence is not likely to be chosen.

So far I have been discussing only phenomenal, intra-personal systems of orientations. Before I turn to a consideration of multi-person systems, let me stop to draw a few threads together. I have stressed the interdependence of various system properties and, without drawing upon other than system-variables (though occasionally I have had to take account of the interdependence of multiple systems in which the same person is involved), I have tried to show how (hypothetically, at least) alternative processes of strain reduction bear orderly relationships to one another. In one respect I have been insufficiently explicit, however. I have noted, but only in passing, that some of these alternatives involve changes following communication while others do not, or at any rate not necessarily.

Since my primary concern is communicative behavior, which by definition is interpersonal, you may be wondering why I have devoted so much time to purely psychological concepts like intrapersonal strain, and to alternative paths to its reduction, some of which do not involve communication at all. My defense is the very general one that the more you know about phenomena closely associated with the particular phenomenon of special interest to you, the better you will understand it. And, in particular, the better you understand what may be considered alternative, or substitute, phenomena, the more you will know about the dynamics of your phenomenon of special interest.

With specific reference to communication, as my phenomenon of special interest, let me draw my threads together as follows: a state of intrapersonal strain toward similarity, hypothetically, is always accompanied by an impulse or motivation to communicate to the person with whom dissimilarity of orientation is perceived. This impulse—which may be regarded as a vector, since it has force and direction—is often countered by other forces. (For example, one doesn't want to argue with a superior, or fears that one will expose one's ignorance; such counterforces can be described as unwelcome changes in A-B relationships.) When such counterforces are strong enough, overt communication will be inhibited. But, as Kurt Lewin has long since pointed out (in connection with his discussion of "the quasi-stationary equilibrium"), such a state of affairs does not mean that there is an absence of forces. It means, rather, that stress is increased. It is this kind of combination of stresses which is responsible, presumably, for much of the impulsive and "irrational" nature of those means of strain reduction which are substitutes for communication.

IV. MULTI-PERSON SYSTEMS

A human organism, as we have long since learned, is a real system which begins life with certain equilibrium demands of physiological nature, and acquires others, of psychological and social nature. These demands require the maintenance of relative constancy of certain relationships, some of which are intraorganismic and some of which are between organism and environment. One of the requirements of the latter kind, for humans, has to do with the social environment, and a necessary adaptive mechanism for meeting the requirement is the ability to receive and to transmit messages—communicative behavior.

But the phrase "social environment" takes for its point of reference one or a set of humans for whom *other* humans (and their behavior) constitute an environment. These "other" humans, however, also constitute part of our problem. Hence an analytic system for the study of communicative behavior, if it is to be applicable to public problems, needs to be extended to include these others in the real system under scrutiny. In turning to a consideration of objective, or multi-person, systems I shall build upon what I have already had to say about intrapersonal systems. The analogy is closer than it may seem. For example, if we consider a group, or a public, as a communicating system, we shall have to deal with problems of both intra-group and inter-group communication. Formally speaking, however, this is the same problem which we have already met in relating the phenomenal systems of two persons to the objective system which they jointly constitute (that is, as seen by the outside observer, who has equal access to the phenomenal systems of both, as well as to their overt behavior).

An objective A-B-X system exists if and only if two or more persons co-orient to each other and to the same X (that is, a potential object of communication). It is not necessary, for theoretical purposes, that the persons be in each others' presence, nor that they co-orient to each other and to the same X simultaneously. But it is simpler, for purposes of this exposition, to assume that they are together and that co-orientation is simultaneous; for simplicity's sake, also, I shall again illustrate with a two-person system.

A potential strain toward similarity exists if and when there is actual, objective discrepancy in orientation toward the object of co-orientation. It becomes an actual strain if and when strain appears in the phenomenal system of either person. The means by which either of them discovers the discrepancy is assumed to be communication. But let me hasten to add, lest I seem to be indulging in circular reasoning, that the strain toward similarity presupposed by the communication in which discrepancy is discovered is not the same as the strain ensuing from that discovery. To give an every-day example, if I am curious about the out-of-doors temperature and know that you have just looked at the thermometer, this cognitive discrepancy may lead me to ask you what the temperature is. Your answer may lead to the discovery of other discrepancies, such as that your thermometer reading is in Centigrade degrees, whereas I had first assumed it to be in Fahrenheit. Communication, in short, is a necessary but not a sufficient step by which discrepancies are both discovered and removed.

The conditions under which existing discrepancy is most likely to be discovered and to be reduced are pretty much the same. I shall stop to mention only one of them—relevance, that is, common dependence upon the object of communication (it might be called "common fate" with respect to it). The importance of this condition seems self-evident; if, like two men on a mid-ocean raft, both are in fact dependent both upon the common object and upon each other (in this case for survival), the likelihood is that they will not only discover their common interdependence but will also arrive at a high degree of consensus—for example, as to the effects of wind and wave upon the raft, and countermeasures to be taken. We feel safe in making this kind of prediction simply because consensus is so important to them—both as precondition and as desired consequence of communication. That is, cognitive consensus makes accurate communication possible, and accurate communication makes possible the continuity of moment-to-moment consensus upon which integrated behavior depends. In this sense, then, existing discrepancy is most likely to be discovered and to be reduced under conditions of high relevance.

It is not part of my assignment to suggest "practical" applications of the kind of analytic scheme which I have been outlining. I do assume, however, that many of you will be interested in whether or not the general point of view and the more specific propositions concerning communicative behavior have any relevance at all to communication on the public scene. I shall try to persuade you that they do, and that (if so) the fact is of some importance.

First, a brief consideration of intra-group communication—or intra-public, if you please. I take it that "a public," by the way, is a set of people who have a common concern. More specifically, it is a group-relevant concern—that is, it has, or is believed to have, some aspects of "common fate." The phrase "or is believed to have" corresponds to "perceived similarity," of "perceived consensus," in the present analytic system. (Perhaps I ought to remind you that I use these terms to represent a continuum; perceived consensus may be negative, that is, perceived non-consensus.) In short, a public may be viewed as a system of orientations provided the necessary conditions are met. The necessary conditions are that there be orientations on the part of two or more persons—orientations of greater than zero cathexis—toward the same object (event, issue, etc.), and that those persons attribute orientations of greater than zero cathexis to others. The A-B-X paradigm is applicable to a public, by such a definition, with the understanding that either the A or the B may be a plurality of persons.

This definition of a public, as you may have noted, includes those public figures often referred to as leaders. This, I think, is as it should be. While it is customary, I believe, to refer to a leader as influencing, or being influenced by, or as speaking to, a public—as if he were outside or somehow apart from it—it is far more consonant with current theoretical development regarding the phenomena of leadership to think of leaders as participating in a system. At any rate, much of the communicative behavior of public leaders is congruent with the kinds of propositions which I have been presenting. When public leaders perceive discrepancies between themselves and their constituencies, via communications of various kinds, they are apt to behave in accordance with one or more of the alternatives I have noted; sometimes they even change their own orientations. When publics perceive similar discrepancies, they too choose among these alternatives—including the toleration of strain and leaving the field (apathy).

The phrase which I have just used—"when publics perceive"—is, of course, hardly more than a metaphor. Perception, strictly speaking, refers to an intra-organismic process of organizing sensory input; collectivities, in any literal sense, are incapable of this. What the figure of speech refers to is very real, however: a distribution of orientations among a plurality of persons and—equally important—a distribution of judgments about orientations of the remainder of "the public." What is sometimes known as "an aroused public opinion" includes as one of its components a high frequency of individual judgments that others, too, are "aroused." The conditions under which high frequencies of such judgments occur are, hypothetically, the two which we have already considered: (1) frequent communication, and (2) the tendency, as a function of strong cathexis, to attribute to attractive others orientations like one's own. This latter, though initially on an "unreal" basis, may lead to communicative behavior which has very real effects; it may, in fact, create the very conditions which did not, in fact, previously exist.

I cannot refrain from reporting, sheerly for purposes of illustrations, some data I obtained from students in several University classes in April of 1951, in a questionnaire dealing with the very recent dismissal of General MacArthur by President Truman. Respondents, who were not representative of any known population, were asked both to indicate their own attitudes and to attribute to various other persons, groups, and categories a modal attitude. Results of this exploratory study included the following:

	Pro-Truman Ss who . . .	Anti-Truman Ss who . . .
attribute to "most of my closest friends"		
pro-Truman attitudes	48	2
anti-Truman attitudes	0	34
neither	4	4
attribute to "most uninformed people"		
pro-Truman attitudes	6	13
anti-Truman attitudes	32	14
neither	4	13

If we assume that "closest friends" are more attractive to university students than "uninformed people," these data provide support for the attraction hypothesis. Comparisons of those whose own attitudes are more and less intense also provide support, though less strikingly, for the hypothesis concerning strength of attitude cathexis.

These, as it happens, are the most striking results of their kind that I have yet seen—perhaps because the issue was at once an ambiguous and a highly salient and controversial one. Except in degree, however, these findings are typical of nearly all others having to do with political issues. Such data do not tell us anything, of course, about the processes by which judgments of others' attitudes were arrived at—whether more or less accurately, following communication (in the case of "closest friends"), or more or less autistically ("wishful-thinkingly"). Such data do suggest, however, a strong force toward the reduction of strain under conditions of strong attraction.

I should like, finally, to make a few observations about "public opinion." If the phrase is regarded as standing for certain properties of one or more systems-in-equilibrium, then the distribution of pro-and-con attitudes within a given population is by no means the only system property—nor even the most important one—in which one will be interested. From the point of view of the kind of equilibrium system which I have been trying to describe, the public opinion researcher would seek information on such points as the following, if he wants the fullest possible understanding about issue X. With what groups and/or persons do respondents co-orient toward this X, and how do respondents feel toward them? (*I.e.,* the significant and salient Bs of the respondents' A-B-X systems must be identified, and attraction toward them must be known.) What attitudes toward the X are attributed to these B's? To what extent do such attributions represent "realistic" information received via communication, and to what extent "autistic" solutions to system strain? To what extent do respondents see a world in which all "good" or attractive B's agree with them, as opposed to seeing a world in which some attractive B's agree and others disagree with them?

Most of these kinds of information, as you will have observed, have to do with the perception of varying degrees of consensus. This may seem to you like saying that second-order public opinion—*i.e.,* public opinion about public opinion—is as important as the first-order phenomenon. I do, indeed, want to say something like that, but at the same time something quite different. The difference is that "the public" to which respondents attribute opinions is by no means the same as "the public" in which the social scientist interests himself. The scientist's problem, from the present point of view, is to discover the nature and the degree of support which members of a given public perceive in the A-B-X systems in which they participate.

Perhaps I can illustrate how research data gathered along these lines might be illuminating. Suppose that a national sample of respondents had been shown to be divided as follows on issue X: 65 per cent pro, 25 per cent con, and 10 per cent not ascertained. Now let us make two different assumptions as to the distributions of the respondents' attributions of support, as shown in Figures 4a and 4b. In these figures the solid lines show the hypothetical attributions of respondents who themselves are "pro" and the broken

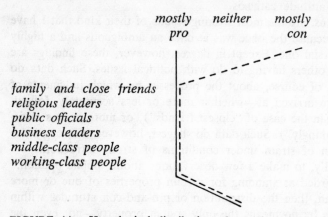

mostly   neither   mostly
pro   con

family and close friends
religious leaders
public officials
business leaders
middle-class people
working-class people

FIGURE 4A. Hypothetical distribution of modal responses showing attributions of pro-con attitudes to selected groups viewed by respondents at "attractive." Solid lines represent attributions of those who are themselves "pro" and broken lines of those who are "con."

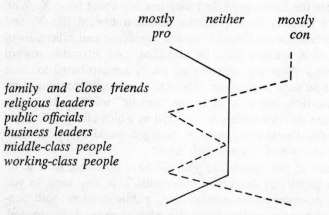

mostly   neither   mostly
pro   con

family and close friends
religious leaders
public officials
business leaders
middle-class people
working-class people

FIGURE 4B. Another hypothetical distribution of respondents, the distribution of whose own responses is the same as in Figure 4a.

lines who are "con." With regard to each group noted at the left, the modal response of all respondents who mention the group as "attractive" is classified as either "mostly pro" (say 60 per cent or more), "mostly con," or "neither." The two sets of profiles are intended to show divergent "states of public opinion," even though the distributions of "own responses" are identical in both cases. Those who might be interested either in following or in modifying public opinion would, I should think, take quite different courses of action under these two divergent conditions of perceived public support.

Frankly, I do not know whether such an analytic system as I have tried to present will ever have any usefulness to political scientists. I do know that, under a wide range of conditions of communication and with widely varying objects of communication—including large government agencies, stratified samples of the adult American population, and student living groups—people behave as if the assumptions on which this analytic system rests were essentially true. My concerns, frankly, are those of understanding as well as I can the why of human behavior as it is related to communication. Beyond this, I suppose I share with the rest of you the basic article of faith that any extension of the frontiers of understanding how things work, no matter how esoteric, eventually finds its niche of usefulness.

HAROLD GUETZKOW

Building Models About Small Groups

WITHIN A CENTURY the social philosopher has been transformed into the social scientist. As Lazarsfeld notes, "A hundred years ago the task seemed to be to make sweeping guesses as to the future development of society. Fifty years ago the interest focused on basic concepts which would properly classify the crucial social phenomena. Today the trend is toward singling out the basic variables from which all specific concepts and interrelationships can be derived" (17, p. 3). The study of small groups epitomizes this trend.

The break-through in small group methodology came in two jumps. The potential of the field experimental in natural, ongoing organizations was demonstrated by the Mayo, Roethlisberger, Dickson efforts [28] in the late 1920's. These studies at the Western Electric Company indicated the productivity of such methodologies as the personal interview and direct observation. The fruitfulness of the laboratory using experimenter-constructed situations was dramatized by Lippitt, White, and Lewin in the late 1930's.[19] Their studies on contrived clubs at the Iowa Child Welfare Station vividly illustrated the possibility of experimental variation in such complex variables as leadership style. After World War II, there has been a consolidation within these two central methodologies as has been documented by Vinacke.[34] The gap between them now is receiving attention and the closure probably will come within the next ten years.[26] The recent efforts to codify methodology (A, B, C) indicate our methods are attaining maturity. Although we can expect continuous and important innovation in methodology, it seems the central focus in contemporary small group study is in the development of theories.

Analytical work in the small group area now is directed toward the building of miniature theoretical systems. A number of investigators have developed such "islands of theory," constructing propositions about a limited number of variables. This paper will overview central trends in the development of these analytical systems, and then indicate their relation to one important methodological problem—the dimensions of groups.

ANALYTICAL SYSTEMS AS COMBINATIONS OF INDEPENDENT AND DEPENDENT VARIABLES

In the earlier work on small groups, researchers tended to limit themselves to hypotheses about two variables. An important trend in the study of small groups has been the construction of models which interrelate more than two variables.

Floyd Allport's early experiments (1, pp. 274–8) on "response within the group" are prototypic of "two-variable" theorizing. Allport asked his subjects to judge the pleasantness of odors when alone and when in small groups. He confirmed his hypothesis that persons in the presence of others tend to shun extreme judgments. Given A (others in the environment), one predicts B (restriction in judgments).

Over the last quarter century the two-variable hypothesis has been the cornerstone of research about small groups. One might diagram the hypothesis as follows:

FIGURE 1:   A ──────────→ B,

wherein the arrow posits a causal relationship. (29, pp. 523–4). A great number of current researches—both experimental and field—on the small group [32] are still concerned with such two-variable relationships. The following paradigm characterizes these researches on groups:

	Certain Independent Variables (describing the group, its task, and/or its members)	Certain Outcome Variables (describing the group, its product, and/or its members)
FIGURE 2:	──────────→	

An example is found in Darley, Gross, and Martin's work [7] with natural groups, women's residence units organized as a cooperative housing project. They found that of some 18 variables describing the groups and their members (variables such as "house scholastic achievement," "strength of leadership," and "volume of participation") 5 of them were related to group productivity in producing a formal plan for better cooperating living.

Independent variables tend to be of two types, those which characterize the members or tasks at the beginning of the observation and those which characterize the internal processes of the group itself. Past scholastic achievement is an example of an initial condition, a characteristic with which each member comes to the group. The volume of participation describes ongoing processes within the group, once members with certain initial characteristics begin working on a task. The tendency within the last ten years in small group research has been to concentrate on these internal processes—sometimes unwisely neglecting the measurement of the initial conditions. Perhaps this emphasis is a reaction against the earlier emphasis on initial conditions as the prime determinants of group outcomes.

This differentiation between variables as characterizations of (A) initial conditions and (G) internal processes, may be thought of as a change in the basic analytic system used in research on small groups to the following:

FIGURE 3: $\qquad$ A $\xrightarrow{\qquad\qquad}$ G $\xrightarrow{\qquad}$ Outcomes

An analogous differentiation has taken place among the measures used to appraise the outcomes. Although many studies continue in the early tradition of determining whether the outcome of the group is "good" or "bad," there is increasing awareness that the outcomes of small group processes are multiple. It is sometimes useful to classify the outcomes of the group's behavior as (L) the group products (things or symbols produced), and (K) changes in the individual members. These changes in the individual may be relatively basic and permanent, as changes in personality due to interaction in the family, as a small group—or changes in skills and knowledge, as in the classroom group. Contrariwise, they may be more superficial, as changes in temporary feelings toward other members of the group, *e.g.*, in the bridge party—or shift in attitudes on social issues, *e.g.*, in the political club. This distinction among outcomes further complicates the model used in small group research as follows:

FIGURE 4: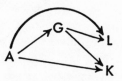

The notion of multiple-outcomes is illustrated in work of the Conference Research project at the University of Michigan which studies the administrative, decision-making meeting in governmental and industrial organizations [23]. The investigators in this project, both in their field and their laboratory experiments, centered on three outcomes, measuring each quite separately: (X) group productivity, (Y) member satisfaction with the meeting, (Z) extent of consensus within the group on the decision. They discovered that

FIGURE 5.

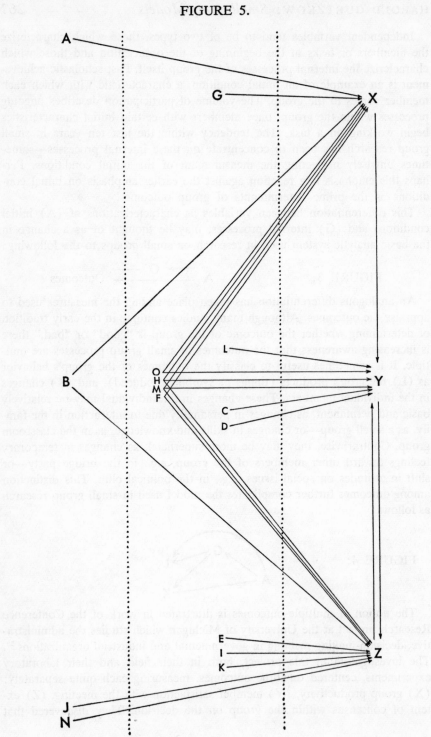

FIGURE 5. Conference Research Model

(see facing page)

Identification of Variables

MEASURES CONCERNED WITH

Nature of Group Task:
A—Urgency of Agenda Problems (Code 13-OB; 14-PR)
B—Adequacy of Group's Authority to Task Requirement (Code 33-OR)

Leadership:
C—Differentiation of Leader's Role (Code 62-OR)
D—Leader's Control over Group's Procedures (Code 58-OR)
E—Percentage Procedural Contributions (Code 71-OT)

Communication:
F—Understandability of Discussion (Code 67-OR)
G—Audibility (Code 66-OR)

Problem-Solving:
H—Orderliness of Topic Treatment (Code 76-OR)

Affective Climate in Group:
I—Conflict During Meeting (Code 53-OR)
J—Disparity as to Means to Goals (Code 51-PR)
K—Amount Group Supports and Accepts Its Members (Code 24-OR)

Motivation:
L—Cohesiveness (Code 121-OR)
M—Expression of Self-oriented Needs (Code 4-OR)
N—Disparity in Values and Goals (Code 3-OR)

Participation:
O—Opportunity to Participate (Code 69-PR)

OUTCOME MEASURES:

X—Group Productivity: proportion of agenda items completed of those attempted. (Code 40-OT)
Y—Satisfaction with Meeting: average of ratings given at end of meeting. (Code 79-PR)
Z—Consensus: participant's judgment as to how much his final opinions differed from the decisions reached by the group. (Code 90-PR)

these three outcomes were only somewhat related to each other. More interesting was their finding that sometimes the same, and sometimes different, variables (measures of both initial conditions and intervening processes) could be used to predict the outcomes. The partial model which was developed on the basis of the preliminary analyses of field and laboratory conferences is presented in Figure 5.

A verbal description of the model is given in Marquis, Guetzkow, and Heyns (23, pp. 59–66). The code numbers refer to the group variable code used in working up the raw data, as presented in "Raw Data and Basic Analyses for Field Observation of Business and Government Conferences," 1949, University Microfilm Publication No. 2791, L of C Mic. A51–852. The code letters tell whether the variable was obtained through an observer rating (OR), an observer tally (OT), or a participant rating (PR).

With differentiations now being made among both predictor and outcome variables, it is easy to understand how researchers on the small group feel quite free to think of any of the intervening processes as outcomes of interest. For example, in the experimental work done at the University of Rochester, Haythorn [14] explored the effects of one individual's personality characteristics upon the individual behavior of others in problem-solving groups. His finding, for example, that an aggressive, self-confident type of behavior on the part of one member induced less aggressive, less self-confident behavior on the part of others in the group is an instance of this focus on the intervening processes themselves as outcomes.

This focus of interest on the intervening processes themselves is very strong in the work of Bales and some of his colleagues at the Harvard Laboratory of Social Relations. With Strodtbeck, study [8] was made of the change in relative emphasis over time which occurs in the interactions of problem-solving groups working toward decision. These researchers coded some 15,000 interactions between individuals in 22 meetings into five broad categories: *orientation* interactions by which ignorance and uncertainty about relevant facts are reduced; *evaluation* activities, in which proposed courses of action are judged in terms of different values and interests; *control* activities, through which the group decisions are made and expectations about further joint action established; and *negative* and *positive* interactions which occur in the handling of the group's social-emotional problems, as contrasted with those more directly task-connected. By plotting the relative frequency of each category they found a progressive change in emphasis given to these different interactions as the groups progressed from the first third through the second third to the last third of its meeting. Orientation activity progressively decreased; evaluative interactions were at their height during the middle part of the meeting; control activities and the affective reactions (both negative and positive) increased from beginning to end. Bales and Strodtbeck then hypothesize, ". . . the interaction process should be considered as a system, with internal tendencies which make each part of the process a condition to other parts" (3, p. 494).

This tendency to be concerned with the internal processes of the group is typical of small group research with sociological roots. Studies of the internal processes of the small group seem to be a compression of the initial conditions-internal processes-outcome paradigm (Figure 3) into a smaller time-span. Thus, in the Bales-Strodtbeck analysis the initial orientation activities lead to evaluations which have their outcome in control activities.

INTERACTION AND FEEDBACK IN ANALYTIC SYSTEMS

As researchers measured three or more variables simultaneously in their attempt to relate initial conditions and intervening processes to different outcomes, they sometimes found there were simultaneous interactions among the variables, and that often there were feedback effects of one variable upon another and even upon itself over time. Attention to these two types of relations among variables demand analytic systems of considerable complexity.

The simultaneous measurement of more than two variables in the small group leads to the location of interaction * effects, finding that the effect of one factor upon an outcome is different in the presence of a second factor. For example, a number of such conditional relationships were found in a special follow-up analysis of Conference Research data.[13] When the conference groups were permeated by conflict deriving from the emotional, affective aspects of the group's interpersonal relations, the efforts on the part of the chairman to seek more information on the agenda topics did not result in significantly more consensus on the group's decisions. Contrariwise, when affective conflict was low, the chairman's activity in soliciting more information resulted in significantly more consensus (13, p. 376, Table IV).

Another example of the "conditioning" effect one variable may have on the operation of another in producing certain outcomes in the small group is found in Pelz' study of work groups in a public utility company (24, pp. 54–55). Certain supervisory practices were found to be very helpful in creating positive attitudes in the employees, if the supervisor himself had power to influence his superior regarding events (such as promotions) within the supervisor's department. But if the supervisor's power was absent, the very same supervisory practices had no relation to the attitudes of his employees.

These conditioning or interaction effects may be diagrammed by using a single-headed arrow in the causal relationship, as follows:

In addition to gaining information about interaction, small group research is concerned with feedback. Kurt Lewin had considerable awareness of the

---

* Small group researchers use the term "interaction" with two meanings: (1) in its statistical meaning, as herewith, and (2) in its social meaning, defining the action and reaction of persons to each other as "interaction."

importance of "circular causal" processes ten years ago, when he commented (18, p. 22) on Lippitt and White's study on leadership: "For instance, if authoritarian control weakens to the point of permitting open intermember aggression, this aggression is likely to weaken still further the level of control

FIGURE 6.

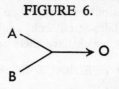

(unless the leader is 'reacting' to the situation by a heightening of control). These circular causal processes have to be taken into account for prediction." "Feedback" is the effect of a variable back upon itself and/or other variable, or its indirect effect upon itself because of its direct effect upon a second variable. These effects are usually diagrammed as direct or indirect "loops":

FIGURE 7.

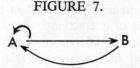

This diagram indicates both types of feedback: that variable A affects itself, and that variable A has an effect upon variable B, which in turn affects A.

Gradually, more students of the small group are using feedback mechanisms as integral parts of their analytic systems. Some students of the small group, especially those who come with psychological backgrounds, tend to develop models which have very short time-perspective. They look at groups over short time periods and then attempt to draw causal interconnections from their observations of concomitant variations. This often makes it difficult for them to discover feedback loops. For example, the psychologist Cattell and his colleagues have observed large numbers of groups for very short periods of time. They state, "One may therefore contingently conclude that the syntality [attributes of the group as a group] of formally leaderless groups, in their first three hours of existence, when exposed to the same but very varied demands, is primarily determined by the pre-group personalities of the component individuals" (6, p. 354). In such situations, there is no feedback probably because there is not time for the variables to feed back upon themselves.

When time depth is put into the research, we begin to straighten out the "Which is first—chicken or egg?" problems. One of the central problems in role theory in the small group is whether the position of the person is obtained because of personal characteristics which lead him into the role, or whether his personal characteristics change, conforming to the situation pressures which develop as the individual enacts the role required by his new position, or both? Lieberman [21] was able to study this feedback problem over a time-span of 14 months in small work groups. Attitudes toward the union and management were obtained originally from some 2,354 rank-and-file workers. During the next twelve months 23 men had been promoted to the position of foreman, and 35 men had been elected by their work groups as union stewards. Fourteen to fifteen months after the original attitude survey, questionnaires were readministered. The results indicated, "that although workers who are made foremen and workers who are made stewards do not appear to be initially selected on the basis of their attitudes toward management or toward the union, their attitudes undergo systematic changes once they are placed in their new roles. The workers who are made foremen tend to become more pro-management, and the workers who are made stewards tend to become more pro-union." This longitudinal study makes it clear as to how feedback is occurring in this situation—the positions feedback into the attitudes.

TWO MODELS

The major components of the analytic systems used by small group theorists now have been outlined. Let us examine two models which embody many of these analytic features, that of Homans and Riecken on sentiment, interaction, and activity, and that of Festinger and his colleagues on pressures toward uniformity in small groups.

A MODEL ON INTERACTION, SENTIMENT, AND ACTIVITY

In 1950 Homans developed a miniature analytic system (16, Chapters 2 through 6) on the basis of his careful analysis of the bank wiring observation room experiments of Roethlisberger and Dickson.[28] In 1954, with Riecken, he examined a great collection of experimental and field data in terms of his model (27, pp. 788–801). The basic variables, as defined in the 1954 summarization, are as follows:

$B(t)$: The extent to which the *behavior* of a member of the group conforms to the norms or values which prescribe what activity is "good" or "important" in the given situation.

$S(t)$: The *sentiment* others have for each member of the group; that is, how well or poorly members feel toward others.

$I(t)$: The frequency of *interaction* among the members.

E : The *external* environment.

As mentioned earlier, an analytic system is constructed by interrelating the variables to each other. Homans and Riecken (27, pp. 789–799) do this as follows:

1. *Ceteris paribus,* "the more nearly a member realizes in his activity [B(t)] the norms and values of the group, the higher his (sociometric) rank [S(t)]."
2. *Ceteris paribus,* "the higher a member's rank [S(t)] the more often he originates interaction [I(t)] as well as the more often he receives it."
3. *Ceteris paribus,* the interaction [I(t)] the member "gives to the other will vary inversely as the 'goodness' or 'importance' of the other's activity [B(t)]. . . ."
4. Changes in I(t) and B(t) may be "enforced upon the system from without" [E].

These propositions may be diagrammed as a miniature analytic system as has been done in Figure 8, using the conventions developed in the earlier parts of our discussion. Although proposition 4 is a bit equivocal, earlier phrasing of this proposition by Homans in 1950 seems to make it clear that he intends a direct feedback loop: "If the interaction between the members of a group are frequent . . . , sentiments of liking will grow up between them, and these sentiments will lead in turn to further interactions. . . ." The Homans model concerns itself with but four variables, contrasted with the eighteen used in the Conference Research model (Figure 5). Yet the Homans analytic system is more complicated in its mechanisms than the Conference Research model, because of the feedbacks. The Homans system makes use of two feedback mechanisms, both indirect: the I-S relationship, and the I-B-S inter-relationship. No conditional relations are hypothesized. Homans conceived the external environment as impinging upon the interaction level (as when a geographic barrier is used to reduce interaction) and the extent to which the activities of the member conform to the group norms (as when an individual is trained outside the group to handle difficult etiquette

FIGURE 8.

The Homans Model of Interaction, Sentiment, and Activity

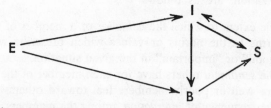

Identification of Variables:
  B: Extent behavioral activity conforms to group norms
  S: Sentiment others have for members of group
  I: Frequency of interaction among members
  E: External environment
A verbal description of the model is given in Riecken and Homans (27)

practices, which then make him able to conform to the group's norms in his activities in the group).

Homans checked the usefulness of his model in 1950 by interpreting other case materials, such as the Norton Street Gang behavior enumerated by Whyte and the operation of the family in Tikopia as described by Firth. In addition, with Riecken in 1954, he re-interpreted with considerable insight many experimental and field observations about small groups. These scholars were able to explain the asymmetry of the interaction matrices of who talks how often to whom in both natural and experimental groups; they were

FIGURE 9.

The Festinger Model of Pressures Toward Uniformity (Aggregative Case)

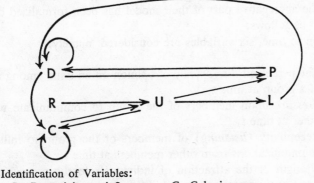

Identification of Variables:

    L: Receptivity to influence   C: Cohesiveness
    D: Discrepancy of opinion   U: Pressure toward uniformity
    P: Pressure to communicate   R: Revelance of issue
    A verbal description of the model is given in Festinger (8)

able to explain why "foreign" relations are particularly the concern of the high ranking members of the groups when two or more different groups have contact; they were able to explain why leisure time interactions differ in their structure from work time interaction. The coverage of their model is impressive.

When one compares the 1950 and 1954 expositions of the Homans model, one notes the implicit shift which has taken place in some definitions of the variables. These shifts are not on the former level. Rather, they are shifts which occur as the model is applied to new data. For example, there is a shift in the term *activity:* in 1950, the term refers "to things that people do: work on the physical environment, with implements, and with other persons" (16, p. 34); in 1954, the term has gathered a nuance, the "actual behavior of a person which others evaluate in terms of their own norms and values" (27, p. 788); and then in the same paper the term is further shifted to mean the conformity of behavior to the norms and values of the group, as is indicated in the quote given as the first proposition above. This tendency for model builders to make extensions of their definitions is quite common.

A MODEL OF BEHAVIOR INVOLVING PRESSURES TOWARD UNIFORMITY

In 1950 Festinger summarized [8] the model building work of himself and his colleagues, K. Back, S. Schachter, and J. Thibault, about pressures toward uniformity in groups.

Part of their model is concerned with aggregative variables (variables which consist of measures made of each individual member and then summed to give an average for the group); another part of their model is concerned with the deviate-member in the group, comparing him with non-deviating members. The aggregative part of their model has been formalized by Simon and myself [30] as follows:

In addition to time, six variables are considered, namely:

"$D(t)$: The perceived *discrepancy* of opinion on an issue among members of a group at time t;

"$P(t)$: *Pressure* upon members of the group to communicate with each other at time t;

"$L(t)$: Receptivity (*listening*) of members of the group to influence by communications from other members at time t;

"$C(t)$: Strength of the attraction of individuals to the group (*cohesiveness*) at time t;

"$U(t)$: Pressure felt by the group to achieve *uniformity* of opinion, *i.e.*, to reduce perceived discrepancy of opinion at time t;

"R : Relevance of the issue to the group. This variable appears as a . . . constant in time" (30, p. 56).

The analytic system then relates these variables to each other, as follows:

1.1 * The more pressure there is upon members to communicate to each other [$P(t)$],
the more receptive the members are to influence by these communications [$L(t)$], and
the greater the present discrepancy of opinion among them [$D(t)$],
the more rapidly they will reduce the discrepancy in opinion among themselves [dC/dt].

1.2 * The greater the present discrepancy of opinion among members of a group [$D(t)$], and

---

* These propositions correspond to the hypotheses numbered similarly in our formalization of the model (30, p. 57).

the more pressure the group feels to achieve uniformity of opinion [U(t)],
>the more pressure will there be upon members of the group to
>communicate to each other [P(t)]

1.3 * The more pressure the group feels to achieve uniformity of opinion [U(t)],
>the greater receptivity will they have to being influenced by com-
>munications from other members [L(t)].

1.4 * The greater the present discrepancy of opinion among the members [D(t)],
>the more pressure is felt to achieve uniformity of opinion [U(t)], and
>the greater the present attraction of the individuals to the group
>[C(t)],
>the more rapidly will the cohesiveness of the group increase
>[dC/dt].

1.5 * The greater the present attractiveness of the individuals [C(t)], and
the more relevant the issue appears to the members [R],
>the greater the pressure to achieve uniformity of opinion [U(t)].

The diagram presented in Figure 9 may be of value in keeping these
propositions in mind. Note the many feedback mechanisms which are
hypothecated in this system. There are direct feedbacks of D and C upon
themselves; there are indirect feedbacks of D upon itself through P, and of
C upon itself through U; there are more complicated feedbacks, as of L
upon itself through D through C through U. Only R is independent of feedback effects. The feedbacks make the Festinger model considerably more
complex than the Homans model, even though the former has only two
more variables than the latter.

The two models are similar in that neither postulates a variable which
is conditional in its effect upon another through its interaction with a third.

The models depart from the simpler paradigms. Except for "relevance"
(R) and "external environment" (E), there are no measures which are independent variables in either model. Thus, they differ radically from the
basic paradigm of independent-dependent variables of Figure 2.

In the paradigm of Figure 3 there is separation of initial conditions, the
internal group processes, and outcomes. In the Homans model the variable
E, representing the initial conditions, plays an important role. In the Festinger
model, the initial conditions (R) are much less important. In both models,
the distinctions between internal processes and outcomes are almost completely obliterated by the rich system of feedbacks.

Like Homans, Festinger wants his analytical system to be of considerable

---

* These propositions correspond to the hypotheses numbered similarly in our formalization of the model (30, p. 57).

generality, so that many experiments and observations may be encompassed. One of his important devices in securing generality has been the employment of relatively abstract definitions of his variables. For example, *cohesiveness* is defined "as the resultant of all the forces acting on the members to remain in the group" (8, p. 274). But this does not mean that no matter what the source of the cohesiveness, its effects will be identical. Back has found, for example, that cohesiveness generated when the group is seen as a means to prestige is qualitatively different from cohesiveness which has its source in the group as a means to task achievement. As Back expresses his findings, the "force exerted increases with cohesiveness but the way in which the increase is effected depends on the basis of cohesiveness" (2, p. 21). This problem in the application of the model to specific experimental situations is the same type of problem Homans and Riecken were meeting by allowing definition "drift."

Besides the sister-model for the deviate-member,[31] Festinger has developed complementary models, such as his analysis of compliant behavior (distinguishing between public conformity and private agreement) [9] and his theory of social comparison,[10] in which he attempts to root the pressures toward uniformity in "the drive for self-evaluation and the necessity for such evaluation being based on comparison with other persons." This tendency for models to breed further models is notable in small group study.

Because of the complicated nature of these models, it is easy to understand why ordinary prose becomes cumbersome for describing analytic systems. There is much impetus toward the use of simpler and more rigorous language, as has been developed in mathematics. For example, Simon and I were able to write the five propositions of the Festinger model given above in five half-column lines using mathematical notation (30, p. 57) as compared with the thirty it took to write the same ideas in prose in this paper. In fact, some believe that empirical findings "even now are adequate for a new and powerful synthesis, in mathematical form, of certain basic aspects of the interaction process" (5, p. vii). In my judgment, this synthesizing is some distance off. Mathematics *may* be its handmaiden. But certainly, there is much need for the qualitative, insightful building of smaller analytic systems. Examination of the few formalizations which have been made to date indicate their extreme dependence upon creative thinking of a nonmathematical variety.

THE DIMENSIONS OF GROUPS

Although small group researchers are making some progress in the construction of models, these models are somewhat like a house of cards because of the variables they incorporate. Once a model has been constructed, its variables must be measured. If they are not independent, isolable entities, empirical checks on the model cannot be made, nor can applications be made of its implications in the work-a-day world.

In concluding the discussions of both the Homans and Festinger models, mention was made of the difficulties encountered in the definition of the variables involved. Shift of meaning was noted in the Riecken-Homans analysis of experimental data; the non-homogeneous effects of different ways of creating cohesiveness was noted in Back's work with the pressures-toward-uniformity model. Our eventual goal, as model developers and users, is to possess definitions of variables which will have wide acceptance among researchers and practitioners. The variables must have meanings which will be communicable; their presence must be easily recognized; and their magnitude must be measurable without too much cost.

But we are a long way from such a goal. Now that we have broken through the methodological frontier and freely observe and experiment in field and laboratory, it seems to me we must settle down to the important task of defining more adequately the variables we're using in our models. There is some work underway. Hemphill and Westie [15] have made an important exploration. Cattell has argued the point vigorously,[5] and with his colleagues, has isolated some small group variables.[6]

Let us examine the problem of definition and measurement of the variables in more concreteness. In the Homans model, there is much use of "sociometric" rank as a measure of "sentiment." The usual sociometric question asks each member of the group to indicate in private a number of individuals with whom he would and would not like to carry on some particular activity (like play ball, serve as follower). Different persons use different bases for answering the question; some tend to choose more individuals than others, even though a subsequent interview indicates they have the same sentiments toward the "forgotten" as toward the "chosen." But then what does the measure mean? As Lindzey and Borgatta's survey [22] of sociometric measurement indicates, the variables defined in sociometry are not easy to isolate; there is much multidimensionality in each sociometric question.

Although this looseness of meaning may make for difficulties, one does obtain significant relations between sociometric measures on the one hand and cultural, demographic, attitudinal, and personality variables on the other, some as predicted by Homans. More attention is being paid to the definition problem. Proctor and Loomis [25] have recently codified the indices used in the analysis of sociometric data. This will aid in making research studies more comparable to each other. One study has already been undertaken using factor analysis, a technique which has been of major importance in isolating intellectual and personal dimensions [11, 12] in the study of individual behavior.

The definitions of variables used in the Festinger model may be operationalized in many different ways. Yet, consider the difficulty Libo had in assessing the variable, *cohesiveness*. In his methodological study Libo used three ways of appraising the "resultant of forces acting on each member to remain in the group" (20, p. 2). (1) His locomotion criterion allowed the member to indicate whether the individual did or did not "wish to continue being a member" and "want to attend future meetings" by walking into a "Meeting Room" or a "Checkout Room" (20, pp. 26–28). (2) His questionnaire measure of attraction consisted of a number of sub-questions, as "Do you want to remain a member of this group?" and "If this group broke up for a considerable length of time and some people were trying to get it started again, would you want to rejoin?" (20, pp. 24–25). (3) His projective technique asked members to tell short stories about three pictures of groups; a score was derived from the stories "according to a scheme which assigns a +1 to every mention of the positive attributes of group membership, every mention of a desire to join a group, and every mention of locomotion toward a group; a −1 is assigned to every mention of the negative counterparts of the above" (20, pp. 25–26). Although all three measures reflect the experimental conditions of high or low cohesiveness which Libo attempted to induce, they are not well related to each other. The scores derived from the questionnaire and the projective stories correlated +.35, sharing only about 12 per cent of their variance. Bi-serial correlations of these two measure with the locomotion criterion of leaving or staying were +.63 and +.39, respectively. Such intercorrelations indicate these measures have only a small core of common meaning.

The lack of commonality among measures of the basic, underlying variables is a serious limitation in the use of empirical findings to disprove relationships postulated in our models. One can readily retort to the researcher who comes up with a negative finding, "But your way of measuring the variable I defined in my model was inadequate. Your negative result merely indicates your inability to operationalize the variable with which my model is concerned." Such discounting of empirical tests is not conducive to improvement of models. Could it be that the failure to make substantial developments in Homans model from 1950 to 1954 is due to an almost unscientific tenet: "We have cited apparent exceptions to the hypothesis, but our faith is that they cannot be true contradictions but rather the effect of variables other than those we have considered so far" (27, p. 794)?

Factor analysis techniques strive to explain a set of correlations among measures in terms of a more limited number of common factors.[33] Thus, the basic technique—and its variants—are useful in consolidating a number of overlapping measures of the same basic variable. The findings of the correlational studies of Hemphill [15] and Cattell [6] already mentioned are only moderately promising. Measures sometimes correlate with one another because of cause-and-effect relationships, not because they are measuring the same basic entity. For example, although one can reasonably well discriminate between dominance and submission, the correlation between their occurrences in a group is appreciable. But under many circumstances one cannot distinguish as easily between correlations which are due to cause-and-effect relationship and those which are due to redundancy in the measures being used.

It is for this reason that work on models and measures must go forward together. Models hypothecate the cause-and-effect interrelations; methodological work on operational definitions aids in deciding whether one variable is influencing another, or whether the researcher is merely measuring the same thing twice.

STRATEGY IN SYSTEM BUILDING

Given the foregoing characteristics of our analytic systems of small groups, how can the efforts of researchers in the field be made more effective? May I submit the following suggestions:

1) Let us use each other's variables to a greater extent in both field and laboratory work, so that we can check each other's findings more easily.
    —Specify in the research report (or in a special document intended for more limited circulation) the operations used in measuring the variables you studied, so that they may be replicated by others.
    —Insert an additional variable or two in each study to tie it into other studies, so that our islands of theory can be bridged.
    —When you want to use a variable of another researcher, measure it in the identical way he does, even though you may want to try a second way of estimating its magnitude to suit the requirements of your own study.
2) For the moment, let us continue building solid islands of theory, not trying to master-mind the small group in its entirety.
    —Avoid encompassing too many variables at the same time, even though this may mean temporarily avoiding study of the more complicated groups; models rapidly become unmanageable.
    —Study small groups over sufficiently long periods, so that the important feedbacks are not missed.
    —Locate unnoticed conditioning variables by trying to organize a well-established segment of a model into what superficially seem to be quite different small group settings.

Advances in our models will require changes in our methodologies; advances in our methodologies, especially those concerned with definition and measurement of the variables, will importantly sharpen our models.

TALCOTT PARSONS

Some Highlights of the General Theory of Action

I HAVE BEEN asked to submit a general sketch of some of the main concepts and propositions of the "theory of action" without special reference to their relevance to the concerns of political science. I shall hence make only a few remarks toward the end of the paper on the latter subject.

By the theory of action I presume is meant the line of analysis advanced a few years ago in the collaborative volume *Toward a General Theory of Action* [1] and other work similar to or associated with this and following it up. At the outset I wish to stress both the elementary nature of the present stage in the development of that conceptual scheme, and the fact that it is in no sense a highly distinctive theory to be sharply differentiated from others. What was attempted at that time was to explore common ground, not only among the contributors to that volume, but more broadly in their own and neighboring disciplines. We felt that there was a very substantial common ground, but also certain divergences of varying kinds and degrees of significance; indeed the volume itself documented some of these divergences. Nevertheless it is my own conviction that if due allowance is made for difference of specific empirical interest and competence, of reference points and perspective, of uneven empirical development in different fields, and of course of terminology and specific mode of formulation, there is far more common ground than is apparent at first sight in these areas. Also, we felt some new ground was broken.

What I shall do in the present paper is to attempt to present a connected account of some of the highlights as I see them now. I shall not specifically attempt to state only things to which general agreement could be assumed, but can hope that a substantial part of what I say will be in accord with the views, properly "translated," of a large proportion of the best social scientists today. [2]

SOME BASIC CATEGORIES

The theory of action is an attempt to systematize the analysis of the *action* or *behavior* of living organisms (for present purposes the two terms may be regarded as synonymous). Behavior in this sense consists in the "motivated"

282

or "goal-meaningful" relations existing, developing and changing between the organism and the objects which constitute its situation or environment. Behavior must be distinguished in these terms from the anatomical structure and physiological process internal to the organism as a biological system, and from the *biochemical* level of interchange with the environment on which the internal physiological system is dependent. The question of the modes of relation and interdependence between physiological and behavioral systems may be regarded as theoretically and empirically open. But the theory of action is, within this assumption, an autonomous theoretical system; there is no presumption that "reduction" to physiological terms is, if feasible in a particular case, scientifically preferable.

Stated in these terms, action or behavior is centered on the one hand on the relation of a total organism to objects in its situation, but on the other on the relations of behaving organisms to each other. The two primary references of the theory of action to systems therefore is to the system deriving from the behavior of a particular individual organism as a whole in relation to its environment as a whole and, secondly, the system generated by the *interaction* of the behavior or a plurality of organisms in relation to each other. These are the systems which, in technical terms, we refer to as psychological and social systems respectively.

These system-types, however, articulate systematically with two others which also must be interpreted as belonging to the system of action in a more inclusive sense. These are first the organism itself, as a system of "mechanisms" of behavior. Explicit treatment of this system will involve transition from strictly behavioral (psychological) to physiological terms, but in such a way as to preserve direct relevance to the processes of behavior in relation to external objects.

The second reference is to "culture" considered as a system which articulates with that of "behavior" in the first instance through social systems. Cultural systems, which involve generalized categorizations of meaning and the symbolization of objects, will be discussed briefly below.

In the theory of action the behavior of one or more organisms or a subsector of such behavior is to be treated as a system. Such use of the concept system is, so far as I am aware, always found in analytically generalized theoretical schemes. With it goes another fundamental conception, namely that variously named "steady state," "equilibrium," "homeostasis," etc. The essential point is that it is a principal aim of such a theory to attempt to define sets of conditions under which relations between the component parts of the system will tend to remain stable, either in a "static" sense or in one of following an orderly pattern of development. For this to be possible the conditions of a stable state must be discriminated from conditions which lead either to change of state of the system, or to "disintegration" of the system, that is to its disappearance as a system of the relevant type, *e.g.,* through the death and biochemical "dissolution" or an organism. Systems of the type which require a distinction between ordinary changes of state and disintegration are what we call boundary-maintaining systems. I believe all systems of action to be this type.

Equilibrium states of the behavioral relations of organisms, *i.e.*, of actors, to their situations, and the modification of these states or disequilibrium must be categorized in relational terms. With primary reference to the individual actor, these have come, by something approaching common agreement, to be categorized in terms of two fundamental modes or aspects of "orientation," which may be called "cognition" and "cathexis" respectively. Cognition is, in perhaps the most general terms, the process by which the state of external objects, and the trend of change in that state, comes to constitute a set of signs capable of determining or affecting the action of the "observing" actor. It is the category within the frame of reference of action, by which the state of one part of the system which is most independent of the internal state of a second, comes to exert influence on that second. Put differently, cognition is the process by which an input of information into the receiving unit is described.

Cathexis, on the other hand, is, from the point of view of a given actor, the category which describes the significance for his own internal state, of his relations, actual and possible, to another object in his situation. It is the process by which the input of "gratification" or "goal-attainment" into this actor's behavioral system can be described. Both categories are essentially relational, neither refers to properties or states of an organism, as such, but rather properties or states of the behavioral systems of organisms. But cognition stresses the independent process in the situational object system; cathexis the impact on the actor of reference of the situational object system.[3]

It has been conventional in dealing with the frame of reference of action, to develop first the case of the action of the individual organism, from the concepts just reviewed and then from such further concepts as goal-orientation, instrumental activity, etc. (I and my colleagues have done it this way.) This approach tends to think of situational objects as in the first instance "nonsocial," *i.e.*, as not themselves actors, but usually as physical objects. For most purposes of the social sciences, however, it seems to be more useful to deal with the *interaction* of a plurality of actors who in interacting constitute a system, as the "paradigmatic" case. In the theoretical sense it is the more general case since from it, to take the step of dealing with the case of the individual acting in a nonsocial situation, all that is necessary is to suppress certain ranges of freedom for variation which remain open in the interaction case.

On the level of interaction, then, cognitively the actions of each member of the system must be treated as a set of signs which acquire meaning for the other members of the system (and for himself). Similarly the impact

of this action of any one member on the others, acquires "cathectic" or motivational meaning for the others, on what we have called their "gratifica-
tion-deprivation balance." For simplicity of exposition let us confine the
main discussion to two interacting individuals and refer to them as ego and
alter respectively.

When to ego, alter's actions have acquired both cognitive and cathectic
meaning in a reciprocal and generalized sense, then we may speak of ego
being concerned not only with what alter does or is likely to do in terms of
sheer probability, but with his "intentions." And when the meaning of an
act is not merely that put upon it by the recipient of it, but includes for him
an imputation of its meaning to the originator, we may speak of *communication*. In acting the way he did, alter "intended" to convey to ego a meaning in terms of his own motivations which ego in turn more or less clearly
and correctly interprets. Communication, of course, does not occur only on
"conscious" levels. However, the theory of action deals with interactions
which on some level have common meanings both to the originating and the
receiving actors and thus involve communication between them.

Very closely associated with this, in turn, are the two fundamental concepts of goal-orientation and norm. In an evolutionary sense presumably
goal-orientedness is a relevant concept even before we can speak of sign-
behavior. It is simply the equilibrating tendency of a behavior system. But
on the levels which clearly involve sign-behavior, intention and communication, a goal becomes, both to ego and alter, an *intended* goal. It is a state
of the relevant interaction system in relation to its situation toward the attainment or "realization" of which ego's own action can be said to be intention-
ally oriented or "directed." It is, then, of great importance to be clear
about the system of action which is taken as a point of reference in imputing
a goal. Above all, such a goal may be, and in a *psychological* context usually is, a state of the behavior system of the individual actor. But it may also
be a state of the social system of interaction in which both ego and alter
are involved. Concretely, in principle both are always necessarily involved.

From the view or, in a sense, postulate, that goals may be treated as intentional, it seems to follow that they may also be *learned*. That there are
primary drives which define by reference to the organism, goal states which
will be "sought" without any learning process seems to be without doubt,
and of course there is a constitutional factor in all concrete goals. But on an
interactive, communicative, essentially "cultural" level there is necessarily
a meshing between the meanings of goals to the actor in question, and to
others with whom he interacts. I postulate that the concrete pattern of meaning in its reciprocal significance can only in limiting cases be understood in
purely hereditary terms without the intervention of a process of learning
through interaction. In general I shall consider the goals significant to social

interaction to be "culturally defined" and to be learned through the processes of interaction. Psychologically considered they are all "secondary
drives."

Secondly, I have pointed out that interaction which involves intentions
and communication, also involves common meanings. That is in order for
ego to communicate with alter and to impute intentions to him and vice
versa, they must both to some degree of approximation "understand the same
things" by each other's acts. This means in turn that each, if he is to be understood, or if he is properly to understand the intentions of the other, must
conform with the "conventions" of the "language" involved in communication. For it is the essence of communication through signs, that the meaning of the sign is not automatically given with the perception of its occurrence,
but there must be a learned association through experience with something
other than the sign itself. The matching of these learned associations is what
constitutes the common meaning system. Taking account of the relation between the actual overt process of sign production and this learned meaning
system, is what is meant by observing the conventions of the system.

But seen in one perspective, using a sign so that alter will be likely correctly to perceive ego's intended meaning in terms of a common meaning
system is an example of what is meant by conforming with a norm. The
conditions of successful communication in interaction constitute a prototype
of the conditions of stability of a system of interaction where the meanings of
acts must be learned. This applies to the normative significance of "linguistic"
conventions, just as it does to other aspects of such interaction. In so far as
the functioning of a system of interaction depends on the reciprocity of the
communication of intentions, relative conformity with the norms of the system of meanings constitutes a primary condition of stability of the system.
Put only slightly differently, ego's capacity to interact meaningfully with alter
depends on each to a degree fulfilling the expectations of the other as defined by a common system of norms.

The implications of the role of norms in the stability of systems of social
interaction can be generalized in two directions. The first of these concerns
the *consistency* of the normative system governing the process of interaction. The primary reference point for the treatment of this problem is to be
found in the goal-orientations of the individual members. For the normative system to be consistent they need not within considerable limits pursue
the same goals, but they must not, to too great a degree, pursue goals the
attainment of which are mutually incompatible. A normative system which
can successfully define the conditions of stability of an interaction system
must include the definition of the goals to be pursued by interacting units in
the system, at least to the extent of setting limits with reference to their mutual compatibility.

But consistency does not depend only on the goals pursued by units, it also involves the actions taken by them in the course of attaining their goals, in relation to the external situation of the system and in the relations of the units to each other. There must, that is, be a generalized consistency of pattern in normative "definitions of the situation" which includes goal-specifications, adaptive or instrumental procedures and inter-unit or integrative actions. It is as such a normative system generalized to include all of these various functional contexts of relevance that I should like to define the common *value-system* of a system of behavior. I have stated this in terms of the system of interaction, *i.e.,* as a social system, but it applies equally to any system of action, *i.e.,* it includes personality systems.

The specification of learned goals, particularized norms, and the generalized patterns of values which comprise both, are central parts of the *common culture* of a system of social interaction. But even taken together they do not exhaust what is ordinarily meant by a common culture. From the point of view of *functions* for the system of interaction they are, however, the core of it.

For me the starting point for formulating the concept of culture lies in the facts that from the point of view of an actor objects in the situation acquire meaning, that these meanings become organized in systems, and that such meanings, both as particularized and as organized in systems, are shared in common by pluralities of actors who interact with one another. Any such object which in cognitive-cathectic terms has a meaning as defined above is a sign.

Conversely *any* object may acquire sign-meanings to an actor, and this meaning can become common to many actors. For almost-obvious reasons the acts of acting individuals have special significance as objects for systems of action. The meanings of discrete acts, of course, must be organized in systems. A human individual or personality, a person acting in a role, or a collectivity, are such *systems* of discrete acts as they are perceived in interaction. They constitute higher-order meaningful objects than do particularized unit acts; they are "complex objects."

But of course it is not *only* actors and their actions which constitute sign-objects. Many physical objects also have meaning in this sense, as conditional to action, as facilities, as reward-objects, and as various kinds of signs relative to expectations of events both on the levels of action and in other respects. Goals, norms and values as I have defined them thus constitute only part of the meanings of sign-objects in a culture. There are above all two other major categories, namely "languages" or sets of conventions by which "content" meanings may be expressed and communicated, and the meanings of categories of physical objects. The broad imperative of consistency which I stated as applying to a culture of course applies to these and to them in their relations to each other and to the more central action-system culture. Partly for this reason culture inevitably has certain reference points outside a system of interaction, and cannot be adequately treated wholly as a function of the process of social interaction.

The *organization* of cultural meaning-system seems to involve above all relations of discrimination and of generalization. On the one hand specific objects and sub-objects are discriminated from one another in terms of various meaningful criteria, but on the other hand discriminated "instances" are grouped together as belonging to the same generalized category. The categories of universalism and particularism, which we have used extensively, seem to constitute principal modes of such generalized categorization, in the first case by virtue of common properties independent of any specific context or system-membership, on the second, by virtue of belonging together in the same system or context. Thus intelligence as a trait may characterize many different individuals who do not necessarily have any specific interactive relations with each other. On the other hand the "character traits" of a given person may be exceedingly different, but they belong together as all describing the personality of the same individual. This distinction seems to be essentially the same as that formulated by logicians between disjunctive and conjunctive relationships.

Finally, it may be noted that there can be and are many different levels of the generality of cultural meanings. The differentiation and integration of systems of action is most intimately bound up with the differences of these levels, and the spanning, in the same "structure," of several of them. The principal categories of value which for example are important to a culture, are usually on a rather high level of generality, under which very large numbers of more particularized categories can be subsumed. These generalized value-categories constitute both universalistic and particularistic groupings of the more specific ones. The imperative of cultural consistency seems above all to apply to this organization of cultural meanings in an ordered hierarchy of levels of generality, and to the mutual relationships of meanings on the different levels.

The second major direction in which it was necessary, as I stated above, to follow out the implications of the role of norms for the stability of systems of interaction, concerns the *motivation* to conformity—or non-conformity— with the expectations of behavior defined by the norms. The distinction between the structure and consistency of a system of norms on the one hand, the level of conformity with the expectations defined by them on the other, is fundamental to the whole theory of action and interaction.

The essence of the problem here concerns what we have called for social systems the *institutionalization,* for personality systems the *internalization* of norms or values, and secondly, the interplay of performances and sanctions as constituting mechanisms of the control of behavior relative to the institutionalized-internalized values.

There is one sense in which, since motivation is always motivation of the individual personality, the phenomenon of internalization has a certain analytical priority over institutionalization. This concept refers to the fact that the norms or values (or role-expectation goals) defined in a culture come to be constitutive parts of the personality of the individual considered as a system of action. The goals an individual pursues, and the values in terms of which the meanings of these goals are generalized in their application to the whole range of action, are derived from the culture in which he has been "socialized." Once socialized and making due allowance for elements of conflict and malintegration on both the personality and the social system levels, a person cannot act otherwise than in conformity with his internalized values. Put a little differently, the internalized value system acts as a mechanism of control over the more detailed processes of behavior, a mechanism the operation of which, once thoroughly established, is relatively independent of variations in the situation of action.

The process of internalization of a system of values is a special type of process of learning. It is one which must include the learning of at least certain components of the concrete goals pursued by the individual and also of norms operating with reference to the choice of means and to the relations between actors. This occurs through the internalization of a series of social object-systems, of stepwise increasing complexity, which are the relevant roles of the significant persons involved in the social environment of the child: parents, siblings, teachers, peers, etc. Certain of the fundamental conditions of the process are: frustration of previously established motivational complexes, permissiveness for expressing symbolically the products of this disturbance, supportive attitudes which favor development of a diffuse attachment to significant objects, selective rewarding of behavior in accord with the new pattern. In the later stages of a cycle the most important factor is the relatively consistent imposition of a special complex pattern of sanctions in accord with the new values, which are always the values of a newly learned role in a system of interaction not previously participated in.[4]

The patterns of value internalized in the personality of a given individual actor are, except for his own creative or degenerative modifications, received from the general culture through the socializing agents; moreover he continues to interact with others as a member of his society and of many of its subsystems and must do so in terms of a common culture. For both these sets of reasons the imperative of cultural consistency cannot be applicable only within the specific personality, nor can there be one set of values which are "social" and govern interaction, and another which are "personal" and apply only to the particular personality independent of his social relationships. Whatever the differences between personalities and social systems there is *one* basic cultural system of values, in a social system, which is specialized, differentiated, particularized and modified in many different ways, but is still in the last analysis one system.

Seen in this perspective the basic fact about institutionalization of values in a social system is that its values are typically internalized in the personalities of all the individuals interacting to constitute the social system. This conception need not involve any disturbing mystery if it is remembered that *the same* concrete processes of behavior constitute *both* personalities and social systems. These systems are not only interdependent, they interpenetrate; they are parts, one to another. To a degree then, the internalization and the institutionalization of a value system are the same thing, seen in different perspective.

But this is not the whole story. Internalization constitutes the primary link between personalities and the imperatives of social systems. But it is never a perfect link and never stands alone. The personality is a genuinely independent system by virtue of its involvement with the specific biological organism, of the uniqueness of its own life history, and of the lack of exact correspondence between its combination of situational exigencies and social roles and those to which any other individual is exposed. There is always a certain tension between personality and the expectations to which it is exposed in social interaction—tensions which themselves may come to be internalized. Moreover, the value system internalized is never wholly "the" common value system; it is always specialized and individualized, and it may be distorted to varying degrees and in various ways.

These seem to be the fundamental reasons which underlie the fact that no social system ever depends *only* on the internalized value-systems of its members for the fulfillment of roles, and every personality is always having to cope with actions of others which are not simply patterned by the common value system. On the social interaction level, the general conceptual scheme for the analysis of the processes of action and reaction involved in adjustment to varying and deviating pressures in the situation, is what we call the interplay of performances and sanctions.

A performance may be defined as an act, or sequence of action, to some degree oriented by the actor of reference as part of the fulfillment of the expectations of a role, and judged by the observer in terms of its impact on the functioning of the system of reference as a system. A sanction on the other hand is an act or sequence of action, oriented by the performer (*i.e.,* in some sense "intended") to the evaluation of a previous act or sequence of actions of one or more *other* actors in the system, and judged by an observer in terms of its impact on the states (*e.g.,* "attitudes") of the actor(s) to whom it was directed and hence of their probable future performance in their roles.

In so far as the action relevant to the functioning of a social system is not a result of the direct "acting out" of internalized cultural patterns, and of constraints independent of the interaction process altogether, it can be analyzed in terms of the interdependence of performances and sanctions. It would be a serious misunderstanding to think that the importance of sanctions is confined to the "control" of incipiently or overtly "deviant" behavior. A very important part of the function of performance-sanction interplay lies in the "specification" of generalized orientations to the point where performance adequate to a particular concrete situation becomes possible. But the deviance-social control aspect is of course also involved.

A useful methodological model for the analysis of performance and sanction is the schema of supply and demand as used in economic theory (indeed it can be shown to be a special case). Within certain ranges a *set* of performances can be treated as being held "ready," the one to be selected being dependent on expectations of the consequences in the form of sanctions. Correspondingly, on the sanction side, there is a range or "schedule" of possible sanction acts, of such a character that that which is selected will be a consequence of the performances of others experienced or expected. There should, then, be a point of equilibrium where the two "curves" intersect; a level of performance which will produce an optimum level of sanction-behavior. This optimum must, I think, be defined in terms of the functioning of the interaction system, rather than of the goals of the individual actor.

These considerations give us a general basis for a theory of motivation in institutionalized roles. In so far as the individual in question has been adequately socialized in the society as a whole and for the specific role in question, the primary motivational mechanisms will be determined by the internalized value system as a governing mechanism of the personality. This means that, at least on a sufficiently generalized level, the goals as well as the norms governing choice of means and interpersonal relations will normally have been internalized. Thus, to take one case which will be discussed below, commitment to the goal of efficient economic production may be treated as an institutionalized goal in our society which with the appropriate specifications has been internalized in the normal personality. In so far as motivation is governed by an internalized value system, internal sanctions will have primacy over external. These are the well-known sanctions associated with guilt, shame, etc., though it should not be implied that only negative sanctions are important. There are also positive sanctions in the form of self-respect, approval, level of aspiration, and things of that sort.

No motivational system, however, is completely governed by an internalized pattern structure of this sort. It is also in the nature of the case sensitive to success in attaining its goals and to the sanctions encountered in the processes of interaction with other persons. To what sanctions the highest sensitivity exists, and with reference to what objects, will have been determined by the socialization process; but in any case quantity and quality of behavioral output will, within limits, always be a function of the experienced and expected qualitative patterns of intensity of sanction, both positive and negative.

The more general internalized value orientation will have been laid down in the childhood phases of socialization, the critical turning point being the Oedipal transition, after which the child assumes much more active roles outside the family. Basic character structure, as looked at in this light, must be considered to reflect the internalization of family values differentiated in the first instance by sex role. After the Oedipal transition there is a process of further differentiation of roles and corresponding specification of role values and the appropriate goals. For example, "success" in a society like ours may be treated as such a generalized role-goal applying to the occupational system. It always has two components, the relative importance of which may vary from one case to another. The first is commitment to effective performance according to the nature of the activity expected in the particular role. The second is valuation of the sanctions imposed by others in the process of interaction in the role. Thus money remuneration in occupational roles is one particularly important class of sanction, and its valuation is one, but only one, important part of the generalized success goal complex. Similar considerations apply in the field of political motivation.

THE ORGANIZATION OF COMPLEX SYSTEMS OF ACTION

Having laid down these fundamental general considerations I may now turn to a consideration of some of the main aspects of the differentiation and organization of systems of social interaction and their relation to the organization of personality.

Two basic postulates will be assumed for purposes of this discussion. The first is that the characteristics of systems of action which have just been reviewed mean that all such systems have certain features in common. They are boundary-maintaining systems the stability of which is dependent on certain constraints, or in a little different perspective, on the meeting at adequate levels, of certain limited functional "imperatives." This applies, whatever the level or scale of the system in question, all the way, for social systems, from a small experimental group to a large-scale society. The basic conceptual scheme applied at all these levels is the same.

The second postulate is that every larger-scale social system may be conceived as a complex network of subsystems, the main relations of any two of which to each other may be conceived in relatively simple terms. In the first place such subsystems are related to each other through a hierarchy of differentiation, so that the value-system of a lower order system is a differentiated variant of that of the superordinate system. This hierarchy may follow through a considerable number of steps. A second mode of relation consists in the fact that, from the point of view of one system of reference, another, which is also a subsystem of the same society, constitutes part of the situation in which the first subsystem functions, to which it must adapt and in relation to which it must fulfill its goals. In such a case, however, mutual "exploitation" in a situational sense will be limited by the fact that on a superordinate level, both have institutionalized the same value system and are thus bound by ties of integrative solidarity. I should contend that a large proportion of the complexities in social analysis, of which we are all so acutely aware, derive from the complexities of these interrelations of multiple systems, rather than from the inherent complexity of any single social system however elementary.

It has been said that a social system is always characterized by an institutionalized value-system. The first functional imperative of any such system then is the maintenance of the integrity of that value-system and its state of institutionalization. In turn this has two aspects each related to one of the primary sources of change in the value-system which can be relatively independent of the processes of interaction in the specific system of reference. In evaluating these it is important to note that, except for the total society, no personality is totally engaged in any one specific system of social interaction. The part of him which is his specific role-involvement is interdependent with the other parts of the personality system. If this role-unit is to have a modicum of stability it must to a degree be insulated against disturbing effects from this source.

The first of the two sources of change is primarily cultural. This is to say that the imperatives of cultural consistency may operate in such a way that cultural changes taking place outside the relevant value-area, *e.g.,* in part of the belief system, may give rise to pressures to change important values within the role-unit area. The tendency to stabilize these values against pressures to change through cultural channels may be called the "pattern-maintenance" function. The second source of change is on the motivational level. Here motivational "tensions," arising from "strains" in the social situation, including other roles, or from organic or other intrapersonal sources, may threaten the motivation to conformity with role expectations. The function of stabilization against this potential source of change may be called that of "tension-management."

Every social system functions in relation to a situation defined as external to it. The relations to the situation, or the processes of interchange between system and situation are the focus of the second and third major functional imperatives of the system (the first being the maintenance of stability of the institutionalized value-system through pattern-maintenance and tension management).

The first of these relations concerns the significance of the situation as a source of consummatory goal-gratification or attainment. A goal-state, for an individual actor or for a social system, is defined as a *relation* between the action system of reference and a system of objects in the situation which, given the value-system and the mode of its institutionalization, is maximally favorable to the stability of the action system. Such a state, once present, will, other things equal, tend to be maintained, and if absent, will tend to be "sought" by action of one or more units of the system. The necessity for the latter case derives from the simple fact that only in limiting cases are processes in the situation closely "synchronized" with processes in the system of action. The occurrence of goal-states thus cannot be "counted on" in general without processes of control of the situation intervening. Goal-states of course may be of negative significance in that they constitute a minimization of threatening or noxious situational conditions, or they may be positive consisting in maximization of favorable or "gratifying" conditions.

The second basic mode of functional significance of the situation of an action system, lies in the fact that, since relations to the situation are problematical, there arises a *generalized* interest in establishing and improving control over the situation in various respects. The pursuit of particular goal-states of course involves such control. But a different order of problem is involved in the *generalization* of facilities which are available for a variety of goals of the superordinate system and of many subsystems, and hence the development of activity specialized in the direction of producing such facilities. When a social system has a single, simply defined goal or task-orientation, there may be relatively little call to differentiate the two functions; the provision of facilities or the "adaptive" function is simply an aspect of the process of goal-attainment. But in complex systems where a plurality of goals become significant the distinction may become of the first importance.

Finally, there is a fourth basic functional imperative of a system of action. Whatever the units which interact in a system-process, be they the motivational units of personality (need-dispositions) or the roles of individual persons in a social system, or the roles of collectivities in more macroscopic social systems, the actions of the significant units may be such as to be mutually supportive in the functioning of the system, or to some degree mutually obstructive and conflictful. There is, then, the problem of "maintaining solidarity" in the relations between the units, in the interest of effective functioning. This I call the functional imperative of *system-integration*.

I have, then, distinguished four fundamental system-problems or types of functional imperative under which a system of action, in particular a social system, operates. These are respectively (latent) pattern-maintenance (including tension-management), goal-attainment, adaptation, and integration.[5]

That these are all genuine functional imperatives implies that these interests or tendencies of the system cannot all be maximized at once, and that, under given conditions and within a limited time span, "pushing" one or two of them will have to occur at the expense of others. Thus pushing hard for the attainment of a single system goal may relatively reduce the level of general adaptation because of the particularized commitment of resources or facilities in form suitable only for that one goal. Or, similarly, insisting on the maintenance of an institutionalized pattern in the sense of consistency may be detrimental to the integration of the system because it overrides the conditions of effective cooperation among units. Again, overintegration of the system, in the sense of attempting to avoid all possibilities of internal antagonism or disharmony, may occur at the expense of effective goal-attainment or adaptation.

These relative incompatibilities of maximizing movement of the system in several different directions underlie two fundamental features of the "structuring" of system processes. The first of these is the differentiation of *phases* in process in a system over time, the second is differentiation in the functions of different units in the system, without specific reference to time. Both modes of differentiation can have, within limits, a twofold effect, namely an integrative effect through mitigating elements of potential conflict involved in trying to get too many things done at the same time, and an effect on efficiency of adaptation and goal-attainment through the consequences of specialization.

The best authenticated studies of phase movement on the small scale are those of Bales and his associates in the analysis of processes in small groups. Similar patterns on macroscopic levels are best known in the field of economic cycles. But there is every reason to believe that the same basic phenomenon is found in all types of systems of action in the form of oscillations, rhythms, and cycles of a very wide variety of kinds.

A phase movement which is mainly repetitive should be clearly distinguished, theoretically (though the empirical distinctions are often difficult to make), from a process of change over time which results in altering the fundamental structure of the system itself. In all the main types of system of action one of the most important of these is the type of process which changes structure through increasing the complexity of the structural differentiation of the system. Such a process can occur without fundamental change in the institutionalized value-system. It should theoretically be carefully distinguished therefore from processes resulting from the introduction of a new value-system, and from processes resulting in the disorganization, and in the extreme case, dissolution of systems.

STRUCTURAL DIFFERENTIATION, ECONOMY AND POLITY

I shall not attempt any further analysis of phase-differentiations over time here, but will jump to a very brief sketch of some of the principal aspects of the structural differentiation of a complex society with a high level of cultural elaboration.

There are several aspects of the differentiation of a complex society which cut across each other. The most obvious of these is the differentiation into collectivities, or "groups" like the family, the business firm, the local community, the political organization. Another is in terms of the types of normative pattern to which commitment is expected differentially by members of the society, *e.g.,* law, level of education, health, religious virtue, etc.

A third, which is not reducible to either of these, is the differentiation in terms of primary function relative to the society as a system. If societies were only neatly organized mechanisms for communication, and for value-realization on cultural levels, we might expect a differentiation on this basis into four neatly separated subsystems which were, in higher-level societies, all readily identifiable. Unfortunately things are not so simple as this. But nevertheless this is a useful lead to the analysis of certain features of such societies, and will enable me to make a suggestion about the problem-area of political science.

There is, however, one outstanding case which fits with the logical requirements of such a basis of differentiation with dramatic exactness. This is the case of the *economy* as that has come to be conceived in the main tradition of modern economic theory. The economy may be defined as the society so far as it can be conceived as being organized for the production of utilities (or wealth or income—the differences are those of perspective). In a highly differentiated society like our own, the economy may be conceived as a relatively sharply differentiated subsystem of the society. Seen in this way its primary goal-orientation is *production* of goods and services (as "demanded" by other subsystems of the society). Its primary adaptive problem is that of capitalization, *i.e.,* of securing fluid resources which can be utilized as facilities for the process of production. Its integrative problem concerns the institutionalization of basic economic relationships, industrial organization and occupational roles as the modes of channeling motivation and facilities of production, property as the rules governing control of facilities, and contract as governing the relations of holders of the factors of production to each other, and to others in other subsystems. Finally, the economy is governed by a special value-system of its own, that of "economic rationality." This is a differentiated subsystem of the value-system of the total society, which in our own case gives particular relative prominence to economic values.

The structure of the economy as a social system can be analyzed on essentially the same basis as that of any other social system. It is defined in the first instance by reference to the functional imperatives which any system must meet, but which of course have special content in this case, which differentiates them from other types of system. Secondly, it is defined by the type of institutional patterns in the general society which are most relevant to the regulation of economic activity and which serve to integrate it with other parts of the society. Third, it is subject not only to its own special adaptive exigencies, namely those of capitalization, but to those governing the society as a whole, which for example are met by technological means and organization.

Within the structure of the economy continual processes of adjustment go on which, as is done in a good deal of current economic theory, can be analyzed in terms of aggregate inputs into the economy and outputs from it over its boundaries. When the economy is looked at in this way the four cardinal factors of production: namely labor, capital, land and organization, as they have been recognized since Marshall, may be regarded as the appropriate classes of input into the economy and the corresponding shares of income as the classes of output.

Analysis of the boundary-relations of the economy to other parts of the society can be directly articulated with sociologically known functions in other structures so that with few exceptions theoretically significant content can be put into the constraints imposed on economic process by the input-output exchanges in each of three major directions.

There is no space here to follow out these relations, but for purposes of illustration let us discuss one boundary relationship, that between economy and household, a little further. For theoretical reasons which cannot be gone into here the household may be said to belong primarily in the pattern-maintenance subsystem of the society.[6] The relation is then one involving boundaries of pattern-maintenance and adaptive subsystems.

The household is, in an industrial society, the prototypical unit of consumption; it is the most important recipient of the consumers' goods and services for which it spends income. A second interchange, however, also takes place in that members of households, through employment, become the agents of the input of labor services into the economy; they assume occupational roles. In exchange for labor services they receive, as the economist puts it, "wages." The link between the two interchanges on the household side is of course given through the fact that wage income is the primary source of funds to spend for the purchase of goods and services. But the transactions, of employment on the one hand, consumers' purchasing on the other, need not be with the same units of the economy or in any direct way linked with each other.

Another way of looking at it is that, as the economists say, there is one "real" interchange, namely of labor services for consumers' goods, and one monetary interchange, of consumers' spending for wages; there is thus a double balancing linkage.

A far greater degree of elaboration could of course be worked out. But this is perhaps sufficient to suggest that it is proving possible to develop systematic theoretical relations between the conception of an economy as developed in economic theory and the general theory of social systems as developed in the general theory of action. The general nature of the relation is that economic theory can be shown to be a special case of the general theory of social systems; it is the case defined as applicable to certain processes in the economy conceived as a social system, *i.e.*, as a differentiated subsystem of a total society. This assertion of course implies the claim that, given certain parametric assumptions about the special nature of an economy, the main body of economic theory can be deduced from the general categories of the theory of social systems.[7]

The suggestion I now wish to make is that a great deal of current political theory could be codified and systematized, and better articulated with economics and sociology, if an analogous conception of its scope were worked out and placed within the general theory of social systems as another special case. Following ancient usage such a subsystem of the society might be called the "polity" as parallel with the economy. If so, I should conceive it as the subsystem, on a cognate level, which was differentiated from others with special reference to the function of goal-attainment—*for the society as a system*. As such it would have its own goal-orientation, its own adaptive and integrative exigencies and its own specially differentiated subvalue system.

If this is a fruitful approach, then the primary goal of the polity should be to "produce" a generalized something which maximizes the potential of attaining societal goals (not necessarily the goals of discrete individuals or subgroups—a whole range of difficult problems is involved here). Some current concepts of power do not seem to be very far from what this something might be conceived to be. Then eventually we ought to be able to speak of a national "power-potential" in much the same way as we speak of the national income.

Next, it may be suggested that, in terms of our general system-paradigm, it should be possible to work out a classification of the "ingredients" of power, which is parallel to the factors of production, and as output categories from the polity, of "types of power" which are parallel to the shares of income. The following is an exceedingly tentative first attempt, which may perhaps serve as a basis of discussion. Not least, the terms used in this tentative formulation are much in need of clarification and eventual definition.[8]

Table I is a schematic tabulation of the relations between system problems, the categories of input and output of the economy as reviewed above, and a suggested set of corresponding categories for the polity. The first set of such political categories may, as noted above, be thought of as ingredients of power parallel to the factors of production. Every social system, as has been noted, operates from a relatively stable and constant institutionalized base which is to a relative degree insulated from the effects of the normal interplay of performances and sanctions in the course of system process. In the case of the economy this stable base is concentrated in the factor of "land," the definition of which it proves to be necessary to extend from given physical facilities to include also what economists have referred to as the "state of the arts" and also the basic motivational commitments of the population to the valuation of production (Marshall's "activities"). I should suggest that there is in a given society a parallel set of noncontingent political commitments, for example, in our own the most basic loyalties of the population to "their country" and their commitment to constitutional government. There may, however, also be other factors. The great tradition of constitutional law may perhaps be said to be the main symbolic embodiment of this factor.

TABLE I.		
SYSTEM PROBLEM	CATEGORY OF INPUT	
	Economy: Factors of Production	Polity: Ingredients of Power
Pattern Maintenance ...	"Land"	Political Commitments
Goal Attainment	Labor	Contingent Support
Adaptation	Capital	Facilities of Power
Integration	Entrepreneurial Service	Legitimation of Goals
SYSTEM PROBLEM	CATEGORY OF OUTPUT	
	Economy: Shares of Income	Polity: Types of Power
Pattern Maintenance ...	"Rent"	Security; Prestige
Goal Attainment	Wages	Binding Decisions
Adaptation	Interest	Control of Facilities
Integration	Profit	Allocation of Prestige

Secondly, specific goal states are a function of the availability in social interaction of a certain type of performance and attitude on the part of actors external to the system. In the case of the economy the input in this category is what economists have in a technical sense called labor. This is not the total of human services, but the latter so far as they may be regarded as contingent on payment of wages through the labor market. Above all, the input of labor concerns not merely the total volume of input of "services" into the economy but its allocation between different units contingent on different terms and contracts of employment. The parallel in the case of the polity might be called the output of "contingent support." This does not concern the basic commitments of our political system as such to the political welfare of the society, but rather those elements of commitment on the part of various sectors of the population which are treated as legitimately contingent on relatively specific terms. These terms are above all settled by processes of political negotiation and the mobilization of popular support for policies. For example, in our system the obligation to pay taxes is not completely settled by general noncontingent loyalty but is renegotiated from time to time through representatives in the legislative process in the background of public opinion. Again, though an obligation to defend the country may be considered basic, specific liability to military service is not adequately defined in these terms alone but must await specific determination through legislation and executive action.

The adaptive needs of the economy center on control of disposable resources which can be committed to the process of production as capital. There is always a problem of alternative use for other purposes, including consumption, but also support of political operations. The cognate category of importance for the polity may also be conceived as the control of disposable resources which in an advanced society depend above all on money funds. The legitimation of such control, however, in this case concerns their importance for the power position of the society in relation to its system goals. I should include here the ingredients of military force other than the motivational commitment of personnel, but also other facilities needed for other types of societal goal.

Finally, related to the factor of organization of the economy is the input of entrepreneurial services as this has been treated by Schumpeter. The entrepreneurial function in these terms concerns the readjustment of organizational relations within the economy in such a way as to improve productivity. The cognate political category might be called "political adjustment" in the sense in which this is conceived as a function of the politician. His role is to work out new combinations of interest groups, sentiments, and so on which have a bearing on the integration of the political system. In both cases the relation to integration may be either positive or negative; it may concern the promotion of more effective integration or the forestalling of threats to a given level of integration.

We may continue the parallel further by barely mentioning certain possible categories of output of the polity to other sectors of the society, which may be considered to parallel the shares of income as these have been treated in economic theory. Corresponding to the category of rent, which it must be remembered in modern terms is not confined to the rents for the use of fixed physical facilities but also of cultural facilities like technical knowledge and the abilities and motivational commitments of people; corresponding to rent in this sense, we may speak perhaps of the returns received by various sectors of the population and the system as a whole from its noncontingent political commitments. Such concepts as "security" and certain aspects of prestige seem to fit in this context. There may be a reference to the external situation in terms of internal affairs but also to the internal situation in that there seems to be a fundamental relationship between the political security of different parts of the social structure and its legitimation through commitments of fundamental loyalty in the political system.

Secondly, corresponding to wages as an output of the economy, it may be useful to speak of "binding decisions" as a political output category. This would be thought of as capacity through decisions to control the activities of nongovernmental elements of the society in accord with goals accepted as valid for the whole system. The process is that of spelling out the more detailed obligations following from a major political decision, and defining the commitments flowing from these for the various units of the society.

Third, corresponding to the output of interest from the economy, we might refer to "control of facilities or productivity." One primary aspect of this concerns the institution of property and the ways in which they define rights to manipulate opportunities for inducement and coercion in social relationships. Within the limits left open by these institutions, however, there is a line drawn in the course of the political process which allows control of fluid resources as between positive political utilization and the "private" sector. Finally, corresponding to profit in the narrow Schumpeterian sense, we may perhaps speak of the processes of reallocation of internal prestige which are a function of the activities of the politician as referred to above.

As has already been noted, this is the most tentative possible set of suggestions for an approach to some aspects of a theory of political power. There are two bases on which I am inclined to have some confidence that a great deal of further work will be productive in this direction. The first of these is the striking formal correspondence with categories which have already proved themselves in the economic field and the way in which the latter fit into the formal structure of the general theory of social systems. The second is that I do not think the concepts, here very tentatively introduced, are very far distant from some of those which are being successfully used in the current work of some political scientists. To take only two examples, Lasswell and Kaplan's book and also that of David Easton would I am sure provide many points of contact with this type of analysis. I therefore have felt it worthwhile to throw out these very tentative suggestions because they seem to constitute a genuinely integral part of the theory of action as I have sketched it in outline in this paper.[9]

PART FOUR

The Community

In the final section, the essays are directed toward a more concrete research area, the study of the community—and the community is used here as an integrating concept which has applicability for several types and areas of inquiry. Some concrete research projects are described.

GORDON W. BLACKWELL
Community Analysis

IN THIS paper we shall first sketch the nature of community as viewed by a sociologist in the hope that this will provide a helpful framework for consideration of the more specialized papers to follow. We shall then discuss some of the methods of community analysis which have been used by sociologists.

I. DIMENSIONS OF COMMUNITY [1]

Sociological analysis of the nature of the local community reveals at least seven factors operative in the dynamics of community structure and function. These we call sociological dimensions of community.

Population characteristics. To illustrate the nature of these different dimensions, let us take as the first example a situation with which many public officials are confronted in southern cities. They often find among Negro population a high illiteracy rate, a loose type of family organization, and departure from middle class mores of sex behavior. Often the husband-father is not in the home. Such a situation has implications for various community agencies. Many reasons are given for it, but if the matter is studied carefully, one may find that a basic reason lies in the sex ratio of the Negro population, which in southern cities as a whole is about 93, meaning only 93 males for every 100 females. In some southern cities it is as low as 80 or a little less (Montgomery, Alabama, 78; Albany, Georgia, 79). Such behavior is perhaps not unexpected in a population with a sex ratio as askew as that. This, then, illustrates the first dimension of community, namely, the population characteristics. Age, sex, density, racial and ethnic composition, mobility, the various vital statistics, and population trends come into this first dimension of community.

Institutional structure. Let us take another example, a community of 10,-000 people. A study will reveal that there are perhaps 150 organized groups and formally established agencies operating in that community. We find among those governmental and voluntary agencies and organized groups 20 which are particularly concerned with children and youth, and we may find them getting into each other's hair a bit: some bickering and jealousies, a lot of misunderstanding as to what each is doing. The need, of course, is for some type of coordination and planning among both public and private associations in community situations in which government is becoming increasingly important.

Perhaps the analogy is not too farfetched to say that a community of that

size is somewhat analogous to the River Rouge plant that Ford has in Detroit. Thousands of workers are there. The plant has a particular objective,
the finished automobile. It is organized into many departments, and the
proper relationship between those departments in operation is vital if the
industry is to be successful. Any part of the plant that does not do its job
well or get behind, upsets the whole schedule of production. The efficiency
we have achieved in large-scale mass production has been due to careful
planning and coordination—in a dictatorial fashion, very largely, it is true,
but it has worked. In contrast, most American communities have had little
or no planning or coordination, often no machinery for it, and the result is
that each is functioning as a community at perhaps 25 or 50 per cent efficiency. If we were competing as businessmen in the meeting of human needs,
many of our communities would go bankrupt. The problem we face in this
aspect of community life is how we can democratically work out procedures
and machinery for planning and coordination.

This point illustrates the second dimension of community which sociologists call the institutional structure: formal associational groupings which can
be distinguished as either administrative agencies or organized groups.

Many organized groups touch only a few of the people in a community.
Studies in cities reveal that 40 to 60 per cent of adults are members of these
organized groups if church membership is excluded. In rural communities
the percentage is usually smaller. So when we bring in representatives from
these organized groups, we should not pretend that we are getting a complete
representation of the people of the community. The American practice of
"joining" is not as universal as popularly assumed.

Value systems. For the next dimension of community, let us take the illustration of two communities side by side in the South. They are both rural
communities with the same climate and the same natural resources. But in
one we find the typical picture of a southern sharecropping community—
soil erosion, poor housing, low standards of living, poor school attendance,
illiteracy, poor health—and in the other, right next door, we find well-kept
homes, green fields, stable and healthy families, bright-eyed children.

What is the explanation of these differences? Inquiry would reveal that
the second community was settled generations ago by an immigrant group
from central Europe who brought with them values very different from those
the southern cotton plantation economy has developed. Thrift, love of the
soil, careful farming practices are a part of the value systems of the people
in this locality. There is all the difference in the world between the communities.

The third dimension, then, is the value systems of a community, which involve the folkways thought to be essential for the group, *i.e.,* the mores—
things that people hold dear. Here we find many of the motivating forces
for what happens in a community. We may ask, "How highly is public serv-

ice rated in the community? Where does it really rank among the values of the people? How do the people value the right of the ballot?"

Social stratification. If we look for another illustration, we might come upon a school superintendent who finds that the schools are not successfully meeting the needs of some segments of the population—perhaps the group across the railroad tracks or a particular racial group—and inquiry reveals that what we call social stratification is functioning to the detriment of a community-wide program of public education. By social stratification we mean the process and resulting social structures through which rights and privileges, duties and obligations, are distributed unequally among socially designated "inferior" and "superior" grades of people. The bases for this ranking vary from one culture to another and between communities in American society.

Numerous studies have shown that American communities are stratified into social classes—it is debatable whether the rigidity of these classes is increasing or decreasing—and into minority groups, racial and ethnic. This social stratification dimension must be understood if we are to work effectively in the community setting. It presents a problem, too, as we attempt to coordinate the schools with other community agencies.

The relationships between social stratification, voting behavior, and political leadership have been explored by political scientists as well as sociologists.

Interpersonal relationships. A newly formed Good Government Association starts off with a bang. Americans are the easiest people in the world to organize if you just go out and talk something up a bit! In the beginning there is a great deal of enthusiasm, and the leaders are sure that much can be done for improving government in the community. If you look in on the community in a year or so you may find that the Association has died. Nothing of consequence has happened, and you wonder why. It may possibly be because those developing the organization failed to bring into the program many of the real leaders in the community. They may have co-opted some of the nominal leaders, the officeholders, but failed to understand that the real leaders are those who have prestige and enjoy the confidence of the community whether or not they hold official positions. These influence relationships are not identical with social stratification along class or racial lines, although patterns of stratification and influence affect each other and may coincide at some points. Techniques exist for locating the real leaders in the community, and failure to use such leaders may be why this Association did not succeed.

Another dimension of community, then, is the extremely complex patterns of interpersonal relationships which may range from social visiting patterns, to mutual aid practices, to clique behavior, to "advice" relationships, to patterns of influence and informal leadership.

In a small southern community several years ago we analyzed patterns of local leadership. Since the community is biracial in its social organization, we asked the white people who they thought the Negro leaders were, and then we asked the Negroes to designate the leaders in their own group. We got very different responses from the two sources. Verification of our findings came shortly after when one of the men identified as a top leader by the Negroes, but not by the whites, stood for election to the town Board of Aldermen. He was soundly defeated. Negroes constitute only 10 to 15 per cent of the local voters, and a Negro candidate must depend largely on white support. In the election two years later the Negroes ran one of their members who in our study had been most frequently named as a leader by whites, less frequently by Negroes. He was elected to office by an overwhelming vote, leading all five white candidates.

Often members of the majority group decide who will take part in community organization, that is, who will participate in decisions, and in doing this they fail to select the real leaders from a minority group.

Power structure. In another situation we find the community aroused about a different kind of problem. It may be smoke control or rat control or narcotics control, or it may be enforcement of a housing code. Many of the organized groups in town go on record as opposing the undesirable situation and urging community action. The newspapers, radio and television support the movement, and there is a great hullabaloo. Yet nothing happens. Agencies of local government, which could take effective action, do not do so. One wonders why. If we look beneath the surface we may find that certain people of power in the community whose vested interests are threatened have, under cover, informally, and in certain patterned relationships with each other, worked out a way to keep anything from happening.

A very important dimension of American communities, then, is the power structure. The locus of power may be found in the political organization of a community—but not always. Often it is in the economic organization of the community. Perhaps a labor union has become so powerful that its leaders informally determine what happens in the community. More frequently it has been management of business or industry that has pulled the strings behind the scenes and has determined what really happens in a community. In a company town we can see this situation clearly.

In other communities the locus of power may be the church. Some years ago in a German Lutheran community in the Midwest, the minister customairily decided to whom a family could sell its land. Here a single institution exercised almost all the effective means of controlling the actions of individuals in the community.

The man who owns a community's only newspaper, radio and television station, as happens in some small cities, by controlling these media of mass communication may be of great importance in the local power structure.

In our meaning of the term, however, the power structure is not synonymous with the top nominal leadership which functions through the institutional structure. The two may overlap some, it is true, but the power structure operates not according to the organizational charts of institutions but on
the basis of informal, though patterned, relationships between individuals.

Ecological patterning. Finally, the seventh dimension of community is
revealed when we look at something that can be seen in many communities—
a fine old residential section is gradually being invaded by business or small
industry. The old homes turn into boardinghouses. Prostitution, poverty, poor
health, delinquency and crime flourish—the combination we all know so
well in city slums. What is happening is a change in the land-use patterns of
the community, in what we call the ecological patterning—a term designating
the processes resulting in division of a community into many different kinds of
land use, with different kinds of residential neighborhoods among the results.
These neighborhoods or zones gradually invade each other, and sometimes
social problems come in the wake of such changes. The implications for location of schools and other public facilities are evident.

One answer to this situation is adequate physical planning, usually by an
official city planning board, which can greatly alleviate the results of these
changes in the land-use patterns.

The question of the outer boundaries of the community—the real sociological community—is also involved in ecology, with its implications for the
problem of city annexation.

The essential meaning of community. These are the seven sociological
dimensions of community. We cannot understand the true nature of a community without considering all of these factors.

What, then, can we say a community is? In a recent article, Hillery [2] has
analyzed 94 definitions of community covering the period 1901 to 1950. He
concludes that a majority of the definitions include the following as important
elements of community: area, common ties, and social interaction. Hollingshead,[3] in an article reviewing the field of community research, concluded
that, regardless of varying definitions, the community has been "assumed
to be an organized structural and functional entity with spatial, temporal,
and sociological dimensions."

For our purposes we have found it most helpful to view the community as
a locus for a set of basic, interacting institutions through the functioning of
which a majority of the residents find it possible to meet their needs and have
developed something of a sense of togetherness, with a consequent potential
ability to act together as an entity. Local areas inhabited by people in relatively close physical proximity do not always clearly exhibit the characteristics of community—particularly large urban agglomerations. Rather than
designating a local area as "a community" or "not a community," specific

localities may be identified as conforming "more" or "less" closely to our concept of community. We think of community in its more restricted, local sense as compared with MacIver's more generalized concept.[4]

It will be noted that our operational definition does not make direct reference to several of the sociological dimensions of community. These factors are viewed as the functions of people living together and meeting their needs through institutional (associational) structures. True, these dimensions—value systems, stratification, interpersonal relationships, power structure, and ecological patterning—are also social structures which in turn condition the institutional processes. The community may be best understood as an organic entity, a web of social relationships, with its various social structures all interrelated. These structures result in a complex of statuses which in turn prescribe multitudinous roles for individuals. Through the fulfillment of these roles we have institutional functioning.

This, we suggest, is the nature of the local community to which political scientists are increasingly turning their research attention. This is the socio-cultural arena in which local government is operating, where much decision-making takes place, where the lower echelons of political parties function, and where voters make up their minds and cast their ballots. It is a highly complex socio-cultural arena with constantly changing modes of social interaction, fluctuating formal organizational relationships, and nuclei of increasing and waning power.

II. OBJECTIVES AND METHODS OF COMMUNITY ANALYSIS

We turn now to the second objective of this paper, namely, a discussion of some of the methods of community analysis which have been used by sociologists. Our approach will be somewhat historical in an effort to indicate the general nature of methodological trends in this area of research.

The social survey movement. It is perhaps not important whether we trace the origins of the social survey to the *Domesday Book* compiled for William the Conqueror in the eleventh century, or to the books by the Englishman, John Howard, on social conditions in the latter part of the eighteenth century, or to the surveys of worker families by the Frenchman, Frederick LePlay, in the middle of the nineteenth century, or to Charles Booth's monumental *Life and Labour of the People of London* which appeared in 17 volumes near the close of that century. The last mentioned, because it focussed on a single community, is more directly related to our present concern.[5]

In his survey of laboring people in London, Booth focussed on "representative groups" in "representative districts," thus using a principle now popularly known as sampling. Furthermore, he combined the statistical and case study methods. He used documentary records, interviewing, and participant observation among his techniques of data collection.

Some of the early work between 1890 and 1910 by faculty and students of the Department of Sociology at the University of Chicago was in the social survey tradition, being essentially normative in nature.

Then between 1909 and 1914, the six-volume *Pittsburgh Survey* was completed under the direction of Paul U. Kellogg, probably the first American use of the concept of social survey in the strict sense of the term: a broad study of living conditions and social institutions in a given locale conducted by a staff of specialists using a variety of data collection techniques and directed toward social reform. The Russell Sage Foundation, from the Pittsburgh Survey to the 1940's, provided guidance and support for the survey movement.[6]

In 1939 the Russell Sage Foundation published Joanna C. Colcord's *Your Community* as a guide to studying urban communities in the social survey tradition. In 1955 the Foundation published Roland L. Warren's *Studying Your Community* to serve much the same purpose but with less emphasis on formal agencies and with attention to "more recent orientation or tools of analysis in intergroup relations, informal group processes, social class, and other such matters." Warren's book contains more discussion of survey procedures, both in the organizational and methodological aspects. Chapters include: Your Community: Its Background and Setting; Your Community's Economic Life; Government, Politics, and Law Enforcement; Community Planning; Housing; Education; Recreation; Religious Activities; Social Insurance and Public Assistance; Aids to Family Living and Child Welfare; Health; Provision for Special Groups; Communication; Intergroup Relations; Associations; Community Organization; Organizing a Community Survey; Aids to the Survey; Some Important Aspects of the Community.

Analytical, comprehensive community studies. The appearance in 1906 of James M. Williams, *An American Town,* marked the first analytical community study in the United States. Although some of its methods today seem crude and some of its concepts outmoded, this research was pioneering in both methodology and theoretical insights. Stimulated by Giddings at Columbia University, this was the first of several similar doctoral dissertations by his students, each based on a community study in the first decade of the century. Williams used documentary sources, especially newspaper files, minute books, diaries, and census data. Furthermore, he was a native of the subject community and lived in it during the period of research, gathering much data through what has now come to be called field work techniques, including participant observation and interviewing. He obtained statistics to show trends in the price of hops and related these to quantified data concerning social activities in the community. He mapped the community and its dozen constituent neighborhoods, thus laying the groundwork for later work in community ecology.

In 1915 Charles J. Galpin's *Social Anatomy of an Agricultural Community* was published by the Agricultural Experiment Station of the University of Wisconsin. In this he demonstrated a technique of field study, based largely on interviewing, which described the functional relationships between town and country people, and made it possible to delineate the boundaries of a village-centered rural community. Data were obtained from merchants, bankers, milk wholesalers, ministers and similar people concerning the area which their institutions served around the town; these data were then verified in interviews with many of the rural residents.

Although some of the research in Chicago by students of the University's Sociology Department became more analytical than normative as early as 1900, it was largely the work of Park and Burgess in human ecology [7] which gave rise to the series of studies of parts of Chicago in the 1920's.[8] Combining use of census data with participant observation and interviewing, these analyses have stood up as sound contributions even when the ecological approach has been under considerable theoretical attack.

Middletown [9] by the Lynds in 1929 was a landmark among analytical studies of whole communities. With a staff of field workers and a framework which was comprehensive, if somewhat static, the Lynds provided accurate description and keen insight into a small midwestern city in terms of its economic organization, family life, education, leisure time activities, religion, government, press, welfare and health. The authors justified this "survey-like" approach as follows:

> By and large, social research seems. . . . to make larger gains by digging vertically rather than by raking together the top-soil horizontally; and a disproportinate amount of energy in current social research appears. . . . to be going into the latter sort of work. . . . The original *Middletown* study. . . . may perhaps qualify. . . . as integrating many scattered vertical research borings, not without some useful redefition of focus at certain points.[10]

By the mid 1930's the research focus in community study was more frequently directed to the "vertical borings" mentioned by the Lynds, though often there was need for some description of the general community situation in which the more specific factors were functioning. We turn attention now to community studies which have focussed on some selected aspect of community structure and function.

Studies of community stratification. Much research has inquired into only one dimension of community or has had a single dimension as its primary focus. Of particular methodological concern are community oriented studies of social stratification, interpersonal relationships, and power structure. We shall give brief attention to each of these types of research.

Stratification studies of American communities have come to be quite the fashion. Since this kind of community research is generally familiar to political scientists, we shall here merely list some of the ways by which sociologists have attempted operationally to define social class. Among the more frequently used techniques for discovering or describing stratification are (a) single, direct, indicators such as income,[11] occupation,[12] housing,[13] or education; (b) composite scales such as Chapin's living-room scale of social status,[14] or Warner's index of status characteristics (combining occupation, source of income, house type, residential area);[15] (c) associational participation by individuals (*i.e.*, Warner's index of "evaluated participation");[16] (d) ranking of occupations according to social prestige by a sample of the adult population;[17] (e) self-identification with social class;[18] and (f) ranking of prestige of individuals by selected judges.[19]

Sociometric community studies. Patterns of informal social interaction within the community context has been less well explored by sociologists than has stratification. These patterns of informal interpersonal relationships may be viewed as channels or networks of communication and influence. For analysis of this dimension of community we suggest a continuum ranging from the most informal kind of repetitive social contact as in social visiting, to more intimate interaction between members of a neighbor group or clique, to informal relationships involving influence and leadership. Except in the very small community it is difficult to chart these relationships in all their complexities.

Early work by Cooley and Simmel laid the groundwork for sociological study of groups and interpersonal relationships. However, it remained for J. L. Moreno to develop a simple research technique for revealing interpersonal relationships. His sociometric test, foreshadowed by the social distance test of Bogardus, was designed to lay bare the relationships which selected individuals would like to have with other individuals under specified circumstances. It is, therefore, actually a measure of preferences in regard to relationships with other individuals. Characteristically, the subject is asked to choose a prescribed number of individuals in rank order of their desirability as associates, either in general or in specific activities. Moreno has written as follows:[20]

> The requirements of a good sociometric test are: (a) that it reaches and measures two-way relations; (b) that the participants in the situation are drawn to one another by one or more criteria; (c) that a criterion is selected to which the participants are bound to respond, at the moment of the test, with a high degree of spontaneity; (d) that the subjects are *adequately motivated* so that their responses may be sincere; (e) that the criterion selected for testing is strong, enduring and definite and not weak, transitory and indefinite.

Moreno has contended that "psychological currents and networks can be disclosed by sociometric procedures and placed under direct or remote control."[21]

While the sociometric technique was originally developed for use in formal organizations such as correctional institutions or children's homes, Moreno himself saw the possibility of its use in larger community settings. On this point he has written as follows: [22]

It had been seen that the individuals, who in the sociometric study of a whole community, form a social aggregate around one criterion form other social aggregates around other criteria and that the individuals who produce structures of chain-relations in one aggregate may produce them in other aggregates. If these chain-relations are traced as they cross through the boundaries of each particular aggregate, a new and larger configuration is seen developing,—a psychological network. The simple fact that individuals are more attracted to some individuals and not to others has many consequences. It leaves out those with whom reciprocal relations have not been established and even within the same group there may be formed different networks which do not cross or break through one another.

The dynamic meaning of chain-relations in social structure is better understood in view of a network hypothesis. The chain-relations in each aggregate are often not only contributing to network formation but are themselves a network effect. As chain-relations develop between different social aggregates, existing networks stimulate and increase the development of chain-relations in each single structure.

Moreno developed a form of graphic presentation of sociometric choices revealed through this technique. This chart, called a sociogram, provides a visual representation through the use of circles representing individuals and lines of different types standing for various kinds of interpersonal relationships. While the sociogram is useful for many purposes, it can serve to present the results of sociometric study only in rather small groups. Furthermore, it does not show degree of intensity nor the content of the choices except as they may be positive or negative.

While Moreno's sociometry dealt exclusively with preferences in social relationships, the research technique has been taken over for analysis of other aspects of interpersonal relationships. In this regard we are concerned especially with studies which reveal patterns of social contact, whether or not they may be preferred relationships. Although most of one's social contacts in a community setting are undoubtedly influenced by personal choice, many contacts of a more or less regular nature are not of one's own choosing and yet serve definite functions both for the individual and for the larger social organization. The sociometric technique can be used to reveal patterns of social contacts which actually exist without regard to personal choices.

The first community study of patterns of interpersonal relationships was by George A. Lundberg in the mid 1930's.[23] He summarized his objective as follows:

> In short, can the informal and private affinities and nucleations of an ordinary community be discovered and charted with any degree of accuracy, and if so, what does this elementary and basic societary structure reveal? [24]

The research technique was the structured interview in a complete house-to-house canvass. The study suffered from "doorbell bias" since wives were most frequently the informants. Following identification questions and use of the Chapin living-room scale of social status, each informant was asked to name his or her "most intimate friends in the community." Confidentiality was promised. Lundberg summarized his conclusion as follows: [25]

> 1) The population of a village divides itself on the basis of friendship groupings in a relatively few well-defined and frequently quite exclusive constellations centering on conspicuous individuals, the "lady bountiful," the politicians, the physicians, etc. One of these was named as friend by seventeen different people, the maximum number of choices received by anyone.
>
> 2) At the opposite extreme there are isolated individuals who are designated as friends by nobody, and who designate none. Some of these have friends in the area adjoining the village. Others have such connections elsewhere, with whom they communicate through correspondence, telephone or occasional visits. Only three cases out of the 256 successfully interviewed were entirely isolated, admitting no connections and never mentioned by anyone else in the village. Age, organic defects, and migration from other places figured in these situations.
>
> 3) The average number of choices *made* by people in different socio-economic groups did not vary significantly, but remained within a fraction of the average for the whole group namely, 2.3 choices per person, the range being between 0 and 8. The number of choices *received,* however, increased conspicuously with increasing socio-economic status.
>
> 4) As was to be expected from the preceding point, there is a tendency for people with average or lower socio-economic scores to choose friends of higher socio-economic status than themselves. If we consider only the group with socio-economic scores between 93 and 143, i.e., about 25 points immediately above and 25 points below the median, we find that 60% of the choices were of friends with higher socio-economic scores.

Loomis, perhaps more than anyone else, has made use of the sociometric technique in studies of small communities. His 1940 study of El Cerrito, New Mexico, is a good example.[26] His charting of interpersonal relationships included visiting patterns, borrowing-lending, and mutual aid as related to such factors as kinship, status, and ecology.

As already noted, the sociometric technique of analyzing patterns of interpersonal relationships is most easily adapted to the study of small communities. There are instances, however, in which it has been used in urban situations. A study by Deutschberger in selected neighborhoods in New York City and Pittsburgh in 1945 affords an example.[27] The sample studied were white males 9 to 16 years of age, regarding English as their native tongue and with family income of less than $2,000 a year. This was a "best friends" sort of study.

Studies of influence and informal leadership. The techniques of studying patterns of social interaction as described above were easily applicable to the task of charting influence and informal leadership relationships. Three examples will suffice. Ryan,[28] using the interview technique with a sample of farm operators, sought to discover *real* leaders as characterized by influence rather than office holding. His primary contribution was the identification of three types of leaders: advisors, organizers, representatives.

Stewart,[29] also using the interview technique with a sample of white permanent residents of a village of 6,000 population, attempted to locate persons in the community with influence as related to job advice, educational advice, personal advice, politics, a community drive, and similar matters. Of some 500 persons mentioned as having influence on some matter, 55 or 11 per cent were mentioned by 10 or more respondents, 20 or 4 per cent by 25 or more respondents. Of the then current office holders in organized groups in the community, slightly more than half appeared in the top leadership group mentioned by 10 or more informants.

Chapin[30] combined a study of nominal leaders (office holders) with real leaders who emerged in interviews with a random sample of adults, "a 'selected' group of civic leaders, recognized and identified as such by their contemporaries," and a group of labor leaders. He compared the nominal leaders with the real leaders on a number of counts. He concluded:

> The limited overlap of the two groups and their similarity in measured characteristics strongly suggest the existence of an inexhaustible reservoir of potential leaders in the freely organized American community and point up a valuable attribute of the American way of social life.[31]

As a model for the analysis of different kinds of community leadership, always remembering that leadership must be studied in its social situational context, we suggest the following:

Attribute of the Individual	Type of Leadership
Influence	Advice
Prestige	Representation
Esteem	Organization and promotion
Power	Policy determination

The wielding of power in policy determination on matters of broad community concern and the patterned relationships between those with power have been the object of a recent series of community studies.

Studies of community power structure. The dimension of community which we call community power structure was largely unexplored until the insightful work of Floyd Hunter.[32] Using semi-structured and unstructured interviews in a metropolitan center, he identified 40 top power leaders. His technique was first to compile a preliminary list of perhaps 200 leaders in community affairs. These names were provided by the Community Council, Chamber of Commerce, League of Women Voters, newspaper editors, and selected civic leaders. The next step was to select 14 judges who had lived in the community for some years and who had knowledge of community affairs. These judges were asked to choose the top power leaders from the compiled list. Power was defined simply as the ability of men to move other men to move goods and services. Hunter described the power leaders of the community, and more importantly he analyzed the relationships between persons in the power structure as it actually operated in respect to selected issues. He further analyzed the power structure of the Negro subcommunity and described methods of its articulation with power leaders in the dominant structure.

Hunter more recently has conducted power structure studies in several smaller communities and generally has verified the findings of his pioneer inquiry.

This concludes our review of objectives and methods of community analysis. The trend followed by sociologists away from normative surveys toward more rigorous and analytical inquiry with theoretical orientation is unmistakable. Community studies have moved from the macroscopic in the direction of the microscopic with focus upon particular parameters. There has been a trend also from static descriptive studies to explanatory inquiry concerning community processes.

This review has sought to be selective. It has therefore slighted some approaches, particularly ecological studies and action-oriented community self-studies. Although sketchily at best, we have gone into somewhat more detail concerning those approaches which may be of peculiar interest to students of political behavior: studies of interpersonal relationships including preference, influence, leadership, and power.

ANGUS CAMPBELL

The Political Implications of
Community Identification

THE CONCEPT of community has been dealt with in various ways by other paper writers. I am here concerned with the psychological phenomenon of sense of community—the feeling of identification and attachment to the geographically localized society of which one perceives himself to be a member. I propose to consider the implications which this sense of community membership has for political attitudes and actions, to put forward certain hypotheses regarding the conditions under which this influence is effective, to mention certain relevant research findings and to suggest some of the problems of research method which are present in this area of inquiry.

It is apparent at once that the term "community" is a very imprecise one and that it is commonly applied to social aggregates of very different character. Neighborhoods, suburban developments, towns, and metropolises are all spoken of as communities, with the result that the term has become so broad that it does not have great scientific usefulness. We clearly need to differentiate these different types of communities in some way which will be meaningful for political analysis.

There are a great many different ways of describing communities, depending for the most part on indices or aggregates derived from the decennial census or other population data. In the realm of political behavior such data have made it possible to study community stability as in V. O. Key's [1] analysis of Republican enclaves in southern Ohio and to trace community change as in the various studies of the shifting partisanship of localized ethnic and religious groups.[2, 3, 4] On the basis of election statistics Louis Harris [5] concludes in his study of the 1952 vote that the increasing Republican vote in the metropolitan suburbs is the result of community pressure on the newcomers who move into these traditionally Republican communities. Since Harris had no information as to the political disposition of these new suburbanites before they came into these communities, it is not clear whether his conclusion regarding community pressure is justified or not.

There have also been attempts through the use of sample surveys to demonstrate that the political character of the local community has effects on the behavior of the residents. This is suggested by the authors of the

318

Elmira study [6] who comment at one point on "the effect of the distant community" as an influence separate from that of the more immediate primary groups. The Elmira study is not very well adapted to the demonstration of community effects since it deals with only a single community. Moreover, the authors do not attempt to measure the degree of community identification directly but infer its influence from the appearance of persistently higher Republican votes in their tables than they can explain on the basis of other factors. They conclude that "in general, the Republicans get more than their random share of the adjustment to a conflicting environment, because of the pervasive Republican atmosphere of Elmira."

A somewhat different analysis of the relation of community political atmosphere to the political characteristics of community members has recently been carried out by my associate, Warren Miller. Dr. Miller has conceived a very ingenious analysis which combines aggregative data available from election statistics and individual data available from the University of Michigan's study of the 1952 election.[7] The independent variable in his study was the degree of one-party dominance in the counties which served as the sampling areas for the 1952 survey. This was determined by examining the election statistics for these counties. They ranged from strongly Republican to strongly Democratic. Then, using survey data, Dr. Miller sorted the residents of these different areas on the basis of their votes in the 1952 elections and compared Republican and Democratic voters in the different types of community as to their attitudes on parties, issues, and candidates. His findings show a somewhat greater tendency for people who vote with the majority in their county to support their vote with a strong and consistent stand on issues and candidates than do people who vote with the minority. Minority voters, both Republicans and Democrats, seem to have a minimum commitment to the party for which they vote. Majority voters, Republicans in Republican counties and Democrats in Democratic counties, tend to reflect the full "party line." We cannot say with assurance that living in a predominantly Republican or Democratic community gives a stronger partisan coloration to those who conform to the prevailing political climate and dilutes the partisanship of those who are out of step. It is possible that factors we have not considered may be responsible for both the extensity and intensity of partisanship in the individual counties. However, Dr. Miller's data suggest that even so diffuse a community as a county may have influence on the political views of its members.

I am very much interested in Dr. Miller's paper not only because of the specific findings which he has reported but because of the unique combination of aggregative and survey data which made his analysis possible. Aggregative analysis has typically concerned itself with the interrelations of one aggregate or index with another; for example, as in Samuel Lubell's analysis, the relation of the proportion of people with Germanic descent in a county to the proportion voting Democratic in the county. Typically, in survey analysis we relate one individual attribute to another. Thus we enter each individual respondent in a correlation table to show the relationship between income and party preference, for example. Miller's analysis demonstrates the manner in which the data obtained from all of the respondents in a particular community or area can be combined to form an index score for that community. These index scores can then be entered, community by community, into a correlation table with scores obtained from sources other than the survey. When one considers the vast range of data that can be obtained through survey procedures and the fact that we know a great deal about the history and contemporary characteristics of the communities in which survey interviews are taken, the possibilities inherent in this type of research seem very great indeed.

None of these studies which I have mentioned has dealt directly with what I have called the sense of community identification. They tell us that the communities in question demonstrate political consensus and in some cases they permit us to infer at least that some part of this consensus is the result of community influences on individual members. Our inquiry into the problem of community effects will remain severely limited, however, unless we can move to the investigation of the way in which individuals perceive and react to the communities of which they are at least nominally members.

The study of community identification will require the use of concepts, hypotheses and data which are, I suspect, less familiar to political scientists than those employed in the studies mentioned earlier. We will need to consider communities as groups and describe them in terms of their group properties. Our hypotheses will deal with the way group properties and the behavior of groups interrelate. Our data for the most part will have to come from individual group members since we will need to know their identifications, perceptions, and values and there is no satisfactory source of this information other than the individual himself.

While there is a substantial and growing literature of research on the effects and characteristics of membership in small face-to-face groups, there is not, to my knowledge, a corresponding literature on membership in large, heterogeneous communities. There has been a great deal of speculation among sociologists as to the relation of the individual to his surrounding community, dating back at least to Durkheim's well-known studies of integration and anomie. There have also been a series of field reports from the social anthropologists which emphasize the control which the small communities they study exercise over their members. The record so far as quantitative studies of community membership is concerned is not so extensive. Even the Erie County [8] and Elmira Studies which were intensive studies done within limited communities were more concerned with membership with subgroups within the community than they were with community membership itself. Robert Angell's [9] study of moral integration in four American cities deals in great detail with the way the residents of these cities perceive their communities and while his concept of moral integration does not correspond exactly with what I have called community identification and while his analysis employs his measure of moral integration as a dependent rather than an independent variable, there is much in his study to interest students of community identification.

If there is to be an effort on the part of political scientists and others to push into the question of community influences on political behavior, it would seem wise to examine the closely related problem of group effects in the large dispersed population categories, those segments of the population differing in sex, race, income, education, or other personal-social characteristics. These demographic and social collectivities are not communities geographically but the phenomenon of identification with these groups is probably not essentially different from community identification. The research which has been done on the political implications of identification with the population groups should suggest some of the possibilities and hazards to be expected in the study of geographical communities.

One of the most firmly established facts in American politics is the persistent tendency of certain ethnic, religious, economic and geographical groups to support one or the other of the major political parties. This phenomenon of bloc voting has come into particular prominence during the last twenty-five years and it has been the inspiration of much slate-building, platform-writing and election year campaigning.

Concensus in the political attitudes and preferences of these major population groups is brought about in either of two ways: It may occur because individual members of a group react independently but similarly to some outside stimulus which affects them similarly; thus we find that people in the older age categories have a stronger interest in social security than people of the younger age levels. Their common reaction to a situation held in common creates what we might call "coincidental consensus."

Group positions in politics may also result from the direct influence of the group on its individual members. When the members of a group are strongly identified with the group and there are clearly apparent group standards, true group effects may be expected to occur. Thus we know that for the last several years members of labor unions have been strongly opposed to the Taft-Hartley Act. There is reason to believe that they are not well informed as to the content of this Act and may even approve of many of its individual clauses if they are not specifically identified with the Act. Their position is apparently influenced by the fact that they are strongly identified with their unions and that the union line is clearly and strongly anti-Taft-Hartley. In such cases, consensus depends not so much on common circumstances in the lives of individual group members as on the direct influence of group membership itself.

This might be called group-induced consensus. Most people are included, voluntarily or not, in a variety of social categories. Some of these groupings have far-reaching significance for their members; others are purely nominal. I would judge, for example, that most Americans whose families have been in this country for several generations are not much moved by the fact that there are other members of the total population with whom they share an ancestral birthplace. On the other hand, it would be difficult for members of the more visible and discriminated minority groups to escape the implications of their dissociation from these groups.

It may also be observed that different group memberships may have relevance in different areas of the values and behavior of the members. For example, being a Unitarian undoubtedly has important implications in matters of religious belief but it would appear to have little significance in one's preferences in art and music. Being a graduate of Siwash University may call forth appropriate behavior on homecoming week end but not on election Tuesday. Being a Negro may influence where one stands on desegregation but have no relationship to how he feels about foreign affairs.

It is also apparent from casual observation that not all members of these groups are equally identified with them. Not all of the graduates of Siwash U. come back to the campus for homecoming. Some of them don't even answer the mail they get from the Siwash Alumni Council. Some members of labor unions are obviously members in name only. They do not identify themselves with their union and they reject its claims on their loyalty. Minority group members differ a great deal in the sense of attachment they feel to their racial or religious groups, some of them being consumed with the special interests of their particular group and others going to great lengths to dissociate themselves from them.

If we attempt now to convert these commonplace generalities into more formally stated propositions, we will emerge with something like the following list: (1) Group consensus may result either from independent but similar reactions to a common outside stimulus or from conformity to perceived group standards; (2) consensus resulting from conformity will be highest in those groups having the strongest membership identification; (3) consensus in such groups will be highest on those attitudes and behaviors regarding which group standards are strongest; (4) within such groups, consensus will be highest among those group members whose identification is strongest.

In order to test hypotheses of this kind we will need to find measures of the three major variables: group consensus, group identification, and group standards.

Most studies of the political characteristics of the major population groups have had to do with the vote. It is not difficult to establish group consensus in voting and this has been done in a number of sample surveys. The vote itself, however, is a very narrow expression of the political complexion of either an individual or a group. The vote is highly categorical and tells nothing of the perceptions, values and attitudes which lie behind it. When we broaden our inquiry to include these latter kinds of data, we find that the pattern of political consensus varies from group to group and is related to the essential characteristics of these groups.

Some groups, men and women for example, or the different age groups, seem to have very little political individuality.[10] Others may show a strong group position on one political measure but not on others. Negroes, for example, are strongly Democratic in their vote but they do not differ from the rest of the electorate in their response to many broad political issues. In some cases we find what might be called a "partial" pattern of consensus. In this category labor union members are prominent. There are a number of issues of domestic policy on which the attitudes of these people are clearly different from those of similar occupational status who are not union members. On questions of foreign affairs, however, their positions seem to be indistinguishable.

Then there are other groups tending to be small and rather distinctive in character which demonstrate consensus on a broad range of political measures. The three or four per cent of the population who are of the Jewish religion are such a group. They are highly Democratic in their votes, liberal on economic and civil liberties issues, internationalist in their world outlook, critical of the Republican administration and very unfavorably disposed to Senator McCarthy.

It is clear then that group consensus can vary both in intensity and extensity and, as we observed earlier, we would expect consensus to be strongest and broadest in those groups in which membership identification and group standards are strongest.

Group identification is a psychological concept and it is usually measured by asking the individual group member to estimate the strength of his attachment to the group. The scales which are usually used for this purpose in small group research are not readily adaptable to the study of membership in communities or other large social aggregates.[11] The problem is not to discover whether an individual is properly classified as being inside or outside a particular group. There is little trouble in finding out whether people are Bostonians, farmers, union members, or college graduates. The problem is to find out what significance this fact has for them. The authors of the Elmira study asked their respondents to select "Which of these groups are most important to you?" in an attempt to note the degree of belonging they felt toward the groups of which they were members. For the most part these ratings of group importance were not highly related to the political behavior of the group members.

During a series of studies over the last five years the Survey Research Center has been interested in the problem of identification with political party. Most people are quite ready to classify themselves as Republicans or Democrats; the question is to find out whether this is a merely nominal attachment or something of deeper significance. After some exploration with more elaborate procedures, we are currently asking our respondents simply to rate themselves as "strong" or "not very strong" Republicans or Democrats. This has the obvious weakness of permitting each individual to make his own definition of what is strong and what is not strong. The resulting unreliability is not so great however as to destroy the usefulness of this intensity measure on a group basis. The people who rate themselves as "strong" partisans are clearly different from the weak partisans on all measures where political partisanship might be expected to have an effect.

These measures of the intensity of group identification are crude and clearly need improvement. The measurement of community identification may prove to be even more difficult. The concept of community membership may not be as immediately clear in people's minds as membership in a party, labor union, or church and it will probably be necessary to use more delicate procedures to find out how much significance in fact this kind of memship has.

It is probably true that all groups that have any degree of self-consciousness have group standards of one kind or another. Among teen-agers it may be standards of dress and current patois. Among white Southerners it may be standards of belief and practice regarding questions of race. Among the upward mobile it is likely to be standards of consumption. One can hardly doubt that various population groups also have standards of approved political attitudes and preferences. One can imagine the weight of group disapproval that would come down on a union member so misguided as to stand up in a meeting of his CIO local and make a statement favorable to the present Republican administration. It would probably not differ very much from the reception one might get if he spoke out in favor of ex-President Truman at a meeting of the North Shore Country Club.

The population groups we have been discussing undoubtedly differ a great deal both in the intensity and breadth of their political standards. The two minority groups, Negroes and Jews, make an interesting contrast in this regard. As Fuchs has recently pointed out, there are many values imbedded in the Jewish tradition which have reflections in the political attitudes of contemporary American Jews. There are also issues of a contemporary character on which there is a clear group position; for example, support for the State of Israel. American Jews are a relatively cohesive group and individual members are relatively likely to know where their group stands on important issues. American Negroes, on the other hand, are neither highly cohesive nor highly politicized. While, over the last thirty years they have moved strongly from the party of Lincoln to the party of Roosevelt, there is very little evidence in this group of consensus on other political matters. It is interesting to speculate as to whether the current conflict over desegregation will have the effect of heightening Negro awareness of a racial position on a broadening range of political issues.

There may be a difference of course between "pronounced" group standards and "effective" group standards. There is reason to believe that the pronouncements of union leadership regarding certain political issues have an influence on the opinions of union membership. One wonders, on the other hand, if the pronouncements of the American Legion leadership have effects on the membership of that organization. Pronounced standards may be ineffective either because the membership is not actually identified with the group or because the membership is not sufficiently well informed to know what its group standards are. As we discovered in one of our studies several years ago,[12] well informed party identifiers were considerably more likely to follow the party line on political issues than poorly informed identifiers. The latter apparently did not know where their party stood.

Pronounced standards may also prove ineffective if they are rejected by the membership as inappropriate to the character of the group. Church congregations, for example, are occasionally upset by excursions into political comment by their minister. Such groups apparently have a relatively well-defined image of the proper orbit of the group's interest. When group leadership goes beyond the limits of perceived legitimacy it endangers its role as leader.

It must also be recognized that some group standards are never pronounced in any formal way. It is probably true that a large proportion of the American public take on the peculiar coloration of their social class, for example, by a form of social osmosis, by a quiet and largely unconscious absorption of the values and standards of the people around them. Once strongly identified with one class or the other, they then tend to follow that class line although not necessarily being aware that they are conforming to its standards.

When we consider the possibility of group standards associated with community membership, we are likely to conclude that the range of their effective operation will be relatively narrow. Most communities, even small ones, are very heterogeneous. They are cut through with all the ethnic, economic, and religious strata, some of which we know to have political standards of their own. Community standards are very likely to come into conflict with the standards of these subcommunities. Thus, it would be easier to get the members of most communities to agree that a campaign to keep trash off the streets would be a desirable thing than to agree that trash collection should be paid for by a tax on amusements rather than property.

The measurement of the presence and strength of group standards may be approached on either an objective or subjective level. Objectively, it is possible to analyze the content of public statements by community leaders or other expressions of approved opinion on matters of community interest. A rough estimate of the degree of unanimity of these status-supported statements and of the frequency of their enunciation should be feasible. It must be recognized, however, that such an objective measurement of expressed community standards may be very imperfectly correlated with the subjective perception of these standards by community members. One cannot fail to be impressed with the ability of the average citizen to ignore a substantial part of the total volume of public expression to which he is exposed. Surveys of public information lead me to conclude that most of the time most people do not listen to most of what appears in the media of public communication. It is also true of course that perception is a very dynamic process and that the way people perceive objective fact is often influenced by their own values and needs. This phenomenon which has been observed many times in psychological experiments is demonstrated in the findings of the Elmira study that voters tend to see the candidate of their choice holding the same position on important issues as they do themselves even though this may not in fact be true.

Sociological studies of group standards or group values tend to follow the Middletown tradition, wherein a persistent and presumably perceptive field worker or group of field workers, after a period of intense participant observation, comes to a statement of the prevailing ethos of the community. Such studies are subject to the criticisms which apply to all such ethnographic reports. They place a great deal more reliance on the perceptions of the field observer than one can feel comfortable about and they tend inevitably to lose the divergent individual in the search for prevailing patterns.

The most direct approach to the measurement of the subjective reality of community standards is, of course, through the individual community member himself. His perception that his community approves or disapproves of this or that opinion or action is the ultimate test of the presence for him of community-related group standards. Granting the possibility of unconscious motivation, it is unlikely that a person who does not see his community holding a position on an issue will be influenced by the community in his own opinion regarding the issue.

Turning now from questions of measurement to questions of research design, it occurs to me that there are three basic approaches to the study of the influence of community membership: cross sectional analysis, comparative analysis, and change analysis.

The analysis of cross sectional data is becoming a familiar exercise in the repertory of those social scientists who choose to deal with quantitative measures. The development of practical methods of sampling randomly from large populations has made it possible to deal with a wide range of research problems which were until recently quite beyond our reach. The analysis of the influence of membership in the various population groups on political behavior is a case in point. Paul Lazarfeld's early studies of the index of political predisposition and of cross pressures are familiar to everyone. In this type of analysis, group influence is typically shown by comparing members and nonmembers within brackets of other variables which are known to be correlated. Thus, in a recent study we have found that the Democratic preference of labor union members remains about constant regardless of their educational or income status; whereas the Republican preference of nonunion members increases as their educational and income levels rise. Factors associated with being a union member appear to be a more important consideration in the voting decisions of these people than educational or economic status.

Comparative analysis does not differ essentially from cross sectional analysis. The comparative study of communities would presumably be designed in such a way that the communities to be compared differed in one of the major variables to be studied; for example, strength of group standards. The influences of group standards might be inferred from comparing the characteristics of the members of the contrasting communities. This is simply a variation of the basic cross sectional design. Unhappily, comparative studies are sometimes based on selections of units of observation which are chosen neither randomly nor according to any systematic design. Selections which are determined by considerations of availability or convenience may be economical but they are often very inefficient in terms of research design.

As everyone knows, it is easy to demonstrate correlation in cross sectional studies but difficult to establish causation. It is often possible, through careful study planning, to build up a strong weight of inference, but the possibility of unmeasured influences always remains. The experimental method is not ordinarily practical for the study of large populations and the nearest approach we have to it is the study of change resulting from the natural flow of social events. It may be possible, for example, to find situations where we can study the consequences on individual attitudes and actions of changes in group membership. We know from some of our recent industrial studies at the Survey Research Center that when workers are promoted to the status of foremen or shop stewards of their unions and then moved back again later to their rank and file positions, their attitudes toward the company and union change quite remarkably to suit the position in which they find themselves.

Similarly, we should expect that if community influence is important, people who move into a community atmosphere different from the one they have left should adapt to their new situation. The paradigm of this type of change is found perhaps in the movement from the metropolitan centers to the suburban communities. It is of interest that when we examined the 1952 votes of new suburbanites, people who had moved to the suburbs, the only point at which we found evidence of conversion to a Republican vote was among the high status professional, college-educated people. Those of lower status were no more or less likely to vote Democratic than similar people in the metropolitan centers. One may surmise that these high status people on coming to the suburbs identified themselves with the strongly Republican high status people they found there and tended to conform to their group standards. Lower status people, integrating at a different level of society, where the political outlook may not have been very different from their own, were less likely to respond to the political standards of a social stratum with which they did not directly identify themselves.

It may also be possible to demonstrate the effect of community influence if we can find situations in which community standards have changed. If a community or group changes its position on important issues, we should expect the strongly identified members to change their positions with it. For the past eight years we have been studying the attitudes regarding foreign policy held by people who identify with either of the two major political parties. In 1948 Republicans and Democrats were not appreciably different in their answers to our questions. This was at the time of the bipartisan foreign policy. In 1951 and 1952 during the Korean War Republicans moved sharply toward the isolationist end of our scales. In 1954, after two years of the Eisenhower administration, they were back almost precisely at the same level as the Democrats. While our data are not very substantial, they appear to demonstrate changes in the foreign policy attitudes of the Republican rank and file, reflecting changes in the Republican party line as enunciated by the party leadership.

It is clear that studies of change must almost necessarily be studies in depth. We know that public attitudes can change very quickly in response to world events, but changes associated with community or group membership of the kind we are discussing here are not likely to occur so rapidly. In order to follow these changes we must have recordings through time. The indicated instrument for the study of individual change is of course the panel survey. Repeated interviews with the same respondents provide data of unsurpassed detail and sensitivity. It must be remarked, however, that there are serious technical problems implicit in the panel method and that the less complex method of successive samples is adequate to answer many questions regarding the nature and location of change.

CONCLUSION

I have not attempted in these remarks about community identification to enumerate specific research projects which might be undertaken. Individual researchers will undoubtedly pursue those lines of investigation which happen to interest them. It does occur to me, however, that certain types of community situations appear to offer promising research possibilities. Communities where high identification and cohesiveness have been objectively demonstrated, for example, are obviously attractive locations for the study of community influences. Communities which are absorbing new members provide the opportunity for the study of the development of community identification and the inculcation of community standards. Communities which have serious internal schisms, such as currently exist in certain Southern cities, present dramatic demonstrations of the workings of community forces. Specific critical episodes in the life of a community, such as a flood, epidemic, or riot, may also provide particularly favorable circumstances for the observation of community phenomena.

How community identification influences behavior is only one aspect of the larger question of how the individual citizen uses his various group attachments to help solve the highly complex problem of living in our modern society. There is little doubt that group attachments give structure and order alternatives in the life-space of group members. The students of small groups have made impressive headway in their analysis of the dynamics of groups in laboratories and other specialized situations. Those of us who are more interested in the larger social aggregates have not been equally aggressive in our analysis of the psychological implications of membership in communities and other large population groups.

SCOTT GREER

Individual Participation in Mass Society

THE PARTICIPATION of the individual in his community is of importance on two grounds. Theoretically, an understanding of such behavior aids in the clarification and extension of our picture of modern society as a system. And, from a normative point of view, the nature and degree of such participation sets the limits and indicates the possibilities of social control in a nonhierarchical society. The dissolution of traditional orders, reflected in our fluid class structure and the uncertain basis for legitimacy, presents a major problem for modern society. Further, if we assume that the solvents destroying these older forms of order emanate from the process of rational transformation and increase in scale in the society, we may be confident that the problems experienced in America and the West are potentially universal problems.

The general ideology identifying the problem and indicating its solution is for Westerners some variation of the democratic dogma. We assume that for the hierarchical order of the past we may substitute an order based on individual option, control through the consent of the governed. In making such normative decisions, however, we are also making certain empirical assumptions about the nature of modern society. We assume the existence, at some level, of subcommittees, in which the individual has interest, influence, and concerning which he has some realistic information. Such subcommittees are the necessary condition for individual participation in the vast totality of society (though they are not sufficient conditions), and whoever says "democracy" is, in effect, positing such groups.

However, the western societies in which modern democratic political systems were first devised have changed radically since their democratic birth. America, approximately five per cent urban at the time of the Revolution, is today over sixty per cent urban and this predominantly urban, centralized society differs radically from the nation assumed by the framers of the democratic constitutions. While the rural population and the smaller cities still have their importance, the social structure of the large urban complex is crucial for the study of social participation and democratic process in contemporary society. It is upon individual participation in very large cities that this paper is focused.

Many current interpretations of the large city sharply contradict the empirical assumptions implied in the democratic dogma. The analyses of Louis Wirth[1] and Georg Simmel[2] emphasize these aspects of the city: (*a*) its heterogeneity (*b*) its impersonality (*c*) its anonymity and (*d*) the consequent social fragmentation of the individuals who make up the urban world. Such views are congruent with the long-run trends envisaged by Durkheim,[3] Tonnies,[4] Park,[6] and others—trends from a simple homogeneous society possessing an automatic *consensus universalis* and resulting solidarity, towards a complex, heterogeneous society, in which order results from functional interdependence of differentiated groups, and solidarity within groups leads to dynamic relations between them. In this view (there are important differences between these theorists, but in major respects they are similar) the primary-group structure of society is in a process of rapid dissolution. Kinship groups, neighborhood groups, the church, and the local community are losing their importance. Their strength in controlling individual behavior is shifted to formal, secondary groups, which organize work, religion and politics. Even play is controlled by the large commercial organization.

From such a position, the theorist who wishes to emphasize the viability of democratic structure and process must, like MacIver,[7] accept the formal organization as the effective subcommunity—one which is capable of performing the function of organizing individuals in meaningful wholes which may then participate in the control of the larger society. The "Associational Society" is seen as the alternative to the hierarchical society of the past, based upon primary communities and hereditary strata.

These formulations concerning urban social structure are largely the result of keen observation and analysis, rather than large scale empirical studies. Their influence is largely due to two facts: (*a*) they are based upon observations available at random in any large city, and (*b*) they fill, neatly, a gap in the theoretical system of sociology. However, in the past decade, and even more in the last few years, a substantial body of work has been accumulated dealing with the specific area of participation in the urban community. It is possible, on the basis of this work, to sketch a tentative description of the modes of participation which occur among urbanites—a snapshot of the organizational topography of the modern city. Such a description serves as a test of earlier assumptions and the basis for new interpretation.

THE DISENCHANTMENT OF THE CITY: EMPIRICAL RESEARCH

The studies to be summarized are focused upon participation in formal organizations—Kommarovsky,[8]—the local area as community—Janowitz,[9] —the urban neighborhood—Foley,[10]—and these together with other areas of participation—Axelrod,[11] Bell,[12, 13] Greer.[14, 15] The urban complexes included are: New York (Kommarovsky), Chicago (Janowitz), Los Angeles (Greer), San Francisco (Bell), Detroit (Axelrod) and Rochester (Foley). The net is thus spread wide, and the results are remarkably consistent—so much so that the discussion of findings will emphasize common trends, rather than variations. The following loci of participation will be discussed: kinship, the neighborhood, the local area, formal organizations, friends, work associates, and the mass media.

Some Empirical Findings. A) Kinship. One of the most striking results of this research is the extreme importance of kin relations for the urban residents. The results, in Detroit, Los Angeles, and San Francisco, all indicate the same fact: kin relations, as measured by visiting patterns, are the most important social relations for all types of urban populations. Half of the urbanites visit their kin at least once a week, and large majorities visit them at least once a month. Even the extended family is important; one-third of the Los Angeles sample visited uncles, cousins, and the like at least monthly. The conjugal family is of basic importance; the urbanite, in any local area, is apt to spend most of his evenings in the bosom of his family; this is true even in Hollywood, and extremely so in the suburbs.

B) The neighborhood. There is much more differentiation here—the range is from a substantial number of people who are intense neighbors to a substantial number who hardly neighbor at all. The degree of neighboring varies by local area, and within the city there is a wide range, but the average urban resident has some informal neighboring relationships.

C) The local area. Much like their neighboring behavior, urban residents indicate wide variation in their degree of "local community" identification and participation. Janowitz found a majority of his Chicago samples to be identified with their local area as their "true home," and in Los Angeles this was true of some areas, but varied considerably between areas.

D) Formal organizations. Although a majority of urban residents belong to churches, a minority which varies around forty per cent attend as frequently as once a month. Aside from church participation, most urban individuals belong to one organization or none. Low socio-economic rank individuals, and middle-rank individuals, usually belong to one organization at most, and it is usually work-connected for men, child- and church-connected for women. Only in the upper socio-economic levels is the "joiner" to be found with any frequency. When attendance at organizations is studied, some twenty per cent of the memberships are usually "paper" memberships.

E) Friendship. Informal participation in friendship relations, with individual friends or friendship circles, is an extremely frequent occurrence. Friendship, outside any organizational context, is a near-universal in the city. The urbanite is seldom isolated from this type of primary group.

F) Work associates as friends. Here one of the important hypotheses of urban theory is in question. As the primary community and neighborhood decline, friendship was expected to be more closely related to work organization. However, studies by Axelrod, Bell, and Greer all indicate that work associates are a minor proportion of the individual's primary relations when he is away from the job. Only in the upper socio-economic levels (where friendship is frequently instrumental for economic ends) is there a change. Work relations are usually insulated from free primary-group participation of the urban-dweller.

G) Mass entertainment. Cultural participation in organized entertainment is relatively unimportant for urban adults. Most of the Los Angeles samples attended fewer than three events a month. One-third attended no event, one-third one or two, and a few attended as many as ten or more. Most attendance was at movies, but the real importance of the mass entertainment media was in the home—television and radio are extremely important, but it is in the context of family participation.

In summary, the urbanite's individual "path" through social structure crosses these six areas of possible involvement and participation. According to one theory of urban society, his involvement should be increasingly intense with respect to formal organizations, work associates as friends, and mass entertainment; it should be correspondingly weak with respect to kin, neighbors, the local community, and primary groups other than these. The studies cited indicate no such clear-cut development. Instead, the usual individual's involvement in formal organizations and work-based friendship is weak; the mass media are most important in a family context; participation with kin and friendship circles is powerful, and with neighbors and the local community's groups it varies immensely by area.

The picture that emerges is of a society in which the conjugal family is extremely powerful among all types of population. This small, primary group structure is the basic area of involvement; at the other pole is work, a massive absorber of time, but an activity which is rarely related to the family through "outside" friendship with on-the-job associates. Instead, the family-friendship group is relatively free-floating, within the world of large scale secondary associations. The family is usually identified, although weakly, with the local community; it "neighbors," but strictly "within bounds." By and large, the conjugal family group keeps itself to itself; outside is the world—formal organizations, work, and the communities.

Such a picture is remarkably similar to that which Oeser and Hammond [16] present, from their studies in Melbourne, Australia. Melbourne, like the American cities studied, is a mushrooming metropolitan complex in a highly urbanized society. Its people are largely "middle rank" economically, neither poor nor wealthy. Its social order centers around the single family dwelling unit, the conjugal family, selected kinfolk, the job, and the mass media— the latter largely consumed in the home. Neither in Melbourne nor in American cities do we find much participation, by most people, in formal organizations or the community. The family retires to its domain, to work in the garden, listen to radio or television, care for children, and read.

A Typology of Urban Populations. Such findings as these are important in two respects: first, in their sharp departures from what would be considered the conventional picture of metropolitan life, and, second, in their consistency. The agreement between the various American studies, and between these and the Australian study, leads us to suspect that such participation patterns are a result of powerful trends in modern Western society. In explaining the average, and variations from it, it is useful to base a description upon social trends.

The Shevky-Bell typology of urban subpopulations [17,18] is one such method of describing and accounting for the varieties of urban areas. Based upon Colin Clark's studies of economic history,[19] and on analysis of the long-term changes in the nature of production, the organization of work, and the composition of the total society, the typology posits three dimensions along which urban subpopulations vary. These are: social rank (economic and occupational status), segregation (the proportion of segregated ethnic populations in a community), and urbanization. The latter refers to variations in life-styles; it ranges from the family-centered, home-centered life at the low-urbanization pole to an opposite pole where one finds many single individuals and couples without children. In this kind of subarea, among the highly urbanized populations, many women work outside the home, most people live in multiple dwelling units, and the market is of great importance as a center of cultural life.

Studies have indicated that the urbanizations of an area is closely associated with the importance of the local area as a "social fact," as a community. And this, in turn, is associated with political participation.

The results of the Los Angeles study of four census-tract populations at middle social rank, without segregated populations, but varying from very highly-urban to very low-urban areas, were summarized as follows:

> In general, our findings indicate a growing importance of the local area as a social fact, as we go from the highly urbanized areas . . . to the low-urban areas. Neighboring, organizational location in the area, the residences of the members of organizations in the area, the location and composition of church congregations, all vary with urbanization and increase as urbanization decreases. Readership of the local community press also increases, as does the ability to name local leaders and intention to remain in the area indefinitely.
>
> Thus the studies of the small community, with its local organizational structure and stratification system, may apply in the low-urban areas; they are not likely to fit in the highly-urban area. We may think of the urbanization dimension as having, at the low pole, communities much like those studied by W. Lloyd Warner, August Hollingshead, and others. At the highly urbanized pole, we encounter the big city population of the stereotype, organized not in community terms, but in terms of the corporation, politics, the mass media, and the popular culture. But predominantly, the highly urban populations associate in small, informal groups, with friends and kinfolk.[15]

A comparison was made between the political attitudes and behavior of the very highly-urbanized populaton and the very low-urban population studied in Los Angeles. The latter were more involved in their local community (they could name more local leaders), had a more consistent voting record, were more certain of the social class position of their "community" (middle-class) and of their political preferences. This data is reinforced by that of Janowitz, who found that, among his Chicago sample:

> Family cohesion and primary group contacts seemed more relevant for predisposing an individual toward acceptance of the community's controlling institutions and associations.[9]

Janowitz took community newspaper readership and identification with the local community as indexes of community participation.

Regardless of the respondents' political affiliations, relative confidence in the effectiveness and honesty of local politics—projective measures of personal political competence—tended to be associated with high community newspaper readership.[9]

We may summarize the findings in this manner: (*a*) urban subpopulations may be arranged in a meaningful typology, based upon their place in arrays derived from indexes of social rank, segregation, and urbanization. (*b*) As the type of area varies, participation patterns vary. As urbanization declines, there is an increase in neighboring and participation in the local community in all its forms. (*c*) This participation is associated with more political involvement and a higher degree of political competence.

The picture of participation in the metropolis must be qualified in these ways: the highly-urbanized populations are atypical—they are an extreme of a continuum. Their behavior deviates from the stereotype of the atomistic man in their great involvement in the family and their intensive participation in primary groups. However, the majority of the population in a great urban complex does not lie in the highly-urbanized segments; instead, it is of middle to low urbanization, and middle social rank. At the extremely low-urban pole, the local area becomes a definite community—it is a social fact, as well as a geographical fact.

The galaxy of local residential areas which make up a great city may be seen as differing in their level of living (social rank) and their style of living (urbanization). At each level of social rank there are vast differences between areas of high and low urbanization. In general, the highly urban areas lie within the central city, and the low-urban areas lie towards the suburbs. One may keep in mind the image of the urban apartment house districts, on the one hand, and the tract developments and suburbs on the other. As one moves towards the latter, community participation in the local area increases, and political behavior in general changes.

However, even as few urban subareas approach the anonymity and fragmentation of the stereotype, fewer still approach the kind of subcommunity envisaged in the democratic ideology. Although more respondents can name local leaders in the suburbs than in the highly-urbanized areas, less than forty per cent can do so anywhere. And the percentage who cannot even name one city-wide leader is considerable. With this qualification in mind, the differences between the polar extremes are sharp and suggestive. What is the meaning of this great variation in "normal life style"—what accounts for it, and what are its consequences?

COMMUNITY—AND MODERN URBAN SOCIETY

The word *community* is an ambiguous one, with many theoretical meanings and varying empirical referents. Two core meanings, however, stand out in the theoretical and empirical uses of the term. In one, community connotes certain modes of relationship, in which the individual shares values, is understood and identifies with the aggregate. In the other meaning community indicates a spatially-defined social unit having functional significance, reflecting the interdependence of individuals and groups. In the first sense, the modern metropolis is not a community; in the second, it must be by definition.

Rather than choose one meaning, it is preferable to indicate the empirical interrelation of the two aspects. For it is likely that, when we refer to community, we have in the back of our mind the picture of the *primary community*—preliterate society, feudal holding, or peasant village. Such communities fulfilled both definitions: they were extremely significant functionally, providing all or most of the conditions for individual and group life, and they had a high degree of consensus and communion. Such is manifestly not the case with the urban community today, and the reasons lie deep in the nature of modern society.

The chief difference between societies based upon primary communities and urban societies is one of scale—modern urban society is the result of a vast increase in scale. Wilson and Wilson [20] have studied this process in Central Africa, tracing its nature and its effects upon three small village cultures. They noted the autonomy of the societies at the early stage—each small group had its own means of subsistence and order, and each was independent of the other. The process of increase in scale was one of increasing commitments to widespread social groups and dwindling dependence upon immediate associates. The wealthy Central African farmer, for example, became free of local economic coercion by the village head man at the same time he became dependent upon the international ground-nuts market. Thus, if one conceives of social organization as a network of mutually-sustaining activities, based upon necessary functions, one may say that the radius of this network was short in the primary community of village society; with the increase of scale, there is a lengthening of these radii of functional interdependence.

Such extension of interdependence is not necessarily the result of rational undertaking, nor are the results all functional. However, once such interdependence exists, the human need for predictability (and the demand for predictability in ongoing organized groups) tends to result in a flow of communication and a mutual ordering of behavior. To paraphrase Freud, "Where interdependence is, there shall organization be."

The process may be traced in the development of modern industry— Florence.[21] The need for a predictable source of supplies results in "vertical integration"; the need for a predictable market results in monopoly, oligopoly, and cartels; the need for predictable work-flow results in bureaucracy, and indirectly in some form of labor organization. The organization of one function acts as a catalyst producing further organization; thus industrial cartels produce national labor unions, and unions in turn force the further integration of management groups.

Returning now to the concept of the primary community, we note that in such communities the radii of many functional interdependencies were short, coinciding with the same aggregate of persons. The result was, for the individual, a complete dependence upon this community leaving him few choices; for the community, it was autonomy from outside groups. There was a coincidence of many organizational networks, based upon functional interdependence for various social products in the same small aggregate. The result was an extreme density of interaction. When such density of interaction occurs, a secondary function results: the social process. This may be defined as communication as an end in itself; it is identical with many meanings of *communion,* and it is the basis for that aspect of association which we call the primary group.

Interdependence based upon the need for the various social products (protection, economic production and consumption, etc.) and upon the need for the social process, or communion, thus creates an extremely strong social group coterminous with the spatially-defined collective. Such a group satisfies both the meanings of community advanced earlier: it is both a mode of relationships and a spatially-defined social unit having functional significance. In such a society the village is, to a large degree, one primary group. (For a more extended presentation of this theory, see Greer.[22])

The process of increase in scale, however, results in both the lengthening of the radii of interdependence (spatially and socially) and the disjunction of the different radii, representing the organizations fulfilling different functions. Not only is the small local area no longer autonomous—the boundaries of the organizations upon which it is dependent no longer coincide. Work, government, education, religion—each is a congeries of organizations which include parts of the local area's population in their various spans, while this area is thrown with many others into various society-wide networks.

In this sense of the word, America has never been to any large degree a society based upon primary community for Western society was already large in scale and rapidly expanding when America became a colony; the very nature of colonialism insured dependence upon the imperial and international markets. There are, however, degrees and it is likely that, until the twentieth century, community existed in a widespread fashion in open-country neighborhoods, villages, and the country town. Such community, less complete than in the peasant village to be sure, was infinitely stronger than that to be found in any part of the modern metropolis. Scattered data from the novels celebrating the "revolt from the village," the criticisms by intellectuals like Thorstein Veblen, and studies of contemporary backwoods settlements in the Hispanola country and the southern Appalachians indicate that spatial isolation produced a marked degree of community.

Such community disappears under urban conditions; it has no hold over the individual, for its functions are preempted by large specialized organizations in the interest of rational control, while the individual is highly mobile and is isolated in the local area only when he chooses to be. As the functional bases for intense interaction disappear, communion goes with them.

As this occurs, the small conjugal family becomes increasingly important for the individual and, indirectly, for the total society. The reason is partly one of default; as the primary community leaves the spatially defined group, the conjugal family remains and is today probably the strongest basis for communion available to most people in the large city. At the same time, in a society of increasing scale, the family is relatively free from community norms (where there is little interaction there can be neither surveillance nor sanctions), and great individuation of family patterns is possible. With the surplus of freedom, of leisure, and of money, the individual can choose between family and nonfamily living—and the family can choose between community-oriented and noncommunity local areas to live in.

Thus the variations in urbanization, and in local community participation, found in the various studies cited can be understood as part of the large-scale process which (*a*) destroys the primary community, (*b*) releases its individual components for duty in large, segmental organizations, and (*c*) releases much time, expenditure, and behavior from community-enforced norms. The large scale society is, in this sense, one of emerging freedoms.

IMPLICATIONS FOR POLITICAL CONTROL

The results of this brief excursus may now be compared with the empirical assumptions underlying democratic political structures. Much of that ideal pattern relies upon the belief in stable subcommunities, viable wholes through which the individual may clarify in social discourse and affect through social action the objects of his grievances and desires. Such a group requires sufficient communication and involvement to result in the ordering of individual behavior. It must then be important to a large part of its constituency. Our ideal example from the past is the New England township, and its image still has an overweening importance in our thinking. It is something of an archetype.

The local area today, however, particularly in the metropolis, no longer represents such a community. Instead of a primary community it is necessarily what Janowitz calls a "community of limited liability." The individual's investment is always small, and if he "loses" he can cut his losses by getting out—the community cannot hold him. Even among the most community-oriented, "small town" areas, those at the low-urbanization pole within the city, there is great variation in the importance of the area to the individual. The local merchants have more of a stake than the home-owning residents with children, and these are more invested than the couple without children who rent an apartment. However, even the most deeply involved can withdraw from the local community, and satisfy all needs elsewhere—and the withdrawal need not be physical.

The reasons may be restated: by community in the double sense we mean a spatially defined aggregate which is a powerful social group. Such groups exist only where there is functional interdependence (as the local community in the suburbs is most functional for the merchants, least so for the childless couple who rent). Only where such functional interdependence occurs is participation strong: constraint is, in this sense, the key to community.

If this is true, then it follows that primary communities are not possible in modern society save in a very few areas—in such survivals as the backwoods communities noted earlier, and in such institutional aggregates as the prison, the monastery, and the army. However, aside from such atypical collectives, there are other groups in which the individual must interact continuously and for a large share of his waking life. One such is the work organization.

The functional interdependence, the flow of communication, and the consequent ordering of behavior at the place of work bulk large in the individual's life. Some theorists, of whom Mayo [23] is the best known, imply that a primary community of work is therefore possible. Certainly economic production, a share in the surplus, and status in the general society are basic functional supports of such primary communities as the peasant village. However in a most cursory inspection of modern industry, several factors appear which make such a strong work community very unlikely. These include freedom of labor, the conflicting functions of the work organization, and their results in the labor union on one hand and the hierarchical organization of industry on the other.

Free labor, which is functional for the total economic system, allows the individual to leave a given work group and join another. His needs may be served as well or better—and likewise the functional demands of industry; however, his relations with others in the group are conditioned by this freedom. Even work is a commitment of limited liability.

Equally important is the hierarchical organization of work in our society. The "scalar principle" is undoubtedly necessary in large organized groups; still the net effect is that the most important social group outside the family is ordered in a way which contradicts the assumptions of democratic process. Further, the common interest of workers and management is so channeled, through the unstable division of the product into profits and wages, as to create a well-structured division of interest as well. This schism between the leaders of work and their followers drastically reduces the common ground of values, and the unions have arisen in response.

Finally, the division of labor at present is so great as to weaken the common conscience of the different levels of workmen. Durkheim postulated a solidarity, a group *élan,* based upon teamwork; however, to the routine worker his job is frequently merely the payment of a pound of flesh (Oeser and Hammond).[24] A large proportion of most work organizations is made up of routine workers, and their lack of control over their work, their competition with management for economic rewards, their organized voice, the union, and their ability to leave the job, all represent limiting conditions. It is difficult to see how strong communities could arise within such market-oriented organizations.

Thus the major institutional order of work is unable to supply the basis for primary community; the local area is functionally weak; the kinship system is important chiefly at the level of the small conjugal family. The remaining possible structure for individual participation is the formal voluntary organization. A brief review of the findings cited earlier, however, indicates that such organizations are relatively unimportant "at the grass roots." They are arenas for intensive participation to only a small minority of their members, and many individuals have no formal organizational membership at all.

One possible exception is the labor union. Here is an organization whose functional importance is great indeed for its members. Unlike industry, it is an organization based upon the assumptions of the democratic ideology: participation in decision-making is quite easy. Finally, it is an organizational type which is extremely widespread—it is probably the most important single kind of formal organization outside the churches. What of union participation?

Many studies indicate that the average attendance of members at a local union's routine meetings is extremely low—from less than one per cent to perhaps 20 per cent.[25,27] Most of those who attend are the same group, over and over, and these, together with the paid professional staff, have undue influence upon the organization. For the average member, on the other hand, the union is almost an aspect of government. He pays his dues, and, as in the national elections, frequently does not vote. His leaders, with the best will in the world, far overreach their responsibility—for there is nobody else to take responsibility. Most often the leaders "run the locals" (with some restraint from the small cadres of actives) and the members act as a "plebiscitary body" in Herberg's phrase.[26] Far from constituting a "real community" for the workers, the union is simply another service organization. It can mobilize the members to strike, but not to participate in the organization's routine functioning where the basic grounds for strikes are considered and argued out.

In summary, it is apparent that in a society with a democratic political structure and ideology democratic processes are relatively rare. Shared decision-making, control through consent, is most common in the conjugal family and friendship groups, but it is hardly transmitted through them to larger entities. The other areas where individual participation is possible, local community and formal organization, engage only a minority in more than token participation, and the organizations of work—most important of all in many respects—are structurally unfit for democratic processes. The following picture of participation in urban society results.

There is a plethora of formal organizations, labor unions, business and professional groups, churches and church-related groups, parent-teacher's associations, and the like. They exert pressure and they influence the political party—another formal organization. However, the leadership in such organizations is largely professionalized and bureaucratized, and such leaders become, in effect, oligarchs. At the same time the members participate in an erratic manner, and frequently "stay away in droves" from the meetings. The organization is a holding company for the members' interests; they exercise an occasional veto right in the plebiscites.

The local area is either not a community in any sense, as in the highly urban areas of the city, or it is a community "of limited liability"; communication and participation are apt to be segmental here as in any formal organization that is extraterritorial. And many are utterly uninvolved, even in the strongest "communities."

Formal government is highly bureaucratized and, aside from votes in national elections and (very occasionally) in local elections, the individual participates very little. Most party "clubs" are made up of professionals, semiprofessionals, and a handful of "actives."

The organization of work is nondemocratic in its nature, and the individual's participation is largely a matter of conforming to directions and decisions made far above him in the hierarchy. This is of great importance, for with the rise of professional leadership in all formal organizations—from labor unions to churches, Boy Scouts, and even recreation in general—the most intense participation in all groups is apt to be that of the official, for whom the organization is his *job* in a job hierarchy.

Thus interpreting the participation of the average individual in democratic society is a somewhat bizarre experience: by and large he does not participate. Since this is true, it is difficult to make a case for the widespread importance of the democratic processes for most people, except in the home and friendship circle. The Democracy we inhabit is, instead, largely a democracy of substantive freedoms, or what Fromm [28] calls "freedom from." Produced by the struggles between various professionally directed interest groups, largely quite undemocratic in their control processes, freedom of choice for the individual is something of a by-product. It exists, perhaps, through the balance of "countervailing forces."

This freedom is, however, a considerable area of the average person's "life space." It is manifest in the urbanite's ability to choose his marital and family status, his local area and degree of community participation—his life style. He may privatize his nonworking world, and turn inward to his single family dwelling unit and his conjugal family (which he does); he may refuse to participate in many activities and yield only a token participation in others (and he does).

Though his commitments to the job and the family are constant and have a priority in time and energy, he exercises freedom of choice—in the market, the large sphere which Riesman [29] calls consumership. He also has a freedom in the symbol spheres which has never been widespread before in any society—the variety of media and of messages is overwhelming. (There are approximately 1,000 hours of television available each week to the Los Angeleno.) His relative wealth, literacy, and privacy allow an exploration of meaning never possible before. In his homelife he experiments with leisure —the hobby industries, the do-it-yourself industries, the flood of specialized publications and programs bear testimony to the increasing use the urbanite makes of this choice. He is part of the *nouveaux riche* of leisure.

His rise is a measure of the leveling of the hierarchical orders; their remnants remain in the relatively higher rates of participation and leadership for the "upper ranks" in most of the formal organizations. Most people, however, are the equivalents and descendants of the illiterates of a hundred years ago. They have neither the vested interest nor the tradition of responsible participation—and they have a great freedom from forced participation in work. They exercise it in fashioning the typical life-patterns adumbrated, in avoiding organizations, politely giving lip-service to the neighbors and local leaders, avoiding work associates off the job, orienting themselves towards evening, week ends, and vacations, which they spend *en famille* looking at television, gossiping and eating with friends and kin, and cultivating the garden.

The bureaucratic leadership and the plebiscitary membership, the community of limited liability, and the privatized citizen are not images many of us hold of a proper democratic society. Perhaps it cannot last—perhaps power is accumulating too rapidly and in too few centers. On the other hand, the picture is less frightening than that of the atomistic man adrift in mass society, *anomic* and destructive. Furthermore, the picture of participation in the primary community is a rather strenuous one. Perhaps a revision downwards, toward effective "limited community" participation, and effective "plebiscites" might result in an adequate check upon the formal leadership groups—enough to represent a modest achievement of democratic participation and control through consent.

FLOYD HUNTER
Studying Associations and Organization Structures

$\mathbf{M}$ Y OWN feeling for a baseline of social research leads me to select first the community level and then I turn my efforts toward trying to understand the interrelationships between individuals and groups at the society level, engaged in activities within complex organizations—policy groups, civic organizations and corporate structures. I would differentiate my work from class structure analysis. There is a reality, I feel, in the study of formal and informal organizations that one does not find in research that is *completely* class oriented. However, the use of hierarchical concepts drawn from class analysis may fit into the study of organizational groupings and be useful.

Neither do I believe that the institutional frame of reference is completely adequate for a study of community action processes. A word on these ideas is in order, perhaps, before we move to a discussion of organizational research per se. As the discussion proceeds I also shall use the concepts of action, power, and social change to illustrate my meanings.

Institutions (if we mean the broad social institution of economics, religion, education, the family, politics, welfare, and the like) are society-wide in scope, and furthermore they are products, in some measure, of analytical constructs on the part of sociologists and other social scientists who have given us a convenient term (as also in the case of class analysis) to designate broad-scale human groupings. In life and in reality all of the so-called institutions are interwoven, almost inextricably, into a total scheme of action we call society, but the associations in society make the whole operate.

The associations in American life and formal organizations rooted in law and custom can be physically located, examined, and researched. Institutions, as such, cannot be. We can talk about institutions but we cannot find them when we look for them. We can find factories, church buildings, homes, school houses, and a host of organizations devoted to keeping these manifestations of institutions alive.

Operationally, no specific community group can attack a problem of insufficient income by approaching the "economic institution," but almost every day working men and women bind themselves together into specific unions to demand specific amounts of money from specific corporations and busi-

343

ness houses. Working men know where to look for what they want, and social researchers might take a lesson from them. We may look for the *places* at which things are happening if we want to do action research. Research at the job point of industry and commerce will be much more productive than research related to the generalized notion of economic institutions. And so on, for the other so-called institutions. Action must be examined in terms of specifics rather than by the use of generalities.

If we pose the question of social change and action in relation to making changes possible, the facts of life dictate to us that men organize themselves formally and informally into associations for effecting specific purposes. To get things done on a community basis, men organize themselves into associations that are characterized by power gradations. Because this can be observed to be true, it would seem that an analysis of power relationships might give us something in trying to come to an understanding of community dynamics.

During the past few years I and other members of the Institute for Research in Social Science at the University of North Carolina have been engaged in several studies of "power structures" in communities. To date we have explored the possibilities of this type of research in seven communities ranging in population size from a few hundred to a half million. Six of these communities are located in the South, and one, a community of 40,000 in New England. Two of the studies have been published to date. Another study with which I have been concerned over the past three years deals with interrelationships between community leaders and some of the major cities of the country, and we shall speak briefly of this latter study after touching upon the specific community studies.

If one begins with the premise that communities are basic locations of action—concerted action in relation to major social enterprises—then obviously some one group or series of groups are involved. If power be simply defined as the ability of men to move other men to move goods and services or to stop such movement, then the problem of power delineation can be attacked. Any community, even the smallest, is the locus of thousands upon thousands of individual actions in any one day. Some actions are obviously more important than others in relation to the community as a whole. In like manner, some of the actors in moving goods and services are relatively more important than others in relation to the community as a whole. In like manner, some of the actors in moving goods and services are relatively more important in specific situations than others. Some men and women are instrumental in furnishing a sense of direction for concerted effort. They are policy makers—decision makers—and they hold special positions in the community's scheme of things. These are then people to look for in sighting the direction of action.

We find that such concepts as status, role, position, and prestige, that have been widely used in stratification studies have been useful in researching limited groups contained in a community as a whole. But if we stopped at merely defining and describing the structures that one may observe in a community, and in the terms indicated, we would not have a complete action picture. We must know how various groups function in relation to each other. The word function is important here and is related to the process of research widely known these days as "structural-functional analysis." The approach merely means that we isolate and identify groups that are engaged in doing something and we relate the action of the group to a greater social whole. A series of interviews with members of various groups that have been related to each other in getting something done reveals "functional" relationships between the groups.

An over-all function of group combinations may well be that of maintaining class dominance within the total community structure (certainly there is a latent function involved), but most men that we have interviewed within the past four or five years have had more short-range goals in mind. Most of them have been interested, first of all, in bettering their positions within bureaucratic structures, within their own "crowds," or within an informal but real pyramid of power.

Within the communities we have studied on a power basis, there appears to be various pyramids of power—business, labor, civic associations, church groupings, political organizations—that relate rather specifically to each other in matters of policy and direction of community ventures. The structures of such pyramids of power can be identified and described easily enough. Within the community context there are many activities, year by year, in which most of these groupings are functionally related. If one asks for issues or projects that confront any community at a given time, the officers and leaders within the associational groupings mentioned, can tell the researcher rather quickly the nature of these larger ventures. And more importantly still, they can indicate who is "behind all the movement." Research carried on during a specific project, and reconstruction research carried on in relation to projects recently completed, gives one a dynamic picture of community movement. Projects, for example that require large bond issues, manifold man hours of labor, and intricate meshing of individual talents and organizational work are liable to reveal a great deal about how things get done in any individual community. An investigation of such projects may also reveal that there is a relatively stable policy-making group related to the larger projects and issues that may act as a capstone in an informal pyramid of power relations within the community, *i.e.,* it is possible to find certain uniformities of behavior on the part of specific individuals who act in such a way as to direct the activities of others, and the whole pattern of action can be described as a power structure.

Informal "clearances," formal conference procedures, methods of "putting pressure on key people," and means of "carrying the story to the public" (or not carrying it) can all be found if one digs at trying to find out "how things get done." This is, I believe, a partial answer to what we mean when we say that we wish to study "structural dynamics," "interaction patterns," and "systems of communication." Analyzing the processes of project formulation, authority delegation, and final execution—both within formal organization limits and without—reveals community structural dynamics.

In the process of study of power structures, it becomes apparent that certain community groupings are considered more potent than others. Economic associations, individual industrial groupings, and business groups in general seem to "carry a lot of weight" in the decision-making process and in finally getting things done. This will come as no surprise to anyone, but the fact can be demonstrated empirically. The role of certain civic organizations, well-intentioned as they may be, or church groupings in some communities, or those who are considered the socially elite, and many other organizational groupings may be functional to the whole in getting things done in a power way, but they do not wield the influence of the economic powers. These are organizational status positions that must be recognized in action analyses.

The man sitting at the job point of power as the head of a large corporate enterprise has much influence regardless of the size of the community studied thus far, and if we are looking for spots to study in the future, it may well be that a closer look at the network of business-community relationships in politics, education, mass communications, and religion would be a good place to begin. These are the points that are all functionally related to one another in the structures of communities.

While communities and groups within communities may be instruments of social change, communities standing alone cannot solve some of the problems that face them. In relation to the larger issues, those, for example, related to such items as segregation, fiscal policy, welfare policy (including housing, health measures, and the like), the community often finds itself helpless to cope with the bigness of the problems presented.

One learns rather quickly, in community work on the level of community organization, that certain problems transcend community abilities and that communities are a part of the greater whole of American society. The community may be a good starting place for discussion and various approaches at solving problems, but sooner or later with some of the larger problems we must link ourselves up with state and national groups to solve our local difficulties.

Many may not like the idea of forswearing complete local autonomy, but in relation to some of the problems that face us we need clearing houses located at national and state levels to help us. Housing is a classical example of a problem that, communities acting alone, community by community, have not solved. We will continue to fuss about this issue, perhaps for sometime to come, but in North Carolina (specifically) we are finding that we need federal aid if we are going to really do a wholesale job in relation to housing. There are many who oppose "going to Washington" and the opposition is momentarily in the ascendency. The opposition is not, however, solving our problem. They are advising that we forget about it and that is hard to do. People still need houses in North Carolina.

Communities are functional parts of the American societal system. There are organizational links, ties between individuals, conference groups, propaganda groups, pressure groups, and many other types of gearing that makes us a nation that produces food, clothing, shelter, recreation, and a host of services for our whole people. If we wish to research problems in the area of intercommunity relationships, we may pose a few questions that might guide such research.

What are the links between various communities? Who are some of the key persons in the linking process? Are trade associations as vital as they are said to be in the literature about them? Does America have sixty families who are as potent as George Lundberg said they were? Does steel dominate the price picture? Who in steel decides on price? Is NAM more potent really than the other lobby groups? How is the community function of Detroit, making cars, related to the community function of Chicago, packing meat? Do the auto makers have any kind of relationship with the meat packers—personal or otherwise? Do corporate managers represent "a new breed of cats" in relation to public policy? How do all of these questions relate to the individual community?

These are researchable questions. There are many more. There are national groups that are concerned with these questions. There are some communication links between these associational groups and community groups. And in a very real sense national groups and community groups are extentions of and complementary to each other. The larger national associations and corporations are structural parts of communities operating at a level where change within them presages and reflects social change because many of them are society-wide in scope. Communities have a responsibility of making known to the larger organizations in society their particular needs and desires, but here one often finds breaks in communication. We need to know why such breaks exist.

We need more empirical study conducted upon a societal level—national level—to fit the community concept into some perspective and to see what role individual communities and groups within communities play in the societal scheme of affairs.

A beginning of such study may flow from some of the facts picked up in community power structure researches. In these pieces of research one finds that certain individuals in specific communities tend to operate on a national level. Key community individuals have a knowledge of other national figures. Corporate executives know other corporate executives in distant cities. They talk with each other about business affairs and about matters of national policy. Some of the national policies discussed related to key issues within community life.

I have had the opportunity in the course of making the national study of power, of visiting some of the major cities in the nation and talking with persons within these cities who are called, by many, "community leaders," and in some instances, "national leaders." This talking with leaders had as one of its research tasks the problem of determining whether or not there is communication between top community leaders, city by city, on matters of "national policy in the making." What has been done begins to give some clues and cues to more intensive research in specifiable areas.

"What part do communities play in development of national policy?" is a valid research question. By merely asking the question, one is compelled to work out research means, however rough, to get it answered. In the process of getting some answers from selected personnel in some of the larger cities, it becomes apparent that there are regional groupings of leaders concerned with specific issues, there are large-scale national associations concerned with specific issues, there is a status and prestige hierarchy, informal in nature, operative at the national level. It is further apparent that there is a network of relationships rooted in communities that extends across the nation and the network concerns itself with the development and extension of national policy.

Specific Background for the Study of Associations. The materials to be given here as theoretical assumptions of a study of associations were drawn together primarily for the larger study of national policy making and power structures. The larger study began with a study of 106 national associations selected from a universe of 1093 such organizations. A summary of results of this segment of research will be given after a brief review of some facts about associations and after we have set down the general set of hypotheses that guided the larger study.

Associations grow up around the interests of men. When individuals and groups want to get something done, almost anything in our society, they form an association to accomplish their ends. In the process they may involve various institutional groupings, church bodies, units of government, or business establishments, but the relatively fluid structure of an association is the effective means employed, time and again, to accomplish limited or long-range objectives. Sometimes such associations are fostered by institutional groups, and the specific association becomes an integral part and instrument of one or more institutional bodies.

The extent to which our citizenry is organized along associational lines is suggested, in summary, by Robin Williams: [1]

> According to their own reports, the major fraternal orders in the United States claim a total membership of about 20,000,000 persons.[2]

As of the late 1930's, there were over 1,500 chapters of national college fraternities and 600 sorority chapters.[3] The distinctive "service clubs" (Rotary, Kiwanis, Lions, Civitans, Optimists, etc.) cover the nation, with some unit in practically every urban center.

Among special women's organizations, the National Federation of Women's Clubs includes 14,000 member organizations claiming 3 million individual members.

There are giant veteran's organizations—the American Legion, Veterans of Foreign Wars, the American Veterans Committee.

In rural areas, there are about 11,000 agricultural co-operatives with well over 3 million members; the American Farm Bureau (about 1½ million members) has state bureaus in 47 states;[4] the National Grange lists approximately 800,000 dues-paying members; the 4H clubs enrolled in 1935 about 2 million youth.

As of 1945, there were 123 national organizations devoted in whole or in part to work on problems of interracial and intercultural relations.[5]

As long ago as 1940, the CIO was composed of 42 national and international unions and organizing committees, with 225 state, county and local union councils and 419 local industrial unions.

There are 1,500 national trade associations, 4,000 chambers of commerce, 70,000 labor unions—and 100,000 women's organizations.[6] At the time of the AFL-CIO merger in 1955 it was estimated that more than 40,000,000 persons belonged to unions.

And so it goes. These, note, are in addition to the elaborate formal organizations represented by business enterprises, foundations, and many other forms of private associations.

There is an enormous proliferation of formally organized special interest associations of the most diverse kinds. Specialized associations have multiplied, whereas the parts played by traditionalized groupings based on proximity, diffuse common values, and direct and inclusive personal relations have all diminished.[7]

It has often been said that America is a nation of "joiners." The figures just cited would seem to bear out this statement, and if we look at some figures cited by Warner and Lunt in their study of "Yankee City," we may be further convinced of the joining propensity of community citizens.[8] These investigators were able to identify almost 900 associations in a city of approximately 17,000 people. More than 350 of these associations were relatively permanent (formal) and important associations. The groupings studied were composed of almost 13,000 memberships held by less than 7,000 individuals. The local community is strategic in associational organization.

Associations are common phenomena at national, regional, state, and county levels of social organization, but it is the local community level at which the associations operate most effectively. The most powerful of the national and superstructured organizations are devoted to a "grass roots" approach to united effort, and thus, what happens in the way of movement and action at the local level of associations is crucial to the upper reaches of organizations. With the growing complex organization of industry and government on all levels of national organization, a host of service, educational and coordinating associations have developed with the local community as a focal point in the organization process.

Williams puts the matter of growing complexity in this way: [9]

> Local communities are highly open chains of interaction initiated at far removed centers of organization . . .
>
> Multiplication of specialized formal associations, especially of the centralized, hierarchical types, leads to the development of numerous mediating, co-ordinating, or tangential organizations:
>
> *Items:* co-ordinating committees, clearing house organizations; councils; multiplication of offices and associations charged with mediating and co-ordinating tasks; federated associations.
>
> Both the total social structure *and* the internal structures of large formal organizations are highly complex: in the latter, numerous specialized statuses are arranged in intricate systems within systems; in the former, varied groups, communities, and associations are interrelated in extended networks, chains and subsidiary social systems.

It was to chart relations between the interlocking system of national organizations and policy-makers at the national level of affairs that was of concern at the outset of my field study.

It seemed apparent to me that to use the national associations as primary indicators of national leadership would be a logical first step. It would be treating the notion as a commitment for study purposes.

Of the hypotheses that guided the national study, the first two of the five to follow were more directly related than the others to an analysis of associations and their place and role in the development of national policy. The hypotheses were:

1) The nation can be thought of as a community.

2) In the nation as in the community there is a power structure inside and outside of government—not synonymous with government or any other formal organization—influencing policy development. The national power structure is not a single pyramid of influence and authority but rather a kind of informal executive committee of the many major influence groups. It represents different geographic sections, different segments of the economy, and different organized groups. While dis-

agreements may arise on specific issues, the common aspirations of the larger corporate interests bring about a working unity.

3) Principal cities, containing concentrations of major industries, are anchor points of power and furnish a large proportion of the active personnel. The national power structure is held together, city by city, mainly by a network of informal association.

4) Because of its unique authority, government is of special concern to the rest of the power structure, which acts through government and upon government in relation to specific policies.

5) Being diffuse and informal in character, a large portion of the total power structure is not seen in operation.

With these hypotheses in mind, we may now turn to a summary of findings related to national organizations.

II. FIELD STUDY

Over a period of several years as a commitment organization worker, I have kept a tally of national organizations considered to be influential. Out of an estimated 10,000 national organizations in the United States, something over 1,000, I was informed during a work period with the Office of Civilian Defense during World War II, could within a matter of hours communicate any message of importance to every citizen of the country. Some of the organizations listed by various governmental organizations are obviously more important than others in relation to the influence they wield.

Having determined to use national associations to lead me to a nucleus of policy-and-decision-makers, my problem was to weed out those organizations that might waste my time in naming and identifying national leaders. My first step was that of arbitrarily eliminating a great mass of organization names from my list of 1,093. I felt confident that one could ask help of the top influential organizations of the nation, as I had previously asked help of influential community organizations in local studies, to lead me to top power leaders in the country, whereas minor associations might be of little help.

With four other persons, whom I felt knew, at least in part, the national organization picture, my list was pared to 106. These organizations were then sent a questionnaire in which, among other items, the secretaries of single associations were asked to rate the list according to an individual estimate and in terms of power and a "top twenty" rank order. The results of this section of our poll was as follows:

First Twenty in Rank Order of 106 National Organizations According to Power and Influence in Affecting the Formulation of National Policy—A Self-Evaluation of All Organizations, 1953
Chamber of Commerce, USA
American Federation of Labor

American Legion
American Medical Association
Congress of Industrial Organizations
National Association of Manufacturers
American Farm Bureau Federation
National Council of Churches of Christ in the USA
National Education Association
National Grange
American Bankers Association
Veterans of Foreign Wars, USA
National Association for the Advancement of Colored People
National League of Women Voters
Council of State Governments
National Congress of Parents and Teachers
Federal Bar Association
U. S. Conference of Mayors
U. S. Junior Chamber of Commerce
Brotherhood of Railroad Trainmen

These associations and others listed in the poll represented a broad cross section of organized national life. The whole list of associations was drawn from listings of women's organizations; veterans, civic, minority, fraternal groups; professional, welfare, youth, education, religious, and business associations.

Other organizations presumed to have considerable influence, but less than the 20 listed, are the following: National Association of American Railroads, National Association of Real Estate Boards, National Better Business Bureau, Rotary International, Automobile Manufacturer's Association, Foreign Policy Association, American Petroleum Institute, and American Jewish Congress.

The organizations that did not rate in the top brackets of power prestige were mainly fraternal, civic, commercial, and professional in character.

The associations polled were asked to add the names of influential organizations that we might have overlooked, and to give us names of persons known to them who might be considered policy makers at the national level of affairs.

Several association names were added to our listing by this process, and these were also polled, but the latter polling did not basically change the ratings of the major associations as given above. The names of persons given provided a basic list of persons, 104, to whom a questionnaire was eventually addressed and with whom I had a sample of interviews designed to relate leaders to leaders and leaders to the development of public policy. Thirty associational secretaries, mostly in New York, Washington, and Chicago where more than half the national associations were located, were interviewed in the early stages of the study to underscore and complement the materials gathered by mailed questionnaire.

In the course of these interviews, and in later interviews with men considered to be top policy-makers in the nation, I was led to believe that many of the associations that are highly rated power-wise in open political circles are not indeed as powerful as deemed. Some of the smaller, less publicly known associations, committees, and fluid power cliques may operate more successfully in moving legislation, for example, than the large publicly known, and sometimes feared tocsins of public opinion. Depending on the matter under consideration and the situation, committee-board organizations like the Committee for Economic Development, the Industrial Relations Board, or the Advisory Committee for the Department of Commerce were extremely important but relatively small policy-making organizations. The latter organizations, along with a sprinkling of foreign policy associations and educational bodies, represent elite groupings of national leadership.

After concluding the more exhaustive study, I feel that the membership lists of the boards of the National Industrial Conference, the Committee for Economic Development, and the Advisory Committee for the Department of Commerce provide good starting points for anyone interested in a quick and partial run-down of national leadership. These boards are highly selective in recruiting members and represent a stable cross section of top business leadership. They are made up of persons who have access to each other and who have channels to persons in other power networks of civic, professional, political, and religious leaders.

A few generalizations and concrete examples drawn from the organizational and top leadership interviews may now be given. Following the examples, a tie-up summary of all the materials will be made.

It became apparent during the process of interviewing associational secretaries and lay leaders that there is a generalized pattern of action in the national organizations. In some degree each of them is dedicated to a "grass roots" approach to organization. Some of them go further down to the grass roots than others but a general reliance on "getting the organization's story across" to as many people as possible and particularly to associational members seems to be a general pattern. Each, of course, differs in some degree in their general scheme of organization. For example, the Investment Bankers Association reaches down only to top level men within local investment banking houses. The organization pyramids up to an executive committee on the national level through a series of operating committees appointed by the executive committee. Policy within the association is pretty well formulated, on a formal basis, by the central executive committee. Operating committees within the organization are advisory.

The Farm Bureau organization, on the other hand, attempts to organize

down to the individual farmer living within townships and counties. Policy
for the Association, on the formal level, is initiated at the township committee
level and is carried through to county, state, and finally to the national organization. Through a long series of meetings on the various levels policy
is finally formulated on the national level in annual meetings and is published for consideration and approval by all subunits. A corps of technical
organizers operating through regional jurisdictions is in the constant process
of educating the members of the Farm Bureau in relation to general policy.
Of all the associations visited, the Farm Bureau seemed to be the most
highly and efficiently organized. Some of the others apparently have a rather
tenuous relationship with their local affiliates.

Some of the top leaders are not too fond of "being educated," as we shall
presently see in an interview held with a man who first describes one phase
of organized activity in relation to a state problem. Many top leaders have
grave questions concerning the potency of organization activities and the
power status of front leadership in associated groups. Such top leaders felt
that personal contact in a quiet way was more effective than large-scale activities.

> Mr. Schwartz said that back a few years ago there was a lynching in
> Southern California and some of the top leaders in the state were asked
> to get together to see what could be done in relation to the situation.
> He said that five men were put on the commission, including himself,
> and out of thirty-five meetings of this group there were only two ab-
> sences from it and those were excusable. This commission met with a
> legislative committee in the state and put four propositions before them
> which were unanimously passed by the legislature and he feels that most
> things go along in that way no matter what the proposition may be and
> no matter what level the government upon which one may be interested
> in action. He was on a committee which was national in scope in 1919
> which was set up to counteract Bolshevism in the country. He feels
> that the people of the country should be educated concerning what the
> Constitution is all about.
>
> Yet, he feels that many of the associations are very competitive and
> they send out too much literature. In anticipation of my call upon him
> he had been saving in a file various materials that had been sent to
> him during the past three weeks prior to my visit. It was a sizable
> amount of literature. He feels that there is an essential weakness in the
> fact that there are so many organizations and associations trying to ed-
> ucate everybody along similar lines.

A West Coast leader, more interested in the individual approach to problems—particularly the approach of the individual company and executive—
speaks in this way:

Mr. Horner, discussing the development of national policy, says he feels that individual effort such as speechmaking and the writing of articles directed toward selected business groups are the most effective means of "getting stories across." He said, "One can be more forthright when you are talking to groups that have the same interests involved in any given matter as you have." He feels that the national associations are important and can come into play *after* decisions have been made.

At a luncheon at the California Club, a gathering place of influentials, Mr. Horner pointed out some of the people who represent top influence in the Los Angeles area. As in some of the other clubs, there seems to be two or three very large tables at which men, who have no definite appointments for lunch, eat and consort with their fellows. During the luncheon period Mr. Horner expanded on many of his ideas.

He said, in speaking of decision-making, that the corporate executive has an extreme number of choices to make each day. Matters of the quality of production, the volume of trade, the distribution of goods, the setting of prices, dealing with employees and human relation choices in general—all matters in which men are "associated" but as a single company unit. The price of labor is something that is constantly in the lap of top executives and the executive has to think in terms of the satisfactions of work and the general satisfactions of life of his employees. He feels that these things are within the new trend of executive management but are of private concern to each company.

He said that, on the civic side of company affairs, many choices of financing research work in the educational field come before the corporate manager—a fact that associates him with University groups. His own company carries on considerable basic research in California Tech and many corporations give grants to this school. Whenever a new product has to be researched and new methods of launching the product on the market are involved they often use the universities as a primary source. They are interested in getting a supply of qualified students who can come into industry. He said that he is also personally interested in liberal education for students because he feels that a university should be a place in which there is development of new truths. He feels that new truths should be developed even though they might put his company out of business.

In speaking of charitable enterprises engaged in by his corporation, he says that they have made a top rule in the company that officers of the corporation can only take on one thing at a time. They may belong to School Boards, Community Chest, Chamber of Commerce, or any other thing that interests them but they feel that they are better qualified to do this work if they take on only one such enterprise.

His executive vice-president is engaged in Boy Scout work in the Los

Angeles area and is a member of the National Board. Another fellow
that he mentioned is involved in the Red Cross. His own interest has
been the Community Chest organization. He feels that the Federal Social Security program has been a fraud. He believes that the Reserve
building activities of this operation in government is completely unsound
economically. He feels that corporation financed plans would be much
better than the Social Security program.

In one way or another all of the associations visited have lobbying or legislative pressure functions. The general technique of such operations seems
to boil down to having paid professional secretaries in Washington or in the
State capitals who approach legislators and legislative committees directly or
utilize the service of lay members of their associations or from communities
in general within states or in the nation at large.

The listing of powerful individuals on national executive committees and
boards of directors is a common practice and it would appear on cursory
observation that some of the men named on the executive committees of the
associations would be top power figures in their own right. Persons named on
this level of organization would not necessarily be "out front" on active
work for the association, but their names on a letterhead seem to carry meaning for the associational secretaries at least. An example of this type of operation would be this:

> It is rather generally agreed, among the informants interviewed of
> Mid-City, that General T. Sherman, of a large retail company, is one
> of the top local power leaders. His name appears on the literature of a
> federal trade association as a policy figure. Within the past two years,
> however, General Sherman has not been extremely active in national
> affairs as a front person but put forward Bill Williams as a working
> representative. Within the corporate organization General Sherman
> holds policy position as chairman of the board of the corporation. He
> has a president of the corporation who is a power figure within it. Bill
> Williams, before he went to Washington and became a national politi-
> cal figure, was considered to be the third ranking man within his cor-
> poration. I was assured that Bill Williams had been in pretty close con-
> tact with General Sherman in relation to the things that he did in Wash-
> ington.

There is some evidence to indicate that interaction between associations on
a formal level is not a very tight knit affair. Some attempts by the Farm
Bureau and the National Manufacturers Association have been made to coordinate national policy interests in Washington. The National Manufacturers Association has a unit in New York which is titled "The Association
of National Organizations."

The general tendency within the association seems to be to key activities around the specific interest of the trade association and a great deal of effort is made to educate members within the individual association rather than spending too much time in trying to bring along another group of associations. Leaders within the commercial and trade organization groupings seem to constitute a top echelon of power and there was consensus of opinion among the informants as to the top policy leaders.

Mr. McCurdy, a man from the Middle West, said that he knew most of the national figures through his connections with NAM. Others he knew from membership on Advisory Committee of the Secretary of Commerce and through his connection on the Board of Directors of a railroad company and the Blanton Trust Bank. He indicated that he was interested in the Chamber of Commerce of the United States and he felt that if one really wanted to get grass roots opinions this organization was the best one to go to. He said, "If you really want to know what people are thinking on any given issue, the Chamber of Commerce is closer to the people than such an organization as NAM. I know that Z. T. Jones would not agree with me on this because he is a great NAM champion. I think, though, that the NAM is pretty well tied up with the industrial people and represents the industrial point of view. In our company we are not only industrial but we have a great deal of retail trade and consequently we are interested also in the Chamber of Commerce."

In discussing conflict in developing national policy, Mr. McCurdy said, "You have to understand that industries are never together on any given policy in spite of the fact that many people think they are. They may get together on civic and welfare issues but on a matter like tariff, for example, they could never be together. If you went out to the chairman of the board of the Smith Watch Company they would be very much against lowering or doing away with tariffs. My own company would be neutral on this subject because we have always been competitive around the world on the products that we produce and we have never asked for any tariff on our products. One of the big auto men has created a lot of discussion on his stand in this matter but we remain neutral. The NAM never could take a stand on a top level policy board but within the NAM there may be a subcommittee that would be quite active on the matter and might even go to Washington to try to get something done in relation to tariff. They could not, however, commit the whole organization to one specific policy. The policy would have to be flexible to include the various interests of members of the organization."

The next, and last, concrete example to be given here, is related to the dynamic process of policy development as seen through the eyes of a man in a lower drawer position of top management of a large middlewestern commercial company.

Mr. Miller went over the list of national organizations with the writer and, as all other informants, selected out those national associations which he considered important in national affairs. When he came to the name "Federation of Commercial Associations" he said, "Now here is an interesting situation that you probably would not pick up unless you got ahold of a guy like me. Our store belongs to the local Commercial Association. We support the Association with a sizable annual contribution and we have a lot to say in relation to its policy.

"However, the activities of the local Association is not nearly so important to us as the National Federation of Commercial Associations. The National Federation is an organization which goes to bat for us in the State capital and in Washington. We have a gentleman's agreement with the local Association that 80 per cent of the contribution we make to them will be passed on to the National Federation. Thus the local Association is actually a 'front' for us.

"As a corporation we would not want to directly support a lobbying organization such as the National Federation represents. Mr. Watts, Mr. Scotty or myself might be on the board or on operating committees of the National Federation but we would be on there as lay persons and not as direct contributors to it. We just do not want to be in the position of lobbying as a corporation but we do want our interests protected by the National Federation."

Mr. Miller said at another point, "Joe Casey, president of the National Federation happens to be a neighbor of mine. I see him every once in a while in the evening and I think he is one of the smartest operators in the game. Joe is a fellow who works very closely with our company, that is, with the top officials, but this would not generally be known. If there is a bill up before the State legislature or before the national Congress, Joe would call on little fellows from Alton, Illinois; Paducah, Kentucky; or Crossroads, Nebraska, to go before Congressional committees or to get in touch with Congressmen. I think this is a rather general pattern of the various national associations. None of them want to have the legislators think that 'big business' is trying to dominate legislation. The 'grass roots approach' is the most satisfactory all the way around. Our interests are satisfied and so are the interests of the little fellow. One, two or three of the big outfits such as Fellers in Atlanta or ourselves will be placed on the program but the bulk of the representatives on any get-together will be little fellows from the smaller towns. It makes the little fellow feel good because they think they are coming into national prominence and as matter of fact I guess they do. Of course the fellow that has his finger on the pulse of this whole thing is Joe Casey."

III. SOME GENERALIZATIONS ON PROCESS

The fact that the men chosen for interview on a self-selected basis tended to be the managerial type of person raises a lot of questions about Lundberg's thesis of the sixty ruling families. Over and over again the men that I interviewed assured me that the managerial type of personnel that I have gathered in the two lists are the persons of top rate power and influence in the development of public policy in the nation. The old families in some instances may exercise power if they are active and are "doers." However, some of the old family members are considered to be wastrels by many of the men who have beat their way up from the bottom of the corporate hierarchies. While the incomes of these men, I am told, tend to be high, they are still salaried men and do not have personal moneys at their disposal to contribute huge sums in political campaigns and the like. Their power would seem to stem from the fact that they are "organization men," and by holding positions on various organizational groupings and in the top echelons of these organizations they are able to exercise considerable power and influence in the decision making processes. The list of organizations to which some of these men belong are impressive indeed and will be tabulated in a final report of this project.

A generalized process of the development of any particular public policy would appear to me to go somewhat in this wise. If the needs of a particular industry are such that public law or administrative policy of the government is damaging to the industry involved or if the industry cannot get what it wants it does several things. The top executive who shuttles back and forth across the country, as does some of his under staff, is in constant touch with other men in other industries and within the industry to which the individual belongs. There is a constant talking together at luncheons, private parties, at conferences, trade meetings, recreational outings, in the citadels of finance, and in other types of get-together in which a line is hammered out on what should be done in a given situation. Innumerable committees are gathered together to make studies of policy. A current case in point is that of the question of free trade versus high tariffs.

There has been much informal discussion of this matter since a few of the top industrial leaders came out in favor of free trade. The commercial men running large department stores tend to be in favor of free trade also. Large industries that have overseas plants favor free trade. On the other hand there are many persons in the business scale of things who do not favor free trade and consequently there was considerable controversy about this matter in the nation.

Clarence Randall of the Inland Steel Company in Chicago is a person who has been a spokesman for large industry over the past several years. President Eisenhower was asked by a group of businessmen to appoint him to a large national committee that has made a report (thought in some quarters to be too much of a compromise) on the question of free trade versus high tariffs. During the course of this study there were many informal discussions going on, there were meetings between individual members of various industries, and there were discussions within the formal national organizations related to the questions involved. Hearings were arranged before Congressional committees. In the final analysis Mr. Randall's committee came out with some policy pronouncements which, as suggested, represent a lot of compromise. Individual industries and business leaders can now choose the parts of the compromise that fit their own needs and any policies that are developed in the future will be guided to some extent by judgments created during this process of study and discussion.

National associations apparently have two or three functions that they perform during the process of policy development. First of all they act as coordinating devices for gathering and distributing information among their members. They hold conferences at which papers are given and men are able to exchange their ideas informally. Another type of association within an industrial grouping may be a purely technical one which gets up facts and which can be used by the conference type of organization. A third type of national organization within a single industry may be that of a pure lobby which puts pressure in Washington when things need to be done. In a concrete situation such as the getting of the tidelands oil for the individual states, the national associations, and the whole gamut of national leaders may not have been primarily interested in the process but there is a lot of back scratching in the whole activity. The large electric companies give a lot of moral aid and support to the oil people and, I am told, when their turn comes, as it seems now to be coming, the oil interests will support the electric people in their bid for taking over the building and operation of dam sites. The rubber industry also has been involved in the log rolling process so that when their turn came they too could purchase some of the government factories with the aid and assent of the industrial groupings.

While the whole process of public policy development sometimes seems to be obscure to the writer (because of its bigness and complexity), it becomes increasingly obvious, as persons are interviewed city to city, that the country may not be as big as we sometimes think it is. It is complex but it is not complex beyond the understanding of those who apparently know the ropes in relation to given policies. It can be generally comprehended and empirically so.

MORE GENERALIZATIONS

There is a general network of individuals who stand behind and sometimes aloof from the formal associations but who use the associations as foils

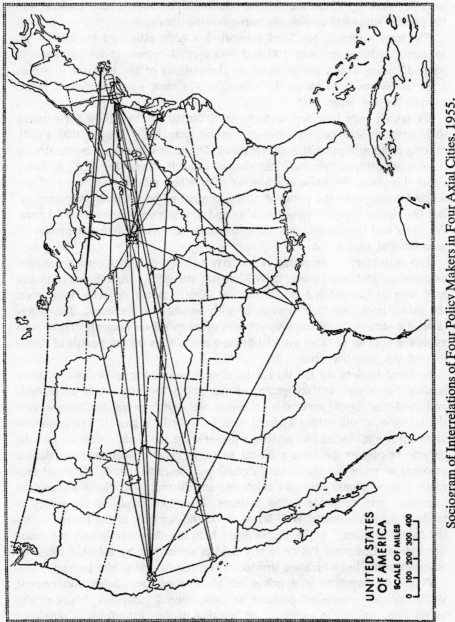

Sociogram of Interrelations of Four Policy Makers in Four Axial Cities, 1955.

in policy making. There are definite relationships between such leaders, and the present study has empirically borne out this thesis.

The total informal, top level network has been estimated by various informants as being between 100 and 300 men. I believe about 200 men in some 13 cities would easily constitute the nucleus of the network of which I speak. However, to be on the safe side, 471 men were selected as broad sample for the large study.

By taking only four top leaders—men turned up by utilizing (in part) their associational connections—it can be graphically shown that policy making relationships exist between them. The least common denominator of their relationship is "personal knowledge" of each other. (*See* Map, p. 361.) From this point, the point of knowing each other, relationships were of differing intensity—to the point of actual control of one person over another. But the story of specific policy making and development cannot be told here. We must end this discourse with a summary statement on the dynamics of associational interaction.

The customary assumption, as we have pointed out, that certain national associations and their lobbies at Washington are mighty strongholds of power may have to be modified. Some national leaders, not a majority, look upon the associations and their secretaries with hostility or contempt. The secretaries are seen as "paid employees," who often go off on tangents. Those who guide the policies of these associations are not always on the boards of directors of the member firms.

National leaders tell me they have a wide acquaintanceship among other leaders. Some men are recognized as top policy makers, others as second- and third-rate figures amenable to reason through informal discussions with the higher-ups, still others as front men for specific interests. The acquaintanceship is not confined to persons who serve on the same corporate boards, or who belong to the same political party, or who happen to have similar amounts of money in the bank. Friendships, committee work, club and recreation associations, customer relations, and financial problems all tend to intertwine into definable action patterns. It is too simple to say policy is made at the curbstone of Wall Street or on the doorsills of the bosses, or by the "sixty families," or by the struggle between the liberals and the reactionaries in Congress. Policy in any field is developed by a broad range of activities, not all of which are sinister or contrary to the public interest.

Policy development is a prime social function that defies confinement within formally organized political or associational groupings. Many of the associations utilize the technique of bringing in the "little fellow"—the corner druggist, the hardware dealer, or the small-town banker—to promote their interests before government officials or committees. The technique is effective when these individuals are backed by the big fellows; most politicians know who is behind the carefully coached witness on a particular matter. Any community organizer, community-chest director, or real-estate board executive uses similar methods. The choice of a person to present a case before any authoritative body is usually well thought out in advance. Deliberations are not published in the newspapers; the final choice may be. Behind the whole process, of course, are innumerable "clearances."

The national associations are, admittedly, excellent clearing houses. They are housed in the larger of the national cities but their affiliates are dotted across the map. Most often they represent an important community link to the world.

PETER H. ROSSI
Community Decision-Making

I. INTRODUCTION

Perhaps the most striking and hence obvious feature of contemporary communities is their ceaselessly changing nature. Within decades demographic shifts have transformed hamlets into towns, towns into cities, and cities into metropolises. Physical appearances also undergo transformations, often making painful experiences of our visits to the scenes of our childhood memories.

Less obvious, but equally important, are the social structural changes which accompany the growth or decline measured in population and building plant terms. On the institutional side innovation after innovation in the forms of local government have been designed to "catch up" with the problems presented by the increasing complexity of our predominantly urban life. To cite another example, in the last few decades our public school systems have increased tremendously in their coverage of our youth and in the same period have been transformed from one form to a variety of forms. Private associations, on the order of Community Chests, Chambers of Commerce, etc., have arisen to fill the needs of "community organization" brought on by the urban transformation.

Many of the changes which appear so dramatic are the end products of "ecological" processes. Individual citizens and private organizations in the course of working out their individual destinies make decisions which, when compounded in the mass, affect profoundly the physical and social structure of our communities. The market or location decisions of an industrial organization can bring relative prosperity or its opposite to the smaller community. On the level of the individual, migration decisions may depopulate an area or flood a labor market. And so on. Such changes in the "ecological" order, while purposive from the point of view of the individual or subsystem of the community, are nonpurposive from the point of view of the community as such. It goes without saying, however, that the net effect of such decisions may be considerable.

In contrast, some part of the community changes may be allocated to the self-conscious actions of individuals and organizations—actions directed at the transformation or maintenance of status quo of the community. It is to these actions that we must look for our understanding of much of the change in the formal social structure of the community, the local government, such "community organizations" as the Community Chest, the public school system, etc.

Our purpose in this paper is to review research on *community decisions* —choices among alternative lines of action directed at affecting community-wide institutions. We shall outline and evaluate the major approaches to empirical research on this topic, and present a few hypotheses concerning how such decisions are made.

Community Decisions: Definition and Location of a Problem. First of all, we must make clear what is to be meant in this paper by "community decisions." [1]

> A community decision is a choice among alternative modes of action whose goals are the change or maintenance of community-wide institutions or facilities, and which is made by an authoritative person or group within the community institutions.

We shall not be concerned whether the motives of the actors involved are personal profit, "power," or the general welfare of the community. If a decision undertaken by an authoritative group or person involves actions directed towards change or non-change within the community-as-such, this is what is meant by a community decision.

Note that this definition contains two specifications: To qualify as a community decision, a choice must be made by an authoritative person or group, *i.e.,* one which either by law or by custom has the legitimate and recognized right to make the decision in question. The second specification indicates that the decision must involve community-wide institutions on the order of local government, locally oriented private associations, and so on.

What sorts of decisions does this concept exclude? It excludes, first, the myriad decisions whose goals are not community oriented, *e.g.,* the market decisions of business organizations, migration decisions of individuals, etc. Secondly, decisions made by "outside" agencies or persons, *e.g.,* state and national government, are not covered. Finally, it excludes decisions made by persons who are not in authoritative positions.

The range of decisions included is considerable. On the broadest level, the citizen casting his vote in a local election is an authoritative decision-maker in his role as voter. A mayor acting in the capacity of his office makes community decisions of a wide variety. So do the members of the board of directors of community organizations such as the Community Chest.

Implicit in our concept of community decisions is the idea of "community issues," which may be defined as choices as to policy open to the authoritative decision-makers. Thus the issue before the voters in a local election are choices among slates of candidates, approval or disapproval of referenda, etc. The issues before a City Council may involve decisions within each of a wide variety of sets of alternatives, ranging from budget allocation for the whole municipality to the repair of a sidewalk in front of a particular citizen's house. Note that the issue defines the relevant decision-maker according to the rules laid down by law and customs.

Issues, of course, involve more persons and groups than just the decision-makers to which they are ultimately referred. Other members and groups within the community express preferences to each other and to the decision-makers, attempt to persuade or even coerce decision-makers, and so on. Each issue thus has its partisans, a category which may include—depending on the issue involved—almost the entire community or just one or two individuals. A *partisan* is some one person or group who is concerned to see that one or another alternative is chosen by a decision-maker.

The definitions offered are not as precise as might be desired optimally. It is not always easy to locate who is the decision-maker for a given issue, although there never is any problem post facto. Nor is it always clear whether an issue involves the community and its status or non-community matters. Our definitions are designed to make rough distinctions and their utility can be judged in the discussion which follows.

Our objective is to review and evaluate research on community decisions. How are such decisions made? How are issues settled? What factors have been found to be crucial in affecting the outcomes of issues? What general statements may be made about the decision-making process? What are the research designs employed and the problems which they seem best suited to study?

There are, of course, approaches to decision-making which we shall not consider here, either because they are not empirically oriented or because they are not concerned with decision-making on the community level.[2] For example, we shall not touch upon the attempts to construct mathematical models for rational decision-making. (32) Nor will we consider in detail most studies of the decision processes conducted in psychological laboratories. (10) We will confine the discussion to attempts to describe and generalize about the decision-making processes within local communities.

II. THREE APPROACHES TO THE STUDY OF COMMUNITY DECISIONS

The small number of empirical researches on community decisions display a variety of approaches and research methods. However, without doing too much violence to the significant differences among such studies, most empirical work on this topic can be classified as employing one or another of three basic research designs. In some studies, several approaches have been employed, although for our present purposes we will treat each approach separately.

One basic approach to the study of decision-making has been concerned with the characteristics of *decision-makers,* attempting to relate the social and personal differences among decision-makers to the kinds of decisions made. The research techniques employed have ranged from the analysis of detailed quasi-clinical case histories through the statistical analysis of official biographical notes.

A second approach has given central attention to the *partisans* of issues, seeking to find in their actions *vis-à-vis* the decision-makers, the "ultimate" determinants of the outcome of decisions. Studies which focus on "pressure groups," or propaganda, or which search for the "power structure," belong to this class of research designs.

A third approach employs *decisions* as its reference point, seeking to understand the choices of decision-makers as the outcome of relatively complex processes. Studies of decision-making in contrived groups within laboratory settings fall into this category as well as analyses of retrospective accounts of the decision-making process obtained from interviews with the decision-makers.

The remainder of this section will be devoted to taking up each approach in turn, presenting a few examples of each, abstracting the major substantive findings and evaluating each approach.

The Decision-Maker Approach. In outline form, the typical design of research in this category is constructed along the following lines: Decision-makers, usually of a particular type, *e.g.,* precinct captains, school board members, voters, etc., are located, certain of their characteristics noted, and compared with some sort of reference population. The technique furnishing the essential characteristics of the decision-makers may range from extensive life histories, as in the case of Salter's study of Philadelphia "bosses" (31)—to published official biographical notes—as in the case of Matthew's study (23) of national and state legislators. The characteristics studied may range from the relatively simple ones of age, occupation, education, to the more complex attitudinal data such as are supplied in detailed interviews.

From a consideration of the ways in which the decision-makers differ from the general population or from some other norm, inferences are made concerning the types of decisions which they are thereby disposed to make. Thus from the finding that the age of city councilmen is higher than that of the voters, the conclusion might be drawn that city councils tend to be conservative and resistant to change.

Several brief examples follow:

An early study by George S. Counts (9) showed that school board members throughout the nation are primarily recruited from among the business and professional occupations. Hence the essentially conservative and "business oriented" character of the public schools.

As part of a study of adolescent behavior in a small midwest community, Hollingshead (13) made a detailed study of the social class membership of the community's school board and top school officials. Finding that school board members and school officials were recruited entirely from among the upper strata of the community, he concluded that the "middle class" character of the school system stemmed at least in part from this pattern of recruitment.

W. Lloyd Warner's (38, 39) now classic study of "Yankee City" contains data showing that the higher the office held in the local government, the higher the social class of the office holder. The "class character" of the local political system is inferred from this pattern of office holding.

In a very recent study of attitudes toward political nonconformists, Stouffer (36) found that "community leaders" (mayors, heads of library boards, etc.) were more tolerant towards nonconformists than the general population of their communities. He suggests that those responsible for important decisions concerning civil liberties on the local level are more tolerant in their actions than would be the average citizen.

Garceau's (11) study of the compositions of Library Boards in a sample of American communities indicated that there was little relationship to be discerned between the composition of these boards and the excellence of the library's services. The members of Library Boards tended to be concentrated in the higher social and economic strata of their communities.

Practically every modern study of voting behavior has relied heavily on the analysis of the way in which classes and regional groups display different electoral choices. *See* Lipset *et al.* (21) for a resume of these studies.

The most strongly established finding of these studies of decision-makers concerns their differential recruitment. As a group, whether we are concerned with the electorate or with elected or appointed officials, decision-makers tend to be drawn disproportionately from the higher age, class, and ethnic groups. Furthermore the higher the authority level of the decision-maker, the more marked are the differences between decision-makers and ordinary citizens. In other words, the upper, as compared with the lower status groups, are somewhat more likely to participate in elections, and are much more likely to hold public or semi-public offices.[3]

However, most of the studies cited above go beyond the fact of differential recruitment to make inferences concerning how decision-making is affected by this pattern. This approach has been most successful when applied to mass voting behavior as a decision-making process where, for most national and local elections, clear divisions may be discerned in the electorate along class, ethnic, and regional lines.

When applied to decision-makers on higher levels, the inferences drawn from the differential recruitment pattern are somewhat shaky. For example, to demonstrate that a school board composed of business and professional men are bound to show a "class bias," it is necessary first to demonstrate that on the issues confronting a school board, the classes in the community hold different opinions. Is there, for example, a "class position" on educational policy? Or, on the alternative solutions to a community's traffic problems?

In other words, it is open to question whether for many issues, there are clear and consistent differences among class groups, ethnic groups, age levels, and so on, which could manifest themselves in different decisions dependent on what kind of decision-maker hold office. The substitution of sets of decision-makers of radically different background need not necessarily result in groups holding radically different positions on many issues.[4]

Secondly, there is an assumption of a close association between an individual's background and personal characteristics and the behavior which he will manifest in office.[5] While it is true that *in the general population,* class position correlates with opinion on a variety of issues (*See* Centers (7) and Bendix and Lipset (4)) these correlations are low enough to ensure a rather large number of deviants from the majority opinion on every class level. *It is precisely to these deviants on the upper occupational levels that the popular support of the lower strata of the community may be attracted.* Among elected decision-makers, at least, social background may be a very poor predictor of decisions made, particularly on class-related issues. In the other nonelected positions, *e.g.,* membership on Library boards, Community Chest, etc., some decision-makers may owe their appointments to the fact that they represent deviant views among the upper strata.

Thirdly, to look to social background and personal characteristics as the major explanation of a man's behavior in a decision-maker role, is to deny that a given individual may act differently when placed in different roles. It is noteworthy that this approach has been most successful when applied to the decision-making role of voter, which is the least demanding of all such roles under discussion. The higher level decision-maker roles with which we are mainly concerned here are ordinarily rather well-defined in both law and custom, by virtue of the concern with which the community has regarded them. Each role involves its incumbents in a set of structured relationships to other roles, and is accompanied by formally and informally defined criteria for its proper performance. Thus a local bank executive on a local school board is pressured to come to grips with the organizational problems of his school system in a way that he would never do as just a private citizen. His actions on the school board are at least in part determined by the demands of his role as school board member.[6] Especially when the role is professionalized—as in the case of school officials, public health officials, social workers, etc.,—and incumbents are specially trained to fill their positions, role expectations will probably be particularly important determinants of decisions. A school superintendent trained in a teachers' college will have been exposed to a very self-conscious view of educational policy and how a superintendent should behave in his role.

Finally, the decision-maker does not operate entirely within a "social vacuum." On many issues, particularly those which intimately affect the "interests" of significant persons or groups, he is bombarded with communications from partisans of one or another policy alternative. Attempts are made to persuade, influence, or coerce him to support particular policies. He is supplied with information, presented with arguments, offered rewards from the intangibles of "social" acceptance to the hard reality of money, and threatened with reprisals either to himself or to his organization. Undoubtedly, the actions of partisans play some part, over and above predisposition and role, in the outcome of many issues.

The evaluation given above of the decision-maker approach should not be taken as a denial that an individual's social and personal characteristics have any effect on the performance of a decision-maker role. Our criticisms are offered as a warning, that, beyond the voter level, such characteristics will not be related to decision-making in a simple and direct fashion, and that the assumption of differences among decision-makers corresponding to their social backgrounds must be tested empirically rather than asserted as fiat.[7]

The "Partisan Approach": Studies of Power and Influence. So dramatic have been the documented instances in which partisans have managed to affect the outcome of issues, that we can hardly overlook their actions as an important set of determinants of community decisions. The dramatic quality of these incidents stems in large part from their semilegitimate status in the light of our democratic values: on the one hand, we recognize the right of citizens to advocate and defend their individual interests as against the individual interests of others. On the other hand, we demand that the decision-maker should be *above* partisan views and should act in line with "the interests of the community," without, however, specifying how one might identify in any particular issue what they may be. *Hence when we examine the outcome of an issue, it is easier to see which individual interests have been served, than to judge whether the community interests as such have been upheld.*

The effects of partisan activity have been studied on many levels of decision-making. Recent research on voting has documented the existence of informal opinion leaders, persons of more than ordinary concern with politics, who affect the behavior of those voters with whom they may be in personal contact. On higher levels of decision-making, the concept of power has been used to describe how persons and organizations controlling significant amounts of wealth or solidarity employ their resources to affect the outcome of issues. Power and influence are both relational terms, concepts employed to describe relationships between persons and/or groups. When we say that a man is influential or powerful for some other persons, in the case of power, we imply a relationship in which individual A affects the behavior of individual B, because B wishes to avoid the sanctions which A would employ if B did not comply with his wishes. In the case of influence, B's behavior is affected in the absence of sanctions. Thus, although the process in each case by which A affects B is different, the general form of the relationship is the same, and hence researches on power and influence tend to follow the same basic designs. Indeed, so close is the relationship between power and influence that it is difficult empirically to distinguish between the two.

Roughly, there are three basic research designs which have been employed in the study of power and influence: First, we have studies of the "potentials" for power and influence, inventories of persons and organizations in a community who are in positions to influence or apply power to decision-makers. Secondly, we have studies of power or influence "reputations," researches on what community members consider the influence or power structures to be. Finally, there are researches on "actual" influence or power, studies of particular issues in which influence or power have played a part in the determination of the outcomes.

Power and Influence as Potential. Since social relationships are notoriously difficult to study directly, some researchers have centered their attention on producing inventories of those positions in the community which have the necessary attributes for the wielding of influence or power. In the case of power, these studies document who within a community controls significant amounts of economic resources. By virtue of their control over economic organizations—banks, industrial and commercial enterprises, public utilities, etc.—such persons are in a position to wield sanctions of an economic sort over decision-makers. In the case of influence studies, inventories of "leaders" are obtained, persons at the heads of various private associations or occupying important public offices. By virtue of their position, they can influence the opinions of their followers on a variety of issues.

A few examples of these researches follow:

> In his study of Middletown, Lynd (22) devotes a chapter to the X family showing how this family group either owns or controls a large

number of enterprises, and has representation in most of the other significant enterprises in the community.

Advising students how they may undertake surveys of communities, Robert K. Lamb (17) stresses obtaining a list of the banking and industrial officials, newspaper editors, owners of large blocks of real estate, etc. Such lists may be used to outline the power structure of the community.

The "community leaders" studied by Stouffer (36) in his research on attitudes towards political nonconformity were chosen in part because their positions made them the likely leaders of public opinion in their communities.

Mills and Ullmer (28) in a study of single and diversified industry cities, identify the "real" leaders of their communities as the industrial and mercantile elite within each community. See also Mills' latest work (27) where he describes the power structure of the United States.

Implicit in this approach is the assumption that the potential for power or influence will undoubtedly be employed. Business leaders, in fact, exercise their power to affect the decisions made by formal authorities. Furthermore, the potential for power is often regarded as equally effective regardless of the point at which it is applied—whether within the Community Chest or within the City Council—and results in decisions which are different from those which will occur in the absence of such power. Similarly, the potential for influence is often regarded as equally effective regardless of the topic involved—whether political opinions, attitudes towards mental disease, etc.—and when employed, results in a different distribution of opinion among the public than would have occurred in its absence.

The studies of power cited above also contain anecdotal examples of the exercise of power in specific situations. Mills and Ullmer (28) quote from an interview with a former mayor who stated that he had to "clear" even such matters as sidewalk repairs with the head of the largest industrial plant in his community.[8] Examples cited are generally ones in which economic powers have blocked or vetoed proposed changed in the community, *e.g.,* new legislation, "public improvements," the entry of new industry, etc.

Studies of Power or Influence Reputation: The Perceived Power or Influence Structure. With the development of the sociometric techniques,[9] it was almost inevitable that these devices be applied to the study of both power and influence in the local community. These techniques allow the researcher to literally chart the interrelationships within a group of people. Obviously, except for communities below a small minimum size, some modification of sociometry was necessary before this technique could be used in either the study of power or influence. In the case of power reputation studies, informants are asked whom they perceive to be powerful within the community. Persons receiving a large number of "votes" from informants are identified as constituting the "power structure." Similarly, in the case of "influence reputation" studies, informants are asked to designate whose opinion would influence them on a variety of topics.

Several examples of research along these lines follow:

Floyd Hunter (14) in his study of the power structure of "Regional City" asked a sample of community organization leaders to designate who were the "top" as "civic, governmental, business and status" leaders in the community. The persons receiving the highest numbers of "votes" were designated as comprising the power structure of the community.[10]

Robert K. Merton (24) asked a sample of "Revere" citizens to designate to whom they would look for advice on a variety of topics, *e.g.*, on educational problems, political matters, health problems, etc. Persons receiving more than a minimum number of designations were termed "influentials." Their characteristics were studied in direct interviews.

My associates and I (30) in a study of "Bay City," a small Massachusetts industrial city, asked members of the community's elite to choose the most important persons on a prepared list of some 25 names culled from among industrial, political, religious and civic leaders. Interviews were obtained from members of this group and an analysis made of the factors which lead them to be frequently chosen by their fellows.

Katz and Lazarsfeld (15) report on a study of women who were asked to designate persons whom they "could trust to let them know what was really going on." Designated persons were then interviewed in order to identify their characteristics as compared with the persons who designated them.

In a study of the public administrators in "Bay City," Freeman (30) obtained ratings from each public official of the "importance" for their operations of other officials and various groups in the city, *e.g.*, the City Council, Mayor, Chamber of Commerce, *etc.* Persons designated as "important" for an official were considered potential sources of influence upon him.

Note that the power or influence "structure" is defined in terms of the "reputations" accorded to individuals by a set of judges. While the "reputations" involved are probably deserved in the sense that these are persons who are *likely* to exercise power or influence, it is still open to question whether on a variety, let alone a majority, of issues, outcomes of issues are heavily affected by their actions.

For example, in the case of Hunter's study, the range of issues with which the power "structure" concerns itself is delimited by example. The instances cited in which members of the power "structure" undertook to provide the leadership for community projects cover a considerable ground. The implication is left that there are few areas of community life in which the power structure does not take a hand. Yet the total set of issues is unspecified and hence the impact of the power structure on the life of the community is hard to assess.

Similarly, Merton's study of influentials is also on a general plane. Influentials are persons who are regarded as potential sources of trusted advice by members of the community: we do not know how frequently, in fact, they are employed as sources. That this is a relevant issue to raise is demonstrated in Katz and Lazarsfeld (15) where it is shown that *the persons who actually influenced specific opinion changes are likely to be very different from persons designated as potential sources of influence.*[11]

The same question may be raised about the power "reputation" studies. It seems likely that they specify one of the important ways in which the outcomes of issues are settled, but we are not confident that this represents either the *typical* way for *every decision* or for *every decision-maker role.*

What have these studies established? First, it is clear that some individuals by virtue of their economic strength can and, on occasion, do exercise more than ordinary influence over decision-makers. Secondly, this control is especially effective over some rather than other decision-makers. Civic associations dependent on voluntary financial contributions seem particularly vulnerable.[12] Thirdly, informal opinion leaders exist on all levels of the community and on occasion affect the opinions of the mass of citizens. It can be shown, furthermore, that these opinion leaders do not entirely overlap with the official public and organizational leaders of the community. (*See especially* Stewart (35).)

Nevertheless, there remain to be answered a number of questions:

Granted that power is wielded and influence exists, as we must concede from the number of examples which these researches have collected, the question still remains as to the *proportion* of all decisions affected in this way. The method of *collecting examples* probably emphasizes the efficacy of the power or influence "structure," as compared, for example, with some of the researches cited later which focus on decisions rather than partisans. It seems obvious, furthermore, that for any urban community of any size, the number of decision-makers and the decisions made is so great that complete monitoring by the power "structure" is impossible, especially since the persons involved are usually engaged in other enterprises as well.

Secondly, assuming that some decisions are heavily affected by the power or influence structure of a community, it is relevant to ask what are the kinds of decisions involved? Lynd and Mills cite examples which suggest that the powers primarily attempt to exercise control over issues which directly affect their economic well-being and social status—public taxation, labor union organization, social club membership, etc. The "power" employed is primarily in the form of an attempted veto, used to block changes which might adversely affect their status and class position.[13] In contrast, Hunter emphasizes innovation as the characteristic concern of the power "structure" in Regional City. His "powers" are "leaders" in getting new "projects" under way, *e.g.,* deciding on a new plan for the community, building a municipal auditorium, getting new industry into town, etc. Furthermore, many of the projects apparently involve raising considerable sums of money through voluntary contributions, a large proportion to be supplied by themselves.[14] Parenthetically, it may be noted that it is hardly surprising that these persons pay such careful attention to the working out of the details of such community "projects," since it is their financial backing which pays for them.

In this connection, we may raise the question of whether all decision-makers are equally vulnerable to the actions of a power "structure"? Our own research in Massachusetts indicated that the decision-makers in the *voluntary civic associations* are particularly vulnerable to the power wielded by heavy contributors, but that the decision-makers within the local government are more sensitive to sanctions wielded by the leaders of the solidary groups.[15] This last point futher suggests that control over economic and financial resources do not exhaust bases for power. Leaders of solidary organizations—labor unions, business and professional associations, churches, etc.—also derive some degree of strength from their positions as organizational leaders, presumably based on their reputed ability to affect the opinions and behavior of their membership.

Finally, we may raise questions concerning what forms the exercise of power takes. We conceive of power as the wielding of sanctions over decision-makers. How are sanctions wielded? The powerful individuals in Regional City, for example, are primarily men of wealth in control of large industrial or financial enterprises. How do they use their positions? Is wealth used directly or converted into other sanctions, perhaps centering around status? More generally, what are the sanctions employed and what sanctions are effective for which decision-makers?

Studies of Decisions: The Process Approach. Up to this point, none of the researchers discussed has paid central attention to decisions as such except to illustrate the operations of power, influence or the background characteristics of decision-makers. Even the concept of decision itself has been used rather ambiguously in our treatment, copying in large part the use of the authors whose work we have reviewed.

The blame for the neglect of decisions as a major research focus must be placed to a large degree on the nature of the phenomenon itself. Most of the issues in which we are most interested ordinarily entail a settlement process in which complicated chains of choices are made by a large number of decision-makers. A description of the events involved, for example, in the approval of a municipal budget by a City Council would result in a large document, while more complicated issues would demand even more complicated descriptions.

Nor would our task be more manageable if we concentrated on the choices made by a decision-maker rather than on issues. The work of a mayor or city councilman involves a large number of choices of a great variety. Few of the decisions would be comparable in content and those which were, are likely to be relatively trivial, *e.g.,* a councilman's votes on public works maintenance orders.

For these reasons the study of decisions has ordinarily been carried out either within the controlled environment of the laboratory, or, in the field, on decisions which are relatively simple and hence comparable. Only a few studies have attempted to follow a particular issue from start to settlement.

The Controlled Observation Approach: Laboratory studies of decision-making have been at the heart of researchers in general psychology. Most of the work done in learning, perceptual discrimination, etc., might be viewed as studies of decision-making processes of a very elementary kind. Although basic to an eventual definitive theory of decision-making, the contributions of the general psychologist (10) have not been immediately useful.

More relevant has been the laboratory study of small groups at work in the cooperative solution of experimental tasks. Since much of the decision-making on the community level takes place within a group context, small legislative or semilegislative bodies—as *e.g.,* City Councils, Library Boards, Community Chest boards, etc.—as a study of the interaction processes which occur as people are brought together to solve given problems must to some extent illumine our understanding of the decision-making process in the "natural" setting.

The typical research design involves bringing together a small number of individuals, setting before them some simple task, and observing the interaction occurring between members of the group. The interaction is ordinarily classified according to some scheme of categories and analyzed quantitatively. In the large number of experiments which have been conducted in the last few years, tasks have been varied; group size effects have been systematically probed and the structure of the group manipulated through the use of role players and fixed communications patterns. (Strodtbeck, (37) Cartwright and Zander, (6) Hare, Borgatia and Bales (12).)

Examples of the more relevant researches follow:

Strodtbeck (37) is currently studying the decision-making processes of juries. Jurors are selected from official panels and are brought to a jury room to listen to recorded cases. The interaction among the jurors is analyzed to provide data on how different elements of cases affect verdicts; on how the jurors affect each other; and how the verdict is affected by the kinds of jurors involved. (Note how in one research design, the concerns of the previously discussed researchers might be met: Strodtbeck is studying how kinds of *jurors,* acting in different *interpersonal environments,* come to decisions on different *issues* (cases).)

The long series of studies conducted by R. Freed Bales (12) has shown that groups engaged in the solution of simple tasks go through typical phases of activity, alternating attacks on the task with behavior designed to weld the group together into a solidary unit. He finds that often two types of leaders emerge, an "instrumental leader" who contributes much to the solution of the task, and an "integrative leader" who helps keep the group interpersonal tension level down.

The Issue Career Approach. Outside of the laboratory, the study of decisions has been most successful when confined to mass observations of simple issues, as in mass voting behavior. Observations are made of large numbers of decision-makers each of whom has to make much the same choice among a small number of alternatives. A small group of researchers have attempted to follow the career of more complicated issues, observing the decisions made with respect to them by a large number of decision-makers acting in different capacities.

Typically, a population is isolated which has either made a decision of a particular kind or will shortly be faced with the necessity for doing so. The decision-makers are interviewed either concerning their past decisions or periodically as they come to a choice on an issue which faces them.

Vote decisions are particularly suited to this approach. The issues before each voter and the form of the decision are identical. Two of the most valuable studies of vote behavior (Lazarsfeld, Berelson and Gaudet (18) and Berelson, Lazarsfeld and McPhee (15)) studied the decisions made by samples of voters interviewed repeatedly during the presidential campaigns of 1940 and 1948. Voters who came to their choice or shifted their preferences during the period of the interviewing were asked to tell how they came to their decision. Using the same research design, my associates and I have studied vote decisions in two local elections, finding much the same patterns. (30)

Katz and Lazarsfeld (15) report a study of changes in marketing habits, fashions and political opinions. A sample of women were interviewed concerning the reasons for their shifts of preference and opinion, with particular emphasis on the roles of the mass media and interpersonal contacts.

Studies of more complicated issues have been relatively rare:

Perhaps the most elaborate study of the career of an issue is the description of how sites were selected in Chicago during 1949 and 1950 for new public housing. Meyerson and Banfield (25) (the former was Planning Director of the Chicago Housing Authority during the period under study) have provided a fascinating account of his way in which sites were finally selected, after much pulling and hauling among the Housing Authority, the City Council and Mayor, local neighborhood groups, etc. Basic data for the study came from documents of the various groups involved, and interviews with participants.

A number of the cases collected by the Inter-University Case Program bear on community decisions. (34). Presented as descriptive accounts, each case follows through a controversy from initial beginnings to final settlement.

In our own study (30) an attempt was made to account for the outcome of two local issues: the selection of a Superintendent of Schools by a local school board; and the approval of a municipal budget by a City Council. School board members and councilmen were intensively interviewed concerning their relationships to each other, their contact with persons outside the decision-making groups, and their reasons for their particular positions on the issues.

What of a general nature can be learned from these studies of the decision-making process? Concerning the findings of controlled observation studies, it is difficult to transfer easily their findings to the "natural" group situation. Yet several major conclusions do emerge: First of all, these studies highlight the effects of the internal organization on decision-making groups. In the course of pursuing a task, groups of individuals, who had hitherto no enduring relationship to each other, rapidly develop a social organization the nature of which affects the way in which they come to decisions and the sort of decisions made. Out of the necessity for cooperation, needs develop, the satisfaction of which becomes a pressing matter. Since in the "natural" world the decision-maker is always found embedded in an organizational context and under some necessity of working out mutually satisfactory relationships with the persons within that context, these studies highlight the importance of this set of factors. For example, a legislative body like a City Council or a school board or a Housing Authority develops its own social organization, with codes of behavior, sets of mutual obligations, etc. How this organization affects the outcome of decisions is documented heavily in Meyerson and Banfield. (25)

Secondly, there are many "natural" situations confronted by decision-makers which bear more than a superficial resemblance to the artificial situations studied in the laboratory. To the extent that we find such correspondences, generalizations may be more easily transferred from the one to the other context. For example, many experiments (*see especially* Asch (1)) concern the effects of group contexts on the interpretation of ambiguous stimuli. Many of the issues faced by a decision-maker lack clarity and definition, *e.g.*, the voter presented with a list of unknown candidates for equally unknown public offices. In the laboratory the subject accepts cues for interpretation offered by the group about him. In real life, the voter is influenced heavily by his family, friends, co-workers, a precinct captain, etc.

Of course, persons working in the area of decision-making need not wait for the small groups field to produce spontaneously the relevant researches. It seems profitable to expend ingenuity on contriving experimental work which can be directly transferred to our major problems. For example, it is conceivable that "experimental city councils" may be devised and studied.

At first glance, it would appear that field studies of decisions would yield the most valuable information concerning decision-making. And this is the case for studies of voting. The pioneer work done by Lazarsfeld and his associates, (5), (18) has increased enormously our understanding of voting behavior. These studies have documented the group basis of voting, contributed the notion of opinion leadership, and shown how the mass media's effects are channelled through opinion leaders to the persons whom they influenced.

The field studies of more complicated decisions, however, have not been very valuable. The very complexity and apparent uniqueness of the processes they have unveiled makes generalization going beyond the specific issues studied very hazardous. These studies provide fascinating reading (especially Meyerson and Banfield) (25), but because they are primarily single cases, it is hard to draw upon them for general knowledge. Only through a comparative approach, studies of large numbers of decisions on comparable issues, will be possible to go beyond the particular.[17] It is to be hoped that the Inter-University Case Program may eventually provide the comparative materials that are called for.

Surprisingly, little attention has been paid to the intrinsic features of the issues involved in the decisions studied. Laboratory studies of decision-making, of course, have been concerned in how the characteristics of the task set before the experimental animal affect the choices he may make. The decision-making models constructed by the mathematical economists also have been concerned with choices made among alternatives, each of which is considered in terms of its probable outcome. (10) But the consideration of how an issue, or even issues, are viewed by decision-makers, has not been given much attention in the studies of the decision-making process within the community context. The decision-maker is almost regarded as having no "internal" dynamics of his own but is "ruled by his group affiliations and interaction patterns."

III. SOME CONCLUSIONS AND QUESTIONS FOR FURTHER RESEARCH

Each of the approaches outlined in the previous section has contributed important substantive knowledge to out understanding of how community decisions are made. Yet it cannot be said that the definitive account of the decision-making process can be constructed now through the results of any one or a simple combination of studies.

The *decision-makers studies* have contributed an emphasis on what the decision-maker brings to his role in the way of general social background, attitudes and values. A person occupying an office retains the personality and attitudinal sets acquired during his life's experiences. Under some conditions, these factors affect the choices he makes among alternatives.

Studies of the decision process emphasize that the decision-maker is embedded in a web of social relationships. The voter acts not as an individual so much as the resultant of his group memberships. The higher level decision-maker's role is embedded in an organization, which has needs and demands of its own.

Finally, *the study of partisans* and their actions highlight the effects of persons standing outside the organizational context of the decision-maker. Under some conditions, partisans are able to affect the outcome of issues. Furthermore, we know that this ability accrues heavily to the upper strata of our communities.

There is a sense, however, in which these studies tend to contradict each other. For any particular decision, it cannot be equally true that the decision was determined by the decision-maker's background, the pressure put on him by the wealthier elements in his community, and the loyalties he might feel to his staff or coequals. Since each approach has been able to present convincing evidence of the importance of its findings for *some* decisions and for *some* decision-makers, the important question appears to be not, for example, whether there is a structure of power or whether the social background of a decision affects his choices, but *under what conditions does each type of explanation best fit the case?*

The three types of determinants (decision-maker qualities, partisan activities and organizational contexts) are best thought of as *latent* possibilities inherent in any issue. Latency implies only some probability of a determinant manifesting itself in any particular situation. Thus, not all issues engage the attention of the power "structure"; nor does the decision-maker's organization care about all his decisions, and so on. Hence it seems reasonable that the search for the understanding of any *particular* decision is not likely to be as fruitful as looking for tendencies within *classes* of decisions and *types* of decision-makers. It is only when we examine and compare a number of decisions that the tendencies characterizing different issues and decision-makers can be discerned.

In other words, *research on decision-making should be extensive rather than intensive, and comparative rather than case studies.* Three levels of comparisons should be made: Decision-makers of *different types,* operating within *different community and institutional settings,* should be compared as they come to the settlement of a *range of issues.* This approach implies a *sampling* of decision-makers, of issues and communities.

Our identification of these dimensions as the major points of comparison to be made, stems for the most part from the findings of the researches we have reviewed in this paper. Each has contributed knowledge about variations which should be taken into account in designing research. As a summary statement, these major findings and some of the questions they raise are recapitulated below:

Concerning Decision-Makers. It seems likely that the most important source of variation among decision-makers lies in their roles rather than in the personal qualities which they bring to their offices. The more of the decision-maker's total interests and activities is invested in the role itself, the more likely are role expectations to determine his decision-making behavior. Thus, at the one extreme, we would expect that the role of voter, being poorly defined and undemanding, would have little effect on the voter's choices; while at the other extreme, the professional social worker in charge of a community organization would be acting according to a well-defined conception of the best way he might fill the demands of his office.

At the higher level of decision-making, roles vary widely in three respects, each of which seems likely to affect the vulnerability of the decision-maker's role to both the demands of the would-be power wielder and those of his organization. First, the higher the prestige of the office, the more the decision-maker will be able to act independently. In this connection, we may note that Supreme Court Justices achieved the highest prestige rating of all the occupations studied by the National Opinion Research Center. (29) Secondly, decision-maker roles in organizations which have an independent financial base are less vulnerable than those in organizations dependent on support controlled by other persons or organizations. Thus, the vulnerability of the civic associations dependent on voluntary contributions, and the relatively greater independence of public officials whose organizations are supported by taxing powers. Finally, decision-makers may derive independence from their basis of tenure: tenurial officials might be expected to be more independent than elected officials who in turn may be more independent than those who are removable at will.

Concerning Variations in Communities. Unfortunately, it is not possible to make clear statements about the variations in decision-making processes which we might expect in diverse types of communities. The number of communities which have been studied is relatively small and their points of difference and comparability are not clearly discernable. Yet several differences seem pertinent.

At the one extreme, we have the one-industry towns and at the other, the economically diversified metropolis. It appears likely, as is suggested by Mills and Ullmer, (28) that the less diversified the economic base of the community, the more clustered is the potential for power. The political homogeneity of a community also seems to be a contributing factor. In one-party Regional City, (14) the power "structure" seems much more organized than in two-party Bay City, (30) where the political strength of the industrial workers acts as a check on the free exercise of power by the industrialists.

Other differences between communities suggest themselves: The cities studied have all been relatively self-contained. What would the decision-making process look like in the satellite suburb? What kind of power structure would arise in a community with no independent economic base and with a relatively homogeneous population?

Communities also vary in the extent to which their dynamics of growth and change raise issues which demand solution. A growing community faces a number of problems which the matured town has faced and solved to some extent in the past. At least part of the differences we have noted between Bay City—a stationary community—and Regional City—still in its stage of great growth—must be allocated to this factor. The issues in Bay City may be more trivial than those in Regional City, engaging the attention of but a few partisans.

Concerning Issues. None of the studies reviewed here have considered the full range of issues which come before a particular decision-maker. The closest to such consideration is in the studies of voting, but there are few studies of electoral behavior in local elections, primaries, etc. The issues which have been subjected to study have been on the more dramatic side, perhaps more properly labelled "controversies."

By and large, we can expect that most issues up for decision are settled without becoming controversies. The routine business of any office or legislative body consists mainly of noncontroversial issues. How are these settled? Is this the point at which we should look for the effects of the personal characteristics of the decision-maker?

What makes an issue into a controversy? Of course, the content of an issue makes a major contribution here: For example, few controversies will arise in a school board over appointments to the lowest levels of the teaching staff, but appointments on the administrative level are more likely to engage the attention of board members and partisans. In addition, some issues are *made* into controversies, often as channels for the expression of cleavages which cannot be expressed more directly. The recent controversies over fluoridation, for example, are most profitably viewed not as content controversies but as expressing the malaise of the older residents in communities experiencing rapid growth. Parenthetically, we may note that the ability to raise issues into controversies is an important source of power.

Our purpose in this review was to assess the present status of research in decision analysis and to raise what appear to us to be important questions concerning method and substance. Any such attempt must necessarily be critical: we hope our critical comments are mostly on the constructive side.

Notes

SNYDER: *A Decision-Making Approach* (pp. 3–38)

AUTHOR'S NOTE: Because this paper was not in any way revised for publication, the bibliographical references are three or more years old. The literature on various kinds and facets of decision-making analysis is already very extensive and is growing rapidly. The following more recent items represent only a small sample of relevant materials and are presented as a supplement to the writings cited in the text and end notes: James Bates, "A Model for the Science of Decision," *Philosophy of Science,* XXI (1954), 326–339; Anthony Downs, *An Economic Theory of Government Decision-Making in a Democracy,* Ph.D. Thesis, Department of Economics, Stanford University, 1957; Ward Edwards, "The Theory of Decision-Making," *Psychological Bulletin,* LI (1954), 380–417; Thrall, Coombs, and Davis, *Decision Processes* (New York, 1954); Harold Guetzkow and John Gyr, "An Analysis of Conflict in Decision-making Groups," *Human Relations,* VII (1954), 367–382; James March, "An Introduction to the Theory and Measurement of Influence," *American Political Science Review,* XLIX (1955), 431–451; Peter Rossi, "Community Decision-making," elsewhere in this volume; Harold Lasswell, "Current Studies of the Decision Process: Automation Versus Creativity," *Western Political Quarterly,* VIII (1955), 381–400; Editors of *Fortune, The Executive Life* (New York, 1956), ch. 10; Jacob Marschak, "Probability in the Social Sciences," in Lazarsfeld, *Mathematical Thinking in the Social Sciences* (Glencoe, 1954), pp. 166–216; James Buchanan, "Social Choice, Democracy, and Free Markets," *Journal of Political Economy,* LXII (1954), 114–123; J. Block and P. Petersen, "Some Personality Correlates of Confidence, Caution, and Speech in a Decision Situation," *Journal of Abnormal and Social Psychology,* LI (1955), 34–41; Nicholas Smith, *et al.,* "The Theory of Value and the Science of Decision," *Journal of the Operational Research Society of America,* I (1953), 103–113; Kurt Riezler, "Political Decisions in Modern Society," *Ethics,* LXV (supplement to January 1954 issue); Paul Diesing, "Noneconomic Decision-making," *Ethics,* LXVI (1955), 18–35; Donald Davidson and Patrick Suppes in collaboration with Sidney Siegel, *Decision-making—An Experimental Approach* (Stanford, 1957); Herbert Simon, "Rational Choice and the Structure of the Environments," *Psychological Review,* LXIII (1956), 129–138; Herbert Simon, "Some Strategic Considerations in the Construction of Social Science Models," in Lazarsfeld, ed., *Mathematical Thinking in the Social Sciences* (Glencoe, 1954), pp. 388–416; Herbert Simon, "Recent Advances in Organization Theory" in *Research Frontiers in Politics and Government* (Washington, D. C., 1955), pp. 23–45; Robert A. Dahl, "Hierarchy, Democracy, and Bargaining in Politics and Economics," *Research Frontiers in Politics and Government,* pp. 45–70; R. C. Snyder, "Game Theory and the Analysis of Political Behavior," *Research Frontiers in Politics and Government,* pp. 70–104; Donald Matthews, *Social Background of Political Decision-makers* (Doubleday Short Studies in Political Science, 1954); Walter Crockett, "Emergent Leadership in Small Decision-making Groups," *Journal of Abnormal and Social Psychology,* LI (1955), 378–383; J. C. Harsanyi, "Approaches to the Bargaining Problem Before and After the Theory of Games," *Econometrika,* XXIV (1956), 144–157; W. D. Oliver, "Rational Choice and Political Control," *Ethics,* LXVI (1956), 92–97; M. Flood, "Management Science Today and Tomorrow: Decision-making," *Management Science,* VI (1955), 167–170; J. Marschak, "Probability in the Social Sciences," in Lazarsfeld, ed., *Mathematical Thinking in the Social Sciences,* pp. 166–216; R. Cyert, "Observation of a Business Decision," *Journal of Business,* October, 1956; W. J. Harris, "Decision," *Military Review,* XXXVI (1956), 33; M. H. Jones, *Executive Decision-Making* (R. D. Irwin, 1957); Harold

ix

Lasswell, *The Decision Process*, Bureau of Government Research, College of Business and Public Administration; and Karl Deutsch, "Mass Communications and the Loss of Freedom in National Decision-making: a Possible Research Approach to Interstate Conflicts," *Journal of Conflict Resolution*, I (June, 1957), 200–211.

1. See, for example, David Easton, *The Political System* (1953), chapters 1–5 particularly; also Lasswell and Kaplan, *Power and Society* (1950). It might be useful for many political scientists to examine Marion Levy's *Structure of Society* (1952) on this point—chapter 10. Levy's "Some Basic Methodological Difficulties in the Social Sciences," *Philosophy of Science*, XVII (1950), 287–301, is also very useful.

2. Interestingly enough, there appears to be little clear understanding of what an "approach" consists of, or of how and why "approaches" differ. For example, the differences between an institutional and a behavioral approach may appear on the surface to be clear, but such is not the case.

3. I shall return to this point later on. Again, exceptions would be Dahl and Lindblom, *Politics, Economics, and Welfare* (1953), and Riesman, *The Lonely Crowd* (1950).

4. *Politics, Economics, and Welfare* (1953).

5. The reader can obtain a reliable introduction to the general nature of action analysis in Talcott Parson's essay elsewhere in this volume.

6. McLeod, "The Place of Phenomenological Analysis in Social Psychological Theory," in Rohrer and Sherif, *Social Psychology at the Crossroads* (1951), p. 225.

7. However, see Easton, *op. cit.*, and Dahl-Lindblom, *op. cit.*

8. It is highly instructive to observe the reactions of some social scientists to the Parsons-Shils volume. Apart from scientifically responsible criticism, at least a few reputable critics appear to feel threatened by the implications of general theories for their own lifetime intellectual framework.

9. Consult Schuetz, "Multiple Realities," *Philosophy and Phenomenological Research*, XV (1945), 523 *ff.*

10. Event here is used as an analytic term, not as meaning a discrete occurrence.

11. Other forms of static analysis are: requisite analysis (a modification of structural-functional analysis), equilibrium analysis, head-counting, and description of structure in the formal sense.

12. It may be true that analysis and investigation will show that social change can take place without conscious choice—if so, it will be necessary to take this into account.

13. For example, see David Easton, "Limits of the Equilibrium Model in Social Research," *Chicago Behavioral Science Publications*, Number 1, pp. 26 *ff.*

14. "Two Types of Social Analysis," *Philosophy of Science* (October, 1953), 266–275.

15. *Op. cit.*, pp. 3–30.

16. See especially, "Choosing Among Projects of Action," *Philosophy and Phenomenological Research*, XII (1951), 161–184.

17. I also hesitate to introduce this troublesome term but it points to an important quality of my analysis. See Rohrer and Sherif, *Social Psychology at the Crossroads* (1951), pp. 215–242.

18. This problem of rationality is more troublesome than we have recognized. I cannot go into the matter here. However, I do not deny that rationality may be a useful concept for some purposes. Cf., Schuetz, "The Problems of Rationality in the Social World," *Economics* (N.S.), X (1943), 130–149.

19. One of the first efforts at explicit conceptualization is James McCamy's "Analysis of the Process of Decision-Making," *Public Administration Review*, VII (1947), 41–48. See also the clear and helpful exposition in Irwin Bross, *Design for Decision* (New York, 1953).

20. There are naturally exceptions to such a broad statement. For example, see Paul Appleby, *Policy and Administration* (1949), pp. 1–26, 47–65; Carl Friedrich, ed., *Public Policy*, IV (1953), pp. 271 *ff.*; and Simon, Smithburg, and Thompson, *Public Administration* (1950), pp. 261–271. However, a very suggestive recent book on business administration says, for example, that "policies are simply guid-

ing principles. . . ." See C. Redfield, *Communication in Management* (1953), p. 17.

21. *Functions of the Executive* (1938).
22. *Administrative Behavior* (2nd ed., 1957).
23. For example, a recent work, E. Gladden, *The Essentials of Public Administration* (1953); ch. 1 on definitions is not concerned with phenomena of administrative behavior and ch. 5 entitled the "Policy-maker" exhibits no conceptualization.
24. For an exception see Waldo, *Ideas and Issues in Public Administration* (1953), ch. 1–5, 9, 14, 16; Simon, "Comments on a Theory of Organizations," *American Political Science Review*, XLVI (1952), 1130–39. See also, Feely, "An Analysis of Administrative Purpose," *American Political Science Review*, XLV (1951), 1069–1080.
25. *Cf.* Snyder and Moore, "The Conference on Theory of Organization," *Items* (SSRC) (December, 1952), p. 41.
26. *Op. cit.*, p. 202.
27. Snyder, Bruck and Sapin, *Decision-making as an Approach to the Study of International Politics* (Foreign Policy Analysis Series No. 3) (1954), where it is argued that decision-making analysis offers a fruitful method of organizing the study of state behavior.
28. Valuable case studies are exemplified by Feis, *The China Tangle* (1953), and Sapin, *The Role of the Military in the Formulation of the Japanese Peace Treaty* (Foreign Policy Analysis Series No. 1) (1954); Almond, *The American People and Foreign Policy* (1950), and Dahl, *Congress and Foreign Policy* (1950), certainly represent long strides forward.
29. For example, the supporting papers of the Hoover Commission and the hearings on the removal of General MacArthur and on the Marshall Plan.
30. *Cf.* Craig and Gilbert, *The Diplomats* (1953). Memoirs naturally should be included.
31. See however Jerome Frank, *Courts on Trial* (1949), ch. 3, 10–12, 19, 20, 25. As usual, Harold Lasswell turns up with a pertinent essay: "Self-Analysis and Judicial Thinking," *International*

Journal of Ethics, XL (1928–30), 354–62.
32. *Cf.* Landis, *The Administrative Process* (1938), ch. 2.
33. Bailey, *Congress Makes a Law* (1950); Cheever and Haviland, *American Foreign Policy and the Separation of Powers* (1952).
34. Numerous works might be cited here. Outstanding, however, are Merriam, *Political Power* (1934); Lasswell, *Power and Personality* (1948); Riesman, *The Lonely Crowd* (1950) and *Faces in the Crowd* (1952); see also Salter, *Personality in Politics* (1948); Stanton and Perry, *Personality and Political Crisis* (1951); Millett and Macmahon, *Federal Administrators* (1939). Some social background theories and researches are reviewed in Matthews, *The Social Background of Political Decision-Makers* (1954).
35. *The Governmental Process* (1951).
36. Apparently some writers and teachers in public administration who are interested in non-governmental administration and who recognize the usefulness of what they regard as psychology and sociology do not necessarily believe in organizational theories or in the search for concepts relevant to complex organizations in *general*.
37. *Cf.* Grodzins, "Public Administration and the Science of Human Relations," *Public Administration Review*, XI (Spring, 1951), 88–102.
38. Pages dealing more specifically with decision-making are: 185–194; 202–221; 233–241.
39. See especially pp. 199–228.
40. Pages 100–117, 330–341, 644–679. See also his newer work, *Patterns of Industrial Bureaucracy* (1954).
41. For example: Selznick, "Foundations of the Theory of Organization," XIII, *American Sociological Review* (February, 1948), 25–35; Bendix, "Bureaucracy: The Problem and Its Setting," *American Sociological Review*, XII (October, 1947), 493–506.
42. For example: Copeland, *The Executive at Work* (1952); and Learned, *et al.*, *Executive Action* (1951).
43. *Fundamental Research in Administration*, Graduate School of Business Administration, Carnegie Institute of Technology (Pittsburgh, 1953), es-

pecially pp. 70–74; also Andrews, *The Case Method of Teaching Human Relations and Administration* (1951), Introductory Note and pp. 3–34. See also Dale, "New Perspectives in Managerial Decision-Making" *Journal of Business* (January, 1953), 1–8.

44. To take one example: Paul Pigors, "The Symbolic Significance of Management Decisions," in Bryson, *et al.*, *13th Symposium of the Conference on Science, Philosophy and Religion* (1954), pp. 733–744. To take another: C. Redfield, *Communication in Management* (1953), ch. 14, on the conference process.

45. Hugh Aitken, "The Analysis of Decisions," *Exploration in Entrepreneurial History*, I (February, 1949), 17; also Deutsch, "A Note on the History of Entrepreneurship, Innovation, and Decision-making," *ibid.* (May, 1949), 8–16.

46. Cartwright and Zander, eds., *Group Dynamics: Research and Theory* (1953), chs. 12–14, 16, 21–22, 26, 31, 33, 34, 38; especially Jennings, "The Significance of Choice in Human Behavior," pp. 62–72, and Lewin, "Studies in Group Decision," pp. 287–304. Guetzkow, *Groups, Leadership and Men*, pp. 55–67. Guetzkow, "An Exploratory Empirical Study of the Role of Conflict in Decision-making Conferences," *International Social Science Bulletin*, V (1953), pp. 286–300. Cartwright and Festinger, "A Quantitative Theory of Decision," *Psychological Review*, L (1943), 595–621.

47. See also Paul Miller, "The Process of Decision-making Within the Context of Community Organization," *Rural Sociology*, XVII (1952), 153–161. An excellent essay is that of Green and Mayo, "Framework for Research in the Actions of Community," *Social Forces* (May, 1953), 320–26.

48. Oppenheim, "Rational Choice," *Journal of Philosophy* (June, 1953), 341–350; Cerf, "Value Decisions," *Philosophy of Science* (January, 1951), 26–34.

49. *Op. cit.;* also "Multiple Realities," *Philosophy and Phenomenological Research*, V (1945), 533 *ff.*

50. Katona, *The Psychological Analysis of Economic Behavior* (1951), chs. 1–5; also chs. 10 and 11 on business decisions.

51. Black and Newing, *Committee Decisions with Complementary Valuation* (1951).

52. *Social Choice and Individual Values* (1951), pp. 1–22, 61–92; see also Little's review in *Journal of Political Economy*, LX (1952), 422–432. See also Black's "The Unity of Political and Economic Science," *The Economic Journal*, LX (1950), 506 *ff.*

53. Von Neumann and Morgenstern, *Theory of Games and Economic Behavior* (1947); Blackwell and Grischick, *Theory of Games and Statistical Decisions* (1954).

54. Mathematical analysis of social behavioral phenomena is not completely synonymous with game theory which is only one possible application. See for example Bales, *Interaction Process Analysis* (1953).

55. "Game Theory and International Politics" in Martin Shubik, *Game Theory and Political Behavior* (1954).

56. Some modifications would have to be made to fit in the decisions of the individual in a non-organizational (in the sense used here) setting.

57. I owe a great debt for many ideas and formulations to the Organizational Behavior Project at Princeton under the direction of Wilbert E. Moore and to my colleagues Henry Bruck and Burton Sapin of the Foreign Policy Analysis Project at Princeton.

58. See Snyder, Bruck and Sapin, *op. cit.*, p. 7 *ff.* This is an important distinction. It implies no bias against general theories. Hopefully, the frame of reference may grow into a sound basis for a general theory.

59. Contrast this with the position taken by Lasswell in *Studies in the Scope and Method of "The Authoritarian Personality,"* (R. Christie, ed., 1954) "The Selective Effort of Personality on Political Participation," pp. 197 *ff.*

60. *Ibid.* Lasswell makes a distinction between a *conventional* definition of political decision and a functional one which makes *all* "important" decisions political. He goes on to say that in order to locate functional elite, it is necessary to locate those making "actual" decisions (pp. 203–204). This

implies that there is a difference between actual and nominal decisions.

61. For example: Garceau, "Research in the Political Process," *American Political Science Review,* XLV (1951), 69–85.
62. To be explained below.
63. Situational analysis is discussed in Easton, *The Political System* (1953), pp. 149–170; Carr, *Situational Analysis* (1948), pp. 1–38, 45–61, 90–100; Cole, *Human Behavior* (1953), pp. 357–388; Cartwright, ed., *Lewin's Field Theory in Social Science* (1951), pp. 30–60, 238–304. Compare the first chapter of Arthur Macmahon's excellent little book, *Administration in Foreign Affairs* (1953). This chapter is entitled the "Concept of Judgment" and should be compared with my concept of definition of the situation.
64. I have reservations on the formal-informal dichotomy, but I shall here let conventional meaning prevail.
65. The lack of a commonly accepted, general concept of decision-making or decision-making process has already been commented on. However, that there are theories of decision-making is clear from the previous section.
66. Typologies would not be as necessary for historical studies as they would be for prediction.
67. The phrase is Gabriel Almond's, *op. cit.,* ch. 1.
68. Adoption of "competence" in preference to "office" or "authority" or "role" is due partly to ambiguities and misleading usages and partly because a more inclusive term was necessary.

69. See Sapin and Snyder, *The Role of the Military in American Foreign Policy* (1954), pp. 35–39; *cf.* Sapin, Snyder, and Bruck, *An Appropriate Role for the Military in American Foreign Policy-making: A Research Note* (1954).
70. See for example: Deutsch, "On Communication Models in the Social Sciences," *Public Opinion Quarterly* (Fall, 1952); Deutsch, "Self-Referent Symbols and Self-Referent Communication Patterns: A Note on Some Pessimistic Theories of Politics," in Bryson, et al., *13th Symposium of Conference on Science, Philosophy and Religion* (1954), p. 619; C. Redfield, *Communication in Management* (1953); Newcomb, "An Approach to the Study of Communicative Acts," *Psychological Review,* LX (1953), 393–404. See also Special Issue on International Communications Research, *Public Opinion Quarterly,* XVI (Winter, 1952–53).
71. Newcomb, *op. cit.* Cf. Hartley and Hartley, *Social Psychology* (1952)— a text cast in terms of communication analyses.
72. *Character and Social Structure,* ch. 5.
73. Lasswell and Leites, *Languages of Politics* (1949).
74. That is, as defined by the actors not by the observer.
75. Black and Newing, *op. cit.;* Arrow, *op cit.,* Oppenheim, *op. cit.* See also, Black, "The Rationale of Group Decision-making," *Journal of Political Economy,* LVI (1948), 23–24.

HAGAN: *The Group in a Political Science* (pp. 38–51)

1. This paper also appeared in the volume, *Life, Language, Law,* Richard W. Taylor, editor, published by the Antioch Press, Yellow Springs, Ohio, in 1957; reprinted by permission.

LEVY: *"Structural Functional" Analysis* (pp. 52–66)

1. The concepts have been taken more or less verbatim from my book, *The Structure of Society* (Princeton, 1952). There is not space here to go into an extended discussion of the limitations and applications of these concepts. An extended discussion of these matters may be found in that volume.
2. See "Definitions," p. XV.
3. For reasons that would take us afield from the present interest, I happen to believe that there is a sense in which the "requisite" form of "structural-functional" analysis is a somewhat more general or basic form than the others. Whatever the merits of this

prejudice may turn out to be, it can be safely asserted that the problem to which the analysis is addressed will determine which combinations of these concepts are most fruitfully taken as primary and which auxiliary.

4. There are, of course, many theoretical elements in the erection of schemes of analysis in terms of which empirical studies leading to comparative work are carried out. In the volume cited above I have tried at numerous points to indicate methods of checking, as it were, on this unavoidable "preliminary" theorizing. *E.g.*, pp. 68–70, 213–217.

5. This does not imply that the unit must continue to exist as defined, but merely asks what conditions would have to exist if it were to persist.

6. The statements about dangers and tentativeness are not to be taken lightly. For extended discussion of these matters see the volume mentioned in footnote no. 1 above.

7. Some of the many problems raised by this definition are discussed in detail in the volume mentioned above in footnote no. 1. See especially pp. 122–136.

8. *Ibid.*, pp. 68–71, 211–226.

9. For the time being the reader is asked to grant as defined the subsidiary terms in these definitions.

10. For present purposes I should like to avoid certain problems. In the first place, I should like to avoid the problem of whether it is possible to do scientific work in the field of social analysis. For present purposes it is assumed to be possible. This position can be based on argument rather than assumption, however. In the second place, I should like to avoid the question of how much of the work done under the heading of "political science," or any of the other social sciences for that matter, is in fact scientific if any rigorous criteria of science are used. Whatever the mixture of science, engineering, "simple" description, philosophy, moralizing, history, etc., there may in fact be in the field, this paper is only interested in those portions of the field that are interested in scientific analysis. This is in no way intended as an invidious dis-

tinction. It is not the assumption here that scientific work is "better" than non-scientific work—just that the two are different.

11. It has been noted above that what is power from one point of view is responsibility from another; *e.g.*, that if A has power over B, then B has responsibilty to A. This is, of course, true *by definition* as the terms have been set up here. It does not follow however that power and responsibility are by definition always in balance. The term balance as used here involves reference to the general system in which a relationship occurs. For these purposes power and responsibility in a system are not considered in balance unless all of those wielding power are responsible for their wielding of it and all those owing responsibility have the power necessary to execute those responsibilities.

12. Certain necessary modifications have already become apparent in other work. Present illustrative purposes would not be served by going into these details nor do they materially affect the purposes for which the proposition will be used here.

13. This latter is true despite the fact that what is power from one point of view is responsibility from another.

14. References to Chinese materials here are taken largely from my volume, *The Family Revolution in Modern China* (Cambridge, Mass., 1949), and two articles, "Some Problems of Modernization in China," *Institute of Pacific Relations* (1949), and "Contrasting Factors in the Modernization of China and Japan," *Economic Development and Cultural Change*, II (Oct., 1953), 161–197.

15. The terms *ideal* and *actual* are used in their conventional social science senses. The term *ideal* refers to what is considered correct and proper and preferable from the point of view of those actors in the system concerned to whom reference is being made. The term *actual* refers to the state of affairs as it appears from the point of view of a scientific observer.

16. Examples can be given of this from many sources. Most descriptions of the "traditional" Chinese family system

given by Chinese and others, with no intent to deceive, are pictures of a family system that is the ideal type for virtually everyone in that society and the actual type for virtually no one—certainly for very few outside the gentry. Many American discussions of strata distinctions in United States society take this form. One could go on.

17. It is not out of the question to maintain that this must be the case if there is to be stability. Considerations of this sort need not detain us here.

18. This is by no means always the case since the father's father may be alive and functioning as the family head.

19. This is one major respect in which the Chinese and Japanese family systems differ.

20. The italics in this paragraph are intended to call attention to a special manner of looking at phenomena that is sometimes of use to the social scientist. The ideas referred to about the governmental system of the United States are obviously not true in fact and of course are not held to in any naive sense either by political scientists or by the numerous people of much experience with the governmental system as such. What is referred to here is a view widely held by members of the system—a view of what the members feel the governmental system should be and where it should be "summed up." It is essential in social analysis to draw such distinctions. Even when the members of a system (let alone scientific observers of that system) know that their ideal picture of it does not coincide with the actual facts, it may be essential that one consider their ideal picture in trying to understand the actual operation of the system.

21. The Chinese sages held that "Of the three unfilial sins the greatest is not to have descendents." They were so horrified by this one that they neglected to mention the other two, and these have remained a minor textual mystery ever since. The interpretations of this "greatest of the unfilial sins" make it clear that the mere production of offspring is not enough; everything possible must be done to lay the basis

for their continuing the family line.

22. In at least one period of Chinese history a major movement in the direction of conversion to Catholicism was brought to an immediate halt when, as a result of policy considerations in the Vatican, the Jesuits were ordered to instruct their converts that they could no longer continue Ancestor Worship and remain Catholics. There is at least room for the educated guess that had Ancestor Worship been rejected and the conversion continued the social structure of China would have been revolutionized at that time.

Definitions

a. *function*—a function is a condtion, or state of affairs, resultant from the operation (including in the term operation mere persistence) of a structure through time.

b. *structure*—a structure is a pattern, i.e., an observable uniformity, of action or operation.

c. *functional requisites*—a functional requisite is a generalized condition necessary for the maintenance of the unit with which it is associated, given the level of generalization of the definition of that unit and the most general setting of such a unit.

d. *structural requisites*—a structural requisite is a pattern (or observable uniformity) of action (or operation) necessary for the continued existence of the unit with which it is associated, given the level of generalization of the definition of the unit and the most general setting of such a unit.

e. *functional prerequisites*—a functional prerequisite is a function that must pre-exist if a given unit in its setting is to come into being.

f. *structural prerequisites*—a structural prerequisite is a structure that must pre-exist if a given unit in its setting is to come into being.

g. *eufunction*—a eufunction is a condition, or state of affairs, that (1) results from the operation (including the term operation mere persistence) of a structure of a given unit through time and (2) increases or maintains adaptation or adjustment to the unit's setting, thus making for the persistence of the unit as defined of which the structure concerned is a part or aspect.

h. *dysfunction*—a dysfunction is a condition, or state of affairs, that (1) results from the operation (including in the term operation mere persistence) of a structure of a given unit through time and (2) lessens the adaptation or adjustment to the unit's setting, thus making for the lack of persistence of the unit as defined of which the structure concerned is a part or aspect.

i. *eustructure*—a eustructure is a structure such that operation in terms of it results in eufunctions.

j. *dysstructure*—a dysstructure is a structure such that operation in terms of it results in dysfunctions.

k. *manifest* (as applied to function or structure)—a factor will be termed manifest if it is intended and recognized by the participants in the system.

l. *latent* (as applied to function or structure)—a factor will be termed latent if it is neither intended nor recognized

by the participants in the system.

m. *IUR* (as applied to function or structure)—a factor will be termed IUR if it is intended but unreocognized by the participants in the system.

n. *UIR* (as applied to function or structure)—a factor will be termed UIR if it is unintended but recognized by the participants in the system.

o. *concrete structure*—those patterns that define the character of units that are at least in theory capable of physical separation (in time and/or space) from other units of the same sort.

p. *analytic structure*—analytic structures are those patterned aspects of action that are not even theoretically capable of concrete separation from other patterned aspects of action.

q. *microscopic and macroscopic structures* —the more inclusive is one structure relative to another the more macroscopic or less microscopic it is relative to that other.

MORGENTHAU: *Power as a Political Concept* (pp. 66–77)

1. A revision of this paper was published in *The Review of Politics*, XVII (Oct., 1955), 431–460; reprinted by permission.

HARTZ: *The Problem of Political Ideas* (pp. 78–86)

1. Since the delivery of this paper, the author has developed the thesis described here in *The Liberal Tradition in America* (New York, 1955).

2. Introduction to G. Gatti, *Le Socialism et L'Agriculture*, p. 20. (My translation).

3. The case of the Diggers obviously differs greatly from that of Babeuf, but we can agree with Petegorsky that it had in common with it the notion of completing a social revolution that the middle class had begun. This notion was absent in America.

SHERWOOD: *Role of Public Law in Political Science* (pp. 86–96)

1. Anna Haddow, *Political Science in American Colleges and Universities* (New York, 1939), *passim*.

2. I. M. Bochanski, *Europäische Philosophie Der Gegenwort* (Bern, 1947), pp. 20 *ff*.

3. It is not without significance to note that the French preoccupation with formal written law to the exclusion of the study of judicial discretion lasted almost a century from the Napoleonic codes to François Geny, *Méthode d'Interpretation et Sources en Droit Privé Positif* (Paris, 1899).

4. Christopher C. Langdell, "Teaching Law as a Science," *American Law Review*, XXI (1887), 123.

5. Many excellent illustrations of the structural and positive law emphasis are to be found in the dissertations of the students of Goodnow published in the volumes of the Columbia Studies in History, Economics and Public Law in the years immediately before and following the turn of the century.

6. For a lawyer's criticism of the state of legal theory in the 1930's, see Thurman W. Arnold, "Apologies for Juris-

prudence" *Yale Law Journal*, XLIV (1935), 729, 736.

7. David Easton, *The Political System* (New York, 1953), pp. 115 *ff.*

8. J. Willard Hurst, *The Growth of American Law* (Boston, 1950).

9. Edward A. Ross, *Social Control* (New York, 1901), p. 106.

10. Ihering does this largely in the second volume of *Der Zweck im Recht* (Leip-sig, 1923) which, significantly, has not been translated.

11. *Cf.* Hans Kelsen, "Pure Theory of Law and Analytical Jurisprudence," *Harvard Law Review*, LV (1942), 44, 54, where a similar distinction is made but for quite different purposes.

12. Harold Stein, *Public Administration and Policy Development* (New York, 1952).

WALDO: *"Values" in the Political Science Curriculum* (pp. 96–111)

1. From "Introduction," by James G. Miller, to *Symposium: Profits and Problems of Homeostatic Models in the Behavioral Sciences,* Chicago Behavioral Publications, I (1953) 7.

2. These paragraphs are under a debt to the opening section of Gunnar Myrdal's "The Relation Between Social Theory and Social Policy," *British Journal of Sociology,* IV (Sept. 1953), 210–242.

3. Myrdal, *op. cit.,* p. 213.

4. *Ibid.*

5. A. J. Ayres, *Language, Truth and Logic* (London, 1953), p. 108. Obviously, in this three-paragraph summary I cannot deal with the subtleties of a major philosophical movement, one now ramified and schismatic. I can only hope to have stated correctly some of the major tenets for present purposes.

6. I am assuming general understanding of and agreement on this point. One supporting statement by a social scientist of acknowledged distinction is appropriate, however: "Quite apart from drawing any policy conclusions from social research or forming any ideas about what is desirable or undesirable, we employ and we need value premises in making scientific observations of facts and in analyzing their causal interrelations. Chaos does not organize itself into any cosmos. We need viewpoints and they presume valuations. A 'disinterested social science' is, from this viewpoint, pure nonsense. It never existed and it will never exist. We can strive to make our thinking rational in spite of this, but only by facing the valuations, not by evading them." Myrdal, *op. cit.,* p. 242. (I understand that it is possible to argue for a very strict separation of "science" and "values"—as Myrdal does—and still recognize this point as valid. There is the further question, however, of what one does when he "faces the valuations.")

7. Richard Bendix, *Social Science and the Distrust of Reason* (Berkeley, 1951).

8. *Op. cit.,* pp. 37–38.

9. *Op. cit.,* p. 38. "The serious questions which we all confront is thereby posed: must we pay for the greater empiricism of modern social science with the unconscious and uncritical subordination of intellectual endeavor to the social and political forces of our time?" p. 41.

10. Myrdal, *op. cit.* "The fact is less and less labour is being applied to major problems," p. 273.

11. *Ibid.*

12. Read before the Conference on Reason and Value of the Pacific Coast Committee for the Humanities, American Council of Learned Socities, Mills College, 1952. Mimeo. Speaking of scientific fetishism he writes: "It is a strange science indeed which establishes as the ultimate test of theoretical worth the rigor with which a methodological formulation is defended rather than the significance of the hypothesis advanced. . . . Rarely has a philosophy inspired by science afforded so much aid and comfort to the mystic."

13. David Easton, *The Political System* (New York, 1953), p. 264.

* For a report of the theory conference, see Harry Eckstein, "Political Theory and the Study of Politics: A report of a Conference, *The American Political Science Review,* L (June, 1956), 475–487.

JACOBSON: *The Unity of Political Theory* (pp. 115–124)

1. In what I have said above and in what I am about to say I should like to make it perfectly clear that I have reference *only* to the study of political theory. I do not pretend to consider methods in political or social science generally. As I will indicate later on, political theory is concerned ultimately with a certain kind of statement of knowledge and not with the acquisition of all knowledge. Any careful analysis of politics and society may be relevant to the construction or evaluation of political theory.

SIBLEY: *Theory in the Study of Politics* (pp. 125–148)

1. Karl Popper, *The Open Society and Its Enemies*, I, *The Spell of Plato* (London, 1945).
2. Warner Fite, *The Platonic Legend* (New York, 1934).
3. Bertrand Russell, *History of Western Philosophy* (New York, 1945); *Philosophy and Politics* (London, 1947).
4. R. H. S. Crossman, *Plato Today* (New York, 1939).
5. John Wild, *Plato's Theory of Man* (Cambridge, Mass., 1946); *Plato's Modern Enemies and the Theory of Natural Law* (Chicago, 1953).
6. Ronald B. Levinson, *In Defense of Plato* (Cambridge, Mass., 1953).
7. Fite, *The Platonic Legend*, p. 265.
8. Leo Strauss, "On a New Interpretation of Plato's Political Philosophy," Social Research, XIII (1946), 351.
9. R. G. Collingwood, *An Autobiography* (Oxford, 1935), pp. 61–66. See also his *The Idea of History* (Oxford, 1946).
10. For example, Andrew Hacker, "Capital and Carbuncles: The Great Books Reappraised," *American Political Science Review*, XLVIII (1954), 775–786.
11. If taken literally, "present" is non-existent for purposes of investigation; all data of politics must be taken from the "past"—even those based on the most direct observations. One may attend a political party convention, for example, and study it with meticulous care; but even as one records one's observations the convention is receding into the "past." One may, of course, mean by "present" the recent "past," but it is difficult to see why there is anything in the study of politics as such which would or should confine the investigator solely to the recent "past."
12. All this, of course, may legitimately raise the problem of terminology. T. D. Weldon's *Vocabulary of Politics* (London, 1953) has rightly criticized many notions implicit or explicit in traditional political philosophy.
13. I realize, of course, that extreme "positivists" would deny that this is true—Pareto, for example.
14. R. W. Carlyle, *Medieval Political Thought in the West* (Edinburgh, 1928), II, pp. 136–37.
15. See W. P. Ker, *The Dark Ages* (New York, 1904), pp. 26–27.
16. Ernest Barker, *Greek Political Theory: Plato and his Predecessors* (London, 1918), p. 383.
17. *Utopia*, Book 1.
18. H. G. Wells, *Experiment in Autobiography* (New York, 1933).
19. *The Open Society and Its Enemies*, I, *The Spell of Plato*.
20. Carl Friedrich, *The New Belief in the Common Man* (Boston, 1943), pp. 151, 177.
21. William H. Kilpatrick, "Crucial Issues in Educational Theory," *Educational Theory*, I (1951), 3–5 and 8.
22. D. W. Brogan, *The American Character* (New York, 1944).
23. This term "soul" will have a harsh ring for many modern ears. As used by Plato and Aristotle, however, it need not imply any such religious doctrine as "life after death" or any notion that the "soul" is separable from "body." Perhaps some such term as "personality as a whole" might be substituted.
24. *Republic*, VIII, 544 d 6: IV, 435 e 1–3.
25. H. W. B. Joseph, *Essay in Ancient and Modern Philosophy* (Oxford, 1936), p. 42.
26. *Laws*, 770.

27. R. G. Bury's translation of the *Laws,* Loeb Classical Library (London, 1926), p. 770.
28. For a good discussion of the problem, note C. E. M. Joad, *Guide to the Philosophy of Morals and Politics* (New York, 1936), pp. 759–765.
29. *Principles of Sociology,* I, part ii, ch. 3.
30. *Cf.* Joad, *Guide to the Philosophy of Morals and Politics, op. cit.,* pp. 24–35.
31. *Cf.* John Wild, *Plato's Modern Enemies and the Theory of Natural Law* (Chicago, 1953).
32. Note the discussion of the late Platonist Wincenty Lutoslawski, *The World of Souls* (London, 1924).
33. Joseph, *Ancient and Modern Philosophy,* pp. 47–50.
34. Werner Jaeger, *Paideia: The Ideals of Greek Culture,* trans. by Gilbert Highet (New York, 1943), II, 365–66.
35. At many points in both the *Republic* and the *Laws.*
36. For example, *Civilization and Its Discontents.* See also his discussion with Einstein, *Why War?*
37. Even writers of the caliber of Hans Morgenthau, while they discourse at length on "national interest" and, indeed, seem to make it the center of their analysis, tend to be very vague about the meaning of the term. We urgently need a treatise comparable to Plato's *Republic,* but inquiring, not into the meaning of justice, but into the definition of "national interest." Yet few have essayed the task; and even where the attempt has been made, as in the late Charles A. Beard's *Idea of National Interest* (New York, 1934), the results leave one unsatisfied.
38. This is clearly adumbrated in Book II of the *Republic.*
39. R. L. Nettleship, *Lectures on the Republic of Plato* (second edition reprinted, London, 1951), p. 157.
40. *Cf.* Roscoe Pound, *An Introduction to the Philosophy of Law* (New Haven, 1922), pp. 74–75.
41. Nettleship, pp. 270–71, 273.
42. Barker, *Greek Political Theory,* p. 243.
43. Ronald B. Levinson, *In Defense of Plato* (Cambridge, Mass., 1953), pp. 504–514.
44. Ernst Cassirer, *The Myth of the State* (New Haven, 1946), p. 73.
45. Barker, *Greek Political Theory,* p. 244.
46. Similar observations might be made about two other great "inverse utopias" of the twentieth century, Eugen Zamiatin's *We* and Aldous Huxley's *Brave New World.*
47. Thus A. T. Wright's decentralist and agrarian utopia *Islandia* (New York, 1942) is very helpful in gaining some over-all understanding of the centralized, non-agrarian United States.
48. Barker, *Greek Political Theory,* p. 244.
49. *Republic,* p. 472.

MCCLOSKEY: *American Political Thought* (pp. 155–171)

* A revision of this paper was published in *The American Political Science Review,* LI (March, 1957), 115–129; reprinted by permission.
1. C. M. Wiltse, *The Jeffersonian Tradition in American Democracy* (Chapel Hill, 1935).
2. Daniel Boorstin, *The Genius of American Politics* (Chicago, 1953), p. 169.
3. *Galvan v. Press,* 347 U. S. 522, 531 (1954).
4. *Shaughnessy v. United States,* 345 U. S. 206, 224 (1953).
5. John Emerich Acton, *Essays on Freedom and Power* (Boston, 1948), p. 199.

FRIEDRICH: *Political Philosophy and the Study of Politics* (pp. 172–188)

1. This paper also appeared in the memorial volume for Professor Piero Calamandrei, published by CEDAM, Padua.
2. *Power and Society* (with Abraham Kaplan) (1950), p. xi. Laski's view is stated in *The State in Theory and Practice* (1935), p. 31. It is worth noting that this book contains Laski's most elaborate explication of Marxist

doctrine on the state, and consequently reflects Marx' view on ideology. Lasswell himself discusses ideology *op. cit.,* pp. 123 *ff.* and defines it as "the political myth functioning to preserve the social structure." This view in turn is based upon the Marx-derived analysis of ideology given by Karl Mannheim, *Ideology and Utopia.*

3. In a discriminating review of Lasswell's book in *The Journal of Philosophy* (1951), pp. 690 *ff.* Thomas I. Cook develops the philosophical inadequacies of Lasswell-Kaplan which ceteris paribus applied to that entire body of opinion.

4. This problem is at the heart of a recent and fairly extended controversy over the interpretation of Plato. A group of writers, including Warner Fite, *The Platonic Legend* (1934), R. H. S. Crossman, *Plato Today* (1939), A. D. Winspear, *The Genesis of Plato's Thought* (1940), and Karl Popper, *The Open Society and its Enemies,* vol. I (1945), all of whom in one form or another have attacked Plato's philosophy as elitist, aristocratic, antidemocratic, authoritarian, and even totalitarian. More recently several writers have come to the rescue of Plato, among them John Wild, *Plato's Modern Enemies and the Theory of Natural Law* (1953) and William W. C. Greene, "Platonism and its Critics," in *Harvard Studies in Classical Philosophy,* LXI, 39–71. I lean toward the first position, though I certainly would reject the proposition that Plato was a totalitarian, and for reasons which are enumerated in *The New Belief in the Common Man,* ch. II.

5. Lasswell, following Dewey, speaks of the "problem approach" as the distinctive feature of the policy sciences, including political science, *The Policy Sciences* (1951), p. 12. But has an inquiring mind, including the political philosopher, ever denied the guiding importance of "problems"?

6. I make this point partly because in a very able recent article a younger colleague, arguing against the "great books" approach with considerable acumen and much verve, suggested in a footnote that he is arguing *inter alias* against me, referring to a paper read at

the APSA meetings in 1955. I am afraid he misunderstood me; my writings, more especially *Constitutional Government and Politics* (1937), show me to be much interested in theoretical analysis and actually making some such, besides crying out for it. See pp. 10, 11. I am referring to Andrew Hacker, "Capital and Carbuncles: The Great Books Reappraised," *American Political Science Review,* XLVIII (Sept. 1954), 775–786.

7. *Cf.* such works as Charles H. McIlwain, *The Growth of Political Thought in the West* (1932) and George H. Sabine, *A History of Political Theory* (new ed. 1951). The interrelation between political and legal philosophy is well represented also by the work of Ernest Barker; see more particularly his Introduction to the translation of parts of Gierke's magnum opus, published under the title *Natural Law and the Theory of Society* (1934) and his *Principles of Social and Political Theory* (1951). A legal philosophy in political and historical perspective by myself is found in *Die Philosophie des Rechts in historischer Perspektive* (1955).

8. *Cf.* Charles Grove Haines, *The Revival of Natural Law Concepts* (1930), for a general earlier assessment.

9. *The American College Dictionary* (1947).

10. *The Concise Oxford Dictionary of Current English* (ed. Fowler) (1929).

11. It should be noted, however, that from time to time, a new method may be discovered, too; the process of its adoption resembles that of the new facts and generalizations based upon them.

12. To give one example for many, B. G. Niebuhr's *Römische Geschichte* (1828) marked that kind of advance.

13. *Nicomachean Ethics,* Book I. The passage continues, significantly: "It is evidently equally foolish to accept probable reasoning from a mathematician as to demand from a rhetorician scientific proofs."

14. See for the Ding an Sich *Prolegomena,* par. 26 and elsewhere (in my *Philosophy of Kant,* p. 80). Kant was, by his position, led to the famous overstatement that "the intellect does not

derive its laws (a priori) from nature but prescribes them to nature." (*op. cit.,* p. 91—end of par. 37).

15. The problems of methodology of political science will be more fully developed by the author in a forthcoming study *Wissenschaft und Methods der Politik. Cf.* for an earlier formulation "A Sketch of the Scope and Method of Political Science" in *Constitutional Government and Democracy* (1941), reprinted separately by Ginn and Company in 1951.

16. The unprecedented nature of totalitarian dictatorship is more fully developed by C. J. Friedrich and Z. Brzezinski, *Totalitarian Dictatorship and Autocracy* (1956).

17. Such a demand has been voiced by a number of writers and was the subject of a committee exploration of the APSA in the twenties; e.g., G. E. G. Catlin, *The Science and Method of Politics* (1927) and the writings of Charles E. Merriam, for earlier attempts. Most recently, the work of Lasswell and Kaplan, cited above fn. 2, has advanced this position.

18. Lasswell-Kaplan, *op. cit.,* p. 3, fn. 1.

19. The book was published in 1953; a lengthy review article of it has appeared in *Diogènes* over my name (1955).

20. *Op. cit.,* p. 136. He adds that "no law, and hence no constitution, can be the fundamental political fact, because all laws depend on human beings. Laws have to be adopted, preserved, and administered by men." Many, including myself, might agree to either of these propositions, and yet consider the argument a non sequitur. Incidentally, the references to Plato and Aristotle cited hardly support the contentions of the text, but this is not the place to enter upon this matter.

21. *Political Philosophy of Hobbes* (1936). See my review article of it in *The Journal of Social Philosophy,* III (1938), 251 *ff.*

22. In writing thus, Strauss neglects that all true authority, in developed stages of society, rests upon reason, as Thomas Aquinas had shown (though many have forgotten it). See my "Loyalty and Authority" in *Confluence* (1954).

23. *Federalist,* No. 10.

24. I might mention in passing that on the subject of natural law, which is central to Strauss' discourse, A. Passerin d'Entrèves published a short book, *Natural Law* (1951), which in its simplicity and sound sense is an anticipatory reply to Strauss' subtleties.

25. *Von der Wahrheit* (1947); *cf.* power and government, pp. 3666 *ff.;* power and authority, pp. 803 *ff.;* dual nature, pp. 581 *ff.* In these passages the author's concept of the dual nature of power (*Constitutional Government and Politics,* 1937, pp. 13–14 and later) is confirmed with the broad context of existentialist philosophy.

26. *Cf. L'Etre et le Néant* (1946).

27. *Holzwege* (1950) contains the essay "Nietzsche's Wort: Gott ist tot" which is concerned with Nietzsche's philosophy of the will to power, resulting from his critique of nihilism. Nihilism has been slowly spreading as a term of derogation; cf. e.g., Eric Voegelin, *The New Science of Politics* (1952), passim. H. cites as key to the issue the passage from *Thus Spake Zarathustra,* "Where I found a thing alive, there I found the will to power; even in the will of the servant I found the will to be Master."

28. *Love, Power and Justice* (1954), esp. ch. III.

29. See above fn. 17. The author, while acknowledging the central role of power (CGD, 1941 pp. 583 *ff.*), has criticized these notions and suggested that political science is largely a critical examination of common-sense notions concerning the working of political institutions and procedures. Lasswell merely comments that "this does not entail either that they are worthless (the base line hypotheses derived from common-sense) or that they are most fruitful in the formulations which common-sense gives them." (p. XXII). I agree. Both of these points are made in my analysis. But whereas I stress testing by a scientific exploration of empirical evidence, Lasswell's treatment is largely confined to logical discourse, definitions, and propositions.

30. Tillich (*op. cit.,* pp. 88 *ff.*) recognizes the dual nature of authority which he differentiates as "authority in principle"

and "authority in fact" (a curious terminology, since he means by the first nonrational authority and by the second rational authority). These problems are more fully and deeply explored by Jaspers, *op. cit.*, pp. 862 *ff.*, where genuine authority, based on reason, is contrasted with "catholicity"— whereas Tillich speaks of the pope as "authority" because of "the place he occupies." I might mention here that David Easton, in his interesting discussion of *The Political System* (1953), insists that authority is one of the focal points of political theory, but he interprets it in psychological terms, pp. 134 *ff.*, as does Max Weber to whom he refers; *cf.* my paper as cited above, fn. 22.

31. W. W. Rostow, *The Dynamics of Soviet Society* (1953) argues that the extension of what Lasswell-Kaplan would call "naked power" is the prime goal of the Soviet rulers; he calls this trend "the rule of the priority of power" (pp. 10, 17 and elsewhere). Karl Deutscher, *Russia, What Next* (1954), insists that there is an overwhelming demand for a more rational order to which the rulers will yield. *Cf.* also Barrington Moore, Jr., *Terror and Progress USSR* (1954) for a more balanced assessment, also introducing tradition as a decisive factor.

32. It should, in justice to existentialism, be noted that both Jaspers and Sartre give a more acceptable account of power, as noted above, footnotes 25 and 26.

33. Cranston's brief analysis is sharply at variance with Louis Hartz' emphasis in *The Liberal Tradition in America* (1955). Hartz stresses, and in my opinion overstresses, the Lockean tradition in American which Cranston unduly minimizes. Surely Cranston's opening sentence declaring that "in the United States the word 'liberal' has not the laudatory emotive meaning it enjoys in the United Kingdom," is untenable. How else explain the fact that everyone, from reactionary (Hoover) to leftist radical (Lerner) insists on calling himself a "liberal," as Cranston himself mentions.

34. See Harold J. Laski, *The Rise of Liberalism* (1936), J. H. Hallowell, *The Decline of Liberalism* (1946), and Guido de Ruggiero, *The History of European Liberalism* (1927).

35. The extent to which freedom means absence of constraint, as well as capacity for creative work, is especially clear in a case like academic freedom. Samuel Eliot Morison, in his *Freedom in Contemporary Society* (1956), when discussing academic freedom, makes "the right of a teacher or researcher in a university or other institution of higher learning to search for the truth in his chosen field" the first and foremost aspect of this freedom. He rightly insists that he ought not to be molested by authorities within or without the institution. The way of putting the matter fails to deal, however, with the much more difficult problem of "constraint" by a scholar's professional colleagues.

36. See, for example, *Constitutional Government and Democracy* (1951, 2nd ed.) by the author, or Daniel Wit, *Comparative Political Institutions* (1953). In such works we may not find a general discussion of freedom or liberty, but we will find discussion of freedom of assembly, of enterprise, of speech, of association, of conscience, of the press and of trade, all of which are freedoms to do something; they are practical and concrete ways of behavior in many societies, describing how people go about doing their work. That they are "free" to do it essentially means that they have the capacity to do it.

37. See *Deutsche Ideologie*, pp. 35–6 and elsewhere, esp. *Critique of Political Economy*, pp. 11–12 (ed. Stone).

38. In *Ideology and Utopia* (1953) based upon Mannheim's original German study published in 1929, but enlarged. The quotes are from pp. 111 and 238.

39. So does Talcott Parsons in his *Social System* (1953) pp. 349 *ff.* Integration is, to him, the primary function of ideology, and it encompasses a possible "romantic-utopian" ingredient. Parsons also helpfully extends the concept by including "movement deviant from the main culture" among the groups that may have an ideology.

40. Jaspers, *op. cit.*, p. 769 gives a formulation which may be in line with the

above, though I cannot be certain, because he uses a term, "durchdrungen," where we say "rational comprehen- sion"; the meaning of durchdrungen is not clear to me. *Cf.* also my article, cited in footnote 22.

ROGERS: *Political Philosophy in the Twentieth Century* (pp. 189–214

1. On January 12, 1955, a press dispatch from Moscow reported that the Soviet Union's Communist Party Control Committee had concluded that the 1924 Russian language edition of Marx's *Das Capital* "had serious faults and had decided to bring Marx up to date."
2. *The New Statesman and Nation,* XLVIII (November 27, 1954).
3. The Committee's first report "Theory and Practice in Historical Study" (Bulletin 54) is to my mind the most important document that the SSRC has yet sired. This is the more intriguing since in the days when I knew the SSRC intimately, History was the neglected muse. As Schlesinger (père) and I used to say, the representatives of the other "disciplines" treated History as if it were a lavatory; they resorted to it when it was necessary. But this report sold 5400 copies and still sells; many of us have insisted that our students read it. It was a remarkable document in its bold announcement

that historians could not be scientists but must content themselves with being artists. The SSRC must have felt much as a Eucharistic Congress would have felt, had one of its committees reported that there was nothing in the doctrine of the Virgin Birth. The more recent report seems occasionally nostalgic and there are traces of sadness because the first committee under the leadership of Charles Beard was so forthright.

4. Balfour, *States and Mind,* p. 143.
5. *Political Characters of Shakespeare* (London, 1945), p. 309.
6. "Training for Statesmanship," *The Atlantic Monthly,* May, 1953, Italics added.
7. Perhaps Thucydides, Shakespeare, Milton, Macauley, and Beard were also Acts of God but I doubt whether there has been an adequate answer to the supplication of the Bidding Prayer: "for a due supply of persons fitted to serve God in the Ministry and in the State."

OSGOOD: *Behavior Theory and the Social Sciences* (pp. 217–244)

1. This paper was also published in *Behavioral Science,* I (1956), 167–185; republication by permission.

GUETZKOW: *Building Models about Small Groups* (pp. 265–281)

Basic References
Three Codifications of Methodology, including the methodology for research on the small group:
A. M. Jahoda, M. Deutsch, and S. W. Cook, eds., *Research Methods in Social Relations with Especial Reference to Prejudice* (New York, 1951), Part II: *Selected Techniques.*
B. L. Festinger and D. Katz, *Research Methods in the Behavioral Sciences* (New York, 1953).
C. G. Lindzey, ed., *Handbook of Social Psychology* (Cambridge, Mass., 1954), Part III: *Research Methods,* chs. 7–14.

Two Collections of Research Articles on the Small Group:
D. D. Cartwright and A. Zander, eds., *Group Dynamics: Research and Theory* (Evanston, Ill., 1953).
E. A. P. Hare, E. F. Borgatta, and R. F. Bales, eds., *Small Groups: Studies in Social Interaction* (New York, 1955). This volume includes an annotated bibliography of small group literature.

Bibliography

1. F. H. Allport, *Social Psychology* (New York, 1924).
2. K. Back, "Influence Through Social

Communication," *Journal of Abnormal and Social Psychology,* XLVI (1951), 9–23.

3. R. F. Bales and F. L. Strodtbeck, "Phases in Group Problem Solving," *Journal of Abnormal and Social Psychology,* XLVI (1951), 485–495.

4. R. D. Bock and S. Z. Husain, "An Adaptation of Holzinger's B-Coefficients for the Analysis of Sociometric Data," *Sociometry,* XIII (1950), 146–153.

5. R. B. Cattell, "Determining Syntality Dimensions as a Basis for Morals and Leadership Measurement," in H. Guetzkow, ed., *Groups, Leadership and Men* (Pittsburgh, 1951).

6. R. B. Cattell, D. R. Saunders, and G. F. Stice, "The Dimensions of Syntality in Small Groups," *Human Relations,* VI (1953), 331–356.

7. J. G. Darley, N. Gross, and W. C. Martin, "Studies of Group Behavior: Factors Associated with the Productivity of Groups," *Journal of Applied Psychology,* XXXVI (1952), 396–403.

8. L. Festinger, "Informal Social Communication," *Psychological Review,* LVII (1950), 271–282.

9. L. Festinger, "An Analysis of Compliant Behavior," ch. 10 in M. Sherif and M. O. Wilson, eds., *Group Relations at the Crossroads* (1953), pp. 232–256.

10. L. Festinger, "A Theory of Social Comparison Process," *Human Relations,* VII (1954), 117–140.

11. J. W. French, *The Description of Personality Measurements in Terms of Rotated Factors* (Princeton, 1953).

12. J. W. French, *The Description of Aptitude and Achievement Tests in Terms of Rotated Factors,* Psychometric Monographs No. 5 (Chicago, 1951).

13. H. Guetzkow and J. Gyr, "An Analysis of Conflict in Decision-making Groups," *Human Relations,* VII (1954), 367–382.

14. W. Haythorn, "The Influence of Individual Members on the Characteristics of Small Groups," *Journal of Abnormal and Social Psychology,* XLVIII (1953), 276–284.

15. J. K. Hemphill and C. M. Westie, "The Measurement of Group Dimensions," *Journal of Psychology,* XXIX (1950), 325–342.

16. G. C. Homans, *The Human Group* (New York, 1950).

17. P. F. Lazarsfeld, ed., *Mathematical Thinking in the Social Sciences* (Glencoe, 1954).

18. K. Lewin, "Frontiers in Group Dynamics," *Human Relations,* I (1947), 5–41.

19. K. Lewin and R. Lippitt, "An Experimental Approach to the Study of Autocracy and Democracy: a Preliminary Note," *Sociometry,* I (1938), 292–300.

20. L. M. Libo, *Measuring Group Cohesiveness,* Research Center for Group Dynamics, Institute for Social Research (Ann Arbor, 1953).

21. S. Lieberman, *The Relationship Between Attitudes and Roles: a Natural Field Experiment* (Ph. D. thesis, University of Michigan, 1954). (An abbreviated report on this research appears in *Dun's Review and Modern Industry,* January, 1955, pp. 44–50).

22. G. Lindzey and E. F. Borgatta, "Sociometric Measurement," in G. Lindzey, ed., *Handbook of Social Psychology* (Cambridge, Mass., 1954), I, ch. 11, 405–448.

23. D. G. Marquis, H. Guetzkow, and R. W. Heyns, "A Social Psychological Study of the Decision-Making Conference," in H. Guetzkow, ed., *op. cit.,* pp. 55–67.

24. D. Pelz, "Leadership Within a Hierarchical Organization," *Journal of Social Issues,* VII (No. 3, 1951), 49–55.

25. C. H. Proctor and C. P. Loomis, "Analysis of Sociometric Data," in M. Jahoda et al., eds., *Research Methods in Social Relations,* Part II, *Selected Techniques* (New York, 1951), pp. 561–585.

26. H. W. Riecken, et al., "Narrowing the Gap Between Field Studies and Laboratory Experiments in Social Psychology," *SSRC Items,* VIII (1954), 37–42.

27. H. W. Riecken and G. C. Homans, "Psychological Aspects of Social Structure," in G. Lindzey, ed., *op. cit.,* vol. II, pp. 786–832.

28. F. J. Roethlisberger and W. J. Dickson, *Management and the Worker* (Cambridge, Mass., 1939).

29. H. A. Simon, "On the Definition of the Causal Relation," *The Journal of Philosophy,* XLIX (1952), 517–528.

30. H. A. Simon and H. Guetzkow, "A

Model of Short- and Long-Run Mechanisms Involved in Pressures Toward Uniformity in Groups," *Psychological Review*, LXII (1955), 56–68.

31. H. A. Simon and H. Guetzkow, "Some Mechanisms Involved in Group Pressures Upon Deviate-Members," *British Journal of Psychology* (in press).

32. F. L. Strodtbeck and A. P. Hare, "Bibliography of Small Group Research (from 1900 through 1953)," *Sociometry*, XVII (1954), 107–178.

33. L. L. Thurstone, *Multiple Factor Analysis* (Chicago, 1947).

34. W. E. Vinacke, *The Miniature Social Situation* (Psychological Laboratory, University of Hawaii) (Honolulu, 1954).

PARSONS: *Some Highlights of the General Theory of Action* (pp. 282–301)

1. Talcott Parsons and Edward A. Shils, eds., *Toward a General Theory of Action* (Cambridge, Mass., 1951).

2. My own development of related ideas will, besides the above-mentioned volume, be found principally in Parsons, *The Social System* (Glencoe, Ill., 1951); Parsons, Robert F. Bales, and Edward A. Shils, *Working Papers in the Theory of Action* (Glencoe, 1953); Parsons, *Essays in Sociological Theory, revised edition* (Glencoe, 1954); and Parsons, Bales and Collaborators, *Family, Socialization, and Interaction Process* (Glencoe, 1955). See also Parsons, "Some Comments on the State of the General Theory of Action," *American Sociological Review*, XVIII (1953), 618–31, and Parsons and Neil J. Smelser, *Economy and Society* (Glencoe, 1956).

3. What in *Toward a General Theory of Action* was treated as the third basic category of orientation, namely evaluation, will here be treated as an aspect of the *organization* of action in systems in the discussion immediately following.

4. An analysis of certain highlights of the process of socialization built about the process of internalization will be found in chs. II–IV of Parsons, Bales *et al., Family, Socialization, and Interaction Process.*

5. Those familiar with my own previous work and that of my associates may miss reference to the "pattern variables." The above classification of four fundamental system-problems is, in fact, one version of the pattern variable scheme, namely that put forward in *Working Papers*, chs. III and V. It consolidates the "attitudinal" and the "object-categorization" parts in a single scheme of four dimensions. A schematic representation of the logical relations involved here appears as figure 2, p. 182, in *Working Papers*.

6. The argument is stated in *Economy and Society*, ch. II, pp. 53 *ff.*

7. This general view of the relations between economic theory and the general theory of social systems was first put forward in a very tentative and incomplete way in my Marshall Lectures, University of Cambridge, 1953, on "The Integration of Economic and Sociological Theory" (unpublished). It has been greatly extended and refined since then and the results have recently been published as *Economy and Society*.

8. Power, from this point of view, is not the actual attainment of the goal of a social system, or even the probability that it can be attained, but a *factor* in that probability. To use a military metaphor, it may be likened to the "mobile reserve" at the disposal of a commander. The power of an agency (*e.g.,* a commander) is its capacity to *mobilize* relevant resources for a specific goal if and when occasion to pursue the goal arises. Thus not only the magnitude of the resources available but their mobility are crucial aspects of their relevance to power. From my point of view power is an attribute of a social system. The so-called "zero-sum" concept of power differs from the present one only in terms of system-reference. The power of a given system is a positive quantity; those of two cognate systems interacting with each other may cancel each other out, making either "powerless" to influence

processes in a larger system of which they are both parts.

9. This paper was written in the spring of 1955 and has been left substantially unchanged, with only minor revisions to correct a few statements which in the light of later developments would appear to be positively untenable. The statement of the general action scheme seems to me to hold without essential change though it could be refined and qualified at a number of points. The approach to the conception of the economy, and its relation to that of the polity, outlined at the end, also holds, but with considerably further qualification. In relation to the economy, after writing this manuscript considerable further work went into revision of *Economy and Society* before it went to press in January, 1956, and a good deal of further work has gone into analysis of the polity which has not yet reached a stage of maturity which would justify publication. Hence it is hoped that the bare outline of an approach to these two fields and the relation between them, the essence of which is a classification of cognate factors involved in the inputs and outputs of the two systems, should be taken for what it was originally presented to be, a set of suggestions which requires much fuller and deeper analytical work before it can pretend to be more than that.

BLACKWELL: *Community Analysis* (pp. 305–317)

1. This section draws upon the author's article, "A Sociologist on School-Community Relationships," *Annals,* CCCII (1955), 128–135.

2. George A. Hillery, Jr., "Definitions of Community: Areas of Agreement," *Rural Sociology,* XX (1955), 111–123.

3. August B. Hollingshead, "Community Research: Development and Present Condition," *American Sociological Review,* XIII (1946), 136–146. For other reviews of community research, see L. L. Bernard, ed., *The Fields and Methods of Sociology* (New York, 1934), pp. 52–109, 286–345; Carl C. Taylor, "Techniques of Community Study and Analysis as Applied to Modern Civilized Societies," in Ralph Linton, *The Science of Man in World Crisis* (New York, 1945), pp. 416–441; Albert J. Reiss, Jr., *A Review and Evaluation of Research on Community* (Nashville, Tennessee, Mimeographed, 1954); Conrad M. Arensberg, "The Community-Study Method," *American Journal of Sociology,* LX (1954), 109–124.

4. *Cf.* R. M. MacIver, *Community: A Sociological Study* (London, 1920), pp. 22–23: ". . . any area of common life . . ."

5. For an extended description and evaluation of Booth's work, see Pauline V. Young, *Scientific Social Surveys and Research,* 3rd ed. (Englewood Cliffs, N. J., 1956), pp. 9–14.

6. See Shelby M. Harrison, *The Social Survey* (New York, 1931).

7. Robert E. Park, Ernest W. Burgess, and R. D. McKenzie, *The City* (Chicago, 1925).

8. Nels Anderson, *The Hobo* (Chicago, 1923); Frederic M. Thrasher, *The Gang* (Chicago, 1927); Louis Wirth, *The Ghetto* (Chicago, 1928); Harvey W. Zorbauth, *The Gold Coast and the Slum* (Chicago, 1929).

9. Robert S. Lynd and Helen M. Lynd, *Middletown* (New York, 1929).

10. Robert S. Lynd and Helen M. Lynd, *Middletown in Transition* (New York, 1927), pp. ix–x.

11. Kurt B. Mayer, *Class and Society* (New York, 1955), pp. 31–32.

12. Alba Edwards, "A Social-Economic Grouping of the Gainful Workers in the United States," (Washington, D. C.; Government Printing Office, 1938).

13. Raymond Mack, "Housing as an Index of Social Class," *Social Forces,* XXIX (1951), 391–400.

14. F. S. Chapin, *Contemporary American Institutions* (New York, 1935), ch. XIX.

15. W. L. Warner, Marchia Meeker, and Kenneth Eells, *Social Class in America* (Chicago, 1929), Part Three.

16. *Ibid.,* Part Two.

17. Cecil C. North and Paul K. Hatt, "Jobs and Occupations: A Popular

Evaluation," *Opinion News,* IX (Sept. 1, 1947), 3–13.

18. Richard Centers, *The Psychology of Social Classes* (Princeton, 1949).
19. Harold F. Kaufman, *Defining Prestige in a Rural Community,* Sociometry Monographs, No. 10 (Beacon, New York, 1946).
20. J. L. Moreno, *Sociometry and the Cultural Order,* Sociometry Monographs, No. 2 (Beacon, New York, 1943), p. 327.
21. *Ibid.,* p. 306.
22. J. L. Moreno and Helen H. Jennings, *Sociometric Measurement of Social Configuration,* Sociometry Monographs, No. 3 (Beacon, New York, 1945), p. 23.
23. George A. Lundberg and Margaret Lawsing, "The Sociography of Some Community Relations," *American Sociological Review,* II (1937), 318–335.
24. *Ibid.,* 326.
25. George A. Lundberg, "Social Attraction Patterns in A Rural Village: a

Preliminary Report," *Sociometry,* I (1927), 78–80.
26. Charles P. Loomis, "Informal Groupings of a Spanish American Village," *Sociometry,* IV (1941), 36–51; see also "Tapping Human Power Lines," *Adult Leadership,* I (1953), 12–14.
27. Paul Deutschberger, *Interaction Patterns in Changing Neighborhoods,* Sociometry Monographs, No. 18 (Beacon, New York, 1947).
28. Bryce Ryan, *Social and Ecological Patterns in the Farm Leadership of Four Iowa Townships,* Research Bulletin 306 (Ames: Agricultural Experiment Station, 1942).
29. Frank A. Stewart, "A Sociometric Study of Influence in Southtown," *Sociometry,* X (1947), 11–31, 273–286.
30. F. Stuart Chapin, *The Impact of the War on Community Leadership and Opinion in Red Wing* (Minneapolis, 1945).
31. *Ibid.,* p. 11.
32. Floyd Hunter, *Community Power Structure* (Chapel Hill, 1953).

CAMPBELL: *Political Implications of Community Identification* (pp. 318–329)

1. V. O. Key, Jr., "Partisanship and County Office: The Case of Ohio," *American Political Science Review,* XLVII (1953), 525–532.
2. L. H. Fuchs, "American Jews and the Presidential Vote," Ibid., XLIX (1955), 385–401.
3. E. H. Litchfield, *Voting Behavior in a Metropolitan Area,* Michigan Governmental Studies, No. 7 (1941).
4. Samuel Lubell, *The Future of American Politics* (New York, 1951).
5. Louis Harris, *Is There a Republican Majority?* (New York, 1954).
6. B. Berelson, P. Lazarsfeld, and W. McPhee, *Voting* (Chicago, 1954).
7. A. Campbell, G. Gurin, and W. E. Mil-

ler, *The Voter Decides* (Evanston, 1954).
8. P. Lazarsfeld, B. Berelson, and H. Gaudet, *The People's Choice* (New York, 1944).
9. R. C. Angell, *The Moral Integration of American Cities* (Chicago, 1951).
10. A. Campbell and H. C. Cooper, *Group Differences in Attitudes and Votes* (Ann Arbor, 1956).
11. Lester M. Libo, *Measuring Group Cohesiveness* (Ann Arbor, 1953).
12. G. Belknap and A. Campbell, "Political Party Identification and Attitudes toward Foreign Policy," *The Public Opinion Quarterly,* XII (Winter, 1951–52).

GREER: *Individual Participation in Mass Society* (pp. 329–342)

I. *Images of the City*
1. Louis Wirth, "Urbanism as a Way of Life," *The American Journal of Sociology,* XLIV (July, 1938), 1–24.
2. Kurt Wolff, trans. and ed., *The Soci-

ology of George Simel* (Glencoe, 1950).
3. George Simpson, trans., *Emile Durkheim on the Division of Labor in Society* (New York, 1933).

4. C. P. Loomis, trans. and ed., *Fundamental Concepts of Sociology* (Ferdinand Tonnies, *Gemeinschaft und Gesellschaft*) (New York, 1940).
5. Robert Redfield, *The Folk Culture of Yucatan* (Chicago, 1941).
6. Robert E. Park, *Human Communities* (Glencoe, 1952).
7. Robert M. MacIver and Charles H. Page, *Society: An Introductory Analysis* (New York, 1949).

II. *Empirical Studies*

8. Mirra Kommarovsky, "The Voluntary Associations of Urban Dwellers," *American Sociological Review,* XI (Dec., 1946), 868–896.
9. Morris Janowitz, *The Community Press in an Urban Setting* (Glencoe, 1952).
10. Donald E. Foley, "Neighbors or Urbanites? The Study of a Rochester District," *The University of Rochester's Studies of Metropolitan Rochester* (Rochester, 1952).
11. Morris Axelrod, "Urban Structure and Social Participation," *American Sociological Review,* XXI (Feb., 1956), 13–18.
12. Wendell Bell, "Urban Neighborhood Types and Participation in Formal Organizations," *American Sociological Review,* XXI (Feb., 1956), 25–34.
13. Wendell Bell (with the assistance of Maryanne Force and Marion Boat), "People of the City," (processed) Stanford University Research Facility, Stanford, California (1954).
14. Scott Greer, "Urbanism Reconsidered: A Comparative Study of Local Areas in a Metropolis," *American Sociological Review,* XXI (Feb., 1956), 19–25.
15. Scott Greer and Ella Kube, "Urban Worlds: A Comparative Study of Four Los Angeles Areas," (processed) Laboratory in Urban Culture, Occidental College (1955).
16. O. A. Oeser and S. B. Hammond, eds.,

Social Structure and Personality in a City (New York, 1954).

III. *A Typology of Urban Populations*

17. Eshref Shevky and Marilyn Williams, *The Social Areas of Los Angeles* (Berkeley and Los Angeles, 1948).
18. Eshref Shevky and Wendell Bell, *Social Area Analysis* (Stanford, 1955).
19. Colin Clark, *The Conditions of Economic Progress* (London, 1940).
20. Godfrey Wilson and Monica Wilson, *The Analysis of Social Change* (London, 1945).

IV. *Community—and the City*

21. P. Sargant Florence, *The Logic of British and American Industry* (London, 1953).
22. Scott Greer, *Social Organization* (New York, 1955).
23. Elton Mayo, *Human Problems of an Industrial Civilization* (New York, 1933).
24. Oeser and Hammond, op. cit., Part V, "The Workers: Social Hierarchies."
25. Scott Greer, "The Participation of Ethnic Minorities in the Labor Unions of Los Angeles County," (unpublished Ph. D. dissertation), Department of Anthropology and Sociology, University of California at Los Angeles (1952).
26. Will Herberg, "Bureaucracy and Democracy in Trade Unions," *Antioch Review,* III (Sept., 1943), 405–417.
27. Seymour Martin Lipset, "The Political Process in Trade-Unions: A Theoretical Statement," in *Freedom and Control in Modern Society* (New York, 1954).
28. Erich Fromm, *Escape from Freedom* (New York, 1941).
29. David Riesman (in collaboration with Reuel Denny and Nathan Glazer), *The Lonely Crowd, a Study of the Changing American Character* (New Haven, 1950).

HUNTER: *Studying Associations and Organization Structures* (pp. 343–363)

1. Robin M. Williams, Jr., *American Society* (New York, 1951).
2. *The Encyclopedia Americana,* Vol.

XII (1944 ed.). See also "Fraternal Orders" and "Masonry," ESS.
3. Charles W. Ferguson, *Fifty Million*

Brothers (New York, 1937), p. 35.
4. Figures revised according to 1953 report of Farm Bureau.
5. Charles S. Johnson, "National Organizations in the Field of Race Relations," *The Annals of the American Academy of Political and Social Science,* CCXLIV (1946).
6. See Jay Judkins, *National Associations of the United States* (Washington,

D. C.; Department of Commerce, 1949).
7. Williams, op. cit., p. 462.
8. W. Lloyd Warner and Paul S. Lunt, *The Social Life of a Modern Community* (New Haven, 1941), pp. 303 and 320. Also ch. 16, "The Formal and Informal Associations of Yankee City."
9. Williams, *op. cit.,* p. 463.

ROSSI: *Community Decision-Making* (pp. 363–382)

This paper was also published in *Administrative Science Quarterly,* published by Graduate School of Business and Public Administration, Cornell University, June, 1956, and reprinted by permission.
1. Solomon E. Asch, *Studies on Independence and Submission to Group Pressures* (In press).
2. Stephen Bailey, *Congress Makes a Law* (New York, 1950).
3. Robert F. Bales, *Interaction Process Analysis* (Cambridge, Mass., 1950).
4. Reinhard Bendix and Seymour M. Lipset, *Class, Status and Power* (Glencoe, 1953).
5. Bernard Berleson, Paul F. Lazarsfeld, and William N. McPhee, *Voting* (Chicago, 1954).
6. Dorwin Cartwright and Alvin Zander, *Group Dynamics* (Evanston, 1953).
7. Richard Centers, *The Psychology of Social Classes* (Princeton, 1949).
8. W. W. Charters, Jr., "Social Class Analysis and the Control of Education," *Harvard Educational Review,* XXIII (Fall, 1953).
9. George S. Counts, *The Social Composition of Boards of Education* (New York, 1927).
10. Ward Edwards, "Theory of Decision Making," *Psychological Bulletin,* LI (July, 1954).
11. Oliver Garceau, *The Public Library in the Political Process* (New York, 1949).
12. A. Paul Hare, Edgar F. Borgatta, and Robert F. Bales, eds., *Small Groups* (New York, 1955).
13. August E. Hollingshead, *Elmtown's Youth* (New York, 1949).
14. Floyd A. Hunter, *Community Power Structure* (Chapel Hill, 1953).
15. Elihu Katz and Paul F. Lazarsfeld,

Personal Influence (Glencoe, 1955).
16. Louis C. Kesselman, *The Social Politics of F. E. P. C.* (Chapel Hill, 1948).
17. Robert K. Lamb, "Suggestions for a Study of Your Home Town," *Human Organization,* XI (Summer, 1952).
18. Paul F. Lazarsfeld, Bernard Berelson, and Hazel Gaudet, *The People's Choice* (New York, 1944).
19. Paul F. Lazarsfeld and Morris Rosenberg, *The Language of Social Research* (Glencoe, 1955).
20. Seymour Lipset, *Agrarian Socialism* (Berkeley, 1950).
21. Seymour Lipset, Paul F. Lazarsfeld, Allen Barton, and Juan Lenz, "The Social Psychology of Voting," in G. Lindzey, ed., *Handbook of Social Psychology,* Vol. II (Cambridge, Mass., 1954).
22. Robert S. Lynd, *Middletown in Transition* (New York, 1937).
23. Richard M. Mathews, *The Social Background of Decision-Makers* (New York, 1954).
24. Robert K. Merton, "Patterns of Interpersonal Influence," *Communications Research:* 1948–49 (New York, 1949).
25. Martin Meyerson and Edward C. Banfield, *Politics, Planning and the Public Interest* (Glencoe, 1955).
26. Robert Michels, *Political Parties* (Glencoe, 1949).
27. C. Wright Mills, *The Power Elite* (New York, 1956).
28. C. Wright Mills and Melville Ullmer, "Small Business and Civil Welfare," Report of the Smaller War Plants Corporation, U. S. Senate Doc. 135 (1946).
29. National Opinion Research Center, "Jobs and Occupations: A Popular Evaluation," *Class, Status and Power* (Glencoe, 1953).

30. Peter H. Rossi, J. Leiper Freeman, and James M. Shipton, *Politics and Education in Massachusetts* (Manuscript in Preparation).

31. John T. Salter, *Boss Rule* (New York, 1935).

32. Martin Shubik, *Readings in Game Theory and Political Behavior* (New York, 1954).

33. Richard C. Snyder, H. W. Bruck, and Burton Sapin, *Decision-Making as an Approach to the Study of International Politics,* Foreign Policy Analysis Series No. 3 (Princeton, 1954).

34. Harold Stein, ed., *Public Administration and Policy Development* (New York, 1952).

35. Frank A. Stewart, A Sociometric Study of Influence in Southtown," *Sociometry,* X (1947), 11–31, 273–286.

36. Samuel A. Stouffer, *Communism, Conformity and Civil Liberties* (New York, 1955).

37. Fred L. Strodtbeck, "Special Issue on Small Groups Research," *American Sociological Review,* XIX (December, 1954).

38. W. Lloyd Warner, et al., *The Social Life of a Modern Community* (New Haven, 1941).

39. W. Lloyd Warner, et al., *Democracy in Jonesville* (New York, 1949).

40. Robin M. Williams and Margaret W. Ryan, *Schools in Transition* (Chapel Hill, 1954).